THE LIFE OF
HENRY CLAY

By

GLYNDON G. VAN DEUSEN

LITTLE, BROWN AND COMPANY

Boston *Toronto*

THE LIFE OF HENRY CLAY

TO RUTH

INTRODUCTION

EACH generation, seeking to discover for itself the reasons why the present has evolved out of the past, examines the lives and deeds of great historical figures. The necessity for doing this becomes imperative when research discloses new sources of knowledge and makes possible new appraisals and different interpretations. This biography is the result of a conviction on the part of the author that Henry Clay's career merits such reexamination. It has also been born out of a deep and genuine admiration for one of the most colorful and fascinating characters in American history.

It is impossible to render adequate acknowledgment to all those who have given valuable assistance during the six years of research and writing that have produced this book. The author wishes to acknowledge his gratitude to Mrs. Thomas S. Bullock, who graciously permitted the use of her valuable and hitherto unused collection of Clay letters and gave permission to reproduce original paintings that are in her possession; Professor Dexter Perkins, who has been both counsellor and friend, reading the manuscript and offering many valuable suggestions; Mr. and Mrs. Thomas G. Spencer, for permitting the use of the important Weed Papers; Mr. J. Winston Coleman, Jr., who read the manuscript and gave essential aid in criticism and in procuring source material and illustrations; Professor Thomas D. Clark, who read part of the manuscript, and whose advice and assistance were of most timely value; Mr. M. William Anderson, for the use of hitherto unused Clay letters; Miss Henrietta Clay, for permission to use material collected by her father, Thomas Hart Clay; Mrs. Jouett Taylor Cannon, who furnished Clay letters in her possession; Mrs. Elizabeth M. Graham, for unflagging zeal and efficiency in research; Mr. F. G. Sweet and Mr. F. H. Sweet, for the use of letters in their possession; Mr. Charles Staples, for suggestions and the loan of material; Professor Culver H. Smith, for permission to read "The Washington Press in the Jacksonian Period" in manuscript; Mrs. Dexter Perkins, for constructive criticisms; Professor and Mrs. Walden Moore for helpful criticisms and for aid in securing illustrations; Mr. Reinhard H. Luthin, for the loan of notes on Clay's activities in the period around 1844; Mrs. John Z. Garbutt, for the use of unpublished Clay letters; Mrs. A. V. D. Pierrepont, who furnished genealogical information; Mr. George Fort Milton, for the loan of books and for valuable advice.

Through the courtesy of the Johns Hopkins University Library, Professor Bernard Mayo's doctoral dissertation, "The Early Life of Henry Clay," was seen by me. It has not been used in the preparation of this book, no permission having been received from the author.

Heartfelt thanks are due to the University of Rochester for financial assistance, and to all my colleagues in the History Department at Rochester for their friendly co-operation.

I wish to acknowledge the friendly and courteous assistance of the librarians, archivists and library assistants at the Library of Congress, Transylvania University, New York Public Library, Buffalo Historical Society, the Archives of the Department of State, Wisconsin State Historical Society, Ohio State Historical and Archaeological Society, the University of Chicago, American Antiquarian Society, Massachusetts Historical Society, Lexington Public Library, North Carolina State Historical Commission, the University of North Carolina, Columbia University, Harvard University, the University of Rochester, the Kentucky State Historical Society, the University of Kentucky, the Capital Library at Frankfort, Kentucky, the University of Illinois, Duke University, the Pennsylvania Historical Society, and the Virginia State Library.

Finally, no list of acknowledgments would be complete without special reference to my wife, Ruth Litteer Van Deusen, whose unflagging interest in research, in criticism, and in the typing and retyping of the manuscript has given to this book a large share of whatever merit it may possess.

CHRONOLOGY

April 12, 1777. Born at the family home in Hanover County, Virginia.

November, 1797. Admitted to the Virginia bar. Moved to Lexington, Kentucky.

March 20, 1798. Admitted to the bar in Lexington, Kentucky.

April 11, 1799. Married Lucretia Hart.

1803–1809. Elected to successive terms in the Kentucky legislature.

1807. United States Senator, filling out unexpired term of John Adair.

1809. Duel with Humphrey Marshall.

1810. United States Senator, filling out unexpired term of Buckner Thruston.

1811–1814. Member of the United States House of Representatives. Speaker of the House, Nov. 4, 1811–Jan. 19, 1814.

1814. Member of the United States Peace Commission at Ghent.

1815–1821. Member of the United States House of Representatives. Speaker of the House, Dec. 4, 1815–Nov. 13, 1820.

1823–1825. Member of the United States House of Representatives. Speaker of the House, Dec. 1, 1823–March 3, 1825.

1824. Candidate for the presidency.

1825–1829. Secretary of State.

1826. Duel with John Randolph of Roanoke.

1831–1842. United States Senator.

1832. Candidate for the presidency.

1844. Candidate for the presidency.

1849–1852. United States Senator.

June 29, 1852. Died at the National Hotel, in Washington.

CONTENTS

THE LIFE OF HENRY CLAY

CHAPTER I

THE EARLY YEARS

WHEN April comes to the rolling fields of Hanover County, Virginia, the delicate bluet, the hepatica, and the wild violet lend color to the fence rows and to the forests of ash and oak, cedar and pine. Sassafras grows in neglected pastures, and along the North and the South Anna, the Pamunkey, and Machump's Creek the alders and the willows trace the watercourses with a touch of feathery green. It is the peaceful renaissance of spring, and the Hanover County farmer of to-day goes out into his fields with the confidence and hope that spring always imparts. So have his forebears done for generations before him.

But war lends a discordant note to any springtime harmony, and in 1777 Hanover County's vernal season was less peaceful than usual. The American Revolution was in full swing and musketry fire was crackling throughout the rebellious colonies. Washington had been fighting stubbornly against superior British forces in the North, but rumor had it that his army was in poor condition. No one knew when the tide of battle might sweep into Virginia, and the air was full of news calculated to make any good Hanover patriot anxious. It was a dramatic setting, and, on the twelfth of April in that year,[1] a child was born whose life was filled with drama.

The small gray eyes of Henry Clay first saw the light in

[1] This is the date accepted by Clay himself, and by Z. F. Smith and M. R. Clay, in *The Clay Family* (Louisville, 1899), pp. 6-7, 90. A rumor was started years later that he had been born in 1775. This was done, apparently, to show that he was too old to be a presidential possibility. The rumor seems to have been based on the fact that there was an older brother, Henry, who died in early childhood, whose name was given to the child born in 1777.

Eunice F. Barnard, "To Henry Clay Comes Paradoxical Fame," in the *New York Times*, April 10, 1927, suggests the dramatic setting of Clay's birth.

the Clay homestead, three and one-half miles southeast of
Hanover Court House and fifteen miles north of Richmond.
He was the seventh of the nine children of the Reverend John
Clay and Elizabeth Hudson Clay, a couple whose families, of
English descent, had played for generations respectable though
by no means brilliant parts in the development of Virginia
colony.[2]

Of the Reverend John Clay, sometimes called "Sir" John,
although no one knows just why, little knowledge of historical
value is extant. Tradition connects his name with a Sir John
Clay who is supposed to have come to Virginia in the early
part of the seventeenth century, and there are records of his
ancestors living in Henrico County during the latter part of
that century,[3] but it would take a genealogist skillful indeed to
give the family a coat of arms. The Reverend "Sir" John was
the son of John Clay of Dale Parish, Chesterfield County.[4]
"Sir" John was at one time, it appears, a dancing master,[5] but
forsook such light pursuits for the Baptist ministry, in which he
served with zeal, even though without conspicuous success.
There are stories of his preaching from a rock in the South
Anna River, preparatory to immersions, and organizing Black
Creek Church in 1777, the year of Henry Clay's birth. There
is no reason to doubt that, from the moral point of view, he
was what is called rather blightingly a "good citizen," honest
and respectable, God-fearing, and, probably, a stubborn rebel
in the Revolution.[6] One other point is of interest. The reverend
gentleman was a man of property. His father had willed him
Negroes and four hundred acres of land. At the end of his life
he possessed more than twenty-one slaves, owned "at Eu-
phraim" in Henrico County, about ten miles above Richmond,

[2] Smith and Clay, *op. cit.*, pp. 38, 89–90, passim.

[3] S. O. Southall to *William and Mary Quarterly*, Vol. XXII (Oct., 1913),
p. 129; W. C. Torrence, "Henrico County, Virginia: Beginnings of its
Families," *ibid.*, Vol. XXIV (Oct., 1915), p. 142, note 1.

[4] Smith and Clay, *op. cit.*, p. 78.

[5] This is based on a letter from Henry Clay to Benjamin Gratz, published
in part in an article by T. H. Clay, "Two Years with Old Hickory," in
Atlantic Monthly, Vol. LX (Aug., 1887), pp. 195–196.

[6] Smith and Clay, *op. cit.*, pp. 7, 13, 19; Clay Papers (Lib. of Cong.,
Mss. Div.), III, William Duval to Henry Clay, June 14, 1821.

a plantation "fit to work four or five hands to advantage," and his wife had brought him the occupation of the farm of four hundred and sixty-four acres on Machump's Creek in Hanover County, to which he and his family moved in 1777, not long before Henry Clay was born.[7]

Elizabeth Hudson Clay came of a well-to-do family. Her father, George Hudson, like his father before him, had been an inspector of tobacco in Hanover County, and a good, substantial fellow. Being the eldest son, he had inherited all the family lands. Thirty-one Negroes, four hundred and sixty-four acres of land on Machump's Creek, and other land and money disposed of in his will were divided, after the death of his wife, between his daughters Elizabeth and Mary.[8]

Elizabeth had prospects, and she must have found favor in the sight of swains for other reasons as well. "She was dark-hair'd, dark-eyed," with red cheeks, and a figure that, though a little below the medium stature, was very well turned indeed. Family tradition bears witness to her charm of manner. Industrious and frugal, strong-willed, but kindly, she must have exerted a real influence upon her family. John Clay's will shows clearly his belief that she would marry again, and the expectation was realized. This woman in her early thirties, who had already borne nine children, became the wife of Captain Henry Watkins, who was ten years her junior, and bore seven children more.[9] Something of a record, even for a marrying and childbearing age! She was a remarkable and an attractive woman, and it is easy to see her reflection in her famous son's charm, and in his unquenchable ambition.

Henry Clay loved to dwell, in later years, upon his humble

[7] Virginia Broadsides (Lib. of Cong., Mss. Div.), 179, newspaper item, 1782; Court Records, Hanover Co., Va., 1783–1792 (Va. State Lib., Archives Div.), Vol. II, pp. 418–419; John Clay's will, reprinted in Smith and Clay, *op. cit.*, pp. 55–57.

[8] Clay Papers, I, will of George Hudson (photostat copy), Nov. 30, 1770; Mrs. J. E. Warren, "Tompkins Family," in *William and Mary Quarterly*, Vol. X, ser. 2 (July, 1930), p. 236; Memo. and letters in possession of Mrs. A. V. D. Pierrepont.

[9] Smith and Clay, *op. cit.*, pp. 17–19, 29–30, passim; *The Henry Clay Almanac* (1843), p. 17, quoting a gentleman "now in the United States Senate," who had known her when he was a boy.

background. He was, he said again and again, an orphan boy brought up amid poverty and ignorance. His earlier biographers have accepted the tale, but the facts present a somewhat different picture.

The Clay homestead, it is true, was situated in a region known as "the slashes," not particularly noted for its fertility. There was better land in Hanover County. But John and Elizabeth Clay were not exactly indigent, and Henry Watkins had possessions in his own right. The house where Henry Clay was born rose well above the lowly status of a log cabin. It was a substantial, story-and-a-half frame structure, rectangular in shape, with large chimneys at either end and dormer windows jutting out from the sloping roof.[10] The farm on Machump's Creek was not only considerably larger than the average in the vicinity in 1782, but was also assessed at well over average value during the 1780's and early 1790's.[11]

Personal property was not lacking during Clay's boyhood. The Virginia census of 1782 recorded Elizabeth Clay as the head of a family of nine whites and eighteen blacks,[12] and Henry Watkins' possessions, from 1782 to 1791, in slaves, horses and cattle, while not indicating great wealth, certainly do not suggest penury. No man was poverty-stricken who possessed seventeen Negroes, five horses, twenty-two head of cattle, and two chair carriages, as Watkins did in 1787.[13]

[10] *Waterston Autographs* (Mass. Hist. Soc.), I.

[11] Land Tax Book, Hanover Co., Va., 1782–1802 (Va. Archives). The entry for 1782, p. 5, gives an assessed valuation of seventeen shillings per acre, amid assessments averaging about ten shillings per acre. There are more entries on this page for farms under three hundred acres than over that amount.

[12] *First Census of the United States, 1790, Records of the State Enumerations, 1782–1785, Va., Hanover Co.*, p. 28.

[13] Hanover Property Book, 1782–1791 (Va. Archives). This personal property shifted in amount during these years. It is greatest in 1787, least in 1789, when Watkins had nine slaves, no cattle, and three horses. This latter record seems low, but it was better in 1790 and 1791, and in connection with this it is important to note that he bought the Clay homestead outright in 1788 for "four hundred and thirty-two pounds thirteen shillings & a penny half penny," and that, owing his brother John £250, 14s., 2d. in Oct. 1790, he paid it off by April 4, 1792, though the last installment was not due until Dec. 30, 1793. Court Records, Hanover Co., Va., 1783–1792 (Va. Archives), Vol. II, pp. 418–419, 481–482.

Young Clay's early education was scanty. There were no great educational opportunities available for him, but he was given the advantage of such as were to be had. He had about three years of schooling under a fairly able though intemperate schoolmaster, Peter Deacon by name. His parents probably gave him some additional instruction, for his mother was a person of real ability, and his stepfather took an intelligent interest in the promising youth. Henry was scarcely left in complete ignorance.

But the tradition of his extremely humble origin is easy to understand. Such an origin has always been a political asset, and the real contrast between Clay's own position and that of his forebears, together with his great penchant for believing what he wished to believe, easily convinced him that the legend was the truth.

The first few years of his life were exciting ones. There were always rumors of the war to keep the family perturbed, and early in 1781 the thunder of the guns came in real earnest, for Cornwallis, following Lafayette up through Virginia, sent Colonel Tarleton raiding. The dreaded squadron swept into Hanover County. Near Hanover Court House they found ten brass twenty-four pounders, which they spiked, throwing five or six of them into the Pamunkey. They burned and destroyed tobacco and military supplies, took prisoners, and terrorized the countryside. One June day, so the story goes, they came to the Clay homestead. "Sir" John had been buried only the day before, and the house was deep in mourning, but Elizabeth made the only white man on the place leave by the back way to avoid capture, and gathered her family about her. Tarleton's men searched the house. They ripped open the beds and emptied the feathers out of the windows; they stole Mrs. Clay's white satin wedding gown, and seized some of the slaves; one of them threatened to and perhaps did thrust his sword into the new-made grave, searching for buried treasure. Mrs. Clay complained of the destruction and Tarleton emptied upon the table a sack of coins which she was afraid to refuse, but afterwards, like a good rebel, scraped into her apron and threw into the fire. Then they rode away, leaving chaos and terror behind them, and a lasting memory for the four-year-old boy.[14]

The next ten years were not packed with such dramatic incidents, but there was always a variety of occupations for the gangling, tow-headed youngster with the big mouth. He mastered the three R's in the log-cabin schoolhouse with its dirt floor. He worked on the farm, barefooted like the other boys of his age, learning as he grew up to plough and cultivate. There were pony rides, astride a sack of corn or wheat, to Mrs. Darricott's grist mill on the Pamunkey. He could chaffer with Black Billy, and Sukie, Bob, and Jim, hunt frogs in the marshy places, and set traps along the creek bank and the fence rows for muskrat, mink and skunk. The Watkins and the Clays were blood relations, and when the wealthy Samuel Watkins, Henry Watkins' brother, brought his family over to visit, Henry Clay played with his little cousin Alice. He called her "cousin Ailcey," and she was his boyhood sweetheart.[15]

The boy was growing up in a country that, young though it was historically, had its traditions and was making history for the future. Not far to the east was the place where John Smith had been captured by the Indians, almost two hundred years before. Pamunkey is an Indian name, meaning "where we took a sweat," and Machump's Creek took its name from Powhatan's brother-in-law, who had visited England and had dined at Governor Dale's table.[16] Hanover had been the first county in Virginia to raise troops against the British, Patrick Henry leading a company of volunteers to Williamsburg to check royalist Governor Dunmore's activities, and she had borne her part in the days of disaster and triumph that had followed. When Clay was eleven years old, in 1788, the convention for ratification of the Constitution met in Richmond, and the giants of Virginia clashed in a debate that resounded over the countryside. Marshall, Madison, Wythe, and young George Nicholas

---

[14] Lt. Col. Banastre Tarleton, *A History of the Campaign of 1780 and 1781* (London, 1787), pp. 294–296, 349; Smith and Clay, *op. cit.*, pp. 17–18; R. Page, *Hanover County* (Richmond, 1926), pp. 38–39; J. S. Littell, *Clay Minstrel* (N.Y., 1842), p. 72, quote of Clay; C. H. Peck, *The Jacksonian Epoch* (N.Y., 1899), p. 11.

[15] Authority of Mrs. A. V. D. Pierrepont.

[16] Page, *op. cit.*, pp. 3–5.

urged adoption of the new charter; Monroe, Mason and Henry denounced it as "squinting toward monarchy."

Patrick Henry of Hanover County! The man who, when Clay heard him later in the British debt case in Richmond, rose to such heights that Judge Iredell on the bench exclaimed involuntarily, "Gracious God! he is an orator indeed!" [17] Young Henry Clay may well have been thinking of "Give me liberty, or give me death" when, as a youth, he went out into the cornfield, barn or forest and practiced the art of speaking, that "art of all arts" to which he later confessed he was "indebted for the primary and leading impulses that stimulated my progress and have shaped and moulded my entire destiny." [18]

The years slipped away swiftly, and family changes came. Henry Watkins' brother John, who had married Mary Hudson, Elizabeth's sister, moved to Kentucky and prospered. He was a prominent citizen of Versailles, Woodford County, by 1792, and the family back home heard glowing reports. Henry Watkins became dissatisfied. After all, he was still young, and the call of the West was strong. Four of Elizabeth's children by her first marriage were still living — George, John, Porter and Henry. George should stay and take care of the farm; John and Porter should go to Kentucky with the family, but what of Henry?

No one knows why it was decided to leave Henry in Richmond, but certain inferences are only just. He had shown aptitude in learning, an active and inquiring mind. He had been placed, in 1791, as a clerk in Richard Denny's retail store, near the market-house in Richmond, and in all probability he did not jubilate over the prospect of a life behind the counter. Watkins seems to have had a certain appreciation of the boy's possibilities, and to have felt that it would be more to his advantage to remain in Virginia. [19] The stepfather had a friend at court in the person of Thomas Tinsley, a prominent member of the Virginia House of Burgesses, and through this man's brother, Peter Tinsley, clerk of the High Court of Chancery

[17] J. P. Little, *History of Richmond* (Richmond, 1933), pp. 90–91.
[18] Peck, *op. cit.*, pp. 16–17.
[19] Watkins family records, authority of Mrs. A. V. D. Pierrepont.

at Richmond, a place was made for the fifteen-year-old boy as
a deputy clerk, with maintenance. Then his stepfather and his
mother moved to Kentucky in 1792.[20]

When young Henry appeared among his fellow clerks,
amused smiles passed about the room, for his appearance was
scarcely prepossessing. His mouth was large, his eyes small.
He was still of the country, and the awkwardness of adolescence
enveloped him in a mantle even more mirth-provoking than his
very stiffly starched linen and his pepper-and-salt Figginy suit
of mixed silk and cotton with its coat-tail "standing out from
his legs at an angle of forty-five degrees." [21] What a copyist
was here! The clerks began to bandy remarks with the newcomer, but they found that he had a ready tongue. The quips
soon ceased, even though he did not attempt to share in their
nocturnal ramblings. The gay young blades commented upon
his assiduity and reading, but they stopped attempting to
persecute him, and he made at least one intimate friend among
them in William Sharp, a youth with an erect military carriage,
black hair, and dark brown eyes, who had been born in Henrico
County, not far from Clay's early home.[22] One can picture the
two lads sitting in raptures under the eloquent spell of Patrick
Henry, or gazing in awe at Jefferson, Monroe, Marshall, and
other celebrities when they appeared in the courthouse or on
the city streets. But, for a time at least, the fifteen-year-old
boy devoted himself to his tasks and his reading. He "lived in
the clerk's office," he wrote later to a friend.[23] So about a year
passed away, and then a fortunate turn of events occurred.

The Chancellor of the High Court of Chancery was one of
Virginia's ablest sons. George Wythe, then nearing seventy, had
had a long and distinguished career as a lawyer, a political
leader, and a teacher of law and the classics at William and

[20] J. O. Harrison Papers, Scrapbook (Lib. of Cong.), p. 38; Calvin
Colton, ed., *The Works of Henry Clay*, 10 vols. (N.Y., 1904), Vol. I, p. 42.
Hereafter cited as Clay, *Works*.

[21] H. W. Caldwell, *Henry Clay* (Milwaukee, 1903), p. 151. Quote of
Roland Thomas, senior clerk in the office at the time.

[22] H. B. Grigsby, *Life and Character of the Honorable L. W. Tazewell*
(Norfolk, 1860), p. 37.

[23] *Ninian Edwards Papers* (Chicago, 1884), p. 23, Clay to Edwards,
July 9, 1800.

Mary. Jefferson, Monroe, Marshall, Breckinridge, Buckner Thruston and George Nicholas had been among his pupils. A fervent patriot in the Revolutionary era, a signer of the Declaration of Independence, he was a firm supporter of the Constitution, and as firm an opponent of Negro slavery. Now he was a little bent by age. His head was very bald, and his cheeks and mouth were sunken and thin from loss of teeth, but his chin was still firm and his bright blue eyes could on occasion flash plenty of fire. Kindly and generous, a man of perfect integrity and great learning, he presided ably over the court committed to his care.[24]

Wythe's right hand was crippled by rheumatism or gout, and he needed an amanuensis. He went to Peter Tinsley's office in search of one. The clerk recommended Henry Clay, whose penmanship was clear and legible. Thus began, early in 1793, an association that lasted for four years and was of great importance to the young boy.

The youth could not fail to be impressed by the great erudition of his employer. The reports of cases that young Henry copied opened up vistas of legal knowledge, and Greek and Latin were strange and fascinating fields. He laboriously transcribed the Greek characters for the Chancellor's citations, and sat enraptured, though he understood not a word, when Wythe read aloud, with beautiful enunciation, from Homer.[25] Henry Clay never forgot the wonder of those moments. When he was Secretary of State, he wrote to his son and namesake: —

I think you would do well to refresh your recollection of the dead languages. I never enjoyed the advantage of knowing them, but I have remarked that those who do find a resource in them throughout life, and sometimes at a late period of it.[26]

[24] L. G. Tyler, "George Wythe, 1726–1806," in *Great American Lawyers*, 4 vols. (Phila., 1907), Vol. I, pp. 51–90; *Biography of the Signers of the Declaration of Independence*, 9 vols. (Phila., 1828), Vol. IV, pp. 171–188; G. W. Munford, *The Two Parsons* (Richmond, 1884), p. 364; *Virginia Historical Register*, Vol. V, pp. 162–167, Clay to B. B. Minor, May 3, 1851.

[25] *Va. Hist. Reg.*, Vol. V, pp. 162–167, Clay to B. B. Minor, May 3, 1851.

[26] Anne Clay McDowell Collection, Henry Clay to Henry Clay, Jr., Oct. 21, 1828. These letters have never been published, and I believe that they have never before been used.

When Wythe saw promise he encouraged it, and his diligent helper soon found favor in the Chancellor's eyes. Wythe became more and more interested, opened his library to the youth, discovered a rising ambition which his own intellect told him should be fostered, and finally advised the boy to study law. This advice found a ready response, and Clay began to read for the bar under Wythe's direction. Later, in the fall of 1796 or early in 1797, he left the clerk's office entirely and for about a year studied under Robert Brooke, formerly Governor and later Attorney-General of Virginia.[27]

Such preparation was of necessity brief to the point of superficiality. But Clay had a mind which could grasp with facility a working knowledge of principles, and the standards for admission to the bar were none too high. At the beginning of November, 1797, he was examined and given a license to practise law in the courts of Virginia.[28] He was on the threshold of his career.

Henry's life, meanwhile, had broadened out in a variety of ways. As his mentality developed, he attracted the attention of able men. Chancellor Wythe was one. Robert Brooke, who took him into his home, was another. In Francis Brooke, the brother of his mentor, he found a lifelong friend. Young Tom Ritchie, cousin of the brilliant Spencer Roane, fell under his spell.[29]

Clay was one of the leaders in a debating club formed by himself, Littleton Tazewell, Edmund Root and others, where the burning political questions of the day were vigorously debated and where he developed his oratorical powers.[30] He mingled in the society of the capital, thanks to contacts made through Wythe and Brooke, lost his awkwardness, and became something of a social favorite. And he developed a

[27] *Va. Hist. Reg.*, Vol. V, pp. 162–167, Clay to B. B. Minor, May 3, 1851; T. Ritchie, *Reminiscences of Henry Clay* (Richmond, 1852), p. 2; D. Mallory, *Life and Speeches of Henry Clay*, 2 vols. (N.Y., 1844), Vol. II, p. 572, Clay's speech at Lexington, June 9, 1842; J. O. Harrison Papers, Scrapbook, p. 38.

[28] Clay Papers, I, Nov. 6, 1797, photostat copy of the license.

[29] E. Sargent, *The Life and Public Services of Henry Clay* (N.Y., 1848), p. 4; Ritchie, *op. cit.*, p. 2.

[30] Clay, *Works*, Vol. I, p. 47.

fervent political idealism that was to make him a Jeffersonian Republican, sympathetic with the French Revolution, and with the doctrine of popular rights; a philosophy that made him quote to Tom Ritchie "with delight" the passage from Mackintosh's *Vindiciae Gallicae* which calls upon legislators to "hazard a bolder navigation, and discover, in unexplored regions, the treasure of public felicity." [31] He was alert, intent, keen-witted. The breadth of his experience and culture had increased far beyond the narrow limits that cribbed the awkward clerk of 1792.

Clay was now nearly twenty-one. He stood six feet and one inch and was loosely put together, although his carriage suggested nonchalance rather than awkwardness. His hair was prematurely white, and the face beneath was scarcely less striking. The forehead was high, the eyes small and gray, the nose prominent and slightly arched, the mouth "a long and deep horizontal cut," so large that he himself confessed that he never could learn how to spit. It was a fair, almost pallid face, sensitive, expressive, compelling. [32] His voice was already developing toward the perfection of the later years, when, like some superb instrument, it could be pitched at will to majestic denunciation, withering scorn, light pleasantry, or deep and tender emotion. It was the voice of an actor, and the expressive face and emotional temperament of this man who could move others to tears, and himself quite as easily, belonged to the footlights. Warm, impetuous, generous Thespian! A lifetime part was ready for him which he was to find very difficult to play.

But was he ready to begin it? He had now some social background, an eager, alert mind, the power of emotional appeal, and budding forensic talent. He was ambitious. These were important credits, but there were debits as well.

Systematic instruction, a broad foundation in the humanities — for these one looks in vain. Wythe was an old and a busy man. He could suggest and advise, but it is scarcely probable

---

[31] Ritchie, *op. cit.*, p. 2; C. H. Ambler, *Thomas Ritchie* (Richmond, 1913), p. 23.

[32] J. O. Harrison Papers, Harrison's sketch of Clay.

that he closely superintended the reading of his talented pupil.
A translation of Homer, a grammar, Plutarch's Lives, and
sundry other works, including a little history, Clay read at his
suggestion.[33] These do not indicate a liberal education. Until
Clay went to Brooke, he worked for Wythe and for the clerk
of the court as well, and, unless he became a changed man
after reaching Kentucky, he was not averse to the pursuit of
pleasure. He confessed in later years that his educational
exertions at Richmond were irregular.[34]

His legal preparation was nearly as bad. He studied for about
a year under Brooke, the one period of systematic training in
his whole life. He read some law with Wythe, who had a
reverence for the law, and solemnly adjured his students not
to skim.[35] But Clay's mind was facile, and the temptation to
skim was irresistible. He did it.

"To attain the highest place," he wrote long afterward to
a favorite son in whose abilities he had great confidence, "you
must make up your mind to labor incessantly. I never studied
half enough. I always relied too much upon the resources of
my genius. If I had life to pass over again, and, with my present
information, could control my movements, I would not appear
at the Bar before 24 or 25, nor until after two or three years,
at the least, of close study." [36]

The results of this insufficient training, and of this attitude
toward the dull grind of preparation, must have been apparent
in later years. There was a grain of truth, if only a grain, in
Webster's sour comment that Clay was really "no lawyer"
and "no reasoner." [37]

But here he was, with his license in his pocket. Where should
he hang out his shingle? Richmond did not seem a particularly
inviting field. The bar was brilliant, the community settled in

---

[33] C. Schurz, *Life of Henry Clay*, 2 vols. (Boston, 1892), Vol. I, p. 10.
[34] Clay Ms. (Univ. of Chicago, Mss. Div.), Speech at Lexington, June 9,
1842. *Cf.* his valedictory in the Senate, March 31, 1842, Mallory, *op. cit.*,
Vol. II, p. 565.
[35] Munford, *op. cit.*, p. 364.
[36] McDowell Collection, Henry Clay to Henry Clay, Jr., April 19, 1829.
Cf. the letters of Jan. 14, 1829, and Jan. 3, 1832.
[37] P. Harvey, *Reminiscences of Daniel Webster* (Boston, 1877), p. 217.

its practices and traditions, and it was at that time a Federalist stronghold. Kentucky, on the other hand, was attractive. All Clay's family ties centered there, his only near relative in Richmond, his brother George, having just died of the smallpox. But even more than this, it was a paradise for lawyers. The terrible confusion of land claims in Kentucky, a chaos out of which emerged innumerable law suits and great demand for legal talent, opened an alluring prospect to a lawyer's gaze, whether he were comfortably circumstanced, or aspiring and penniless. John Breckinridge, George Nicholas, James Brown, and other Virginia legists had gone to Kentucky and were prospering. Young Clay decided to follow in their footsteps. He gathered up his simple belongings and, a few days after he had received his license, started out on the dangerous trail that led across the mountains through Cumberland Gap, then up the Wilderness Road that Boone had marked in 1775, to Crab Orchard and Lexington.[38] He was on the threshold of new prospects and new fortunes, and not far distant were the portals of fame.

[38] M. William Anderson Collection, Henry Clay to Col. John Ballenger, Sept. 8, 1806. This collection is unpublished and seems to have been overlooked by other biographers of Clay. M. Taul, "Memoirs," in *Kentucky State Historical Society Register*, Vol. XXVII (Jan., 1929), p. 345; Isaac Weld, *Travels*, etc., 3rd ed., 2 vols. (London, 1800), Vol. I, pp. 233–234; J. Winston Coleman, Jr., *Stage-Coach Days in the Bluegrass* (Louisville, 1935), pp. 19, 32. It was customary to travel in a group, for parts of the way were infested by renegade whites and Indians.

CHAPTER II

A HAZARD OF NEW FORTUNES

KENTUCKY! The name had magic in it for the pioneering spirits of the late eighteenth century, despite the somber significance of its Indian title, "the dark and bloody ground." It conjured up visions of bluegrass, Indians, frontier adventures, opportunities for the acquisition of land and fortune. Daniel Boone, who had left his peaceful home on the banks of the Yadkin in North Carolina to wander "in quest of the country of Kentucky," found it fair as the garden of the Lord.[1] Simon Kenton, the McAfees, and the "Long Hunters" extolled its abundance of game. Richard Henderson and the Hart brothers saw and seized upon its possibilities for land speculation.

Kentucky was populated with great rapidity. James Harrod, in 1774, established the first permanent settlement in the state, where Harrodsburg now stands, and settlers from Virginia, North Carolina and Maryland began to filter in even during the Revolution. The movement was accelerated during the succeeding years, partially due to liberal land grants made by the mother state, Virginia. Kentucky became a state on its own account in 1792 and, by 1797, contained a population of about one hundred and eighty-five thousand souls.

The people of this youthful state were frontiersmen, and they had the characteristics of the frontier, so well described by Frederick Jackson Turner: —

That coarseness and strength combined with acuteness and acquisitiveness; that practical, inventive turn of mind, quick to find expedients; that masterful grasp of material things, lacking in the artistic but powerful to effect great ends; that restless, nervous energy; that dominant individualism, working for good and for evil, and withal that buoyancy and exuberance which come with freedom. . . .[2]

[1] G. Imlay, *A Topographical Description of the Western Territory* (London, 1793), pp. 325–326, *et seq*. Boone's own narrative.

[2] F. J. Turner, *The Frontier in American History* (N.Y., 1921), p. 37.

Such was the Kentucky of 1797, Republican in its politics for the most part, and always ready to defend its rights and to demand respect and fair treatment from the national Government.

Lexington lies in the north central part of Kentucky, and in the Bluegrass country. Named in 1775 in honor of the battle, reports of which had just begun to drift through the wilderness, its growth was fostered by the natural attractions of its surroundings and the exertions of its founders, Colonel Robert Patterson, John Maxwell and others.[3] But it scarcely merited the title of "town" during the Revolutionary era, and it was not until 1784 that the first dry goods store, a welcome sight to the ladies, was opened amid its huddle of log cabins. The following years saw a more rapid development and the appearance of signs of prosperity. The *Kentucke Gazette* appeared in 1787, one of the first if not the first newspaper west of the Alleghenies. Transylvania Seminary was founded in 1788 and when, ten years later, its name was changed to Transylvania University, it could boast, as it still does, of being the first institution of its kind beyond the mountains.

When Henry Clay arrived, the town had about sixteen hundred inhabitants and over two hundred houses, a few brick, some frame, but mostly built of logs. Twenty-four retail stores dispensed all kinds of goods, from axes and rifles to Paisley shawls, nankeens and muslins, and there were silversmiths and vendors of fine china and glassware, and even an attempt at a theater.[4] There was, for a frontier community, considerable pretension to refinement, even though an atmosphere strangely compounded of horses, legal wrangling, poker and liquor seemed to hang about the place.[5] And Lexington could boast, even then, a galaxy of names that were to rank high in the state's history.

John Bradford, "The Kentucky Franklin," as he was some-

[3] G. W. Ranck, *History of Lexington, Kentucky* (Cincinnati, 1872), pp. 19f.

[4] *Ibid.*, pp. 40–42, 105, 124, 202–203; Coleman, *Stage-Coach Days*, p. 29.

[5] F. A. Michaux, *Travels to the West of the Allegheny Mountains* (London, 1805, reprint Cleveland, 1904), pp. 194f.

times called, was the first editor of the *Gazette*. A variety of interests, which ranged from astronomy and mathematics to the founding of the Lexington library, in no wise detracted from his hearty love of sociability or from his enjoyment of a good game of poker. A Republican and a philosopher, as became a follower of Jefferson, he was a leading figure in the political and social life of the town. John Breckinridge had brought a growing family across the mountains in 1792, and almost immediately had become a leader on the frontier. This brilliant and popular humanitarian was one of the ablest lawyers in Kentucky. The luxuriant crop of land suits gave him wealth, and he had already plunged into the political career that was to take him far before his untimely death in 1806. Thomas Hart, land speculator, merchant and trader; James Brown, a Frankfort lawyer who maintained close Lexington connections through his wife, Nancy Hart Brown, daughter of Thomas Hart; James Morrison, the stern, decisive, yet courteous man of business already on the way to amassing a great fortune — these and a few others like them formed, with their families, a social nucleus marked out from the common run by success and achievement.

Clay arrived late in November, 1797. He came, he was wont to say in later years, without friends and penniless, but he must have had letters of introduction from Wythe and Brooke,[6] and his mother and stepfather, whom he visited regularly at their prosperous tavern in Versailles, a few miles away, would not have let him starve. He had, furthermore, a small inheritance from his father which Henry Watkins settled upon him soon after Clay reached Kentucky.[7]

The budding lawyer appeared to be in frail health, his movements characterized by a certain lassitude, but his ambition drove him on. He devoted himself to widening his circle of acquaintances, studying Kentucky law and its practice the while, and during those first few months an event occurred which

[6] J. M. Rogers, *The True Henry Clay* (Phila., 1904), p. 34, asserts that Clay had "letters from the best men in Richmond to the best men in Lexington."

[7] County Clerk's Office, Woodford County, Will Book B, pp. 54–55. Settlement between Henry Watkins and Henry Clay, Dec. 4, 1797.

showed that he was going to fit well into the life of the bustling little village.

He had become a member of a debating club not long after his arrival. One evening, when the discussion was seemingly spent and the chairman was about to put the question to a vote, Clay was heard to remark in a low voice that he did not think the subject had been exhausted. Someone suggested that he speak, and the chairman assented. The young man was still something of a stranger in a strange land and as he rose, feeling all eyes upon him, he became embarrassed. "Gentlemen of the jury . . ." he began, paused, floundered a bit, repeated the phrase, and then gaining courage launched into a brilliant discussion of the subject. His audience listened with attention and at the close gave him a round of applause.[8]

He was admitted to the bar in Lexington on March 20, 1798,[9] and established an office, probably in the house on North Mill Street where his shingle hung for many years.[10]

Clay's health was never robust, but he lived intensely. One of his fortes was his capacity for pursuing several objectives at one and the same time. In the spring of 1798, while he was establishing himself as a debater, and was appearing as a lawyer at Lexington and near-by towns, he plunged into the political questions of the day. His first venture was clearly marked by idealism, perhaps more clearly marked by it than any other action of his whole life, for in it he appeared as the champion of human rights and democratic government.

The Kentuckians had established a charter for themselves in 1792, modeled, by and large, on the Federal Constitution, and providing for universal manhood suffrage. It was a liberal instrument for the times, but the frontier democracy, after trying it out for five years, became restless and demanded altera-

[8] Clay, Works, Vol. I, p. 100; Sargent, op. cit., p. 4. Both Colton and Sargent had the benefit of being contemporaries and friends of Clay, and such anecdotes may be accepted, I think, as being approximately correct. These two authors are likewise the best sources available for stories of his criminal law trials.
[9] Fayette Circuit Court, Order Book A, p. 94. He was admitted on his own motion, but this was quite customary at the time.
[10] Ranck, op. cit., p. 215.

tions. Charges flew about that a favored few were absorbing the land, the money and the slaves; that these men were waxing fat and becoming aristocratic.[11] The discontented clamored against the limitations upon the will of the people, and they were especially fervent in regard to the indirect election of the Governor and the senate. There was also a group that, with humanitarian zeal, sought a gradual emancipation of the state's thirty-five thousand slaves. Both of these movements were vigorously opposed by the conservatively minded. The situation presented an opportunity for a young man who believed himself a liberal, and Clay joined the reformers.

Writing in the *Kentucky Gazette*, under the pseudonym of "Scaevola," he urged on two counts the adoption of a new constitution. The first was that of slavery, which was safeguarded by the existing charter. Clay pictured it in no uncertain terms. How can a humane man, he asked, be happy and contented in the midst of the horrors of slavery? Certainly Kentuckians, with their enthusiasm for liberty, cannot. All America acknowledges that slavery is an evil, injuring slave and master alike. "If it be this enormous evil, the sooner we attempt its destruction the better," and to accomplish this he demanded provision for gradual emancipation. At the same time, he attacked the senate, which he wished to see curbed, if not abolished. A bicameral legislature, he asserted, was not founded upon truly democratic principles. "If it be true that the farther we go from the people, we get men better acquainted with, and more competent to decide upon, the affairs of the republic, why stop at fifteen, why not descend to two or one?" The senate was without value as a check, he argued, because the will of the people should not be checked, and the senate might just as easily impede the progress of good laws as bad ones.[12]

At the ensuing general elections there was no landslide for a new constitution, but the demand was sufficiently strong to

[11] H. Marshall, *History of Kentucky*, 2 vols. (Frankfort, 1824), Vol. II, pp. 246–247.

[12] *Kentucky Gazette*, April 25, 1798. *Cf. Ibid.*, Feb. 28, 1799, where Clay insinuates that the slaveholders are moving toward a freehold qualification of the suffrage.

induce the legislature to summon a convention. This was held in July of 1799, and a new instrument was provided that was to remain in force until 1849. This signalized the march of democracy by establishing the direct election of the senate and of the Governor, and by providing for overruling the Governor's veto by a simple majority. But the convention did nothing toward abolishing slavery, although Clay felt that the exertions of his fellow emancipationists and himself produced the clauses in the constitution which gave the legislature power to prohibit bringing slaves into the state as merchandise, and power to pass laws compelling humane treatment.[13]

What did Breckinridge, who opposed the calling of the convention, George Nicholas, who had helped draft the constitution of 1792, and the well-fed in general think of Clay at this juncture? Was he going to be a demagogue, a caterer to the have-nots? A certain coolness might have been exhibited by the frontier conservatives, had not an incident occurred which drew all Republicans, rich and poor alike, into a boiling vortex of indignation.

Jeffersonian Republicanism favored holding the Federal Government within bounds and fostering an agrarian democracy. It looked upon the French Revolution as a noble experiment enlarging the rights of man. All this appealed to the proud and self-reliant frontier spirit, disgusted with the Federalists' penchant for power, and their delay in freeing Mississippi navigation from the throttle hold of Spain. As early as 1793, democratic clubs on the French model were formed in Kentucky.[14] The one in Lexington, with John Breckinridge as president and Thomas Bodley and Thomas Todd as clerks, campaigned vigorously for open navigation of the Mississippi, exalted France, and denounced Federalism. All the Republicans of Lexington joined it, wore tricolor cock-

[13] McDowell Collection, Henry Clay, Jr.'s diary, 1832; C. S. Morehead, and M. Brown, *A Digest of the Statute Laws of Kentucky*, 2 vols. (Frankfort, 1834), Vol. I, p. 68; A. E. Martin, *The Anti-Slavery Movement in Kentucky* (Louisville, 1918), p. 31.

[14] E. D. Warfield, *The Kentucky Resolutions* (N.Y., 1887), p. 35.

ades and planted liberty poles, with liberty caps atop, on the street corners. The followers of Hamilton wore black cockades, and at times party spirit rode high and fierce.[15]

The excesses of Genêt, the opening of the Mississippi by the Spanish treaty of 1795, and the X Y Z Affair, lessened the spiritual force of this Republicanism, but distrust of a Government that had levied a hated excise tax, and that seemed intent upon forcing federal unity at the expense of the states, scarcely became latent. It flamed with renewed vigor when the Federalists foolishly attempted to crush their opponents by the Alien and Sedition acts of 1798. These laws gave the President wide powers over aliens, and curbed the freedom of speech and of the press. All Kentucky seemed to blaze up,[16] and in the general excitement young Clay took an active although a minor part.[17]

No report of his speeches has been preserved, but at one of the public meetings in Lexington, after George Nicholas had denounced the laws and the despotic tendencies of Federalism, someone shouted Clay's name. He mounted the wagon that served as a speaker's rostrum and poured forth such an impassioned torrent of denunciation that, when he had finished, not a sound came from the crowd. It was silent and raging. William Murray, leading Federalist orator of the region, came forward but was not allowed to speak. He would have been dragged down, had not Nicholas and Clay interfered. Another Federalist speaker was forced into flight by the wrathful assemblage, and then the people took Nicholas and Clay upon their shoulders and bore them away in a triumphal procession.[18]

Clay had no part in framing the Kentucky Resolutions, but there is no doubt that he approved them in principle, and

[15] R. Peter, *History of Fayette County, Kentucky* (Chicago, 1882), pp. 69–70.
[16] M. Butler, *A History of the Commonwealth of Kentucky* (Louisville, 1834), pp. 282f; Marshall, *op. cit.*, Vol. II, p. 254.
[17] Mallory, *op. cit.*, Vol. I, pp. 598–599.
[18] R. Mc. McElroy, *Kentucky in the Nation's History* (N.Y., 1909), pp. 224–225.

Madison's report, which denounced broad construction of the Constitution under the general welfare clause and upheld the right of the states, acting together, to declare federal laws unconstitutional, aroused his enthusiasm, and his determination to make Madison's principles his own.[19] Clay had demonstrated his loyalty to the party, and in the Republican triumph of 1800 he stood by the side of Breckinridge and the other leaders.

The young lawyer had meanwhile taken a step which deepened his connection with the wealthy and more conservative interests of Kentucky. On April 11, 1799, in the brick house which still stands on the southwest corner of Mill and Second Streets, Clay married eighteen-year-old Lucretia Hart, youngest daughter of wealthy Thomas Hart. This marriage was advantageous in many ways. It brought him into direct connection with a prosperous and influential family, and Lucretia Hart, although neither beautiful nor intellectual,[20] was a woman of good sense, discreet and kind, a good manager, and was to be a devoted mother.[21] The latter quality was especially needful. She was to bear him eleven children.

Clay was not certain, at first, that he would be content to remain in Kentucky. The West lay open to him, he was eager to get ahead as rapidly as possible, and, from time to time, he weighed the advantages of moving to Tennessee, or down to New Orleans.[22] But family ties, an auspicious beginning in law and politics, and association with a region that was speedily developing its business opportunities, were considerations that outweighed the wanderlust. Lexington was booming. Ropewalks, manufactories for spinning cotton and hemp, duck

[19] J. Madison, *Letters and Other Writings*, 4 vols. (Phila., 1865), Vol. IV, pp. 515–555, Report on the Virginia Resolutions, House of Delegates, session 1799–1800; *Annals of Cong.*, 15th Cong., 1st sess., 1361; Mallory, *op. cit.*, Vol. II, p. 572.

[20] M. B. Smith, *The First Forty Years of Washington Society* (N.Y., 1906), pp. 86–87, 332. Mrs. Smith was a devoted friend of Mrs. Clay.

[21] *Ibid.*, pp. 85–87, 332, 353; Hart family tradition.

[22] James Brown to Thomas Bedford, Oct. 8, 1799 (Ky. State Hist. Soc. Lib.); Clay Papers, I, James Brown to Henry Clay, Feb. 27, 1806; XVII, Clay to J. B. Harrison, Sept. 11, 1831; Breckinridge Papers, XXV, Clay to John Breckinridge, Nov. 21, 1803.

factories, carriage factories, powder mills, sprang up and flourished apace. Kentucky manufactured $6,181,024 worth of goods in 1810, and Lexington was the principal center of this activity.[23] Law and business go together.

The rising lawyer found himself, too, in sympathy with the spirit and the manner of living of the Kentuckians. They were a boastful and somewhat petulant lot, high-spirited, almost as fond of law suits as they were of horse racing, and mighty men with the bottle and at the card table.[24] The young lawyers of the day fitted into this manner of living without visible signs of reluctance. It was fashionable for them to drink and gamble. Micah Taul observed that "there were Gentlemen, attending the Courts, who studied Hoyle, more than they did Blackstone, & generally *won all the money,* made by others." [25] Clay is supposed to have led a life of the strictest virtue in Richmond, but if he did, he soon got bravely over it. The stories of his wild intemperance can be dismissed as part of the malicious gossip that is so apt to center about prominent men. But he loved good wine, and drank it regularly all his life,[26] and it would have been a strange Kentuckian who looked upon whiskey and brandy as works of the devil. James O. Harrison, his friend and executor, who scorned the stories of his drunkenness, admitted that it was not unheard of for Clay's drinking "to add something to his vivacity," [27] and it is easy to believe the story of one occasion in his early life when, after the dinner had ended and the bottle had circulated freely, he

announced his intention of finishing off the entertainment by a grand Terpsichorean performance on the table, which he accordingly did, executing a *pas seul* from head to foot of the dining table, sixty feet

[23] *American State Papers, Finance* (Washington, 1832), Vol. II, p. 713; Michaux, *op. cit.,* pp. 200–201; F. Cuming, *Sketches of a Tour to the Western Country* (Pittsburg, 1810), pp. 160–167; Wm. Darby, *The Emigrants' Guide* (N.Y., 1818), pp. 205–206.

[24] Michaux, *op. cit.,* pp. 247f; Taul, *op. et loc. cit.,* pp. 357–359; A. Kendall, *Autobiography* (Boston, 1872), p. 126.

[25] Taul, *op. et loc. cit.,* pp. 366–367.

[26] Clay Papers, Duplicate Photostats, J. O. Harrison's reminiscence; XXII, Feb. 2, 1841.

[27] Clay Papers, Duplicate Photostats, J. O. Harrison's reminiscence.

in length, amidst the loud applause of his companions, and to a crashing accompaniment of shivered glass and china: for which expensive music he next morning paid, without demur, a bill of $120! [28]

Such actions were thoroughly in keeping with the robust humor of the West.

Clay was fond of gambling, and he indulged this passion freely, especially during the early part of his life. "You know, Rodney," he wrote to his friend Caesar Rodney, in 1812, "that I have always paid peculiar homage to the fickle goddess." [29] Poker and brag (both essentially games of bluff and betting), claimed a good deal of his time in early years, and his love of whist in later years was notorious.[30] United States Senator William Plumer, who lodged in the same house with Clay in 1807, noted that Clay gambled a great deal. Clay told Plumer, the latter states, that one evening he won fifteen hundred dollars at cards, and on another lost six hundred dollars.[31] Sometimes the stakes were so exorbitant that full payment was not expected, as is illustrated by an incident that passed into a tradition among the inhabitants of Lexington.

Clay and John Bradford were warm friends, and frequently played cards together. At the close of a game one evening, the summing up revealed that Clay had won forty thousand dollars from Bradford. When they met the next day, the debtor asked how they should settle the account. Clay replied that Bradford's note for five hundred dollars would be satisfactory. This was given. A few nights later they had another lengthy game and when they rose Clay was Bradford's debtor by sixty thousand dollars. The five-hundred-dollar note again changed hands and both men were satisfied.[32]

[28] R. T. Coleman, "Jo Daveiss of Kentucky," in *Harpers Monthly Magazine*, Vol. XXI (Aug., 1860), p. 352.

[29] Simon Gratz Collection (Pa. Hist. Soc.), Dec. 29, 1812; see also Clay's speech, *Annals of Cong.*, 16th Cong., 1st sess., 1730.

[30] R. C. Winthrop, *Memoir of Henry Clay* (Cambridge, 1880), pp. 26–27; "Recollections of an Old Stager," in *Harper's Monthly Magazine*, Vol. XLVI (Dec., 1872), pp. 92–97.

[31] E. S. Brown, *William Plumer's Memorandum of Proceedings in the United States Senate, 1803–1807* (N.Y., 1923), p. 608.

[32] W. H. Perrin, *The Pioneer Press of Kentucky* (Louisville, 1888), pp. 15–16.

John Quincy Adams, a shrewd if cynical judge of human nature, repeatedly noted Clay's passion for play. Adams' comment is famous: "In politics, as in private life, Clay is essentially a gamester." [33]

These characteristics, plus a magnetism and charm of manner that made men forgive him his petulance and hauteur and women acknowledge his fascination, endeared Henry Clay to Kentuckians.

The Kentucky bar was a brilliant one. John Breckinridge, George Nicholas, Joseph Hamilton Daveiss, and James Hughes in Fayette County were extremely able men. James Brown, tall, majestic and haughty, Clay's brother-in-law and friend, was then in his early thirties and prominent in the legal profession. The able John Allen and Jesse Bledsoe, and the courtly George Mortimer Bibb, were brilliant rivals of about Clay's own age. As a newcomer Clay had felt that he would do well if he made one hundred pounds, Virginia money, a year, and he was delighted with his first fifteen-shilling fee. But from the very start his practice increased rapidly, and within a few months he was appearing at the courthouses in Winchester and Frankfort as well as in Lexington.[34] His professional activities broadened in a way that showed a real aptitude and a capacity for hard work. Colonel Hart gave him a goodly amount of business; [35] John Breckinridge, who went to the United States Senate in 1801, and later became Attorney-General, entrusted many of his clients to Clay's care.[36] Within a few years he was acting as legal representative in Kentucky for Eastern merchants,[37] and beginning in 1806 Noah Webster, the New

---

[33] J. Q. Adams, *Memoirs of John Quincy Adams*, 12 vols. (Phila., 1874), Vol. V, p. 59, April 6, 1820.

[34] Mallory, *op. cit.*, Vol. II, p. 572; Taul, *op. cit.*, pp. 354–356; L. F. Johnson, *History of Franklin County, Kentucky* (Frankfort, 1912), p. 10.

[35] *Edwards Papers*, pp. 17–23.

[36] Breckinridge Papers, XXV, Clay to Breckinridge, Nov. 21, 1803; XXIX, Clay to Breckinridge, Jan. 5, 1806; XXXI, Mary H. Breckinridge to Breckinridge, Dec. 22, [1806].

[37] Clay Papers, I, Clay to William Taylor, Aug. 31, 1800, *et seq.*; Porter Collection (Buffalo Hist. Soc.), Clay to William Taylor, March 8, 1803; Matthew Carey Accounts (Am. Antiq. Soc., Worcester, Mass.), Vol. XX, p. 27, May, 1804.

England author and lexicographer, employed him to safe-guard his interests in the Western country.[38] A good deal of his business involved land suits that required tedious and careful research, but Clay was equal to the task, and he reaped good profits from his increasing clientèle. His criminal practice was rapidly growing at the same time. He was placed by popular opinion, as early as March 1805, among the leaders of the Kentucky bar.[39] And this in six years' time!

The stories about his practice are legion, the records are few.[40] But such evidence as there is bears witness to his extraordinary success as a criminal lawyer. No prisoner defended by him, it is said, was ever capitally punished,[41] and the tales recounted by Sargent and Colton illustrate his great powers of persuasion, early in his career. He defended a woman clearly guilty of murder, in his first important criminal case. It was before the day of alienists, but Clay pleaded temporary delirium on the part of his client, and this emotional appeal so worked upon the sympathies of the jurors that they brought in a verdict inflicting the lightest possible jail sentence. He succeeded in getting a manslaughter verdict in another case, and then forced from the court an arrest of judgment which resulted in the discharge of the prisoners.

A man named Willis was accused of a peculiarly atrocious murder. Clay defended him, and the jury disagreed. A new trial was granted, Clay not objecting. Then at the second trial, he told the jury that they could not now convict the man, because the law forbade putting a man twice in jeopardy of his life for the same offense. The court forbade his using that argu-

---

[38] Noah Webster Papers (N.Y. Public Lib.), Clay to Webster, Nov. 18, 1806, *et seq.*

[39] Clay Papers, I, James Brown to Clay, March 12, 1805.

[40] No stenographic records of criminal trials were kept in those days. Even the records of civil suits in which he was involved, either as attorney or as plaintiff or defendant, are largely lost, destroyed or stolen. I have examined carefully the records in the Fayette Co. courthouse, at Lexington. Every courtesy was accorded, but it was a grimy and in the main a thankless task.

[41] J. O. Harrison Papers, sketch of Clay; Sargent, *op. cit.*, p. 5; Cassius M. Clay, *Memoirs* (Cincinnati, 1886), p. 87. "Cash" goes so far as to state that Henry Clay never lost a case in criminal practice.

ment. Clay declared he could not proceed unless allowed to take that course, gathered up his books and papers, and left the trial. This threw all responsibility upon the court, which was none too sure of its law, for Clay was invited to come back and proceed as he wished. He did so, convinced the jury that he was right, and, regardless of the evidence, the prisoner was acquitted.[42]

He used the dramatic approach, as in the Willis case, again and again. Joined to his imperious air of command, it was effective and delightful. On one occasion, at the beginning of a trial, he called for the warrant of arrest, and found it defective and illegal. He turned to his client and said, "Go home, sir!" The man hesitated. "Go home," thundered Clay, and the man jumped up and "put out," without an attempt by sheriff or judge to stop him.[43]

Clay distinguished himself also as a friend of the Negro in court. It is true that, during his brief occupancy of the post of district attorney, he secured the execution of a Negro who had killed a brutal overseer, but he always regretted this. He was wont, during his early years as a lawyer, to volunteer his services to slaves who sought their freedom by means of law, and it is traditional that he would never resist the attempt of a Negro to gain his freedom through the courts.[44]

There are several factors that account for this success. It was a day of oratory, and Clay knew how to play upon the emotions of twelve "good men and true." He customarily stood close to the jury box. Movement was confined to graceful gesticulation with one or both hands save when, in making a vital point, he would take a few steps forward.[45] The jurors gazed into a face that could mirror every emotion, and they

[42] Clay, *Works*, Vol. I, pp. 106–108; Sargent, *op. cit.*, pp. 4–5. All his early biographers recount these stories.

[43] Peter, *op. cit.*, p. 353.

[44] J. O. Harrison Papers, sketch of Clay; Peck, *op. cit.*, p. 24. See Clay Papers, I, Feb. 5, 1807, for a letter from a Negro in New Orleans, James Johnson, requesting Clay to purchase for him his brother's freedom. Johnson regrets having to ask this favor, "but there is none else in whom I can place that Confidence."

[45] C. M. Clay, *op. cit.*, p. 88.

felt the spell of a voice whose magic subdued the most obdurate heart. Then, too, the bench was often pathetically inadequate. Kentucky established, in 1802, a circuit court system, with one judge, learned in the law, going on circuit. This in itself was not objectionable, but the judge was always flanked on either hand by two local assistants, unlearned in either law or equity, and with power to overrule him at any time.[46] This asinine procedure resulted in a chaos that enabled lawyers to win case after case with emotional appeals made in utter defiance of right law. Finally, Clay's real ability in the law, plus his facility in using tricks that confused both bench and jury, made him always dangerous as an opponent. But successes gained under such conditions cost him some qualms. "Ah, Willis, poor fellow," he said once to the murderer, "I fear I have saved too many like you, who ought to be hanged." [47]

One other comment may justly be made upon Clay as a lawyer. Brilliant and successful as he was, talented, able and industrious, his mastery of the law was scarcely profound. In part this was due to the fact that the general principles of the common law ruled most cases at the time and a thorough knowledge of precedents was not necessary, in part to his increasing interest in politics and the pleasures of society, and in part to his self-confessed willingness to rely too much upon the resources of his genius. Justice Story's comment, years later, is significant: —

Your friend Clay has argued before us with a good deal of ability; and if he were not a candidate for higher offices, I should think he might attain great eminence at this Bar. But he prefers the fame of popular talents to the steady fame of the Bar.[48]

Clay's professional success brought money, and a place in the community as a substantial citizen. His taxable property in 1799 consisted of one horse. In 1800 he was a little more

[46] Marshall, *op. cit.*, Vol. II, pp. 350–351; *Cong. Debates*, 23d Cong., 2d sess., 591–594. Clay on these circuit courts.

[47] Schurz, *op. cit.*, Vol. I, p. 22.

[48] W. W. Story, *Life and Letters of Joseph Story*, 2 vols. (Boston, 1851), Vol. I, p. 423, Story to the Hon. Mr. Justice Todd, March 4, 1823.

prosperous, owning three slaves and two horses,[49] but in 1805 he was assessed on one hundred and twenty-five acres of first-class land, sixty-four hundred acres second-rate or unspecified, eight slaves, fifteen livestock, and town property to the value of twenty-three hundred dollars. This was a tidy increase in property over five short years. Small wonder that James Brown heard from the Kentuckians who visited New Orleans that Clay was at the head of his profession and rapidly growing rich.[50]

Land holdings ranging, as Clay's did, up to thirteen thousand acres by 1808, might be simply the result of fees or title occupancy in the interest of clients, but there is no question that Clay was interested in land speculation. The lists of his holdings in various parts of Kentucky, his purchase later of a farm in Missouri and a section in Illinois, all show that he had the land fever, a disease that never wholly left him. As late as 1835, when he was heavily in debt and money was tight for him, he embarked with one of his sons upon the purchase of a Bluegrass farm, because he felt that real estate was going up in value.[51] This was entirely apart from Ashland, which grew in size until, at the time of his death, it contained five hundred and thirty-seven acres.

Clay was interested, also, in other investments. Property that he had acquired in Louisville was exchanged by him in 1808 for a stable, houses and lots in Lexington.[52] He owned a tavern in Lexington, Traveller's Hall, and leased it for nine hundred dollars a year. He became one of the proprietors of the Madison Hemp Company, which could run with water power twelve hundred spindles for spinning hemp and flax.[53]

And like so many of his neighbors, Clay was himself in-

[49] Fayette Co. Tax Lists (Ky. State Hist. Soc. Lib.). Col. Hart probably gave him some financial aid (*Edwards Papers*, pp. 17–23, Clay to Edwards, July 4, 1801), but the tax lists, 1799–1802, indicate no sudden influx of real or personal property.

[50] Clay Papers, I, James Brown to Clay, Oct. 31, 1805.

[51] McDowell Collection, Henry Clay to Henry Clay, Jr., Feb. 19, 1835.

[52] Henry Clay *vs.* Lytle, Wickliffe, &c., Fayette Circuit Court, file 823, May 17, 1835.

[53] Cuming, *op. cit.*, pp. 165–166; Wm. Littell, *The Statute Law of Kentucky*, 5 vols. (Frankfort, 1807–1811), Vol. III, p. 532.

volved in many law suits. The records of the Fayette Circuit Court demonstrate the frequency with which he resorted to legal action, either as executor for Thomas Hart or in connection with his own property and money interests. Titles were often cloudy, and men frequently gave notes that they were unable to meet. The real estate that Clay acquired in 1808 eventually involved him in a great law suit with Robert Wickliffe which ran on until the 1830's and cost Clay thousands of dollars.[54] In 1810, he had to file suit to protect his title to land which he had acquired near Lexington.[55] He sued repeatedly to collect notes that those indebted to him were unable or unwilling to pay.[56]

These suits would seem to indicate a certain trustfulness and optimism scarcely consonant with good business methods. The impression thus created is heightened by his ready endorsement of notes for friends and relatives, a practice that cost him large sums of money and repeatedly embarrassed him.[57] One incident of the 1820's illustrates the nonchalance that characterized many of his business transactions. On January 25, 1820, Clay collected and paid over to one Leonard Jacoby $291.22. Four years later, pressed by Jacoby's assignees for this money and forgetting that he had paid it once, he paid over to them $250 more. He sued for the recovery of this money, December 15, 1827, having only then discovered his former slip![58] Such carelessness was, however, thoroughly in consonance with the expansive optimism of the frontier.

The young Virginian's hazard of new fortunes brought him

[54] Henry Clay vs. Lytle, Wickliffe, &c., Fayette Circuit Court, file 823, May 17, 1835.

[55] Henry Clay & Thos. Hart vs. Wilson C. Nicholas, et al., Fayette Circuit Court, file 442, Jan. 11, 1819.

[56] Henry Clay vs. John Jordan, Jr., Fayette Circuit Court, file 119, Feb. 16, 1807; Henry Clay vs. George Adams, Fayette Circuit Court, file 120, June 15, 1807; Henry Clay vs. John South, Fayette Circuit Court, file 135, April 7, 1808; Henry Clay vs. Alfred Grayson, et al., Fayette Circuit Court, file 203, March 30, 1811.

[57] McDowell Collection, passim; Clay Papers, XXIV, D. M. Craig to John Odenhamer, March 5, 1845.

[58] H. Clay vs. the assignees of Leonard Jacoby, Fayette Circuit Court, file 665, Dec. 15, 1827.

wealth, real repute as a successful lawyer, and social position. His friendship was cultivated, his opinions were sought, and he entered into the social and intellectual life of his new home in a variety of ways. Shortly after his arrival, he had become a member of the Masonic lodge in Lexington. He remained active and influential in the order until 1824.[59] He became one of the owners of and gave its name to the Olympian Springs, a resort situated among the high hills of what is now Bath County, forty-seven miles from Lexington. It became the custom for him to go there in the summer, with his growing family.[60] On October 10, 1805, the board of trustees of Transylvania University unanimously elected him Professor of Law and Politics.[61] He served until the fall of 1807. Then he resigned, and was elected a trustee of the institution,[62] an office that he filled actively and intelligently, so far as the somewhat scanty records show, for over twenty years.[63] It was, all in all, a busy life, but, in the midst of these diverse activities, his attention turned more and more to a political career.

[59] J. Winston Coleman, Jr., *Masonry in the Bluegrass* (Lexington, 1933), pp. 51, 67, 75, 92.
[60] Coleman, *Stage-Coach Days*, p. 37, note.
[61] Proceedings of the Board of Trustees.
[62] *Ibid.*, Oct. 7, 1807.
[63] Miscellaneous Papers at Transylvania University. He left the board in 1813, but was re-elected in 1818 and served until 1830.

CHAPTER III

POLITICS, "TREASON," AND A DUEL

CLAY had been interested in politics and government while still
in Richmond, and this interest developed as he made a place
for himself in Kentucky. He took a vigorous part in the discussion of constitutional revision, and the Alien and Sedition
laws. He stood on the "right" side — that is to say, on the
popular side — in the campaign of 1800, and during that
campaign he made an earnest though unsuccessful attempt to
obtain an appointment as clerk of the Kentucky senate.[1] He
had, by 1803, established himself as a brilliant and successful
lawyer, a man who was making money and was harmoniously
connected with the business interests of Fayette County.

These factors made him a suitable candidate for the legislature. They were reinforced by the knowledge that he stood for
the maintenance of the Kentucky Insurance Company, a local
institution already being subjected to a scattered fire from the
hustings. His friends nominated him without his knowledge or
consent, as the story goes, while he was at Olympian Springs
in the summer of 1803, and he won out over several candidates
in the election.[2] The legislature met in Frankfort, and Clay was
there when the house assembled on the second floor of the
rectangular "rough marble" statehouse with its cupola atop. It
was the beginning of a phase of his career that brought him
state-wide recognition as a political leader.[3]

The first session that he attended was not distinguished for
its legislation. The proceedings developed into a grand log-

[1] Ky. State Hist. Soc. Lib., Clay to James Taylor, May 26, 1800; *Edwards
Papers*, p. 23, Clay to Ninian Edwards, July 9, 1800.
[2] Mallory, *op. cit.*, Vol. II, p. 572, Clay's speech at Lexington, June 9,
1842; Sargent, *op. cit.*, p. 6; G. D. Prentice, *Biography of Henry Clay* (N.Y.,
1831), p. 25. Prentice states that Clay returned *during the election*, and
swung it in his favor by an ingenuous speech.
[3] The best sources are the *Journal of the Kentucky House of Representatives*,
1803–1810; the *Kentucky Gazette*; the Breckinridge Papers.

rolling shared by all the members, and most of the sixty-eight laws passed were local in character. One of the exceptions, introduced by Clay, was an act which changed, to the disadvantage of the Federalists, the method of choosing presidential electors.[4]

The New Orleans excitement was one cause of this deficit in statesmanship. Kentucky was seething with rage when the legislature met, for in 1802 the Spanish Intendant, Morales, had refused the United States the right to deposit goods at the mouth of the Mississippi. The furor occasioned by this had been heightened by the news that Spain had ceded Louisiana to France. Governor James Garrard raised troops and handed out commissions for a crusade on New Orleans. Clay was appointed one of the two aides of General Hopkins, the commander of the proposed expedition, and made ready to "go with the croud to endeavour to share the glory of the expedition."[5] Jefferson had, in the meantime, purchased Louisiana, and when the news of this reached Frankfort, the excitement died down. Clay wrote to Breckinridge that he would have been glad to go, "but I nevertheless sincerely rejoice that the affair has terminated pacifically."[6]

The next two sessions of the legislature were much more dramatic, and Clay was active in a variety of useful matters. He was a member of many committees, one of the most important being a committee on finance to consider and suggest revision of the revenue laws.[7] He introduced acts, which were passed, for paving the streets of Lexington and incorporating the Ohio Canal Company.[8] He urged, as he did repeatedly and without effect, the removal of the capital from Frankfort,[9] and he opposed, unsuccessfully, a measure punishing adultery as a

[4] Breckinridge Papers, XXV, Wm. Stevenson to John Breckinridge, Nov. 21, 1803; Thos. Todd to Breckinridge, Dec. 1, 1803.

[5] *Ibid.*, Clay to Breckinridge, Nov. 21, 1803. This is one of the rare examples of bad spelling to be found in Clay's letters.

[6] *Ibid.*, Dec. 30, 1803.

[7] *House Journal, 1805–1806*, p. 10. Clay moved the appointment of this committee.

[8] *Ibid.*, 1804–1805, pp. 12f. The canal company did not prosper.

[9] Marshall, *op. cit.*, Vol. II, p. 10; Prentice, *op. cit.*, p. 28. He wanted to make Lexington the capital, but the members could not agree on any new location.

felony.[10] But his leadership shone forth most clearly in the great struggle of these two sessions over the Kentucky Insurance Company.

This company had been formed in 1802 by a number of men in Lexington, its ostensible purpose being to insure boat cargoes on the Mississippi and its tributaries. William Morton was president, John Bradford cashier, and Thomas Hart was a member of the board of directors. Its charter, a fair, full instrument in twenty-five sections, had passed the legislature without demur. The company was given a tenure of fifteen years, and no similar organization was to be established during that period. It could own property worth one hundred and fifty thousand dollars, and could issue stock up to one hundred thousand dollars. This was fair enough, but, hidden adroitly away among the provisions, was a clause that permitted the unlimited issue of notes payable to bearer. In other words, this insurance company was a bank. The venture prospered, and in 1805 was making profits at the rate of sixteen per cent. a year.[11] Mutters of protest arose, but the business men stood firm. It was the masses against the classes again, as it had been in the case of constitutional revision in 1799, but this time Clay was in the conservative camp.

The great champion of repeal was Felix Grundy. This young gentleman, five months Clay's junior, had come to Kentucky in his family's baggage train in 1780. His education had been meager. He had studied law under George Nicholas, being admitted to the bar in 1797. Two years later he had sat in the constitutional convention, and thereafter took a prominent rôle in politics. Of ordinary stature, ruddy complexion, light brown hair with a reddish tinge, and keen blue eyes, he was the possessor of a winning personality, and great oratorical powers.[12] And in ambition, at least, he was Clay's equal.

[10] *House Journal, 1805–1806*, pp. 103–104.

[11] Littell, *Statute Law of Kentucky*, Vol. III, pp. 25–31; R. T. Durrett, "Early Banking in Kentucky," in *Ky. Bankers Assoc. Proceedings* (1892), p. 40; Marshall, *op. cit.*, Vol. II, pp. 348–350, 374; Ranck, *op. cit.*, p. 222.

[12] J. W. Caldwell, *Sketches of the Bench and Bar of Tennessee* (Knoxville, 1898), p. 60.

Why Grundy fought the Kentucky Insurance Company is an open question. It may have been honest conviction and a love of democracy. It may have been the demagoguery of which his opponents were quick to accuse him.[13] But oppose it he did, and in 1804 he came to the house with a majority at his back. He and Clay fought the issue out, before crowded galleries and with the senators in almost constant attendance. Grundy denounced the company as undemocratic and dangerous, and pointed particularly to the power of unlimited note issue. Clay defended banking in general, and the company in particular.

Grundy succeeded in putting through the house a bill repealing the company's charter. It was defeated in the senate. The malcontents then introduced and passed, December 19, 1804, another bill which limited the company's banking powers. It was deprived of its monopoly, and could now issue notes freely only up to the total value of the company's property, plus the stock, plus the money in the vaults, plus *all* debts due. The president and directors were to be held personally responsible for notes issued above that amount. This had the appearance of a Pyrrhic victory. Feeling remained bitter and the struggle was not yet over.[14]

Repeal had a majority in both houses in the following session, but again Clay came to the support of the company. Grundy renewed his onslaught almost as soon as the legislature met on November 4, 1805. Banks, he said, were undemocratic, for they drove the balance of wealth out of the hands of the people. He denounced the power of note issue, and asserted that the law creating the Lexington bank was unconstitutional. Clay upheld banking as essential for a progressive community, and said that repeal of the law was unconstitutional, for it would mean the destruction of vested rights. His arguments were ineffective,

[13] His later activities in Tennessee suggest the latter. T. P. Abernethy calls him "the first demagogue of Tennessee" — *From Frontier to Plantation in Tennessee* (Chapel Hill, 1932), p. 228. But in 1806 he was a resident of Lexington and a trustee of Transylvania University — Ranck, *op. cit.*, p. 232.

[14] Littell, *Statute Law of Kentucky*, Vol. III, p. 212; Breckinridge Papers, XXVII, Innes to Breckinridge, Dec. 20, 1804; Clay Papers, I, Grundy to Clay, Feb. 4, 1805; Durrett, *op. cit.*, p. 40.

and the repeal passed both houses. Governor Greenup vetoed it, December 5, but despite a desperate struggle by Clay and his group, the house passed it over the Governor's veto by a vote of forty to eighteen,[15] an even greater majority than before. The bill went to the senate, where its passage seemed certain.

Then Clay made a very adroit move.

The legislature, during the preceding ten years, had badly botched the disposal of great tracts of land south of the Green River. A bewildering variety of acts had been passed providing for settlement in that region, acts that verged always toward relief, favoritism and worse. There were undoubtedly many honest, poverty-stricken settlers in the south country, but the "Green River band" in the legislature, with its persistent appeals for relief from land payments, had become a scandal,[16] and these Green River men constituted an important part of Grundy's forces. Just as the repeal of the Lexington bank law was about to pass the senate a second time, Clay introduced in the house a bill to compel the payment of the Green River debts. It was a threatened exposé of the whole mass of corruption in the south country. The repeal project was paralyzed, and the violent opponents of banks in general, including Grundy himself, became, ludicrously enough, the proponents of a state bank which was actually chartered a year later.[17] "I believe our Legeslature in Kentucky are geting higher toaned every year . . . ," wrote a disgruntled Democrat to John Breckinridge.[18]

The contest was over. Grundy became a judge on the court of appeals in 1806. The following year he moved to Tennessee, and Clay and his group were left in control of the situation. But bitterness remained, and, in at least one instance in the next election, the charge was made that Clay had promised to

---

[15] *House Journal, 1805–1806*, pp. 48f.

[16] Marshall, *op. cit.*, Vol. II, pp. 178f. *Cf. Cong. Deb.*, 24th Cong., 1st sess., 1248–1249, for Clay's story of the land scandals in those early days.

[17] Breckinridge Papers, XXIX, F. L. Turner to Breckinridge, Dec. 20, 1805; W. Stevenson to Breckinridge, Jan. 1806 [?]; Collins, *op. cit.*, Vol. I, p. 295; Durrett, *op. cit.*, p. 40.

[18] Breckinridge Papers, XXX, Russell to Breckinridge, March 1, 1806.

supply a pro-bank candidate with money from the Lexington bank.[19]

This triumph of the business interests increased Clay's reputation as a parliamentary tactician and, on the whole, was to his credit. His advocacy of banking indicated intelligence and foresight. The Kentucky Insurance Company would scarcely be tolerated as a bank to-day, but Western banking practices were not exactly cautious in the frontier era. The company, wisely managed, was a valuable aid to the business of the region, although by 1818, when its charter was due to expire, it was in bad financial straits.[20] Perhaps the only real regret left by the struggle is that the young leader did not throw himself into a crusade against the "Green River band" with the same abandon that he showed in saving the bank.

The breath of scandal, one of Clay's deadliest foes in public life, touched him three times in 1806. Two of these occasions had no serious menace. The story of his supplying bank money for political purposes was a mere rumor; no facts substantiating it were ever brought to light, and it can be dismissed as a product of political animosity. The offer of a bribe created a momentary excitement, although his disdainful rejection of it [21] scotched all possibility of its being perverted into a gossip-mongering tale. But the third occasion, though he did not know it at the time, was potent with menace for his future political career, for it linked his name with that of Aaron Burr.

Burr came of good stock. A grandson of Jonathan Edwards, a son of Aaron Burr the theologian and second president of the College of New Jersey, he himself had had a distinguished career. Soldier, lawyer, United States Senator, third Vice-President of the United States, he was a man of brilliant parts. Dignity and the charm of fascinating manners compelled men's admiration. Women and children loved him. He was an able lawyer and an astute politician.

But these qualities were counterbalanced by great defects.

---

[19] Anderson Collection, Clay to Col. John Ballenger, Sept. 8, 1806.

[20] Durrett, *op. cit.*, p. 40f; Ranck, *op. cit.*, p. 222.

[21] *House Journal, 1806–1807*, pp. 35–36. It was offered to gain his influence in putting through the house a private bill of divorce.

Spendthrift, a lover of adventure and intrigue, offending conventional taste by his notorious amours, it was his fate, in some part undeserved, to be constantly enveloped by strange clouds of glory and suspicion which became more and more dark and foreboding.

For several years Burr's star had been swiftly sinking. Bitter political quarrels, constant attacks by his arch-enemy, Alexander Hamilton, and failing personal fortunes, all had played a part. Determined to rid himself of the man who was hounding him down, he had forced Hamilton into the famous duel. They met on July 11, 1804, at Weehawken. Each fired once, and the pistol smoke that hung for a brief instant in the morning air completely smudged a shield already tarnished. Burr's career in the East had ended. Penniless, threatened with disfranchisement in New York and with hanging in New Jersey, he turned his thoughts to the West, and in May of 1805 appeared in Frankfort.[22]

Burr was always adept at conspiracy, and the West fired his imagination. No one knows whether he included the Mississippi Valley in his schemes of a great Western empire. Perhaps he did not know himself. But at any rate his plans meant rapine and destruction, the conquest of Mexico, and a war with Spain.[23]

Burr spent the summer of 1805 in the West, surveying the ground and laying plans. He gained the confidence of Harman Blennerhassett, a wealthy and eccentric Irishman, who had a beautiful estate on an island in the Ohio River, not far from Marietta. He became very friendly with James Wilkinson, the shifty and venal general in charge of the federal troops in Louisiana. More money was necessary, and in the autumn of 1805 Burr went back to Philadelphia where he tried, fruitlessly, to get financial aid from the English Government, and from Spain (!). A year later he was back in the West, where he was received as formerly with great favor. The frontier hated Spain, and it was generally believed that Burr was planning some

<hr />

[22] McElroy, *op. cit.*, pp. 277–278.
[23] The best treatments of his plans are in W. F. McCaleb, *The Aaron Burr Conspiracy* (N.Y., 1903), and S. H. Wandell and M. Minnigerode, *Aaron Burr*, 2 vols. (N.Y., 1925).

great project against her. Andrew Jackson, hot for a stroke against the dons, acted as one of his agents gathering boats and supplies.[24]

Then fate rose up against Burr. On November 5, 1806, he was publicly charged with violating the laws of the Union by setting on foot an unauthorized expedition against Mexico. The charge was made in Judge Harry Innes' court at Frankfort, and the accuser was Joseph Hamilton Daveiss, federal district attorney in Kentucky.[25]

Daveiss took this action for a number of reasons. He was patriotic undoubtedly. He was also an ardent Federalist, and had been a devoted admirer of Hamilton. He was anxious to humiliate the Western Republicans, most of whom believed in Burr, and he may have thought that he could discredit Jefferson. The President had taken no action, although Daveiss had been writing to him for almost a year, denouncing Burr as a traitor. This denunciation was wildly seconded by a sensationalist newspaper, the *Western World*, to which Humphrey Marshall, Daveiss' brother-in-law, and a leader of the Federalist faction in Kentucky, was an efficient contributor.[26] There was only one grave difficulty for the district attorney. Ferociously eager as he was to expose the plotter, he had no real proof of a plot.

Burr promptly looked about for legal advice. It was not hard to find, and he soon had a brilliant array of counsellors, among them Henry Clay and John Allen. But on November 11, the day set for the trial, Daveiss pleaded inability to get his witnesses together, and the grand jury was dismissed.[27] Burr, with sublime effrontery, continued his preparations for the venture. Then, on November 25, Daveiss renewed his motion for an investigation. The grand jury was once more summoned, and again Burr applied to Clay for legal aid.[28]

Clay, in the meantime, had been chosen by the legislature to

[24] McCaleb, *op. cit.*, pp. 182, 252–255; Taul, *op. et loc. cit.*, Vol. XXVII (Sept. 1929), p. 607.
[25] *Kentucky Gazette*, Nov. 10, 1806; McCaleb, *op. cit.*, p. 177.
[26] McCaleb, *op. cit.*, pp. 172f.
[27] *Kentucky Gazette*, Nov. 13, 17, 1806.
[28] Clay Papers, I, Burr to Clay, Nov. 27, 1806.

fill the seat in the United States Senate vacated by John Adair.[29] Like most Westerners, Clay felt that Burr was innocent of wrongdoing, but he hesitated, for the case possibly involved the question of fidelity to the national Government. He consulted his friend John Rowan. They agreed that there was some impropriety in abandoning a client in the midst of litigation, and Rowan suggested that Clay obtain a pledge that no schemes hostile to the peace or union of the country were in prospect. The pledge was asked and, fortunately for Clay, was given in the most unequivocal language.

I have no design [wrote Burr] nor have I taken any measure to promote a dissolution of the Union, or a separation of any one or more States from the residue. . . . I have no design to intermeddle with the Government or to disturb the tranquility of the United States, or of its territories, or any part of them. I have neither issued, nor signed, nor promised a commission to any person for any purpose. I do not own a musket nor a bayonet, nor any single article of military stores, nor does any person for me, by my authority or with my knowledge. . . .

Considering the high station you now fill in our national councils, I have thought these explanations proper, as well as to counteract the chimerical tales which malevolent persons have so industriously circulated, as to satisfy you that you have not espoused the cause of a man in any way unfriendly to the laws, the government, or the interests of his country.[30]

This assurance was a strange compound of truth and falsity, but Clay could not know that. His qualms vanished, and within twenty-four hours he again appeared in court for the defendant.

Daveiss delayed action for three days, against the energetic protests of Burr's counsel, and then, his witnesses being gathered, he renewed his charge that Burr was setting on foot an expedition against a peaceful neighbor.

By this time, excitement in Frankfort was intense. The town was full of people, and crowds jammed into the courthouse to watch the proceedings. Federalists stoutly maintained Burr's

[29] *House Journal, 1806–1807*, pp. 67–68. Clay was elected Nov. 19, 1806.
[30] C. Colton, ed., *Private Correspondence of Henry Clay* (Cincinnati, 1856), pp. 13–14, Burr to Clay, Dec. 1, 1806; Butler, *op. cit.*, p. 315.

villainy, but the masses were firmly convinced that Daveiss was a blackguard, trying to gain notoriety by the vicious persecution of an innocent man. Feeling ran high. Clay and Allen added fuel to the flame by charging that Daveiss' delay was violating the constitutional right of a citizen to a free trial, and that the district attorney was denying them their right of free speech (!).

Then, in the midst of all this furor, came the farcical dénouement of the investigation. Judge Innes, worked upon by Clay, who compared the district attorney's tactics to "the screws and tortures made use of in the dens of despotism," [31] refused Daveiss the right to question the witnesses before the grand jury. The witnesses themselves, including the editors of the *Western World*, had no evidence of any value to give. At two o'clock, on the afternoon of December 5, the jurors completed their examination and filed back into the courtroom to return the indictment "not a true bill." There was nothing for Daveiss but to bow in humiliation, and the jury was dismissed while the courtroom rang with applause, and Burr's attorneys "could scarcely contain their joy."

A brilliant ball was given in Frankfort in Burr's honor. Social gatherings received him as an honored guest. At one of them, Joseph M. Street, one of the editors of the *Western World*, was roughly handled. Burr was a popular hero as he rode out of Lexington, some days later, bound for Nashville. He could not know that General Wilkinson had betrayed him in malignant fashion, that Jefferson had taken fright, and that a presidential proclamation, warning the country to beware of "sundry persons" who were conspiring against Spain, was already being hurried into the West. Nor could he foresee the trial in Virginia that was to develop into a political persecution, with an acquittal leaving him still deeply suspect in the public mind. The debonair descendant of Jonathan Edwards was heading for disaster.

Clay's part in Burr's defense might have meant disaster for the Kentuckian as well. Both he and Allen, regarding the

[31] *National Intelligencer*, Jan. 12, 1807. This gives the account of the trial published in the *Western World* of Dec. 18, 1806.

Easterner as a wronged and persecuted man, had refused the fee he offered them, and had defended him without charge. The night before Clay left for Washington, Burr came to see him, and gave him letters of introduction. They were accepted, even though not used.[32] Clay left Kentucky convinced that Burr was innocent, and he publicly defended his erstwhile client on his way east.[33] All these circumstances were warped and twisted in later years to show that he was implicated in the project.

Such charges were based only on partisan malignity. There is not a shred of evidence that connects him with Burr's plans. He simply shared that Western temper of mind which made Andrew Jackson one of Burr's active supporters. It was perfectly natural that Clay should accept his client's pledge of innocence. Finally, Clay's letters written after his arrival in Washington are obviously those of a man who was surprised and shocked by the discoveries he had made. "Colonel Burr has supplied much fund of conversation," he wrote to Thomas M. Prentiss. "No doubt is now entertained here of his having engaged in schemes of the most daring and illegal kind. Having left Kentucky under a belief that he was innocent, it was with no little surprise upon my arrival here that I found I had been deceived." [34] Some of the Ohio papers attacked Clay for defending Burr, and the young Senator picked his way carefully that winter in Washington. When, in connection with the investigation of the conspiracy, suspension of the writ of *habeas corpus* came up in the Senate, Clay voted for it, although he told Senator Plumer that he did so only because of his delicate position as late counsel for Burr.[35]

The Kentuckian's about-face might suggest political expediency were it not that thereafter he remained convinced of

[32] Colton, *Correspondence*, pp. 206–208, Clay to Pindell, Oct. 15, 1828.

[33] *Ibid.*, Clay to T. M. Prentiss, Feb. 15, 1807; Thos. H. Clay's Scrapbook, an unidentified newspaper reprint of a letter from Clay to Thos. Hart, Feb. 1, 1807.

[34] Colton, *Correspondence*, pp. 14–15. *Cf.* Durrett Collection (Univ. of Chicago), Clay to Innes, Jan. 16, 1807; T. H. Clay, Scrapbook, Clay to Thos. Hart, Feb. 1, 1807; J. J. Crittenden Papers (Duke Univ.), Clay to Thos. Todd, June 24, 1807.

[35] Brown, *Plumer's Memorandum*, pp. 565, 589; Prentice, *op. cit.*, p. 38, says Clay voted against the motion, but Plumer is the more reliable authority.

his erstwhile client's guilt. Years later, when they met in New York, Clay refused to take Burr's proffered hand. But it is to Clay's everlasting credit that he was courageous enough, and kindly enough, to act as legal agent for Blennerhassett in settling his financial affairs after dreams of grandeur had vanished before the hard realities of plunder and disgrace.[36]

Clay had started for Washington as soon as the Burr investigation at Frankfort had been concluded. The journey was long and tiresome and it was not until December 29 that he took his seat in the Senate chamber. He seems to have had some difficulty in finding a boarding place that suited him, and eventually lodged among Federalists, at Frost and Quinn's boarding house, about eighty rods from the Capitol.[37]

It would be pleasant to picture him as inspired by his first sight of the nation's capital. But Washington at that time, and for years afterward, was only a rude and provincial town. "The city of magnificent distances," as the Portuguese minister ironically called it a few years later, was a sorry place to look at. The broad streets were unpaved. They froze into the roughest of ruts; the rains converted them into morasses; and in the summer the winds swept up clouds of dust to blind the eyes and choke the throats of the passers-by. Hogs roamed at large and rooted up the city commons. Quail and other birds were shot within one hundred yards of the Capitol. The houses were widely scattered and it was easy for a traveler to reach the middle of the town before he realized that he was not in the open country.[38] The parks were planned but not laid out. The public buildings, classic in design, were few, and the north wing of the unfinished Capitol was so leaky and insecure that great chunks of plaster were liable to crash down from the ceiling, and during every storm the members sat in terror lest

[36] Blennerhassett Papers (Lib. of Cong., Mss. Div.), Clay to Blennerhassett, July 22, 1807; Draper Collection, 26CC29 — an old, unidentified newspaper account of Clay's presentation of Mrs. Blennerhassett's claim for damage done to her home.

[37] Brown, *Plumer's Memorandum*, pp. 523, 570.

[38] *National Intelligencer*, April 5, 1809; C. W. Janson, *The Stranger in America* (London, 1807), p. 205; J. Melish, *Travel Through the United States of America, 1806–1811* (Belfast, 1818), p. 144.

they be maimed or killed by the collapse of a wall.[39] "Washington, at present," wrote a keen French observer in 1810, "resembles those Russian towns traced in the deserts of Tartary, in whose enclosures we behold nothing but naked fields, and a few groupes of houses."[40]

Clay could not have been awed by any aspect of the capital. Neither did he regard his entrance upon the national scene as the beginning of a great public career. Business would prevent his being a candidate for the next Congress, and he had come to this one because he could make money by doing so, he told William Plumer.[41] Clients who wanted him to attend to their affairs in the Supreme Court had given him a purse of three thousand dollars. Apparently it was then not an impropriety for a Senator to practise law in the midst of his legislative activities, and he spent part of his time in the basement of the Capitol, in the dark and badly ventilated room then occupied by the nation's highest tribunal.[42]

Social activities claimed a goodly share of his time. The New Hampshire Senator noted that Clay read little, but gambled a great deal; that he was "out almost every night," and that he promptly established himself as a great favorite with the ladies. He frankly confessed that he meant the session to be a "tour of pleasure."[43]

He was not, however, inattentive to his political duties. The fact that he was a few months below the constitutional age for a Senator troubled neither him nor his constituents, and seems to have excited no comment at the capital.[44] The small matter that he was making his first bow in Washington was brushed

[39] Brown, *Plumer's Memorandum*, pp. 526–527.

[40] Felix de Beaujour, *Sketch of the United States of North America* (London, 1814), p. 78.

[41] Brown, *Plumer's Memorandum*, p. 565.

[42] He was admitted to practice at the Supreme Court bar, Feb. 3, 1807 — Roll of Counsellors, Clerk's Office, Supreme Court. The name of Humphrey Marshall, his Federalist enemy in Kentucky, who argued one of these suits against him, appears on the same roll.

[43] Brown, *Plumer's Memorandum*, p. 608. Mrs. Clay had not come with her husband. She was expecting her fifth child, Anne Clay, born April 7, 1807.

[44] Clay referred to it in later years as a "juvenile indiscretion." *Cf.* R. C. Winthrop, *Memoir of Henry Clay* (Cambridge, 1880), p. 5.

aside as he plunged into the Senate's business. The day after he took his seat he was put on a committee, and during this short session he was put on at least three others, twice as chairman. His first speech, on the question of building a bridge across the Potomac, gave him an opportunity not only to support the bill,[45] but to amuse the Senate by comparing an opponent, the Federalist Uriah Tracy of Connecticut, to Peter Pindar's magpie: —

> Thus have I seen a magpie in the street,
> A chattering bird, we often meet;
> A bird for curiosity well known,
> With head awry, and cunning eye,
> Peep knowingly into a marrow bone.[46]

He made another speech, on January 15, 1807, upon a bill forbidding the importation of slaves. No report of his remarks is preserved, unfortunately, but a Senator from Massachusetts, John Quincy Adams by name, remarked that it was "ardent," and solemnly recorded in his diary that the newcomer from Kentucky was "quite a young man — an orator — and a republican of the first fire." [47] Clay was also responsible for a bill that extended the Federal circuit court system to Kentucky, Tennessee and Ohio. But his chief interest lay in the subject of internal improvements, of which he demonstrated that he was an eager champion.

This was not a new subject. Transportation facilities throughout the Union were in a wretched state. A few coastwise canals were in the project stage. Turnpike construction was being pushed in New England and the middle states. Albert Gallatin, a year later, could dwell with delight upon the many wooden bridges which, "uniting boldness to elegance," spanned the broadest and deepest rivers of the East; but he had to confess that south of the Potomac there were few artificial roads or

---

[45] It became law, Feb. 5, 1808 — *National Intelligencer*, Feb. 15, 1808.

[46] Sargent, *op. cit.*, p. 8; Prentice, *op. cit.*, p. 37. See Plumer's withering comment on Tracy and this bill — "Under the mask of sanctity he practises much deception." Brown, *Plumer's Memorandum*, p. 594.

[47] Adams, *Memoirs*, Vol. I, p. 444. Clay voted for the bill. *African Repository*, 68 vols. (Washington, 1826–1892), Vol. VI, p. 5.

bridges; he had no evidence of such improvements in the poorer Western states; and his suggestion of four roads connecting the greatest Atlantic and Western rivers bears striking witness to the deficiencies of communication between the sections.[48] When Pennsylvania Avenue could be described as "the great Serbonian bog," [49] the condition of the highways throughout the country can be imagined. Crossroads were bad all the time, main roads, even in the East, were good only in summer. Ruts, mudholes, rocks and stumps made every journey a terror. Travel was expensive, postage was high. Freight charges across the mountains frequently came to one third the value of the goods carried. The development of the West was impeded, the establishment of a close union delayed, and the situation called for action.

Some steps had been taken. The Cumberland Road bill, establishing a national highway from Cumberland, Maryland, to Ohio, had become a law March 29, 1806. In his annual message, December 2 of that year, Jefferson coupled a rosy picture of the finances with a reference to internal improvements. He suggested using the public funds for such objects although, with an indifference to consistency that was almost sublime in one who had purchased an empire without constitutional warrant and had signed the Cumberland Road bill, he stated that an amendment to the Constitution was necessary.[50]

Clay was not greatly troubled by such scruples. He felt that local and national necessity warranted a broad interpretation of the sacred instrument, and he acted accordingly. He spoke for the Potomac bridge bill; he was a zealous advocate of Government aid for the Chesapeake and Delaware Canal, which was called by the committee that reported on the project "the basis of a vast scheme of interior navigation"; [51] he supported a motion requesting the Secretary of the Treasury to furnish the

[48] *American State Papers, Miscellaneous* (Washington, 1834), Vol. I, pp. 724–741.

[49] H. P. Caemmerer, *Washington, the National Capital* (Washington, 1932), p. 41.

[50] J. D. Richardson, *Messages and Papers of the Presidents*, 20 vols. (N.Y., 1897–1927), Vol. I, pp. 397–398.

[51] *Annals of Cong.*, 9th Cong., 2d sess., 34.

Senate, at the next session, with a report on the general status of internal improvements, and a plan for applying the means within the power of Congress to the making of roads and canals; [52] and he tried earnestly to push through legislation providing for a canal at the rapids of the Ohio. The report of the committee on the Ohio Canal, of which Clay was chairman, asserted that the constitutionality of government aid for such projects was not relevant to this one. It argued that "both policy and power" favored promoting an undertaking by which government property would be "incidentally benefitted." The Senate, by a vote of eighteen to eight, passed a bill authorizing the President to appoint a commission to ascertain if the canal were practicable, and if it should be on the Kentucky or the Ohio shore.

Clay's record in the Senate was a good one. He had pushed vigorously the interests of his state, and he had taken an active part in legislation of more general importance. But, in the midst of all this, his thoughts turned homeward, to his wife, who was soon to bear him their fifth child, and to the farm that he was improving. "After all that I have seen," he wrote to his father-in-law, "Kentucky is still my favorite country. There, amidst my dear family, I shall find happiness in a degree to be met with nowhere else." [53] When the Senate adjourned he went back to Kentucky, and in that summer's elections Fayette County sent him once again to the state legislature, where he was to serve two more years.

He was now unquestionably an outstanding man in the Kentucky assembly, and the leader of his party there. When seventy-six members of the legislature met at the Eagle Tavern in Frankfort on February 17, 1808, they unanimously approved and signed an address prepared and presented by Clay which recommended James Madison for President of the United States. Clay's influence was felt in many of the acts of these sessions. When a contested election developed in Hardin County, he was the foremost in settling the dispute. The report of the committee of which he was chairman laid down effectively

[52] *Ibid.*, 9th Cong., 2d sess., 96–97. Gallatin sent a lengthy report to the next session.
[53] T. H. Clay's Scrapbook, Clay to Col. Thos. Hart, Feb. 1, 1807.

the principle that the will of the majority must prevail, and that to seat the loser in the election simply because his opponent was technically ineligible, "would operate as a deception of the people." His bitter political enemy, Humphrey Marshall, introduced a bill facilitating the speedy adjustment of land claims by shortening the period of outlawry from twenty to seven years. Its passage was of the utmost importance; and Clay, dropping personal animosity for the time being, worked side by side with Marshall to put the measure through.[54]

When the Speaker of the House, William Logan, resigned in January, 1808, Clay was elected to fill the vacancy.[55] The journal of the house does not record the speeches made there, but more than once Clay left the chair to come down on the floor and engage in the debates. On one of these occasions he gave a striking exhibition of sanity in the face of popular clamor.

On June 22, 1807, the British frigate *Leopard* had stopped the United States frigate *Chesapeake* off the Virginia coast, and, upon her refusal to surrender supposed British deserters, had fired into her and forced her to strike her flag. It was one of many incidents in a quarrel of some years' standing over neutral rights, and search and seizure. War seemed inevitable during the latter part of 1807, and Kentucky shared the excitement. The patriots in her legislature wished to retaliate, and blindly proposed to do so by a measure that would have harmed only themselves. They proposed to forbid the use of all citations of British law in the Kentucky courts. This meant virtually the abandonment of the common law, the very basis of the legal system, but so intense was popular feeling that a large majority of the members supported the motion. Clay was no Anglophile, but he was not ready to plunge into chaos as a means of punishing a foreign power. His opposition was vigorous and eloquent, and finally he obtained a compromise limiting the prohibition to the period after July 4, 1776.[56] He must have subscribed heartily, on the other hand, to the resolution of the general assembly, on January 22, 1808, commending the Administration, and flaying British conduct as "outrageous and insulting

---

[54] Butler, *op. cit.*, p. 333.

[55] *House Journal, 1807–1808*, pp. 44–46.

[56] Marshall, *op. cit.*, Vol. II, p. 454; Sargent, *op. cit.*, p. 8.

in the extreme." [57] His dislike of British measures was very strong, and that, together with political rivalry, brought him into his first duel.

Humphrey Marshall was a cousin of Chief Justice John Marshall, whose sister he had married. Now in his middle forties, he was a commanding figure of a man, six feet two in height, well built, lithe and muscular. His hair was black and thick, and his piercing eyes were blacker than his hair. He was proud, aristocratic, fearless, and he had a blistering tongue and a biting pen. [58]

Marshall had employed Clay in some of his law suits, and their relations had been generally amicable before the Burr incident. [59] But that case, involving politics as well as patriotism, had produced a bitter hostility. This was heightened by the change in the attitude of John Wood, one of the editors of the *Western World*, who publicly recanted the part he had in bringing on the trial. Marshall always believed that this was due to Clay's influence, and when he wrote his history of Kentucky, years afterward, he took pains to charge that Wood had been "seduced . . . principally by the address and solicitation of Henry Clay." [60]

The Burr episode only whetted Marshall's appetite for a treason hunt. Judge Harry Innes' method of conducting the trial had provoked Marshall's animosity, and he determined to force an investigation of the judge.

Innes was not altogether above suspicion. He had been for a long time an intimate friend of General James Wilkinson, whose close connection with Burr was under fire, and of another Western figure, Judge Benjamin Sebastian, who had been involved in treasonable correspondence with Spain in 1795. An investigation thoroughly besmirched Sebastian's past character and drove him from the bench and public life. It was understood that Sebastian's correspondence with Spain had been known to

[57] *National Intelligencer*, March 9, 1808.
[58] A. C. Quisenberry, *The Life and Times of Hon. Humphrey Marshall* (Winchester, Ky., 1892), pp. 17–19.
[59] See the *Kentucky Gazette*, Feb. 18, 1832, for Marshall's account of his relations with Clay, and his story of the duel.
[60] Marshall, *op. cit.*, Vol. II, p. 412.

Innes, and when the Kentucky legislature met, December 28, 1807, the air was full of rumors that the latter would be attacked.

The judge waited in suspense for some three weeks, and then Marshall opened the onslaught by bringing before the legislature a series of resolutions that violently condemned Innes for his connection with the plots of 1795, and demanded an inquiry by the Federal Government. The debate that followed lasted over a week. It was a bitter and impassioned fight, and Clay came down from the Speaker's chair to take part in it.

The Republicans had counseled as to how the attack should be met. Clay, Thruston and others had agreed that Innes, though he had erred in not communicating to the Government his knowledge of the Spanish affair, had done nothing to merit impeachment.[61] Clay considered the honesty and many good qualities of the judge as beyond question,[62] and in answer to Marshall, he moved a series of counter resolutions which threw his opponent into a fury. They expressed confidence that the Administration and Congress would deal adequately with anyone who violated the Constitution or the laws; asserted that the Kentucky legislature had enough to do without meddling with the prerogatives of the Federal Government; and stated that an expression of opinion by the legislature upon the guilt or innocence of Innes would be unjust and prejudicial, especially since he had already requested a Congressional inquiry.[63] These resolutions did not pass, and in all probability Clay did not expect that they would. They did afford a good basis for maneuvers, however, and before Marshall's proposals went through they were stripped of their denunciations and reduced to a simple request that the Government investigate Innes' conduct. This was forwarded to Congress and there a committee of the House exonerated the judge.[64]

[61] Durrett Collection, Clay to Innes, Jan. 16, 1807.

[62] Breckinridge Papers, XXIX, Clay to Breckinridge, Jan. 5, 1806.

[63] Cf. Butler, op. cit., pp. 323–326, and Marshall, op. cit., Vol. II, pp. 447f.

[64] American State Papers, Miscellaneous, Vol. I, p. 922. The committee, headed by John Rowan, reported April 19, 1808. The documents it examined are printed, pp. 922–934.

All this was gall and wormwood to Marshall. He had struggled for almost two years to discredit the Kentucky Republicans, and the net results had been the dismissal of Federalist Daveiss, whom Jefferson had condemned as overhasty and impolitic, and the retention of Republican Innes on the bench. A double defeat, and in each case Clay had been a leader on the winning side. Enmity rode high and within a year came the final clash, tied up this time with the question of foreign policy.

The Napoleonic wars were raging. Britain was attempting to crush Napoleon by a blockade which was steadily extended by a succession of orders in council. Napoleon retaliated with a series of decrees which declared a paper blockade of England and visited punishment upon all neutrals who respected the British orders. The United States, a weak neutral, found herself between the upper and the nether millstones. The violation of her rights became the order of the day.

Jefferson's answer to this was the embargo. He would bring England and France to terms by cutting off trade with them. The policy was a failure, as it proved, but when it was instituted, in 1807, the Republicans rallied to its support. The New England Federalists, whose commercial interests had prospered despite the British and French seizures, were indignant. Their shipping, if it did not engage in illicit commerce, lay rotting at the wharves. Traditional friends of Great Britain, they rose in wrath, and party feeling flamed high.

Marshall, as a Federalist, was violently opposed to the embargo. He regarded it as vicious, dangerous, and involving a threat of war. Clay, on the other hand, was ready for an appeal to the sword on behalf of American rights. "We are anxious to know if a War will take place," he had written to Breckinridge in 1806, almost two years before the embargo was declared. "Such an event is peculiarly interesting to this Country. I believe it would not be unpopular. Perhaps this is a fortunate moment to repress European aggression; and to evince to the world that Americans appreciate their rights in such a way as will induce them, when violated, to engage in War with alacrity and effect." [65] The embargo received his hearty support.

[65] Breckinridge Papers, XXIX, Clay to Breckinridge, Jan. 5, 1806.

When the Kentucky legislature met, December 12, 1808, there was a general feeling that Clay and Marshall would have it out. Clay was not chosen Speaker, and he and his enemy met daily on the floor of the house.[66]

Hostilities were not long delayed. On December 16, Clay acted as one of the sponsors for a series of resolutions supporting the general policy of the Federal Government. These praised the Administration, and approved the embargo. They resolved that the general assembly of Kentucky would view "with the utmost horror" any proposition to submit to the British orders in council or the French decrees. They pledged the assembly "to spend if necessary, the last shilling, and to exhaust the last drop of blood, in resisting these aggressions." They promised cordial support of the Government's policy, whether that policy meant embargo, nonintercourse, or war; and they closed with a pæan of tribute to Jefferson for the "ability, uprightness and intelligence" which he had displayed in handling America's domestic and foreign policies.[67] Marshall stood alone in opposing these spread-eagle resolves. They passed the house by a vote of sixty-four to one.

Successful in this move, Clay followed it with another. He introduced a resolution on January 3 that the members of the general assembly should wear only clothes of American manufacture, and abstain from the use of all European fabrics until the orders and decrees were repealed. This shrewd proposal, which linked Kentucky's patriotism with her already intense interest in domestic manufactures,[68] passed the house the next day by a vote of fifty-seven to two.[69] It also unleashed the flood of Humphrey Marshall's wrath.

Clay and Marshall sat near each other, being separated by only one chair. This was occupied by General Christopher Riffe, a burly German of great size and strength. Clay had customarily worn suits of imported cloth, but with the in-

---

[66] *House Journal, 1808–1809*, p. 1; Prentice, *op. cit.*, p. 42; William Logan was elected by a vote of 36 to 31 over Clay.

[67] *House Journal, 1808–1809*, pp. 30f.

[68] See E. M. Coulter, "The Genesis of Henry Clay's American System," in the *South Atlantic Quarterly*, Vol. XXV (Jan. 1926), pp. 45–54.

[69] *House Journal, 1808–1809*, pp. 91, 101–102.

troduction of his resolution he appeared in a suit of jeans. Marshall, who had worn homespun, now blossomed out in a suit of the best English broadcloth that could be found and strutted down the aisles of the house to annoy Clay.

The Republican championed his measure in the name of justice and patriotism. The Federalist denounced it as sheer demagoguery. Tempers quickly reached the boiling point, and the excitement attending the passage of the resolution brought verbal warfare. Clay made a more than usually stinging speech. Marshall replied in kind, and his characterization of his opponent as a demagogue was so biting in its attack upon Clay's motives that it reached the point of insult. Maddened by the opprobrium, Clay jumped up and rushed toward his willing opponent. They were about to fight, perhaps some blows were actually struck, when Riffe seized each of them with one hand and held them apart, saying, "Come poys, no fighting here. I vips you both." The scene in the house ended, but later that day Clay sent a challenge. That he wanted to fight is obvious, for the challenge was phrased with an additional taunt. He hoped that he would "not be disappointed in the execution of the pledge you gave on that occasion." Marshall immediately accepted.[70]

The meeting took place in Indiana territory at Shippingport, across the Ohio from Louisville. They fought at ten paces. Each fired three times. Clay then insisted "very ardently" on another fire, but as he had been wounded in the thigh, the seconds refused to grant "his importunate request" and the affair was over.[71] Clay wrote an account of the affair to a friend, as soon as he returned to Louisville, which gives something of the vindictive spirit in which he had gone out to fight.

[70] *Kentucky Gazette*, Jan. 31, 1809, Feb. 18, 1832; Clay Papers, I, Clay to Thos. Hart, Jan. 4, 1809; Mrs. J. T. Cannon Collection (Frankfort), letter signed H. Blanton, June 3, 1879 (an eye witness of the scene in the house); Quisenberry, *op. cit.*, pp. 100–103. The original challenge and Marshall's reply are in the possession of the Library of Congress, Manuscripts Division.

[71] *Kentucky Gazette*, Jan. 31, 1809. This is the account of the duel given by the seconds.

Louisville, 19 Jan. –9

Dr. Clarke:

I have this moment returned from the field of battle. We had three shots. On the first I grazed him just above the navel — he missed me. On the Second my damned pistol snapped and he missed me. On the third I rec'd a flesh wound in the thigh, and owing to my receiving his fire first &c., I missed him.

My wound is in no way serious, as the bone is unhurt, but prudence will require me to remain here some days.

Yrs.,

HENRY CLAY.[72]

Clay could reflect upon a political career packed with interest and excitement, as the year 1809 drew to a close. He had become one of the leaders in the Kentucky legislature, and his career there had demonstrated his ability as a shrewd and clever parliamentarian, standing in general for wise legislation, and for the business interests. His career in the United States Senate had been active and thoroughly creditable. He had fought a duel that had demonstrated his coolness and courage, and that had in no wise detracted from his personal popularity.

He was easily re-elected to the house in 1809 for his seventh consecutive term,[73] and when the legislature chose a successor to Buckner Thruston, who had resigned his seat in the United States Senate, Clay was given the preference by a vote of more than two to one over his only rival.[74]

He went to Washington in January, 1810, secure in the knowledge that he commanded a large following in his state, and ready and eager to play a prominent part in the dramatic events then taking place in the national capital.

[72] This letter is reprinted in the *Lexington Daily Press*, Aug. 9, 1873. Marshall attempted to conceal the fact that he was wounded (Memo. of P. U. Major, Ky. State Hist. Soc. Lib.). Peck, *op. cit.*, p. 31, note 1, recounts the tradition that Clay's friends in Louisville, certain that Clay would kill or badly wound Marshall, were prepared to give him a dinner on his return from the duel. His wound prevented this, but he returned the compliment by giving card parties in his room.

[73] *Kentucky Gazette*, Sept. 19, 1809.

[74] *House Journal, 1809–1810*, pp. 117–118.

CHAPTER IV

FOUNDATIONS

THREE elements of the setting in which Clay was placed must
now be understood if we are to appreciate the part he played in
Congress prior to the War of 1812. First, the stage which he
had reached in his own career; second, the immediate aspirations of Kentucky, and of the frontier; and third, the changes
that were taking place in the ideals of the party of which he
was a member.

It was inevitable that the young Kentuckian should have
lofty political aspirations. His ambition, a fire never to be
quenched, drove him on. His achievements, and they were remarkable, added fuel to the flame. Not yet thirty-three years
of age, he was acknowledged as one of the most brilliant and
successful members of the Kentucky bar; he was maintaining
in comfort and luxury a large and growing family,[1] which
could justly deem itself in the first rank of frontier society;
and he had achieved a political prestige second to none in
Kentucky. The man who was soon to begin signing himself
"H. Clay" was far removed from Henry Clay, the boy who
had been glad to get the humblest clerkship in Peter Tinsley's
office. His ability and zest in playing the political game had
brought him increasing prestige ever since those December
days in 1804 when he had measured swords with Felix Grundy,
and proved "too hard for him in all the pinches."[2] It was a
logical step from Frankfort to Washington, and this time there
was no talk of its being a pleasure tour.

Clay went to Washington as a Kentuckian and a Westerner.

[1] Their first child, Henrietta, died in infancy, but by 1810 there were
five children: two sons, Theodore Wythe and Thomas Hart, and three
daughters, Susan Hart, Anne Brown and Lucretia Hart. A third son, Henry,
Jr., was born April 10, 1811. Cf. Young, op. cit., pp. 16f.
[2] Breckinridge Papers, XXVII, J. Jouitt to Breckinridge, Dec. 24, 1804.

Therein lay the primary motivations of at least the early part of his national career, for that section had definite characteristics and aims which he naturally would represent.

The West had industrial ambitions, even in the frontier stage. It was, of course, primarily agrarian, but by 1810 Kentucky, Ohio and Western Tennessee were moving toward industrialization. The two latter were making small but respectable ventures in establishing mills and looms for cotton and wool, iron furnaces and, most of all, distilleries. Ohio manufactured about $2,000,000 worth of goods in 1810, counting domestic industry, and Western Tennessee $1,500,000.[3]

Kentucky was far ahead of them. She had had visions of industry almost from her beginning, a dream of riches to be obtained by the manufacture of goods for the West. "Exportation, not importation, is your way to wealth," declared one of her pioneer industrialists,[4] at the time when young Clay was crossing the mountains for his new home. Kentucky manufactured, in 1810, practically all the cotton bagging in the Union. She had more rope-walks than any other state save Massachusetts. She stood first in the number of powder mills, second in the manufacture of salt, third in distilleries, fourth in cotton and woolen looms. And Lexington was the manufacturing center of the state.[5] These developments had been aided by the embargo. When it was repealed in 1809, Kentucky began asking for protection and she kept on demanding it while Clay was in Congress.[6] She never feared Eastern competition, and was perfectly willing, by 1811, to see protection made uniform for the whole country.[7]

[3] *American State Papers, Finance*, Vol. II, pp. 690–712; *Niles' Weekly Register*, Sept. 7, 1811. Hereafter referred to as *Niles' Register*.

[4] The *Mirror*, Nov. 18, 1797, quoted by E. M. Coulter, "The Genesis etc.," in *South Atlantic Quarterly*, Vol. XXV (Jan. 1926), pp. 48–49.

[5] *American State Papers, Finance*, Vol. II, pp. 690–711; *Kentucky Gazette*, Feb. 19, 1811.

[6] *Annals of Cong.*, 11th Cong., 2d sess., 626–630, Clay's speech; 11th Cong., 3d sess., 101, petition presented by Clay; J. B. McMaster, *History of the People of the United States*, 8 vols. (N.Y., 1927–1928), Vol. III, pp. 505–509.

[7] Coulter, "The Genesis etc.," in *South Atlantic Quarterly*, Vol. XXV (Jan. 1926), pp. 53–54.

Kentucky joined with the whole Western region in other hopes and aims. The West desired security for its lands and waterways. It regarded the Indians and their British friends with a coldly critical eye, and it was always suspicious of the possibilities that might lie in Spain's control of West Florida. There was, also, a passion for wealth and expansion. The Kentuckians, wrote John Adair to Wilkinson in 1804, although not poor were "as greedy after plunder as ever the old Romans were, Mexico glitters in our Eyes — the word is all we wait for." [8] By 1809, adventurers had poured into the lands between the Red and the Sabine, giving the Spanish authorities no end of trouble, and peaceful settlers were moving into West Florida and Texas.[9] Such aspirations, joined to a spirit of patriotism and devotion to the Republican Party, furnished a Western setting for the Congressmen who traveled across the mountains to Washington.

The Republican Party, the political expression of the desires of South and West, had demonstrated by 1810 that its principles were not entirely static. It remained agrarian, it is true, and its opposition to federal centralization was still vigorous. But it had also championed strict construction of the Constitution and as little government as possible. These ideals weakened as control brought responsibility, and responsibility demanded power. Three breaches had been made in the wall of strict construction by 1810, and each of them marked steps in the direction of increased federal power. The purchase of Louisiana was without specific constitutional warrant. The embargo, with its destruction of commerce, had required an extremely elastic interpretation of the regulation of commerce clause. The Cumberland Road had been justified by the subterfuge of getting the consent of the states through which it passed. The Republicans, pushed by the power of national interest, were donning some of the Federalist robes that they had trampled so disdainfully in the dust of 1800. And the rising young leaders, Clay, Calhoun, Lowndes, Cheves, and Grundy, were

[8] Durrett Collection, Misc. Letters, Dec. 10, 1804, quoted by J. W. Pratt, *Expansionists of 1812* (N.Y., 1925), p. 62.

[9] Pratt, *op. cit.*, pp. 62–63.

under no compulsion to stand in awe before the ark of the constitutional covenant.

Ambition, the aspirations of Kentucky and the West in general, and the growing latitudinarianism of the Republican Party laid the foundations for Clay's national career.

Clay took his seat in the Senate on Monday, February 5, 1810, and it was not long before he had an opportunity to champion the industrial desires of his section. A bill came before the Senate providing for the purchase of munitions of war. One section, offered by John Pope of Kentucky, instructed the Secretary of the Navy to give preference, in buying naval supplies, to those of American manufacture. An amendment was offered by James Lloyd of Massachusetts, striking out this section, and Kentucky's second Senator rose in answer.

There was a personal element involved, for the Hart family raised huge quantities of hemp, and Clay himself had become interested in its production. But back of any such consideration lay the industrial ambitions of the section which Clay represented. He pleaded for manufactures in general, and for protection, which, he blithely asserted, meant more and better goods. Not that he wished a change from an agrarian to a manufacturing society. The idea that America should export manufactured goods was rejected emphatically. That way might lie the vice and wretchedness of England. His simple plea was for national self-sufficiency. "The nation that imports its clothing from abroad is but little less dependent than if it imported its bread," and he stressed the danger in dependence upon a foreign supply of naval stores. Cleverly, he joined a sneer at New England with a plea for nationalism. "Dame Commerce . . . is a flirting, flippant, noisy jade, and if we are governed by her fantasies, we shall never put off the muslins of India and the cloths of Europe. But I trust that the yeomanry of this country, the true and genuine landlords of this tenement, called the United States, disregarding her freaks, will persevere in reform until the whole national family is furnished by itself with the clothing necessary for its own use. . . . Others may prefer the cloths of Leeds and of London, but give me those of Humphreysville." His peroration might have been spoken by any Westerner. The Senate had rejected "manly protection" of the rights of commerce; it had postponed internal improvements; would it now refuse a trifling support to manufacturing? [10]

Lloyd's amendment was defeated, nine to twenty-two. The nascent industrial interests had gained a minor victory,[11] and, whether he knew it or not, Clay had laid one of the cornerstones of his American System.[12] For the speech did not exclude the East from protection any more than Clay did a month later when he voted for increasing the duties on all goods imported into the United States.[13]

He took an active part, during the remainder of his term in the Senate, in two other acts of great national importance. These related to the Floridas and to the National Bank, and in both he represented Western interests and ideals.

The dispute with Spain over the Floridas forms an amazing episode in American diplomacy. It sprang naturally out of a transaction equally amazing, the purchase of Louisiana. That empire, bought by a President with a doubtful right to buy, from an Emperor who had no right to sell, was conveyed to us in a fog of ambiguity. No one knew or could possibly tell whether or not it included West Florida to the line of the

[10] *Annals of Cong.*, 11th Cong., 2d sess., 626–630.

[11] No Western Senator voted for Lloyd's amendment. Its support came chiefly from New England.

[12] Carl Schurz's contention (*op. cit.*, Vol. I, pp. 55–57) that Clay's position was not far from that of Gallatin, who was a free-trader in principle, is scarcely tenable. It is true that Gallatin suggested, as did Clay, that manufactures could be encouraged by duties and bounties. But Gallatin, unlike Clay, was critical of these methods, and preferred government loans as aid to manufactures (*American State Papers, Finance*, Vol. II, pp. 430–431, Report on Manufactures, April 17, 1810). Gallatin suggested, December 1810, a "considerable and immediate" increase of duties, but this was only to offset the effects of Macon Bill #2 on the Government's revenue (*ibid.*, Vol. II, pp. 441, State of the Finances, Dec. 12, 1810). Clay stood for higher duties *as an aid to manufacturing.* He approved a 50% increase, because it would encourage manufactures. "As the increase is not contemplated, however, to be permanent, I should prefer a smaller augmentation, and that it should be durable." (Colton, *Correspondence*, pp. 46–47, Clay to Adam Beatty, April 23, 1810.)

[13] *Annals of Cong.*, 11th Cong., 2d sess., 673–674. An amendment to Macon Bill #2, defeated 8 to 19.

Perdido River. The treaty that had transferred Louisiana from Spain to France "defined" its extent in a meaningless jumble of words, and these had not been clarified when Napoleon handed it over to Livingston and Monroe. Livingston had previously contended that West Florida formed no part of Louisiana. Spain always maintained that ground, and the weight of evidence bears out the contention.[14] But the purchase quickly convinced Livingston that West Florida was included, and a similar pleasing conviction rapidly instilled itself into the minds of Jefferson, Madison and Monroe. Spain, curiously enough, remained obdurate, and responded to the American attempts to demonstrate her error by loudly calling upon logic, grammar, common sense, and even history to prove her point.

The "excessive delicacy" of Jefferson and Madison prevented their demanding West Florida when Louisiana was transferred to us,[15] and the Spaniards retained an official possession that grew more and more wobbly during the ensuing years.

Bona fide settlers, adventurers and marauders pushed into the disputed territory. Border incidents developed, provocative of rancor and complaint. Kentucky and Tennessee were in a state of almost constant irritation. Spanish control of the Mobile and Apalachicola, Alabama and Tombigbee Rivers, transportation routes vital to the Mississippi territory and Western Tennessee, produced a succession of jarring discords. The Southwest suspected, too, that the dons were tampering with the Indians.[16] The expansive force of the frontier was battering against the walls of Spain's possessions, and the proud Spanish monarchy, convulsed by the struggle of the Titans in Europe, looked on helplessly while her North American possessions disappeared, piece by piece, under waves of men possessed of land hunger and money lust and armed with long rifles.

The break came in the summer of 1810. The Americans in West Florida rebelled, captured Baton Rouge, and proclaimed

[14] I. J. Cox, *The West Florida Controversy, 1798–1813* (Baltimore, 1918), p. 82.
[15] *Ibid.*, pp. 108, 98.
[16] Pratt, *op. cit.*, pp. 65–67.

their independence. Then they promptly appealed to the United States for annexation.

Jefferson had tried to acquire undisputed possession of both the Floridas, but his tortuous negotiations had resulted only in failure. Madison, also an expansionist, was perfectly willing to keep up the good work. There was a lack of authority, for Congress was not in session, but the situation demanded action, and he moved with celerity. October 27, 1810, he issued a proclamation reasserting the old claim based on the Louisiana purchase, and taking possession of West Florida to the Perdido. Then this curious document proceeded to state that, though we were now in possession, West Florida would "not cease to be a subject of fair and friendly negotiation and adjustment." [17] This was followed by a sharp message to the revolutionists, warning them against frowardness, [18] and when Congress met in December, it was informed of the situation, assured of the legality of the President's action, and urged to pass the necessary legislation for the new province. [19]

A more barefaced steal could not well be imagined, but Congress was equal to the situation, and never was the law of claw and fang more clearly vindicated. Tuesday, December 18, Senator William B. Giles of Virginia reported a bill extending the territory of Orleans to the Perdido, and the debate was on. Pope of Kentucky defended the bill on the ground of expediency and unexceptionable title. The Federalists rallied to the attack, which was opened by Outerbridge Horsey of Delaware. The President, Horsey pointed out, had clearly exceeded his powers; our title was not good; our action was clearly unjust to Spain, and threatened war with that power and perhaps with her ally, England. [20] The Senator from Delaware had thrown down the gauntlet. Henry Clay picked it up on behalf of the Administration.

Clay's speech was a masterpiece of its kind. Clever and

[17] *American State Papers, Foreign Relations* (Washington, 1832), Vol. III, pp. 397–398, Oct. 27, 1810.

[18] *Ibid.*, Vol. III, p. 398, R. Smith to Gov. Holmes of Miss. Territory, Nov. 15, 1810.

[19] *Annals of Cong.*, 11th Cong., 3d sess., 12–13.

[20] *Ibid.*, 11th Cong., 3d sess., 26f, 37–42, 55–64.

sophistical, it displayed his great facility in making the worse appear the better reason, and what it lacked in logic it made up in chauvinism. He began by an ironical commendation of men whose sense of justice led them to espouse the cause of a foreign nation against their own. A series of specious appeals to history established our title to West Florida and the authority of the President to take possession of it. We had hitherto refrained from doing so only because of "the genius of the nation" which was prone to peace and fearful of encouraging a spirit of militarism. If we delayed, Great Britain, Spain's ally, might acquire Cuba and Florida. Did Senators wish to be placed at the mercy of that power? It was better to assert our rights, even though it might mean immediate war with England. "Is the time never to arrive," he exclaimed, "when we may manage our affairs without the fear of insulting His Britannic Majesty? Is the rod of British power to be forever suspended over our heads?" Title or no title, West Florida must be held on the ground of national interest.

I have no hesitation in saying, that if a parent country will not or cannot maintain its authority in a colony adjacent to us, and there exists in it a state of misrule and disorder, menacing our peace, and if moreover such colony, by passing into the hands of any other Power, would become dangerous to the integrity of the Union, and manifestly tend to the subversion of our laws; we have a right, upon eternal principles of self-preservation, to lay hold of it. This principle alone, independent of any title, would warrant our occupation of West Florida. But it is not necessary to resort to it, our title being in my judgment incontestably good.

He finished in a burst of expansionist fury: —

I am not, sir, in favor of cherishing the passion of conquest. But I must be permitted to conclude by declaring my hope to see, ere long, the *new* United States (if you will allow me the expression) embracing not only the old thirteen States, but the entire country east of the Mississippi, including East Florida, and some of the territories to the north of us also.[21]

[21] *Ibid.*, 11th Cong., 3d sess., 55–64.

Such sentiments expressed the greed and Anglophobia of the times. The Senate rallied to them. Pickering read a letter dated December 21, 1804, from Talleyrand to the American Minister at Paris, denying the United States had acquired West Florida with Louisiana. It should have ended the matter, for we could not have purchased more than France had sold, but, instead of retreating, the Republicans attacked the Massachusetts Senator for violating the injunction of secrecy that Jefferson had put upon the letter, and on Clay's motion, Pickering was censured by the Senate.[22]

Expansion was triumphant, and, though Giles's bill was dropped, because of Georgia's opposition to cutting off from the Gulf the territory that later became Alabama and Mississippi, the American claim remained in force. The Government was in a mood to go even further. On January 3, 1811, Madison sent a secret message to Congress virtually asking permission to seize East Florida, in case the Spanish authorities were overthrown and danger developed of occupation by some other foreign power. Clay took the lead in pushing through the necessary legislation, which was reported out by a committee of which he was chairman, debated in Committee of the Whole, and passed, all within a week's time.[23] South and West were determined to have the Floridas.

One last extravagant assertion of the prevailing state of mind remained for the Kentuckian. In the spring of 1812, when West Florida was divided between Louisiana and Mississippi territory, Clay repeated his previous arguments on America's right to possession and buttressed them by the flat statement that Spain could only desire the possession of West Florida for some sinister reason.[24] Jingoism could scarcely have gone further.

The Republicans were willing to stretch the Constitution when the expansionists demanded it, but their old-time theory

[22] *Ibid.*, 11th Cong., 3d sess. 65, 67.

[23] *Ibid.*, 11th Cong., 3d sess. (secret), 370, 371, 375.

[24] *Ibid.*, 12th Cong., 1st sess., 1204–1206. At the same time, he moved, successfully, to keep the territory subject to future negotiation, explaining that he did so to accommodate the views of others, rather than his own. He would "as soon see a part of the State he represented ceded away as this territory."

of strict construction was aroused from its deepening slumber in 1811 to deal with the banking situation.

The Bank of the United States, chartered in 1791 for twenty years, owed its creation to Alexander Hamilton, and members of the party that he had built up owned most of the stock that had remained in the country. Because of this, and on account of its representing the Federalist idea of a strong central government, it was doubly offensive in Republican eyes. Another reason for the disfavor into which it had fallen was that two-thirds of its stock was owned in England, and British investors were receiving comfortable dividends while Anglophobia mounted in the United States. Local interests, too, were jealous of it. Over one hundred state banks had been chartered by 1810, and others were in prospect. Their investors longed for greater profits, and they regarded with suspicion and dislike the strict watch kept over the local institutions by the National Bank, and its uncomfortable habit of calling upon them to redeem their note issues. Kentucky felt this bondage with the rest, and the Kentucky legislature was among those that instructed their Senators to kill the object of their hatred.[25]

There could have been no worse time for such action. Credit was tight in Europe and America. England was trying to withdraw specie from the United States, and our supply was already insufficient to sustain our bank-note circulation. State banks were increasing and their issues were expanding in omnivorous fashion. War with England was lowering on the horizon,[26] making it doubly dangerous to unsettle the currency. But all this counted for nothing against the phrenetic passion that seized the majority party in Congress.

Bravely, for Madison stood aloof, Gallatin threw himself into the struggle. The Bank was strongest in the House, but there, after many speeches, it was voted, sixty-five to sixty-four, to postpone indefinitely the question of recharter. The Senate was the only recourse,[27] and there the Secretary of the Treasury

[25] National Intelligencer, Feb. 19, 1811; McMaster, op. cit., Vol. III, pp. 379–381; H. Adams, History of the United States of America, 9 vols. (N.Y., 1921), Vol. V, pp. 327–330.
[26] Adams, Hist. of the U.S., Vol. V, pp. 330–337.
[27] Ibid., Vol. V, p. 331.

found an able champion in William Harris Crawford of Georgia.

Crawford was blessed with an imposing presence. Six feet two in height, he was the embodiment of health and vigor, and his handsome face, with its fair complexion, high, broad forehead, and brilliant blue eyes produced devastation and despair in the hearts of the ladies. Affable and engaging in manner, he had a fund of ready stories that made him popular on the rostrum and in society. His ability was beyond question, and when he rose to champion a cause the bold and brilliant qualities of his mind commanded alike attention and respect.[28] He was a formidable foe, whether on the dueling ground where he had killed his man, or in the Senate chamber.

On February 5, 1811, Crawford introduced a bill continuing the old Bank charter twenty years, with certain amendments. He accompanied it with a letter from Gallatin, which stated in vigorous terms the difficulties and dangers attendant upon a failure to recharter, and six days later the Georgian made an able speech defending the Bank. He denounced the theory that Congress could exercise no implied powers, and that it was unconstitutional to charter a corporation, in language which his opponents of the time were to copy five years later.

His biting phrases on the Constitution are pertinent to-day.

Upon the most thorough examination of this instrument, I am induced to believe, that many of the various constructions given to it are the result of a belief that it is absolutely perfect. It has become so extremely fashionable to eulogize this Constitution . . . that whenever its eulogium is pronounced, I feel an involuntary apprehension of mischief.

Warning against a blind and unintelligent construction that would "render it wholly imbecile," he pleaded the doctrine of implied powers, and the need for the Bank in carrying on the fiscal concerns of the Government. The vials of his wrath were poured upon the states whose "avarice combined with their love of domination" led them into opposition. He called for patriot-

[28] For a description of Crawford, see W. H. Sparks, *The Memories of Fifty Years* (Philadelphia, 1870), p. 60.

ism, and the sacrifice of pride and greed and political resentments to the country's good.[29]

Giles made an interminable speech three days later, finally concluding against the Bank when he had bored the Senate to exhaustion. Then, on February 15, Clay rose as the real spokesman of the opposition.

Beginning with a satiric compliment to Giles for arguing on both sides of the question, he launched into the attack by twitting Crawford for going over to the Macedonian phalanx of the Federalists. There followed a strict interpretation of the Constitution that, like Banquo's ghost, was to rise up to plague him again and again in after years. He described the power to charter a bank as gypsying through the Constitution, in a vain quest for authority. The fathers had been very careful to leave as little as possible to implication in the charter. There was nothing there that authorized a bank, the treasury could get along just as well without one, and local banks were safer. The precedent already set should be cast aside, for it was dangerous. His fevered imagination pictured it as inciting the creation of other corporations, with capital consisting of land, slaves, and personal estates that might absorb all the property within a state. He spoke mournfully of the East India, the South Sea, the Mississippi companies, and their baneful effects upon Europe.

If the growth of the country created new wants and exigencies, he said, they could be satisfied by constitutional amendment. Then he glorified the written word — "Once substitute practice for principle, the expositions of the Constitution for the text of the Constitution, and in vain shall we look for the instrument in the instrument itself. It will be as diffused and intangible as the pretended Constitution of England. . . ." — and said we should take warning, as to what would happen under broad interpretation, from the "swarms of intolerant and furious sects" produced by the various interpretations of Holy Writ.

Flag-waving came next. About five million dollars, one half of the specie circulation of the country, were in vaults of the Bank, an immense power wielded by only a few men chiefly

[29] *Annals of Cong.* 11th Cong., 3d sess., 134–150.

amenable to foreign stockholders. Did anyone doubt that war with England would mean control of the Bank by the English Premier? He satirized, in his peculiar fashion, the argument that possession of this British capital gave us certain influence over the British Government. Why not then, he exclaimed, turn over all our property to foreigners? "We should then be able to govern foreign nations." The Bank had helped us not a whit with England. What had it done about impressment, or the *Chesapeake*, or the orders in council? On the contrary, it had probably been an aid to England in putting through Jay's treaty and dulling our national sense of honor.[30]

This speech, fittingly enough, was not delivered with Clay's accustomed eloquence. Washington Irving thought that the orator seemed frightened by the expectancy of the crowded galleries.[31] It was strict constructionist, anti-British, Kentucky bombast, and Henry Adams' verdict, that its only excuse was Clay's volte-face five years later, is just. Hot-headed, impulsive, dramatic, and not yet thirty-four, perhaps led on by his admiration for Madison, who had made no move to save the Bank, he had conjured up monstrous apprehensions that Crawford justly called "the chimeras of a fervid and perturbed imagination."[32]

The bill was defeated by the casting vote of the Vice-President, George Clinton. The Bank was dead, and when Clay reported from committee against giving it more time to wind up its affairs, and took a final jibe at the institution for concealing dangerous situations from the public gaze, he had completed his own picture as a first rate anti-Bank man.

Clay worked hard during his first years in the national capital. Indian affairs, the rights of settlers on public land and a variety of other matters claimed his attention, as well as the more important and dramatic questions that concerned domestic and foreign affairs. Washington was becoming for him a second home.

Mrs. Clay began coming with him to Washington while he was in the Senate, and that meant bringing the family. When

[30] *Ibid.*, 11th Cong., 3d sess., 210–219.
[31] Peck, *op. cit.*, p. 41, note 1. Statement of Washington Irving.
[32] *Annals of Cong.*, 11th Cong., 3d sess., 330–346.

he entered the House in 1811, the six children, including baby Henry, who was only seven months old, made the long and arduous trip across the mountains. The whole family came back to Lexington that summer, and then returned to Washington for the following session. This meant particularly slow and tedious traveling, and Clay complained that it gave him scarcely time to turn around at home before setting out again.[33]

The Clays' life in the capital was probably not very gay, for Lucretia, though kind and friendly, had no fondness for society or fashionable amusements. She "is a thousand times better pleased," wrote Margaret Bayard Smith, "sitting in the room with all her children round her, and a pile of work by her side, than in the most brilliant drawing room."[34] But there were children's parties, where Mrs. Clay and Mrs. Smith decked themselves out with flowers, drank punch, ate sugar plums and cakes and oranges, and then, while Lucretia played the piano in the flower-decorated room, the rest "romp'd rather than danced till a late dinner."[35]

They could scarcely have avoided the drawing rooms, nor can it be supposed that Clay, at least, desired to do so. Friends that he had made in 1807 remembered him, and, as he attained greater eminence, social as well as political doors swung open to the charming and gallant Kentuckian. It was at this time, for instance, that the Madisons became his lifelong friends. Clay probably met James Madison for the first time in 1807, although his admiration for the Virginia statesman had begun years before. There is a tradition, entirely within character, that when he went to pay his respects to the great Virginian, a very pretty maid opened the door and bade him come in. Attracted by her smile, he gallantly kissed her. Mr. Madison appeared, and she passed the kiss on to him; whereupon Clay remarked, "Had I, madam, known you were Mrs. Madison, the coin would have been larger."[36] The Clays were favored guests at the executive mansion, when Madison was President, and a grand-nephew of the gorgeous Dolly recalled in later

[33] Clay Papers, I, Clay to ——, Nov. 20, 1812.
[34] M. B. Smith, op. cit., pp. 86–87.
[35] Ibid., pp. 87–88.
[36] A. C. Clark, Life and Letters of Dolly Madison (Washington, 1914), p. 93.

years that, at the "levees" which she introduced, he often saw Clay, Webster and Calhoun about her, and from that time on became accustomed to calling the Kentucky statesman "cousin Henry." [37]

There are various and sundry stories about Clay's attraction for women. That they liked him is certain, whether that liking expressed itself in the "sister's affection" that Mrs. Madison and Mrs. Seaton had for him, [38] or in the vehement, almost indiscreet, protestations of devotion with which Eliza Johnston, wife of his friend, Senator Johnston of Louisiana, showered him. [39] But there is no proof that he was a philanderer at any time, and Mrs. Johnston's idolatrous admiration, the one bit of incriminating evidence, was too frank and open to have been the result of an affair.

Back in Lexington there were always legal cases and family affairs, and a variety of duties and obligations. Clay acted as consultant to James Monroe when the latter wished to sell his Western lands; [40] he was the leading member of a committee, appointed by the Transylvania trustees, that was vigorously hunting down a new president for the languishing University; [41] he was elected Grand Orator of the Grand Lodge of Kentucky Masons, at the Grand Annual Communication; [42] he attended to the great mass of legal business that was connected with the Hart family affairs, and out of that, like a grim phantom of the past, rises a slave auction: —

LIKELY SLAVES FOR SALE

In virtue of a deed of trust made the first day of September last, by John Wilkinson and Thomas Pickett, which is recorded in the

---

[37] *Ibid.*, pp. 461–462; B. P. Poore, *Perley's Reminiscences of Sixty Years*, 2 vols. (Philadelphia, 1886), Vol. I, p. 31.

[38] Clark, *Life and Letters of Dolly Madison*, p. 395, Mrs. Madison to Mrs. Seaton, Aug. 23, 1847.

[39] Clay Papers, XV, July 10, 1829, XVI, Dec. 12, 1829. *Cf.* R. P. Letcher to Clay, XVI, Dec. 26, 1829.

[40] Monroe Correspondence (Lib. of Cong., Mss. Div.), XII, Clay to Monroe, Nov. 13, 1810.

[41] F. H. Sweet Collection, letter signed with the names of Clay, Pope and Mason, Sept. 20, 1813.

[42] *Kentucky Gazette*, Sept. 22, 1812.

office of the County Court of Clarke, the subscriber, appointed by the said deed Trustee, will proceed, on Saturday the sixth day of July next, in the town of Lexington, before the door of the Kentucky Hotel, to sell at public auction, for ready money, upwards of twenty likely slaves, being men women girls and boys, the property of the said Wilkinson and Pickett, to satisfy the two first instalments of a debt due from the said Wilkinson and Pickett to Abraham S. Barton and John Hart surviving partners of Hart Barton and Hart, to secure payment of which debt the said deed of trust was given.

HENRY CLAY
Trustee
3d May 1811.[43]

But of all his private interests, except his family, Ashland undoubtedly lay closest to his heart.

The exact year in which he began the acquisition of this property, which he named for its ash trees, is uncertain. It may have been as early as 1805.[44] The first purchase of which court records now exist was made on October 11, 1811, when he bought one hundred and twenty-three acres of land bordering on the Richmond road from Thomas Bodley. The cost was "one thousand pounds current money of Kentucky."[45] He purchased two hundred and fifty-five acres more in November, at a cost of six thousand three hundred and seventy-five dollars.[46] Small additions were made subsequently and a last substantial purchase of about one hundred and twelve acres came in 1830, at a cost of about thirty-five dollars per acre.[47] Ashland comprised approximately four hundred acres by the beginning of

[43] *Misc. Papers* (N. Y. Public Library). The Kentucky hotel belonged to Clay.
[44] Fayette County Tax Lists, 1805; McDowell Collection, diary of Henry Clay, Jr., entry for Nov. 27, 1840; Peter, *op. cit.*, p. 359.
[45] A. C. V. M. Rogers, *Ashland the Home of Henry Clay*, M. A. thesis (Univ. of Ky. Lib., 1934), p. 64, deed. The transcripts of deeds in this unpublished thesis are valuable.
[46] *Ibid.*, p. 71, deed dated Nov. 16, 1811. This was from Samuel Smith of Maryland and Wilson Carey Nicholas of Virginia. But he had brought suit against them, evidently in an attempt to make good his own title to this land, on June 18, 1810. — Henry Clay & Thos. Hart *vs.* Wilson C. Nicholas *et al.* Fayette Circuit Court, file 442, Jan. 11, 1819.
[47] Rogers, *op. cit.*, pp. 74–83, deeds.

1812, and the land itself had then cost him ten thousand dollars, perhaps more.

The house was a large brick structure, one hundred and twenty-six feet long and fifty-seven feet wide. The main building, two-and-one-half stories high, had one-story wings at both ends. The icehouses and the dairy stood, and still stand, just to the south of the main site. The smokehouse, carriage house, and slave quarters were out beyond. The park to the north and east, where Clay loved to walk, is supposed to have been designed by L'Enfant, but it was laid out in later years.

No one knows when the house was begun. It was certainly not later than 1810, for Henry Clay Junior's diary states that he was born there, April 10, 1811.[48] It was valued at ten thousand dollars in 1812, and insured for eight thousand dollars in that year.[49] There is a tradition that it was designed by Benjamin Latrobe, but that is by no means certain.[50]

This noble country estate, about a mile and a half from the city of Lexington, occupied a great deal of Clay's attention during the years that followed. It aroused in him a deep and tranquil affection, and more than once he found solace there, and rest. The house was torn down and rebuilt in the decade following his death, and the estate has dwindled down to twenty acres, but the grounds that remain are redolent of the memories of old days. There you can see the myrtle beds, as planted by Mrs. Clay; the Chinese ailanthus, the Scotch pine, and other trees and shrubs first brought by the master of Ashland. And, if you have the gift, when evening falls you may catch a glimpse of a tall, spare form with bent head pacing sedately along the winding path under the pines and cedars.

[48] McDowell Collection. The entry, headed "Ashland, Nov. 27, 1840," reads: "I was born on the 10″ April, 1811 in the dining room of this house."

[49] Clay Papers, I, fire insurance policy, Sept. 25, 1812.

[50] F. Kimball, *Domestic Architecture of the American Colonies and of the Early Republic* (N.Y., 1922), p. 274. Kimball states that the house was built in 1813 and the year following from designs by Latrobe, and relies for this on a letter of Latrobe, dated Aug. 13, 1813. It is possible that the letter refers to the house at Mansfield, a neighboring estate in which Clay developed an interest.

CHAPTER V

THE WAR HAWK

THE United States was drifting toward war in 1810. Two years later we were involved in our second struggle with Great Britain. But the War of 1812, upon which we embarked in the name of free trade and seamen's rights, was fought in defiance of the New England commercial element whose interests it was supposed to protect. This paradox requires an explanation. What were the real reasons that Madison "esteemed it necessary to throw forward the flag of the country, sure that the people would press onward and defend it"? [1]

The background was the great duel between Napoleon and England, and it is true that, in one sense, we were forced into the struggle by continued and flagrant violations of our rights as neutrals. The attack upon the *Chesapeake* in 1807, the impressment of thousands of American seamen,[2] the arbitrary seizure of hundreds of American ships by both the French and the English while the Tenth and Eleventh Congresses fumbled about from embargo to nonintercourse, and from that to the humiliating Macon Bill Number Two — these stirred the national pride. Some Republican leaders were criticizing the pacific policy of the Administration as early as 1808, and Clay's old friend, Tom Ritchie, in his *Richmond Enquirer,* was denouncing feebleness and demanding energetic action.[3] But this group of insurgent Republicans, a number of whom were merely factious intriguers opposed to Albert Gallatin, could

[1] H. Adams, *Life of Albert Gallatin* (Philadelphia, 1879,), p. 460, note, Madison to Bancroft.
[2] At least 6,000 from 1803 to 1812, and estimated by contemporaries at from 10,000 to 50,000. — J. F. Zimmerman, *Impressment of American Seamen* (N.Y., 1925), pp. 255–256.
[3] D. R. Anderson, "The Insurgents of 1811," in *Amer. Hist. Assoc. Report* (1911), Vol. I, pp. 167–176; Pratt, *op. cit.*, pp. 30–31.

never have carried the country into war. New England made trading profits even in the midst of adversity, and manifested little desire to have its pride avenged. The philosophy of modern nationalism, still a new force in Europe itself, had small influence in a land where sectionalism played such an important rôle. Patriotism and the concepts of national honor and national pride were present, and they had a part in whipping up a bellicose spirit; but it was a combination of more practical reasons that sent the West and South on their crusade for war.

The West was stirred deeply by an economic depression that began in 1806 and lasted, with one brief and partial interruption, until 1812. Faced by great difficulties in marketing its produce when prices were high and times were peaceful, this era of trade restrictions and falling prices drove the Mississippi Valley into an increasing bitterness against the British orders in council and into a belief that it must mend its failing fortunes by commercial coercion and, that failing, by an appeal to arms.[4]

The Indian menace, pointed by the outbreak under Tecumseh and the Prophet in 1811, was another source of rage and hatred. For the frontiersmen saw the British in Canada back of the Indians, and the whole Ohio Valley believed, with some reason, that the only way to rid itself of the red man, and incidentally acquire control of the rich fur trade, was by a smashing attack that would break the Indians' power and end with the conquest of Canada. General Harrison knew, before he started on the Indian campaign of 1811, that any number of men could be obtained for a march into the Indian country or into British territory.[5] The Battle of Tippecanoe increased the ardor of the West, and the subsequent Indian depredations stimulated the demand for a war which should crush the Indians and their "allies" forever.

Nor were the Southern frontiersmen one whit behind their Western brothers in warlike ardor. General George Mathews of Georgia, a Revolutionary veteran and an enthusiastic an-

[4] G. R. Taylor, *Agrarian Discontent in the Mississippi Valley Preceding the War of 1812* (Chicago, 1931), pp. 486f.

[5] Pratt, *op. cit.*, pp. 42f; C. B. Coleman, "The Ohio Valley in the Preliminaries of the War of 1812," in the *Miss. Valley Hist. Rev.*, Vol. VII (June, 1920), pp. 40f.

nexationist, made an extraordinary attempt in 1811 and 1812 to wrest East Florida from Spain.[6] The Spaniards still held that territory and Mobile, and the demand for annexation was more insistent than ever. Georgians, like Troup and Crawford, believed that it was necessary for the safety of their state. The whole Southern Border was avid for it. Spain was England's ally, and the South commonly assumed that war with England meant war with Spain, or at least forcible occupation of all Florida. The old idea of wresting Mexico from Spain, if not actually annexing it to the United States, was once more abroad in the land.[7]

Along the great drawn bow of the frontier, an arc extending from New Hampshire out through Kentucky and Tennessee and back to Georgia, there vibrated a passion for battle and expansion.[8]

This spirit broke out in unmistakable fashion early in 1810, and Clay was one of its most ardent champions.

Nonintercourse with France and Britain had been tried the year before. Now a bill was introduced that repealed that measure, closed American ports to the ships of the warring nations, and admitted British and French merchandise when directly imported in American vessels. It had passed the House, but in the Senate a factious group of Republicans were tearing it to pieces, when Clay arose. He urged that the bill be recommitted and strengthened, but, more than that, he spoke out boldly for a war which he preferred "with all its calamities and desolation, to the tranquil and putrescent pool of ignominious peace." Such a war would strengthen the national character and preserve the nation's honor. It would extinguish "the torch that lights up savage warfare," and give America entire control of the British fur trade. "The conquest of Canada is in your power. I trust that I shall not be deemed presumptuous when I state that I verily believe that the militia of Kentucky are alone competent to place Montreal and Upper

[6] Pratt, *op. cit.*, pp. 75f. Mathews had the tacit consent, at least, of the United States Government.

[7] *Ibid.*, pp. 120–124.

[8] Pratt plots this "crescent," and comments upon its significance in masterly fashion (*op. cit.*, pp. 126–127).

Canada at your feet," and "the enterprise and valor of your maritime brethren will participate in the spoils of capture." [9]

The motion was lost, and the emasculated bill passed, only to be mired and strangled in a slough of dispute between the House and the Senate. But Clay's speech, although not the first war speech that had been made in Congress, was redolent of the frontier and breathed an energy and courage that were to lead to action, after the fumbling, factious Eleventh Congress had passed to its reward.

It may be noted, in passing, that there was an irony of which he was unconscious in one part of his remarks. It was essential, he said, for the United States to have "a certain portion of military ardor" and "a new race of heroes" in order to avoid the danger of enervation. Perhaps it was. But if the curtain of time could have been rolled up for one brief moment, he might have glimpsed the tall form and stern face of a military hero who was to be created by the very war that Clay was urging. The sight would not have been inspiring.

No further striking manifestations of war psychosis appeared in the strife-torn Eleventh Congress. The principal work of that body was to pass the famous Macon Bill Number Two, another experiment in trade regulation. This opened commerce with the world, but provided that, if one belligerent removed its restrictions on neutral trade, the President should proclaim nonintercourse with the other. Thus, it was hoped, the United States might obtain respect for her rights as a neutral, but the bill simply gave the French Emperor an opportunity to trick the American Government and force it toward war with Great Britain.

On August 5, 1810, Napoleon signed a minute which stated, although in ambiguous language, that his Berlin and Milan decrees were revoked, and that, after November 1, they would cease to have effect. There were plenty of reasons why Madison should have mistrusted this statement, and it was, as a matter of fact, false and misleading. But the President was anxious for peace, and willing to clutch at a straw. On November 2, 1810, he issued a proclamation which declared that the French

[9] *Annals of Cong.*, 11th Cong., 2d sess., 579–582.

decrees had been revoked and warned Great Britain that non-intercourse would be clamped down upon her if she did not repeal her orders in council within three months' time.[10] The British Government would not act until satisfied that France had kept her word, and Madison, refusing to withdraw his threat, waited in vain for proof of the Corsican's good intentions toward the Americans whom he professed to love.[11]

When Kentucky chose her delegation for the Twelfth Congress, Clay stood for the House of Representatives. His decision to do so seems to have been based largely upon personal preference. He had been accustomed at Frankfort to the turbulence of a more crowded chamber, and he preferred it, he told Monroe, to the "solemn stillness" of the Senate. Already committed to a war policy, Clay realized that vigorous action was more apt to emanate from the House, and consultation with friends strengthened his preference for the change.[12] It is possible that hints of the Speakership had been whispered in his ear. At any rate, when Congress convened, November 4, 1811, and the House balloted for its Speaker, "the Western Star" was elected by a large majority.[13]

It was the beginning of a long and able career in that position. Tactful but decisive, genial yet firm, his tenure of the office increased its power while strengthening his own influence. "Decide, decide promptly," he told Robert C. Winthrop, in later years, "and never give your reasons for the decision. The House will sustain your decisions, but there will always be men to cavil and quarrel about your reasons." He used the authority and prestige of the office, sometimes in shrewd and arbitrary fashion, to push through measures that he had at heart,[14] and

[10] Cf. E. Channing, A History of the United States, 7 vols. (N.Y., 1928), Vol. IV, pp. 411–415; Adams, Hist. of the U.S., Vol. V, pp. 254–261, 289f; McMaster, op. cit., Vol. III, pp. 360–369.

[11] Adams, Hist. of the U.S., Vol. V, pp. 256, 300–304, 340f.

[12] Monroe Correspondence, XII, Clay to Monroe, Nov. 13, 1810; Colton, Correspondence, p. 47, Clay to Adam Beatty, May 31, 1810.

[13] Annals of Cong., 12th Cong., 1st sess., 330; Wm. Lowndes to Elizabeth Lowndes, Nov. 2 or 3, 1811, in Mrs. St. J. Ravenel, Life and Times of William Lowndes (Boston, 1901), p. 84.

[14] M. P. Follett, The Speaker of the House of Representatives (N.Y., 1909), pp. 69–82; Winthrop, op. cit., p. 6.

there are plentiful illustrations of this in the dramatic session of 1811–1812.

For the Twelfth Congress was to be a war Congress. The Federalists were in a decided minority, the conservative Republicans lacked unity and constructive leadership, and the War Hawks — the young leaders, eager, aggressive, and contemptuous of Republican dogmas — rode the tide. Henry Clay, John C. Calhoun, William Lowndes, Langdon Cheves, Felix Grundy, Peter B. Porter, and Richard Mentor Johnson pushed on ardently, if somewhat blindly, in a passion for war and conquest.[15]

They had, too, a powerful ally in James Monroe, the Secretary of State. This tall, rawboned, broad-shouldered man, reserved in manner to the point of shyness, transparently honest in character and motives, with an air of respectable mediocrity which seemed wafted straight from a Virginia farm, was to prove a pillar of strength. A long record of public service had included a difficult and unsatisfactory mission to England in 1805, and another failure to obtain a settlement of American grievances after he had become Secretary of State in April, 1811. By December of that year Monroe seems to have felt certain that war could not be avoided.[16] "Gentlemen, *we must fight.* We are forever disgraced if we do not," he is reported as saying, and his influence upon the younger members of Congress, and doubtless upon the President, was great.[17]

Madison's third annual message (November 5, 1811) reviewed the unsatisfactory state of relations with Great Britain. It was full of ominous warning and stressed the need of providing for security.[18] The House answered with alacrity. Clay, as Speaker, put War Hawks on all the principal committees.

[15] Cf. Wm. Reed to Timothy Pickering, Feb. 18, 1812, in the Timothy Pickering Papers (Mass. Hist. Soc.), XXX, folio 17.

[16] He had turned against England definitely in July. Cf. Adams, *Hist. of the U.S.*, Vol. VI, p. 44, and G. Morgan, *The Life of James Monroe* (Boston, 1921), p. 307.

[17] G. Hunt, "Joseph Gales on the War Manifesto of 1812," in the *Amer. Hist. Rev.*, Vol. XII (Jan. 1908), pp. 303–310; Wm. M. Meigs, *Life of John C. Calhoun*, 2 vols. (N.Y., 1917), Vol. I, p. 131.

[18] Richardson, *Messages and Papers*, Vol. II, pp. 476–481.

Porter, Calhoun, Grundy, Harper and Desha were placed on the Committee on Foreign Relations; David R. Williams was made chairman of the Committee on Military Affairs; Langdon Cheves was chairman of the Naval Committee; Ezekiel Bacon and Cheves headed the Committee on Ways and Means.[19] The Foreign Affairs Committee reported, late in November, proposals for increasing the army and furbishing up the navy, and, in the debate that followed, the warlike spirit ran wild and the conquest of Canada was urged continually. The Republican press backed this furor, howling its denunciations of impressment and Indian intrigues. War was the cry, and the conservative Republicans were powerless to stem the tide. John Randolph shook with spasms of violent but impotent invective. Others, like Gideon Granger, the Postmaster-General, contented themselves with gloomy prophecies.

I cannot perceive [Granger wrote to a friend] the grounds on which we can remain at peace without a change of measures which will dishonor the Administration and possibly the Government. Nor do I perceive that under our present circumstances, we can inter [sic] into war, without materially retarding the growth of the nation, without hazarding our republican principles; and incurring all the evils of Federal funding systems, & internal Taxes. As a counter balance for these evils, we shall doubtless acquire the Canadas and other northern british possessions. . . . But will not the addition of these Territories accellerate a dissolution of the Union? Or can it spread securely over the Continent? I fear, I doubt.[20]

Meanwhile, the Senate, where faction was not yet dead, passed and sent down a bill that under the guise of patriotism was designed to embarrass the Administration. Madison had wanted an army increase of only ten thousand men, but William B. Giles, a Republican Senator who hated the President and Gallatin, had sponsored a measure that called for twenty-five thousand men, enlisted for five years, despite the obvious difficulties that this would create for an empty Treasury if, indeed, such a number could be raised. There was logic against the

---

[19] *Annals of Cong.*, 12th Cong., 1st sess., 333, 343.
[20] Granger Papers (Lib. of Cong., Mss. Div.), Granger to John Tod, Dec. 26, 1811.

bill, and all the Federalist help available had been necessary to push it through the Senate, but the War Hawks in the House were careless of the consequences. It is true that the House Committee on Foreign Affairs, probably after consultation with Madison, cut the number of additional troops from twenty-five thousand to fifteen thousand, but when the bill, thus amended, reached the floor, it was met with "a gust of zeal and passion" [21] that abolished the reduction.

The Western Star came down from the chair and joined the debate in the Committee of the Whole. The vehemence of the Kentuckian's bellicosity had increased since the year before. He offered an amendment that provided for gradual appointment of the necessary officers, in order to soothe the feelings of the economically minded, but he stood unequivocally for the increase of twenty-five thousand. He wanted, so he said, a vigorous and short war, not one of "languor and imbecility." He demonstrated the need of the maximum force for conquering Canada. In language comparable for its nationalism to that of Isnard in the French Revolution, he boasted of the character of the American people, and brushed aside the idea that a large army was a threat to republican institutions. The citizens of the United States "possessed more intelligence than any other people on the globe. Such a people, consisting of upward of seven millions, affording a physical power of about a million men, capable of bearing arms, and ardently devoted to liberty, could not be subdued by an army of twenty-five thousand men." Britain must be humbled, for she was an aggressor, seeking to destroy "a Power which, at no very distant day, is to make her tremble for naval superiority." He mentioned the horrors of impressment, and even suggested that failure to protect seamen's rights would result in their leaving the United States and seeking employment abroad, perhaps in England.[22]

The speech was a strange compound of warlike zeal and arrant nonsense, but it suited the temper of the majority. Clay's amendment and a few others were accepted, but the twenty-five thousand figure was reinstated.

[21] *Annals of Cong.*, 12th Cong., 1st sess., 701. Speech of Peter B. Porter.
[22] *Ibid.*, 12th Cong., 1st sess., 596–602.

The bill went back to the Senate, which threw out all the amendments. It came back to the House in its original form, and the War Hawks, led by Porter and Calhoun of the Foreign Relations Committee, abandoned the effort to alter it. In vain John Randolph poured out his vitriolic wrath upon a standing army and the desertion of Republican principles. "After you have raised these twenty-five thousand men," he exclaimed, " . . . shall we form a committee of this House, in quality of a Committee of Public Safety, or shall we depute the power to the Speaker (he should not wish it in safer hands) to carry on the war?" He proposed, after the bill had passed,[23] a motion that the President be authorized to use the army, when not in active service, in constructing roads and canals. The war men raged against this insult to the military arm, which, Randolph asserted, was "cankered to the core." They appealed to Clay if Randolph were in order "thus to abuse the army of the country," but, certain of his majority, the Speaker held that the Virginian was within his rights, and urged decorum in debate. The proposal was rejected, fifteen to one hundred and two.[24]

The bill went through as Giles had first proposed it, and this army, created in times of peace for purposes of conquest, was supplemented by an authorization of fifty thousand militia which Cheves and Clay argued could be used constitutionally for invading Canada(!).[25] Bills for internal taxation were to follow. The Republican Party was cut loose from its old moorings, despite the forebodings of the conservative element.

The big navy men followed hard upon the heels of the military. On January 17, 1812, Langdon Cheves, chairman of the Naval Committee, asked an appropriation to build twelve "seventy-fours" and twenty frigates, at a cost of seven million, five hundred thousand dollars. He pleaded for it as a war necessity, even though he admitted that it was opposed to Republican precedent.[26] The leaders were showing no great respect for the traditions of their Party, but the financial strain

[23] *Ibid.*, 12th Cong., 1st sess., 691.
[24] *Ibid.*, 12th Cong., 1st sess., 727.
[25] *Ibid.*, 12th Cong., 1st sess., 728f.
[26] *Ibid.*, 12th Cong., 1st sess., 803f.

already imposed by the army bill was enough to produce defection.

The Western War Hawks began to fall away. Rhea of Tennessee opposed the bill. He knew of no use that warships could be to the West "except they meant to use them against the Indians." As to New Orleans, "it is defended so well by nature, that no foreign Power can annoy it. The upper country will always maintain it." Grundy was opposed. The cry went up that navies were expensive and dangerous to popular liberty. They bred ruin and corruption. Richard M. Johnson pictured them as fraught with piracy, plunder and disaster. He went back to ancient history for melancholy examples. "I will refer to Tyre and Sidon, Crete and Rhodes, to Athens and Carthage." [27] The spirit of disaffection spread, and for a time Cheves found himself almost alone. Then Lowndes came to his aid, and on January 22 Clay left the chair to speak on the naval question.

The speech was temperate, compared to his effusions on the army. Extensive naval building was, he admitted, impossible at this time, and probably it would never be desirable to have a great navy. Indeed he should consider it madness to attempt to provide a fleet capable of meeting Britain's on even terms. What he wanted was a defensive navy, about twelve ships of the line and fifteen or twenty frigates; a force that would ensure "the command of our own seas." It could not be built at once, but it ought to be started. New Orleans, East Florida, even Cuba, "though he wished her independent," must be guarded against the British menace. Commerce must be protected. Again he conjured up the spectacle of American tars being driven into foreign employment. Lastly, the navy would "form a new bond of connection between the states, concentrating their hopes, their interests, and their affections." [28]

The House refused to build frigates or "seventy-fours," despite these efforts, and a much less pretentious measure became law.[29] But it is interesting that Clay's position here

[27] *Ibid.*, 12th Cong., 1st sess., 875–884.
[28] *Ibid.*, 12th Cong., 1st sess., 910–919.
[29] *Ibid.*, 12th Cong., 1st sess., 2261.

was out of line with the other Westerners. He was nationalist, not sectional, and it is possible that even his moderation was diplomatic rather than real. For, three weeks before, he had boasted that ere long the United States would make Britain tremble for naval superiority.

Slowly the winter months of 1812 wore on, while Clay and his fellow enthusiasts labored with painful ferocity to bring their colleagues into a warlike mood. They succeeded in passing a bill for a loan of eleven millions. A series of resolutions providing for a host of new taxes was jammed through the House. But progress was slow. Over a third of the Republicans in Congress had little liking for a policy that entailed such wholesale subversion of Jeffersonian principles for the sake of the doubtful glories of an appeal to arms. The Federalists, who with a strange fatuity frequently voted for war measures, were only interested in turning their opponents out of office. Delay resulted, delay that irritated the flaming youths of the frontier. Twenty-five years later Clay recalled an incident that showed his mood at the time. He remembered saying to "an illustrious man, now no more: we must stop this everlasting discussion, this endless diplomacy; let us go to work, and appeal to the valor of our countrymen to sustain us; no other alternative is left us. But he replied in his calm and dignified way — 'Mr. Clay, recollect our institutions rest on public opinion, on reasoning and argument.' " [30]

The "illustrious man" may well have been Madison. Short of stature, frail of physique, diffident and formal when appearing before the public, this mild-eyed, weak-voiced man, for all his great learning and devotion to liberal democracy, was not the leader for a time of troubles. Weary and worn by all this storm and stress, unable to cope with the valiant spirits who never tired of chanting their war cry — wondering, doubting, fearing, but unopposing — he fumbled with reluctant hands at the bolts which barred the doors of the temple of Janus. Even after he had apparently given up hope of averting the struggle, he thought of sending Bayard to England in a final

[30] *Cong. Globe*, 25th Cong., 2d sess., 38.

effort. The mission never materialized, and if a Federalist story is true, Clay was chiefly instrumental in thwarting this project, the last chance for peace.[31]

By the Ides of March, the President finally became convinced that war was inevitable. He had obtained possession, in February, of a batch of papers sold to the Government by John Henry, an Irish adventurer. These purported to disclose that Henry had acted as a British agent in fostering a separatist movement in the Eastern United States, and, although they were most unsatisfactory as evidence, Monroe and the War Hawks proposed to use them as a means of hurrying on the crisis.

On March 15, after a conference with Monroe, Clay laid down a program before the Administration. The Henry disclosures, he said, presented an opportunity that should not be missed. He suggested that the President recommend to Congress in a confidential message a thirty-day embargo, to be followed by war; that he also recommend provision for accepting ten thousand volunteers. The tone of the letter clearly showed that he expected presidential action.[32]

There is no reason to believe that the Government's policy was dictated by Clay. But it is certainly interesting that Monroe, in a conversation a few days later with the French Minister, Serurier, used the arguments that Clay had used in this letter, and outlined the same plan in demonstrating the Government's readiness to fight.[33]

On April 1, after Monroe had consulted with the House Committee on Foreign Relations, and had told them that the President meant war, the House, in secret session, received a request from Madison for a sixty-day embargo. The War Hawks, who had a bill already prepared in anticipation, acclaimed the proposal. Clay and Grundy praised the message,

[31] Pickering Papers, XXX, Abraham Shepherd to Pickering, Feb. 20, March 9, 1814; Adams, *Gallatin*, pp. 457–459. The Federalist tale that the War Hawks forced Madison's hand by threatening to oppose his renomination has long been exploded.

[32] Monroe Correspondence, XIII, Clay to Monroe, March 15, 1812.

[33] Adams, *Hist. of the U.S.*, Vol. VI, p. 194, quotes Serurier's account of this conversation.

and openly asserted that it threw down the gage of battle. Randolph solemnly reminded the House that the eyes of God were upon them, and denounced war and this proposal, as an aid to France. Clay replied impatiently. There was no need for Randolph to remind them in this manner "of that Being who watches and surrounds us." [34] Boldly, he minimized the settlement of the *Chesapeake* affair, and asserted that all else was as bad as ever, and that they now had "complete proof" that Britain would do anything to destroy the United States. He wished that war had come in 1809. Public opinion clamored for it now, and it must come.[35]

Randolph and the Federalists fought a vain fight. The bill passed, seventy to forty-one, and, after the Senate had weakened it by extending the time limit to ninety days, it became law on April 4, 1812. It was followed by an act authorizing the President to call out one hundred thousand militia for six months' service; and then, for almost two months, Congress slipped into its former hesitant way, while it awaited news from Europe, watched the Administration's disappointing search for generals and men and money, and descried alarming Federalist victories in New York and Massachusetts. Many of the members went home on leave, and it was generally understood that no action would be taken until the first of June.[36]

Clay remained in Washington during this period. Convinced, despite the delay, that war was at hand, he yearned to welcome

[34] This curious reference to the immanence of the Deity is one of the few sidelights on Clay's early religious life. Another is his proposal in 1807 that the Senate hold a session on Sunday, a proposal that the Senate turned down, the friends of the motion not liking to go on record as favoring it (Brown, *Plumer's Memorandum*, p. 634). In 1805, Thomas Hart, who seems to have been interested in a new religion, the followers of which agreed to settle their differences without recourse to law, gave Clay a published dialogue between a lawyer and a parson, in which the parson got the better of it. Clay refused to return the paper and said that the editor (Duane) was a "damned unprincipled wretch who wished to see anarchy and confusion prevail throughout the Union." (James Brown Papers, Lib. of Cong., Mss. Div., I, Thomas Hart to James Brown, Jan. 27, 1805). It is probable that Clay, if he thought about religion at all, inclined toward Jeffersonian rationalism.

[35] *Annals of Cong.*, 12th Cong., 1st sess., 1588–1598.

[36] Adams, *Hist. of the U.S.*, Vol. VI, pp. 204–215.

it and waited impatiently for decisive action.[37] It was small matter to him and his fellows that Britain had abandoned the irritating diplomatic methods of Canning; that she had modified the orders in council, and offered further modifications; that she had atoned for the *Chesapeake* outrage; [38] that France had sinned as deeply, if not as widely, as England, and had promised what she would not perform; that we were utterly unprepared for war and had a Treasury that was almost empty; that the War Department was inefficient; that the financial condition of the country was completely unstable; that New England was hostile. The War Hawks had passed beyond rational restraint. Federalist Abijah Bigelow was right when he told his wife that to reason with them would be like trying to reason with a madman.[39]

The war party was arrogant in its determination to force the issue. On May 19, dispatches arrived from the British foreign office stating that Great Britain would not rescind the orders in council until Napoleon had "absolutely and unconditionally" rescinded his decrees. Promptly the War Hawks sounded the alarm. It was rumored that Madison was preparing a war message, and appeals to patriotism and party regularity were used with good effect to rally wavering spirits. Ten days after the dispatches had arrived, Randolph was silenced by a ruling from the chair when he attempted to speak, and the House, by a vote of seventy-two to thirty-seven, refused to consider his resolution that it was inexpedient to resort to war with Great Britain.[40]

The crisis was at hand. According to Joseph Gales, a deputation from Congress, headed by Clay, called upon Madison and told him that Congress was ready to throw down the gage of

[37] Clay to Thos. Bodley, May 12, 1812 (Ky. State Hist. Soc. Lib.); Crittenden Papers, I, Clay to Crittenden, May 28, 1812.

[38] *Cf.* Adams, *Hist. of the U.S.*, Vol. V, pp. 525–526.

[39] Bigelow Letters (Amer. Antiq. Soc.), Abijah Bigelow to his wife, March 27, 1812.

[40] *National Intelligencer*, May 30, June 2, 16, 1812. The fiery Virginian carried the case to his constituents, and Clay, stung by this, defended his action in a published letter that provoked a sharp reply from Randolph. *Ibid.*, June 17, July 8, 1812. Clay dropped the matter, on the advice of Langdon Cheves; Clay Papers, I, Cheves to Clay, July 30, 1812.

battle.[41] No one knows in what words Madison replied, but a day or two before June 1, while Clay was taking one of his usual morning horseback rides to Georgetown, he told a colleague that a confidential war message might be expected from the President.[42] Clay rode out toward Georgetown again on the morning of June 1, in a mood of fiery exultation. When he came back and the House session began, the message came. The procedure was cut-and-dried. Two days later, the Committee submitted a report recommending war, a report that had been written by the Secretary of State, James Monroe.[43]

Josiah Quincy and John Randolph moved that debate be public, but the House voted this down, and the discussion was in secret session where the Speaker's power was absolute. Congress, wrote the Washington correspondent of the *New York Evening Post*, sat only "to receive and register the *decrees* of a few inexperienced and hot-headed politicians. The minority are *tied down*, hand and foot, ready to be *trod upon* and cast out by the *lordly men*, who press themselves upon the public view." [44] The deliberations were brief, and the South and West carried the day. The House voted for war, seventy-nine to forty-nine, on June 4, and the resolution went to the Senate. That body delayed majestically for nearly two weeks, and then passed the resolution. On June 19 Madison sent the proclamation of war. The United States had decided to fight, and criers were sent up and down the land, proclaiming the glad tidings. No one knew that, two days before, the British Government had abandoned the orders in council.

There is no question that Clay was one of the leaders in the war movement. The facts speak for themselves. His policy as Speaker, his efforts on the floor of the House, his letter to Monroe, all demonstrate the part he played. But it would be idle to assert that he was *the* leader in the movement. Monroe championed it, and his influence was undoubtedly powerful.

---

[41] Hunt, "Joseph Gales, etc.," in *Amer. Hist. Rev.*, Vol. XIII, p. 309.

[42] *National Intelligencer*, July 8, 1812. Randolph's letter.

[43] Hunt, "Joseph Gales, etc.," in *Amer. Hist. Rev.*, Vol. XIII, pp. 306–309.

[44] *National Intelligencer*, June 6, 1812. Reprint from the *Evening Post*.

Madison certainly did not oppose it. The whole band of War Hawks, who represented the spirit of the South and West, furiously pushed it on. As Speaker of the House, Clay had a singular opportunity to display his zeal effectively. But after all, he was only one among many who sponsored the folly of the day, and at least it can be said in his behalf that the War of 1812 would have come if "Harry of the West" had never lived.

CHAPTER VI

WAR AND PEACE

DAZZLING visions must have danced before the eyes of Kentucky's impetuous leader in June of 1812. That enthusiastic optimism, which seldom deserted him, prophesied a brief struggle brought to a brilliant conclusion by the valor of the American people. Canada captured, England humbled, a victorious nation would dictate terms of peace that would be a concrete representation of American power and might. And then what station in the political firmament could be too high for that Western Star which had blazed the way to victory? What meed of victory might not be bestowed?

Alas for human hopes! The lanky Kentuckian's dreams of glory and grandeur were to be rudely dispelled by a war which had many of the elements of a comic opera. The incompetent General William Hull passed from a mood of boastfulness into a blue funk and surrendered Detroit and an army of twenty-five hundred men to a vastly inferior force of British and Indians. This was the beginning of the "attack" on Canada in 1812. At Niagara and Kingston and above Lake Champlain mutinous militia and incompetent generals staged a series of ludicrous offensives. Commanding officers frittered months away, quarreling among themselves. They marched troops up to the border and then marched them away when the militia refused to cross into enemy territory. General Smyth took some four thousand men up to the Niagara frontier only to have them melt into utter confusion, running away and "discharging their muskets in every direction." Peter B. Porter accused Smyth of cowardice and the two men fought a duel with pistols from which the seconds had removed the bullets.

Oliver Hazard Perry did win the battle of Lake Erie and furnish a militaristic slogan for American schoolboys. His victory opened the way for the defeat of the British and the death of Tecumseh at the Thames but the net result of these exploits was the safeguarding of our Western lands rather than the conquest of Canada. The Americans really had cause to congratulate themselves when Macdonough's victory on Lake Champlain in September of 1814 prevented General Prevost from smashing down along Burgoyne's old route into the Hudson Valley. But the raiding party of American irregulars who burned the Government buildings at York, Ontario, merely gave the British an excuse for summary retaliation when, after our militia ran away at the "Bladensburg races," the British troops occupied Washington and burned the Capitol and the Executive mansion. Occasional victories on the sea could not obscure the stubborn fact that our coast was stringently blockaded, and that the residents of a long stretch of the Maine coast tamely took an oath of allegiance to the conquerors. Even Jackson's brilliant repulse of the British at New Orleans had its ironic aspect, for that battle was fought after the peace treaty had been signed.

By and large, the War of 1812 presented the spectacle of Britain concentrating her main attention upon the mighty Corsican but at the same time dealing us a series of left-handed blows that kept us staggering. And the one great national hero produced by the struggle was destined to be the nemesis of Clay's ambition.

The dismal war record, which filled its sponsors with chagrin, is easily explained. Madison's leadership was suited only for the piping times of peace, and vigorous executive action was conspicuously lacking. The finances were in chaos, despite the heroic efforts of Albert Gallatin. War preparation was utterly inadequate, New England was sourly resentful, and, worst of all, there was no unanimity as to aims. Professor Pratt has described graphically the effect of sectional jealousies upon the conduct of the war.[1] The North cared nothing about the occupation of East Florida, the South and the Administration were indifferent to the idea of annexing Canada. The expansionists had united to bring on the war. They divided as to practical objectives once it had commenced, and the Government's force

[1] Pratt, *op. cit.*, pp. 166–188, 228, 266f.

and energy, already weak enough, were hopelessly vitiated.

Chaos marked the very beginning of the war, when a Federalist movement to repeal the nonimportation acts against Great Britain failed, June 25, 1812, only by Clay's casting vote as Speaker. The financial needs of the Government were so great that even Calhoun and Cheves had inclined toward this idea, and Clay and his followers, who barely kept nonimportation in force, were placed in the unenviable position of including the United States in the Continental System of Napoleon, while at the same time, the French Emperor was plundering and burning American ships at will.[2]

The Kentuckian listened to the reports of Hull's expedition with an enthusiasm quickly tempered by anxiety, and by the end of July he was urging William Henry Harrison upon the attention of the Administration. When Hull was driven back and cooped up in Detroit, Clay acted with Governor Scott and others in making Harrison commander of a relief expedition from Kentucky. This was high-handed dealing with the military arm, but Clay got around that difficulty by telling Monroe that of course the act was provisional, and could be revoked by the President. Harrison besought Clay to come to the Ohio frontier. "Your advice and assistance in determining the course of operations for the army . . . will be highly useful," he wrote,[3] but Clay did not join his future political rival.

Hull's surrender made the Kentuckian rage. In his opinion, he told Monroe, the general deserved to be shot without an investigation. The war should be all the more vigorously prosecuted, and the Indians "must be made to feel the utmost rigor of Government."[4]

[2] *Cf.* Adams, *Hist. of the U.S.*, Vol. VI, pp. 231–234. Clay had the audacity to assert, in 1817, that the American policy had produced the repeal of the French decrees before the War of 1812 — *Annals of Cong.*, 14th Cong., 2d sess., 816–823.

[3] Clay Papers, I, Harrison to Clay, Aug. 30, 1812.

[4] Monroe Correspondence, XIII, Clay to Monroe, Sept. 21, 1812. It was reported that Madison thought of giving Clay command of the forces in the field, but that Gallatin persuaded him that Clay was more valuable in Congress. Madison did think of sending Monroe to take charge of the forces near Detroit. Clay Papers, I, Monroe to Clay, Sept. 17, 1812; Schurz, *op. cit.*, Vol. I, p. 88.

In later years, Clay held an exalted opinion of Madison's judgment and common sense. But the Government's wartime ineptitude disgusted the War Hawk, and by the end of 1812 his estimate of the President was plumbing the depths. On December 29 he wrote of his hopes and fears to his friend Caesar Rodney. He was still optimistic of the outcome of the war; he felt that the spirit of the House of Representatives was excellent, and that the patriotism of the country was holding firm; but Madison filled him with despair.

It is in vain to conceal the fact — at least I will not attempt to disguise it with you — Mr. Madison is wholly unfit for the storms of War. Nature has cast him in too benevolent a mould. Admirably adapted to the tranquil scenes of peace — blending all the mild & amiable virtues, he is not fit for the rough and rude blasts which the conflicts of nations generate. Our hopes then for the future conduct of the War must be placed upon the vigor which he may bring into the administration by the organization of his new Cabinet. And here again he is so hesitating, so tardy, so far behind the national sentiment, in his proceedings towards his War Ministers, that he will lose whatever credit he might otherwise acquire by the introduction of suitable characters in their place.[5]

But the die had been cast, and a week after this gloomy verdict had been handed down, Clay defended the Administration in one of his most eloquent speeches. The Federalists in the House had launched a bitter attack upon the war, and the setting gave Clay an opportunity to deliver a dramatic eulogy of his party and its policy.

On December 29, 1812, the House went into Committee of the Whole to discuss a bill enlisting twenty thousand more men for the invasion of Canada. The opposition, led by Josiah Quincy, pounced upon this with vigor and abandon. They poured scorn upon the policy of providing for additional enlistments, when the present army was not yet filled. They denounced a war of conquest, and pointed their remarks by references to the withdrawal of the orders in council. The Republicans, in their eyes, were the sycophantic tools of Bonaparte. Why attack our peaceful neighbors, the Canadians, exclaimed

[5] Simon Gratz Collection (Pa. Hist. Soc.), Clay to Rodney, Dec. 29, 1812.

Quincy, in a speech remarkable for its unbridled invective. There was more excuse for Kidd, the buccaneer. Those who believed that Britain could be threatened into peace negotiations "must be very young Politicians, their pinfeathers not yet grown, and however they may flutter on this floor, they are not yet fledged for any high or distant flight. . . ." The war men were merely bloodthirsty Anglophobes. "The language of their conduct is that of the giant, in the legends of infancy: —

> Fee, faw, fow, fum
> I smell the blood of an Englishman
> Dead or alive, I will have some."

It was all, he said, a part of the general policy to keep James the First in office four years longer, and then bring James the Second to the succession.[6]

Bitterly the war party resented these insults. Rhea, Grundy, and others answered, defending their program and belaboring the Federalists. On January 8, Clay took up the cudgels in a speech that was continued on the following day.

He was unwell, he said as he arose. (How often, in years to come, this brilliant master of histrionic talents was to use that method of playing upon the sympathies of his hearers!) Then followed an eloquent attempt to silence the opposition and bolster the prosecution of the war. The insinuation of French influence he dismissed as preposterous. He dwelt upon the irenic efforts of the Government and the factiousness of the opposition. The reference to a presidential plot was countered by a significant allusion to a plot to dismember the Union. Quincy had made a fleering comment upon Jefferson, and Clay answered with an impassioned tribute to the great Republican leader.

He snatched from the rude hands of usurpation the violated Constitution of his country, and *that* is his crime. He preserved that instrument, in form and substance and spirit, a precious inheritance for generations to come, and for *this* he can never be forgiven. How impotent is party rage directed against him! He is not more elevated by his

[6] *Annals of Cong.*, 12th Cong., 2d sess., 459f. Quincy spoke January 5, 1813.

lofty residence, upon the summit of his own favorite mountain, than he is lifted by the serenity of his mind, and the consciousness of a well-spent life, above the malignant passions and the turmoils of the day.

On the second day Clay reviewed the causes of the war, and found them in British tyranny. He conveniently forgot the way in which he had muzzled Randolph, and asserted that public opinion had been so powerfully aroused that the opposition had refused openly to attack the declaration of war in its passage through Congress. Impressment, he declared, was sufficient ground for throwing down the gage of battle. The United States had gone to war for her rights and should extort their recognition at all hazards.

He deplored the fact that pacific gestures had been made since the struggle began, and pointed out that they had come to naught. A great majority of the people approved the war, he said, and he urged its vigorous prosecution, and the negotiation of peace at Quebec or Halifax.

In such a cause, with the aid of Providence, we must come out crowned with success; but if we fail, let us fail like men — lash ourselves to our gallant tars, and expire together in one common struggle, fighting for seamen's rights and free trade.

This speech was one of Clay's best efforts, and his eloquence, rising to majestic heights at times, drew tears from those who heard him. Specious in places, amusing, perhaps, in its defense of the Jeffersonian principles which Clay and his party were rapidly tearing into shreds, it urged the war onward, and skillfully pilloried Quincy and his followers for their deficiencies in patriotism. If anything were needed to establish Clay as a leader in the Government, it was supplied by this oration, which had a profound effect throughout the country.

The enlistment bill, after some further debate, passed the House, January 14, by a vote of seventy-seven to forty-two. Eleven days later, the Senate passed it, with amendments. The House concurred in these amendments, and the bill received Madison's signature on Friday, January 29, 1813.[7]

[7] *Ibid.*, 12th Cong., 2d sess., 495f, Appendix 1322.

The Twelfth Congress adjourned *sine die*, on March 3, and the House tendered its unanimous thanks to Clay for his conduct in discharging the duties of Speaker. When the Thirteenth Congress met in special session on May 24, he was again chosen to that office. Two days later, when he took occasion to express himself vehemently on British inhumanity and barbarism in the conduct of the war, it was evident that his war spirit was still aflame.[8]

Nevertheless, he and the other leaders had to face gloomy prospects as the year 1813 wore away. Perry and Harrison gained victories in the West, but elsewhere inefficiency and discord continued to prevail. And, as Napoleon's power began to crumble, there rose the menacing specter of more vigorous British action. Peace became increasingly attractive, even to Henry Clay.

Peace had been in the Administration's thoughts since the beginning of the war. Seven days after the conflict had been formally opened, Monroe had suggested an armistice which Great Britain had refused. Russia offered mediation in 1813, an offer precipitately accepted by Madison. The President appointed John Quincy Adams, then Minister to Russia, James Bayard, a Delaware Federalist and United States Senator, and Albert Gallatin to meet with British representatives at St. Petersburg under the benevolent eye of the Tsar. Gallatin and Bayard went to St. Petersburg, and then news came that Great Britain had declined the proposal. But the humiliating predicament in which this placed the American Government, with two of its negotiators left to wander about in Europe, was ended by a British move for direct negotiations. This offer did not hold out much hope of a settlement of maritime difficulties, but it was accepted, January 5, 1814, and, with the consent of the Senate, the Government appointed Adams, Bayard, Gallatin, Jonathan Russell (a Massachusetts Republican), and Henry Clay to negotiate the terms of peace.

It has been asserted that the Administration's initial preference was Crawford rather than Clay, but the choice of the latter was a natural one. He was ambitious and sensitive, the outstand-

[8] *Ibid.*, 13th Cong., 1st sess., 109. May 26, 1813.

ing leader of the war party, and Serurier, the French Minister, seems to have had a hand in the matter.[9]

The delegation was excellent in many respects. Adams and Gallatin were men of tried worth and long experience in public affairs, and the group as a whole represented the different parts of the nation and the variants in war sentiment. Adams, Bayard and Gallatin, from the Eastern states, were distinctly inclined toward peace. Russell, who was supposed to represent commerce, and Clay as the spokesman for the West and South, were more bellicose, although the latter was supposed to be favorable to peace on "just conditions."[10] But Adams' Puritanical qualities and lack of a sense of humor, the Kentuckian's impulsiveness, and Russell's jealousy provided combustible elements.

Clay received his passport on February 4, but before he sailed a petty question arose in regard to money that was an omen of worse to come. He and Jonathan Russell agreed that they would expect equal compensation with Adams, the senior member of the group, and Monroe was so informed. But Clay told Russell that he had received his outfit and the offer of a full year's salary in advance, and the "representative of commerce" promptly wrote to Monroe that, if a similar indulgence were to be extended to him, he wished to hear about it in New York. The Secretary of State waxed fretful and Clay felt it necessary to assure him that Russell was "altogether uninfluenced by avaricious motives."[11] So began the *rapprochement* that Adams was to note with much bitterness in the ensuing months.

Clay said good-by to his family, and then went to New York where he was joined by the secretary of the mission, Christopher Hughes, Jr. Instructions arrived February 14, and they hoped

[9] Adams, *History of the United States*, Vol. VII, p. 363. Crawford was sent as Minister to France.

[10] James Monroe, *Writings*, 7 vols. (N.Y., 1898–1903), Vol. V, pp. 277, 281. Clay was willing to admit, by December of 1813, that the conquest of Canada was not an absolute essential. — Clay to Dr. Bodley (Ky. State Hist. Soc. Lib.), Dec. 18, 1813.

[11] Monroe Correspondence, XIV, Russell to Monroe, Feb. 6, 1814; Clay to Monroe, Feb. 23, 1814.

to leave on the twentieth for Gothenburg, Sweden, where the conference was first scheduled. Monroe wrote that Clay should sail immediately, without Russell, if necessary; but on February 23, the Kentuckian was still in New York, much to his "mortification."[12] He was not, evidently, in the most happy frame of mind. Two days later he and Russell set sail on the twenty-eight gun corvette *John Adams*, Captain Samuel Angus commanding.

The voyage was a trying one, for the two sides of the ship had been built by different contractors, one of whom had skimped, with such disastrous results that the ship sailed most unevenly. Hughes, thirty years later, referred to their passage with feeling: — ". . . a poor crew and ship & a mad Captain. A Miracle we weren't drownd."[13] After nearly seven weeks on the high seas, they reached their destination, apparently in such a state of mind that they scarcely knew the day of the month on which they arrived.[14]

The outlook for peace was dark. The Allies had taken Paris, Bonaparte was about to abdicate and, with the end of the Napoleonic wars in sight, British feeling ran high against America. Bayard and Gallatin, who were in London, and Crawford, the American Minister to France, were gloomy.[15]

Bayard and Gallatin were informed, toward the latter part of April, that Britain desired a change in the seat of negotiations, to London or some place in the Netherlands. The two Americans were agreeable, Gallatin being willing even to have the conference in London, and they wrote to Clay and Russell for their opinion. The latter had gone to Stockholm, and Clay took the responsibility of replying. He would not go to Lon-

---

[12] *Ibid.*, V, Monroe to Clay, Feb. 18, 1814; XIV, Clay to Monroe, Feb. 23, 1814.

[13] G. F. Emmons, *The Navy of the United States* (Washington, 1853), p. 87; Clay Papers, XXV, Hughes to Clay, Sept. 14, 1847.

[14] Archives of the Ghent Embassy (Dept. of State), Clay and Russell to Adams, April 14, 1814; Clay and Russell to Monroe, April 20, 1814. In the first letter they date their arrival April 13; in the second April 14.

[15] *Ibid.*, Bayard to Clay and Russell, April 20, 1814; Bayard and Gallatin to Monroe, May 6, 1814. Clay Papers, II, Crawford to Clay, June 10, 1814.

don, he said. There was no sense in being too conciliatory toward those "haughty people," the British. America should preserve "a firm and undismayed countenance." He would, however, consent to Holland if the British Government shouldered the responsibility for the change and thus allowed the United States to keep beyond hazard the friendship of Sweden.[16] Bayard and Gallatin accepted this point of view in regard to the change in location, and so informed the other commissioners. On May 16, the British proposed Ghent as the new seat of negotiations. It was accepted, and the Americans, including Adams, who had joined Russell at Stockholm on May 25, gathered slowly in that ancient city.[17]

Clay left Gothenburg on June 2. He might have gone on the *John Adams,* but he left that pleasure for Russell and Adams and proceeded over land, as much as possible. He passed through Hamburg and Amsterdam — traveling slowly, for he wanted to see something of the country — and reached Ghent on June 28. Bayard, Adams and Russell had preceded him by a few days. Gallatin came July 6.[18]

Then the American commissioners settled down for a month of waiting that frayed nerves and tempers. The representatives of Great Britain — Lord Gambier, Henry Goulburn and William Adams, scarcely a scintillating trio — arrived on Saturday evening, August 6. Four and one-half months of negotiations were to ensue before the treaty was signed.

The Treaty of Ghent provides an ironical commentary upon the ways of diplomats. The American representatives came to Europe with instructions to demand that Great Britain abandon impressment; that she consent to a clarification of neutral rights; that she pay damages for wanton destruction of property before and during the war; that she be induced, if possible,

[16] Archives of the Ghent Embassy, Clay to Russell, May 1, 1814; Clay to Bayard and Gallatin, May 2, 1814; F. A. Updyke, *The Diplomacy of the War of 1812* (Baltimore, 1915), pp. 187–190.

[17] Archives of the Ghent Embassy, Bayard and Gallatin to Adams, Russell and Clay, May 17, 1814, Bayard and Gallatin to Monroe, May 23, 1814.

[18] *Ibid.*, Gallatin to Monroe, June 20, 1814; American Commission to Monroe, July 14, 1814; Adams, *Memoirs*, Vol. II, p. 649; Bayard Papers (Lib. of Cong., Mss. Div.), VI, Diary of J. A. Bayard, June 28, 1814.

to cede Canada.[19] The British demanded that what are now Michigan, Wisconsin and Illinois, four-fifths of Indiana and one-third of Ohio, should be set apart forever as an Indian buffer state with which England should have full trading privileges; they insisted upon a territorial settlement based on the principle of *uti possidetis;* they asked rectification of the Canadian frontier, including cession of a part of Maine, the sole right of maintaining armed forces on the Great Lakes, and continuation of the right to navigate the Mississippi. Controversy raged over these questions for months, and then both parties signed a treaty which scarcely mentioned any of them, a treaty that was based upon the restoration of conditions as they were before the fighting started, and that consisted chiefly of clauses referring all the disputed boundary questions to special commissions.

There were various reasons behind this apparently silly dénouement. The American Government wanted peace. Monroe began to modify his instructions before the conference opened, and a majority of the American commission was strongly inclined to end the struggle, even at a real sacrifice of American pretensions. The British Ministry, too, became more and more irenic as the negotiations progressed. Reverses at Baltimore and Plattsburg, the tension at Vienna, financial troubles, and Wellington's contention that conquests in America were not to be obtained under existing conditions moderated the British position. Lastly, both sides were faced by the fact that the end of the Napoleonic struggle had eliminated the fundamental causes of irritation between the two countries. Impressment and the seizure of American shipping had stopped, and, unless the war were to be continued frankly for conquest, it would be idiotic to pour out more blood and treasure over questions of abstract rights. Jesting Pilate's query, "What is truth?" could never be invoked more properly than in an attempt to establish the "rights" of neutrals.

But if the force of circumstances inclined the American dele-

---

[19] *Amer. State Papers, Foreign Relations,* Vol. III, pp. 695–700, 701–702; Updyke, *op. cit.,* pp. 175–185.

gation toward a treaty of peace with Great Britain, the influence of proximity drove them into war with one another. They had made the initial mistake of leasing a house, the Baron de Lovendeghem's residence, where they tried to live and work together. The results were disastrous. John Quincy Adams, the head of the mission, was an able diplomat and a man of culture, but he was tedious, fussy and tiresome. His Puritanical conscience rode him mercilessly, and his sense of humor was conspicuous by its absence. When the delegates first assembled at Ghent, Adams withdrew from the common dining table, because he disapproved of the way in which the rest sat after dinner, drinking bad wine and smoking cigars. Clay expressed regret at this departure and Adams came back,[20] doubtless to prove something of a specter at the feast. Two days later a controversy arose because Adams objected to the way that the other members, particularly Clay, were sending special messengers flitting about Europe at Government expense.[21] In revenge for Adams' strictures the other members fell upon his literary style, and eventually he turned over to Gallatin the drafting of the official correspondence. But his wrangling with Clay continued, and more than once their quarrels threatened to disrupt the mission.

The saving spirit in these brawls was Albert Gallatin. Always tactful and conciliatory, he smoothed over many a bad situation among his colleagues, and between them and the overbearing British delegates. Even the young and supercilious Henry Goulburn fell under the spell of Gallatin — who, he said, was not in the least like an American.[22]

Clay was willing to do his part of the work, but he insisted upon enjoying himself at all-night card games which aroused Adams' scornful disapproval.[23] The Kentuckian sent to Amster-

---

[20] Adams, *Memoirs*, Vol. II, pp. 656–657.

[21] *Ibid.*, Vol. II, pp. 657–658.

[22] C. K. Webster, "The American War and the Treaty of Ghent, 1814," in the *Cambridge History of British Foreign Policy*, 3 vols. (Cambridge, 1922–1923), Vol. I, p. 539; James Gallatin, *Diary* (N.Y., 1916), pp. 27–28; Adams, *Gallatin*, pp. 520, 522.

[23] Adams, *Memoirs*, Vol. III, pp. 32, 39.

dam for the best Spanish "segars," and displayed a free-handed hospitality which was appreciated even by Gambier and Goulburn. Ghent extended its arms to the visitors. There were rounds of dinners and Clay was made an honorary member of the Society of Agriculture and Botany.

No incident better illustrates his sensitivity and pride than one that arose out of this honor. Adams, Gallatin and Bayard had been made members of the Society of Fine Arts and Letters. One of the Ghent members of this body, Mr. Meulemeester, told Gallatin by mistake that all the Americans were invited to a supper celebration of the Society. The Kentuckian went and suffered agonies of mortification, especially when a speech was made explaining why he, Russell and Hughes had been invited to join the other society. The next day Clay entered a formal complaint about his having been misled.[24]

The burden of the negotiations was carried largely by Gallatin and Adams, although Clay participated actively in the discussions and frequently drew up papers that set forth American claims. When the British delegates presented their initial demands, Clay shared the general indignation of the Americans. He told Goulburn that the proposals were equivalent to asking the cession of Boston or New York, and he wrote to Monroe in withering comment upon "the well known arrogance of the British character."[25] Like the rest of the American delegates, he believed at times that the war would have to be continued. But, unlike them, he had the gambler's instinct, and it must have been that which gave him what Adams called the "inconceivable idea" that the British were bluffing, and might back down.[26] The British game was "brag," Clay told his colleagues on December 11, when they were discussing the question of

[24] *Ibid.*, Vol. III, pp. 58–59.

[25] Adams, *Gallatin*, p. 524; James Gallatin, *Diary*, p. 30; Monroe Correspondence, XIV, Aug. 18, 1814.

[26] Adams, *Memoirs*, Vol. III, p. 20; J. E. D. Shipp, *Giant Days* (Americus, Ga., 1909), p. 123, Clay to Crawford, Aug. 22, 1814; *Amer. State Papers, Foreign Relations*, Vol. III, pp. 710–711, American commissioners to Monroe, Oct. 25, 1814; Monroe Correspondence, XIV, Clay to Monroe, Oct. 26, 1814.

the fisheries. The proper thing to do was to "out-brag" them.[27]
There was shrewdness in this point of view, and Clay's optimism in this regard was a real asset to the delegation.

His rigid stand on the Indian question was likewise valuable.
British merchants were anxious to obtain a guarantee of Indian
trading privileges. Clay stood invariably opposed to any such
concession. A majority of the Americans were disposed, at one
point, to offer the status *ante bellum* in a manner that would
have specifically accorded this privilege. The Kentuckian stalked
up and down repeating angrily that he would never sign a
treaty on the general status *ante bellum*, including the British
right to the Indian trade "so help him God to keep him steady
to his purpose." His vehemence carried the day, and the committee gave in.[28]

The course of the negotiations, nevertheless, made Clay
distinctly unhappy. He had been commissioned to conclude a
peace, and he seems to have realized that peace ought to be
made. But the overbearing attitude of the British ministers, the
relinquishment of American claims and prospects that he had so
jauntily portrayed before the war, the certainty that the outcome would not be glorious, made him morose and irritable.
He strove desperately to avoid concessions. Any proposition for
disarmament on the Great Lakes was sure of his opposition.[29]
Alone among the Americans, he continued to urge an article
prohibiting impressment.[30] It was finally included in one of
the American drafts, but it received short shrift from the British.
He regarded the article pledging both parties to make peace
with the Indians as a real sacrifice.[31] When affairs went badly,
he railed at Massachusetts and boasted of what Kentucky would
do if it were attacked.

More than once the Kentuckian manifested a desire to break
off, and trust to the fortunes of war. He was ready to do so

[27] Adams, *Memoirs*, Vol. III, pp. 101–102, 112.

[28] Adams, *Memoirs*, Vol. III, p. 103; Monroe Correspondence, XIV, Clay
to Monroe, Dec. 25, 1814; Updyke, *op. cit.*, pp. 204, 243.

[29] Updyke, *op. cit.*, p. 275.

[30] Adams, *Memoirs*, Vol. III, pp. 63–64.

[31] *Ibid.*, Vol. III, p. 103. *Cf.* Wm. Macdonald, *Select Documents Illustra-
tive of the History of the United States* (N.Y., 1930), p. 197.

on October 31, if Great Britain did not satisfy the commissioners' complaints about delay in furnishing passports for dispatch-vessels. Three years more of war was what he wanted, he told Adams on December 11. That would make us a warlike people. The best possible terms now would leave us with a half-formed army and a military reputation only half-retrieved.[32] His discontent increased as the labors of the commission drew to a close. It "would be a damned bad treaty," he asserted, one that "would break him down entirely," and he had grave doubts about signing.[33] He was apparently ready to throw everything overboard, two days before the negotiations ended.

One of the heaviest crosses Clay had to bear was the controversy over the Mississippi River and the northeast fisheries. The treaty of 1783 had given to America the right to use the northeastern fisheries, and to Britain the privilege of free navigation of the Mississippi. The British now claimed that war had ended the fishing rights, although they continued to assert the right of Mississippi navigation. The American contention was, in general, that the treaty of 1783 was a permanent treaty. But here discord arose between Adams and Clay, for if the fishery rights were permanent, so was the British right to use the Mississippi. John Adams had fought for the fisheries in 1783, and his son, as spokesman for New England, was not disposed to relinquish them. Clay, representing the West, was determined to close the Father of Waters to the British. It looked as though the mission might split apart on this question.

On October 30, the British having refused fishery rights, Gallatin proposed to renew both provisions. Clay was violently opposed. The fisheries were trivial, he said, but the navigation of the Mississippi was important. During the following days the matter was fully discussed. A vote, taken November 5, stood three to two, Clay and Russell voting against Gallatin's plan. Clay then announced that he would not sign the communica-

[32] Adams, *Memoirs*, Vol. III, p. 101.
[33] *Ibid.*, Vol. III, pp. 104, 118.

tion containing the proposal. He might, he said, ultimately accept it, but not then. In deference to him, the commission finally agreed upon his substitute, which simply excluded the fisheries from the discussion.[34]

The British counter-project ignored the fisheries, but contained a clause giving Great Britain the navigation of the river. Clay would have none of it. Again Gallatin brought his proposition forward, and Clay once more flamed up in opposition. He denounced New England; whereupon Adams, with insufferable complacency, observed to him "that he was now speaking under the impulse of passion, and that on such occasions I would wish not to answer anything." But Adams continued, defending the importance of the fisheries to New England, and the right of Great Britain to navigate the Mississippi. Thereupon Clay launched into gloomy prophecies as to British influence in the Mississippi Valley.

Gallatin now brought all his powers of persuasion to bear. The vote on the reciprocal provision was again three to two, Clay and his henchman Russell opposing, but Clay said nothing about refusing to sign the treaty if the Mississippi were opened to the British. He explained somewhat lamely, afterward, that his opposition had been steady and consistent, but that he did not restate his position at this particular juncture "lest it be understood as a menace." What happened finally was that the commission proposed the reciprocal opening of the fisheries and the Mississippi navigation, or else that both be omitted from the treaty.[35]

It is interesting that Clay twice refrained from making the Mississippi navigation question a *sine qua non*. There are two possible reasons for this. One is that the British were almost certain to refuse the fishery rights, while at the same time, they seemed determined to hold for an express sanction of their

---

[34] *Ibid.*, Vol. III, pp. 60–65; *Amer. State Papers, Foreign Relations,* Vol. III, p. 733.

[35] Clay's "Memorandum on the Treaty of Ghent," in the *Lexington* (Ky.) *Herald,* Dec. 27, 1914; Clay to Russell, July 9, 1822, in Prentice, *op. cit.,* pp. 285–289; *Amer. State Papers, Foreign Relations,* Vol. III, p. 742; Adams, *Memoirs,* Vol. III, pp. 71–76; Updyke, *op. cit.,* pp. 321, 327–329.

Mississippi privileges. The other is that Clay felt that these privileges, based as they were in the second proposal, on the treaty of 1783, could be so construed as to give the British no control over that part of the river acquired in the Louisiana Purchase.[36]

The British refused the reciprocal provision, and proposed, in lieu of omitting the subject entirely, to insert an article that would leave both questions to future negotiation. The phraseology of this article implied that both rights had been abrogated by the war, and consequently, it was much to Clay's liking.[37] But it threw out of court the American claim to the fisheries. Adams could not and would not accept this. Finally, at Gallatin's suggestion, the Americans repeated their proposal to omit the whole question, and, December 22, the British accepted this offer.

Gallatin brought to Adams' chamber the note containing the British agreement. Clay read it and was much chagrined. Evidently he had believed that the British would insist upon their last offer. He seems to have been willing to break off the negotiations, but the others would not listen.[38] The last great obstacle to peace was now surmounted, and the treaty was signed, December 24, 1814.

The next day was Christmas, but Clay's heart was not overflowing with peace and good will. The treaty terms were not "very unfavorable," he wrote to Monroe; America lost no territory, and, he thought, no honor. He did not intend to come home right away. News had come, he said, that his constituents had again elected him to Congress, and if there were a special session he would want to be at his post, but it did not seem convenient to sail before April 1. He proposed to spend the next three months at Paris and in England "to see whatever is curious and instructive."[39] The temperamental Kentuckian was in the throes of melancholy, and, when Christo-

---

[36] Adams, *Memoirs*, Vol. III, pp. 62–63, 65.

[37] *Amer. State Papers, Foreign Relations*, Vol. III, pp. 743–745; Adams, *Memoirs*, Vol. III, pp. 120–121.

[38] Adams, *Memoirs*, Vol. III, pp. 120–122.

[39] Monroe Correspondence, XIV, Clay to Monroe, Dec. 25, 1814.

pher Hughes sailed for America, Clay threw his arms about his friend's neck and wept as he said good-by.[40]

The negotiations were not in themselves sufficient cause for such heartburnings. Clay had stoutly and successfully opposed a clear grant of British trading rights with the Indians. The British had not obtained recognition of their right to navigate the Mississippi, and his opposition to that proposal had been vigorous and of real effect. There were many reasons for feeling that he had fought a good fight, and that, as matters had turned out, the West would not feel bitterly toward him. But the sanguine dreams of 1812, the dreams of a leader who had enjoyed brilliant success in accomplishing his objectives until now, had faded into an extremely prosaic reality. The contemplation of that reality afforded small grounds for satisfaction and might legitimately have produced some searching introspection. This was not the case. Self-examination, so familiar to the conscientious Adams, was not one of Clay's characteristics. He was humbled for the time, but his flashing spirit, which never knew repose for long, was soon to lead him into new projects for his country's glory and, incidentally, his personal renown.

Clay was eager to set out for Paris after the treaty was signed, but winding up the affairs of the mission took almost two weeks. It also gave an opportunity for a final bitter and unseemly wrangle with Adams over the custody of the official papers. Adams won, to his great satisfaction. Good relations were patched up to such an extent that Clay and Bayard came to Adams' apartment on the night of January 6 to say good-by, and about six o'clock the next morning they left in the diligence for Lille.[41]

The Kentuckian, under Crawford's guidance, found much to interest him in Paris. He visited the French courts, and saw a legal battle between a father and a mother over the custody of a six-year-old child who was later to be Napoleon III. Madame de Staël invited Clay to her home and he found her

---

[40] Clay Papers, XXIV, Hughes to Clay, Nov. 27, 1844.
[41] Adams, *Memoirs*, Vol. III, pp. 129–144.

"most extraordinary," as indeed she was. Her dinner parties must have impressed him as decidedly different, for at one which he attended Benjamin Constant contradicted everything the lady said, all talk of political economy was imperiously forbidden, and immediately after the meal was over the hostess left her sixteen guests and rushed off to the Théâtre Français.

Mme. de Staël asked Clay on one occasion if he knew that the British had contemplated sending Wellington to America. He replied gallantly that he wished Wellington had come, for defeat by the conqueror of Napoleon would have been no disgrace and to beat him would have meant immortal honor. Madame de Staël subsequently introduced the two men and repeated this conversation, whereupon the Iron Duke remarked that he should have acquired a noble feather in his cap "had he beaten so gallant a people as the Americans." [42]

Paris held the Westerner until March. He seems to have been loath to go to London until he had heard of the Battle of New Orleans. Jackson's triumph, ironically enough, filled Clay's heart with joy and made him feel that he could now visit England without humiliation. [43]

There was another round of social life at the British capital, and there was also some business, for Clay, Adams and Gallatin had been instructed to make a commercial treaty with Great Britain. Another Ghent negotiation on a smaller scale now took place. The British delayed the opening of the negotiations for weeks, and when they were begun, they proceeded at a pace truly majestic. Clay was very anxious to go home, and Gallatin shared this feeling. They did their best to expedite matters, while Adams looked coldly and disapprovingly at their haste. [44] The convention was finally signed July 3. It established most-favored-nation privileges between the United States and Great

[42] Adams, *Memoirs*, Vol. III, pp. 153–158; Carl Schurz Papers (Lib. of Cong., Mss. Div.), LXXX, 17652–17653, Clay to Mrs. Harrison Smith, March 1829 (copy).

[43] Schurz, *op. cit.*, Vol. I, pp. 123–124.

[44] Bayard Papers (Lib. of Cong., Mss. Div.), IV, Clay to Bayard, April 3, 28, May 13, 1815; Dept. of State, Ghent, etc., American Commissioners, Clay and Gallatin to Monroe, May 18, 1815; Adams, *Memoirs*, Vol. III, pp. 218–227.

Britain in Europe, and gave the United States a similar status in the East India trade. The trade with the West Indies, most important of all in American eyes, was not touched, and the American attempts to bring up impressment and blockade were fruitless. The convention was not of any great value, but, such as it was, it favored the United States.[45]

Clay found living extremely expensive in London,[46] but he managed to invest, through Baring Brothers, about forty-five hundred dollars in the six per cent. stock of the United States, and when he sailed he left two hundred pounds in the hands of the bankers.[47] He received about sixteen thousand, five hundred dollars for his expenses and services on these two missions. Such compensation elicited no complaint from him at the time. But in 1821, when his private affairs were not in the best condition, he presented to President Monroe a demand for forty-five hundred dollars more, on the ground that he should have been given half an outfit for the London mission. No other member of the mission had received such a favor. It was without precedent, Adams scornfully asserted, but Monroe, toward whose administration Clay had become very critical, felt that it was awkward to refuse. The Attorney-General, William Wirt, investigated the situation and made two reports, the first favorable, the second equivocal. Monroe finally gave in, and Clay's creditors were that much nearer satisfaction.[48]

Kentucky's representative returned from his first and only trip to Europe in September, 1815. He was received with acclaim, feasted and fêted in Lexington, and when he went to Washington for the opening of Congress in December, he was promptly re-elected Speaker of the House of Representatives.

[45] D. H. Miller, *Treaties and other International Acts of the United States*, 4 vols. completed (Washington, 1931–), Vol. II, pp. 595–600; Updyke, *op. cit.*, p. 396.

[46] Misc. Letters (Dept. of State), Clay to Monroe, April 5, 1816.

[47] Clay Papers, II, Baring Bros. to Clay, June 30, 1815; Colton, *Correspondence*, p. 45, Clay to Mrs. Clay, July 14, 1815.

[48] Misc. Letters (Dept. of State), Wirt to Adams, Oct. 1, 1821; Monroe Papers, XX, Clay to R. M. Johnson, July 12, 1822; Adams, *Memoirs*, Vol. VI, pp. 311, 329; Colton, *Correspondence*, p. 45, Clay to Mrs. Clay, July 14, 1815.

CHAPTER VII

AN AMBITIOUS PATRIOT

THE period immediately following the War of 1812 was marked by a striking manifestation of patriotic feeling in the United States. The salutary lessons of that conflict were still fresh, the peace bore many of the earmarks of a truce, and, as the fervor of sectionalism abated, national development held the center of the stage. The establishment of an effective army and navy, innumerable plans for improving the means of communication, protection for the frontier by the removal of the Indians from great sections of the West and by the acquisition of East Florida, a rising tariff, and a new bank to stabilize and strengthen the national economy, all were received with acclaim. The young Republican leaders, Clay, Calhoun, Lowndes and the rest, worked together in a campaign for increasing national unity and power.

Clay's hopes and plans were in full accord with the spirit of the times. His ardent patriotism, the spirit engendered by acknowledged leadership in public life, and his political ambition, prompted him to assume a vigorously national point of view. He was eager to win fresh laurels for himself and for his country.

"I love true glory," he exclaimed before the House. "It is this sentiment which ought to be cherished; and in spite of cavils and sneers and attempts to put it down, it will finally conduct this nation to that height to which God and nature have destined it." [1]

The omens were still favorable to his leadership, for, perhaps to his surprise, the native had returned from foreign lands with undimmed prestige. He was pampered and petted by his con-

[1] *Annals of Cong.*, 14th Cong., 1st sess., 784.

stituents. He was caressed by the Administration, which, within a year, offered him the mission to Russia and then the War Department.[2] These posts were refused, evidently on account of a belief that the House afforded a greater opportunity for advancing his designs.

There, before the Fourteenth Congress was a month old, the Kentuckian stated that every man in the Union should be given obvious and palpable evidence of the benefits which the National Government afforded,[3] and he proceeded, during the latter part of January, 1816, to lay down his proposals for achieving this result. His aims included internal improvements, aid and protection for business, aid to South America (with an accompanying hint at the danger to our liberties from reactionary Europe), military and naval preparedness for possible trouble with Spain and the Holy Alliance, and for inevitable wars with Great Britain.[4] Most of these ideas were in harmony with those of other leaders, as Congressional legislation speedily proved.

Clay, Calhoun and Lowndes sponsored a bill providing for a substantial increase in the navy.[5] They showed equal zeal in protecting the business interests of the country. The tariff of 1816 was designed in part to offset a lowering of internal taxes, but, though its rates were not high, it was avowedly protective. Every Republican member of note, save John Randolph, declared himself for protection, and the bill, as passed, was designed to aid the producers of cotton and woolen goods. Clay strove to increase duties that would benefit his section, but he also held that the duties placed on cotton goods were too low, and tried valiantly to increase them. He stated that his objective was national self-sufficiency in all articles of necessity, and four years later he asserted that the tariff of 1816 had satisfied his

[2] Clay Papers, II, Monroe to Clay, Oct. 30, 1815; Madison to Clay, Aug. 30, 1816.

[3] Annals of Cong., 14th Cong., 1st sess., 426–430. The discussion concerned a proposal to establish three additional military academies. Calhoun, who followed Clay in supporting the measure, said that "the only question really before the House at this time appeared to be, what was the best mode to produce a national spirit."

[4] Ibid., 14th Cong., 1st sess., 723–730, 776–792.

[5] Ibid., 14th Cong., 1st sess., 1369, 1371, 1886.

desires only partially. It was obvious that he expected a continuous protective policy.[6]

The Republican statesmen also directed their attention to the banking situation, and Clay took a prominent part in the reestablishment of an institution which, five years before, he had helped to destroy.

The currency was in a deplorable condition. With the destruction of the National Bank in 1811, state banks had mushroomed throughout the Union. Some of these were good and some were bad, but all alike, in the Middle and Southern states, had been drained of their specie reserves by the steady flow of hard money into New England to pay for manufactured goods. Every bank from New York to Savannah had suspended specie payment by the close of 1814, and the Western banks speedily followed their example. The Government, millions of its revenue being thus tied up, was reduced to a situation that would have been ludicrous, had it not been tragic, and the Treasury of the United States had to default repeatedly.[7] Meanwhile the country had made shift to get along on all kinds of weird paper currency. Neither did the situation of the people improve materially after peace was declared, for the banks obstinately refused to resume specie payments. This circumstance made a National Bank inevitable.

At the beginning of the Fourteenth Congress, Clay appointed Calhoun, who was an ardent Bank man, chairman of a select committee to consider that part of Madison's message relating to a uniform national currency.[8] The South Carolinian consulted with Secretary of the Treasury Dallas, and then, January 8, 1816, brought in a bill which was Hamilton's Bank all over again.

The Bank was to have a capital of $35,000,000 and 350,000

---

[6] *Ibid.*, 14th Cong., 1st sess., 1237–1247, 1272; 16th Cong., 1st sess., 2034; Adams, *op. cit.*, Vol. IX, pp. 114–116; McMaster, *op. cit.*, Vol. IV, pp. 336–340. There was active lobbying by the manufacturers. — *Cf.* James Kent Papers (Lib. of Cong., Mss. Div.), IV, Moss Kent to James Kent, Jan. 16, 1816.

[7] McMaster, *op. cit.*, Vol. IV, pp. 286–298; R. C. H. Catterall, *The Second Bank of the United States* (Chicago, 1903), pp. 1–7.

[8] *Annals of Cong.*, 14th Cong., 1st sess., 377.

shares of stock. The Government was to subscribe to 70,000 shares, and the President of the United States was given the duty of annually appointing five of the twenty-five directors. The parent bank, located at Philadelphia, had branching power. The notes were receivable in all payments to the United States, and the institution was made the custodian of the public funds. Various provisions for inspection and regulation were included.

The debate over the measure was lengthy, but the Federalist and strict constructionist opposition was unable to stem the tide, and on April 10, President Madison signed the bill.

Credit for the passage through the House should go principally to Calhoun, but Clay had a hand in the proceedings. He had made Calhoun chairman of the special committee, and during the debate the Speaker left the chair to support the bill. His remarks there were not recorded, but a speech to his constituents at Lexington on June 3 contains his point of view.

He had opposed recharter in 1811, he said, for three reasons. First, because he had been instructed to do so by the Kentucky legislature (strange portent of 1825!); second, because he believed it had abused its power and become involved in politics; and third, because of his conviction that Congress lacked the constitutional power to charter such a corporation. Now, he had received no such instructions, and he believed (for a variety of none too cogent reasons) that this Bank would not abuse its prerogatives. On the third point he made a complete and open reversal. He saw, as he had not seen in 1811, that the Bank was necessary to carry into effect powers specifically granted in the national charter. "The Constitution," said he — "The Constitution, it is true, never changes; it is always the same; but the force of circumstances and the lights of experience may evolve to the fallible persons charged with its administration, the fitness and necessity of a particular exercise of constructive power today, which they did not see at a former period." Had he foreseen in 1811, he said, the present condition of affairs, and had there been no other than a constitutional objection to the old Bank, he would have voted for renewal in that year.[9]

[9] *Ibid.*, 14th Cong., 1st sess., 1190–1195.

Hindsight is better than foresight, and there had been nothing in Clay's former tirade against the Bank to justify this last assertion. In fact, most of his interpretation of his previous viewpoint appears rather forced. But the remarkable thing about this speech is the attitude it takes toward constitutional interpretation. That the Constitution should mean what each generation thinks it means is a point of view to which many Americans have scarcely become used, even to-day.

The summer of 1816 is significant as the one time when Harry of the West was nearly abandoned by his constituents. Congress had passed a bill, the preceding March, increasing the pay of its members from six dollars a day (about nine hundred dollars a year) to fifteen hundred dollars per year, and Clay had urged its passage. But the news of this legislation created a countrywide furor of indignation, and the following election resulted in a holocaust of the offending members. The purifying fires raged from Maine to Kentucky, and in the latter state, out of nine Congressmen who were on record as supporting the bill, only two were returned. The campaign was strenuous and bitter. Clay's opponent was John Pope, who, as Senator from Kentucky, had been opposed to the war. This was a fortunate circumstance for Clay, who promptly accused his adversary of being a Federalist and lacking patriotism, and, according to the *Western Monitor*, called upon Pope to prove his Republicanism by joining in a mutual pledge to support the administration of James Monroe.[10] The Popeites accused Clay of having acquired high-toned ideas through his European intercourse with "lords and nabobs"; retorted the Federalist charge, and quoted him as saying that the compensation law was a matter "worthy only of the notice of a nail-gathering, groat-hoarding, stiver-saving people." [11] Clay triumphed, but he had to fight hard to do so.

It is customary to attribute his difficulties in this election to the compensation law, and that was undoubtedly the main cause. There is an amusing story that, when Clay asked an Irish friend

[10] *Western Monitor*, Lexington, March 27, 1819; Draper Collection, Misc. Mss., 8CC173.
[11] Draper Collection, Misc. Mss., 8CC171.

why he had shifted his allegiance to Pope, the answer was: "Och, Misther Clay, I have concluded to vote for the man who has but one arm to sthrust into the streasury." [12] But during the years immediately following his return from Europe, arrogant and domineering ways, and a certain superfine sense of personal honor that was affronted on the least occasion, manifested themselves in such a manner as to excite concern among his supporters and bitter distaste among his opponents. His friend Christopher Hughes felt it necessary to caution him against rushing into altercations. Certain inoffensive remarks by John Rowan, about Clay's rise without regular classic or scientific background, were garbled by political enemies, and Clay became so incensed against Rowan that the latter had to proffer regrets and explanations. Senator Mason of Virginia, who admired the Kentuckian's talents and his zeal for the Republican cause, found his lordliness almost intolerable, and asserted that "his disgusting vanity and inordinate ambition were fast destroying his influence and his usefulness as a public man." [13]

Perhaps some of Clay's constituents were willing to teach him a lesson. At least he came back to Congress to speak for the repeal of the compensation bill, although he still favored a higher *per diem* compensation. [14]

An attempt to put through a bill that provided a national program of internal improvements featured the 1816–1817 session. Calhoun evoked the specter of disunion, horrid to him then, and summoned all his nationalist fervor and subtlety of logic to the task of binding the Republic together with a perfect system of roads and canals. He waved aside objections based on the Constitution as the theses of ingenious logicians. "It ought to be construed with plain good sense," he declared, and he sought the establishment of a fund for internal improvements out of the bank bonus and the dividends from the Government's bank stocks. Clay vigorously supported this ebullition

[12] Ranck, *op. cit.*, p. 163.
[13] Clay Papers, II, Hughes to Clay, Sept. 13, 1816; Rowan to Clay, June 1, 1816; *William and Mary Quarterly*, Vol. XXIII (April 1915), pp. 232–233, A. T. Mason to J. T. Mason, July 15, 1816.
[14] *Annals of Cong.*, 14th Cong., 2d sess., 495–498. The bill was repealed. In 1818, Congress raised the *per diem* compensation from six to eight dollars per day.

of Southern patriotism. He thanked Calhoun for the bill and for his speech, "able and luminous." The Speaker had no constitutional doubts, but if such existed, he would appropriate now and clarify them later.[15] The bill passed House and Senate by narrow margins, New England and some of the Southern states voting heavily against it. Madison received it March 3, and promptly clarified the doubts by vetoing it on constitutional grounds. An attempt at passage over the veto failed, and the struggle ended for the time being.

A measure of preparedness, a degree of tariff protection, and a National Bank had now been put into effect. So much of Clay's program had been realized. Internal improvements at national expense and aid for South America remained. But his advocacy of these measures during the next four years was bound up with another factor, his opposition to the policies of James Monroe. That opposition arose in part out of Clay's ambition and his impetuosity.

A Secretary of State was looked upon at that time as an heir-apparent to the presidency, and his was a much coveted position. It was natural that Clay should hope to possess it, and it was generally known that he was anxious for the honor.[16] But Monroe, acting, as he professed, in the interest of political harmony, avoided candidates from the South and West, and turned to New England's distinguished son, John Quincy Adams.[17] Crawford, another prominent aspirant for the position, was asked to retain his post at the head of the Treasury, and consented to do so. The Kentuckian was then offered the War Department. He refused it, and, according to Crawford, "in the most decided manner." The mission to England was then proffered and also turned down. Clay professed to be satisfied with his position in the House, as giving him a greater opportunity to render public service.[18]

[15] *Ibid.*, 14th Cong., 2d sess., 851–858, 866–868.

[16] E. S. Brown, *The Missouri Compromises and Presidential Politics* (St. Louis, 1926), pp. 51, 81; Ravenel, *op. cit.*, p. 231; A. Gallatin, *Writings*, 3 vols. (Phila., 1879), Vol. II, pp. 24–26, Crawford to Gallatin, March 12, 1817.

[17] Monroe, *Writings*, Vol. VI, pp. 2–4, 5.

[18] Gallatin, *Writings*, Vol. VI, p. 25, Crawford to Gallatin, March 12, 1817; Adams, *Memoirs*, Vol. IV, p. 73.

That he was embittered by the choice of Adams seems almost certain. Josiah Quincy asserted that Clay did not disguise his dissatisfaction.[19] Adams believed, and constantly insisted, that Clay's opposition to Monroe and himself arose out of disappointed ambition, and a determination to run down the Administration and become President by hook or crook in 1824.[20] The Kentuckian's attitude at the time of Monroe's inauguration bears out these observations. First he would not surrender control of the House chamber to the Senate committee in charge of the affair. Then he refused to allow the fine red chairs of the Senate to be brought in, on the ground that "the plain democratic chairs of the House were more becoming," [21] and the committee went away in a huff. Monroe was inaugurated on a temporary platform in front of the house where Congress was holding its sessions, some two hundred yards east of the ruined Capitol, and of all the distinguished men in Washington that day, Clay alone did not attend the ceremony.[22] In vain had Monroe offered honors. In vain did he now give Clay free access to his presence, even when the Cabinet was sitting.[23] In vain did he later signify his willingness to meet Clay's demand for additional compensation for the Ghent mission. Harry of the West remained unpacified. His chief was no longer the "dear Colonel" of former days, and for the next four years gibes, innuendos and criticism nearly drove the President to distraction.

This criticism centered about foreign policy and internal improvements.

Sympathy for the South American attempts to gain independence had been manifested by the people and Government

---

[19] D. C. Gilman, *James Monroe* (Boston, 1911), p. 135.

[20] Adams, *Memoirs*, Vol. IV, pp. 130–131, Vol. V, p. 53, passim. By 1818, Hyde de Neuville, the French minister, described Clay as the leader of the party in opposition to the administration. — Archives des Affaires Etrangères, Corr. Polit. Suppl., vol. 8, fol. 329, Hyde de Neuville to the Duc de Richelieu, June 21, 1818.

[21] *Cong. Deb.*, 24th Cong., 2d sess., 992.

[22] Taul, *op. et loc. cit.*, Vol. XXVII, p. 497; McMaster, *op. cit.*, Vol. IV, pp. 376–377.

[23] M. B. Smith, *op. cit.*, p. 141.

of the United States as early as 1811; and at various times we had sent a number of unofficial agents into Spain's rebellious colonies, to report on the status of their affairs.[24] The hopes of the rebels waned during the years immediately following the downfall of Napoleon, and in 1816 all the centers of disaffection, save Buenos Aires, passed under the rod of the Spanish armies. But in 1817, both Chile and La Plata rose again in revolt, and American interest grew to real proportions.

Clay shared this general feeling. There was a chivalrous side of his nature which responded to any struggle against tyranny, and he had a very lively conception of the glories of liberty, as represented by the institutions of his own country. Also, he felt convinced that economic advantages were involved. These factors formed the basis of his interest in South American unrest.

As early as January, 1813, he had intimated that the internal politics of Europe had only a remote interest as compared with the movements in South America.[25] His attention was concentrated upon our own troubles during the next three years, but by 1816 the swift sequence of events in Europe had presented a dangerous possibility to the restless mind of a man who had seen at first hand just enough of the Old World's political institutions to strengthen his suspicion and distrust.

All Europe was in the throes of reaction, and the liberalism born of the French Revolution seemed to be dying. America, more than ever, appeared to be the hope and the asylum of liberty. Was it not vitally necessary to take action for preventing the overthrow of this last temple? Clay believed that it was. The Congress of Vienna, he said on January 20, 1816, had carried its ideas of legitimate government "to an extent destructive of every principle of liberty; we have seen these doctrines applied to create and overthrow dynasties at will. Do we know whether we shall escape their influence?" And he suggested that the preservation of our own freedom might demand that

---

[24] F. L. Paxson, *The Independence of the South American Republics* (Phila., 1903), pp. 105–106, 110–114.

[25] *Annals of Cong.*, 12th Cong., 2d sess., 663.

we aid the cause of South America.[26] Nine days later, stung by John Randolph's sarcastic remarks about quixotic crusades and snuffing the carnage of Waterloo, Clay spoke again of the danger that a "combination of despots, of men unfriendly to liberty" might reach the United States and subject us to "tyranny and degradation." A little later in the same speech, referring to the South Americans, he asserted that we had a right and an *interest* in taking part with them — "It would undoubtedly be good policy. . . . He considered the release of any part of America from the dominions of the Old World as adding to the general security of the new." [27]

Such a point of view furnished a background of theory for the Monroe Doctrine and Pan Americanism, but more immediately it produced in its proponent a very earnest desire for prompt action. That desire increased as the darkness of oppression deepened over Europe in the immediately ensuing years. The Kentuckian was always ardent in any cause he championed, and not long before Monroe's inauguration, Clay broke out again into defense of struggles against tyranny, and unsuccessfully opposed a bill which was designed to prevent the flagrant violations of our neutrality by South American privateers.[28] Within less than a year, he took still more definite steps.

Monroe's message of December 2, 1817, assured Congress that we had maintained an "impartial neutrality" in the struggle between Spain and her colonies. On the day after this was received in the House, Clay urged that body to instruct its Committee on Foreign Affairs to inquire whether any, and, if any, what laws were necessary to ensure *to the colonies* a just observance of our neutral position. His speech charged that the acts of our Government bore against the provinces, and it was fraught with expressions of sympathy for them. The House agreed to the proposal.[29] It was obvious that the Speaker was not going to be content with any dilatory policy, and that he was ready, if need be, for war with the Administration. He in-

[26] *Ibid.*, 14th Cong., 1st sess., 723–724.
[27] *Ibid.*, 14th Cong., 1st sess., 776–792.
[28] *Ibid.*, 14th Cong., 2d sess., 740–743.
[29] *Ibid.*, 15th Cong., 1st sess., 13, 401–404.

tended to bring forward a motion to recognize the government at Buenos Aires, and perhaps Chile, and Crawford brought proposals from him to the Executive, expressing a wish for harmony in this. Calhoun and Adams, however, were opposed, and Monroe, hesitating a little, agreed with them. The day before Christmas, at a dinner party given by the Crawfords, Clay came out violently against the Government's South American policy. He had, in truth, as Adams observed, "mounted his South American great horse," [30] and Crawford reported him as saying a week later, on an evening when he was gay and warm with wine, that he meant to follow up his attack, and that "I'll beat you, by ——!" [31]

But before this attack developed, Clay's other grievance appeared in a great debate over internal improvements at national expense.

Monroe took ground, as Jefferson and Madison had done, that authority for this was lacking, and suggested a constitutional amendment as a way out of the difficulty. The committee appointed to deal with this part of the message brought in a report, however, which disagreed with this point of view. It proposed to set aside for such objects the bonus and dividends from the National Bank. This was essentially the plan vetoed by Madison the year before.

On Friday, March 6, the House went into Committee of the Whole on the subject, and sparks flew wildly. Constitutional objections at once appeared. The strict constructionists denounced the plan, and New England and Virginia led the Administration forces in the fight which speedily developed. Clay came down from the Speaker's chair to join in the fray, and never were his power in debate and his right to be called a statesman more clearly vindicated.

He spoke as a Westerner when he described the need felt in

[30] Adams, *Memoirs*, Vol. IV, pp. 28, 30–31. The *National Intelligencer* (Dec. 9, 1817) attempted to demonstrate that Clay was not at odds with the Administration, but the effort was feeble.

[31] Adams, *Memoirs*, Vol. IV, p. 40. Clay told Crawford, a day or two later, that he wanted no trouble, and merely wished an appropriation for a minister to Buenos Aires.

the agricultural regions for roads and canals and contrasted the Government's attitude there with its willingness to aid the Eastern commercialists. But he spoke as a great and far-seeing patriot when he urged the necessity of cementing the Union by Governmental action under a wise interpretation of the Constitution. Respect for the rights of the states was avowed; he decried "that spirit of encroachment which would snatch from the States powers not delegated to the General Government." But when justice, patriotism and economic need could be met by a liberal interpretation of the Constitution, he was for that construction.

Every man who looks at the Constitution in the spirit to entitle him to the character of an American statesman, must elevate his views to the height which this nation is destined to reach in the rank of nations. We are not legislating for this moment only, or for the present generation, or for the present populated limits of these States; but our acts must embrace a wider scope — reaching northwestwardly to the Pacific, and more southwardly to the river Del Norte. Imagine this extent of territory covered with sixty, or seventy, or an hundred millions of people. The powers which exist in this Government now will exist then, and those which will exist then exist now.

It was a pity that his remarks were marred by diatribes against Monroe. He read the President a lecture for trying to influence legislation, condemned Monroe's message on the subject in hand as being without a single reason, implied that those who defended the Executive viewpoint were sycophants and parasites, and made utterly unjust comparison of Monroe's reception on his good will tour to that of kings upon their entering the Théâtre Français or Covent Garden. Clay's denial that he had desired any office in the Executive Department and his interpolated tribute to Monroe's character and services were no offset to these gibes. Such thrusts were unworthy. They were almost vindictive.

Despite all these efforts, the program went down to defeat. The House passed one meager resolution, declaring that Congress had power to appropriate money for roads and canals, but had no power to construct them, and there the matter rested.[32] But the West was outraged, and Clay, as its leading representative, felt specially aggrieved. This grievance constituted another reason for his opposition to Monroe's administration.

The development of our South American policy during the next few years hinged to a great extent upon the attitude of Monroe and Adams. Both men were sympathetic with our southern neighbors, and expected to recognize them eventually. Monroe was anxious to lend them a helping hand. Adams was friendly, although he had a very sane scepticism about their capacity for either independent or liberal government, and was more inclined to caution than was the President.[33] Outside of such personal predilections, there were considerations of state that had to be taken into account, and these forbade precipitate action.

Negotiations for the acquisition of East Florida were in progress and it was felt that hasty recognition would damage these, perhaps irretrievably.[34] Furthermore, British policy was skillfully directed toward keeping the United States from winning undue credit and influence in South America. Lord Castlereagh, the British Foreign Secretary, succeeded in conveying an impression that European mediation between Spain and her colonies was probable, and that precipitate American action might give unnecessary offense. This played an important part in the Administration's policy of delay.[35]

These were weighty matters. Clay should have taken them into account. But, armed alike by fervor and resentment, he pushed ahead in a frenzy for immediate recognition that had much more the appearance of factious opposition than of

[32] *Annals of Cong.*, 15th Cong., 1st sess., 1114–1179, 1359–1385.

[33] J. Q. Adams, *Writings*, 7 vols. (N.Y., 1913–1917), Vol. VI, pp. 325–326, 342, 433, Vol. VII, p. 446; *Memoirs*, Vol. IV, pp. 118, 186–187; D. Perkins, *The Monroe Doctrine, 1823–1826* (Cambridge, 1927), pp. 43–45; Paxson, *op. cit.*, pp. 145-154.

[34] Paxson, *op. cit.*, p. 160; H. L. Hopkins, "The Hispanic-American Policy of Henry Clay," in *Hisp. Amer. Hist. Rev.*, Vol. VII (Nov. 1927), p. 464.

[35] Adams, *Memoirs*, Vol. IV, pp. 166–167; C. K. Webster, "Castlereagh and the Spanish Colonies," in *English Hist. Rev.*, Vol. XXVII (Jan. 1912), pp. 90–95.

statesmanlike policy. Had he avowed the intention of aiding the Administration to move toward recognition, he might have acted in harmony with the Executive.[36] Instead, he became a querulous, provocative critic, and his value to the South American cause was diminished accordingly.[37]

The Kentuckian insinuated that foreign influence played a part in the Administration's policy of neutrality. He sneered at Adams' counsel of patience in negotiations with Spain. His gibes about Executive leading strings, directed at the mild John Forsyth, Chairman of the House Committee on Foreign Relations and a supporter of Monroe, almost goaded that gentleman into showing his independence by proposing a bill that Monroe emphatically did not want — a bill authorizing the President to take possession of East Florida.[38] Clay also waxed derisive over the commissioners sent to South America by Monroe in December, 1817, to survey conditions there.

On March 24, 1818, he moved an appropriation of eighteen thousand dollars for a minister who should be sent to the United Provinces of the Rio de La Plata "whenever the President shall deem it expedient." This was supported by a brilliant and bitter speech.

Now was the time to act, Clay said, while Spain was weak. He would demand, "in temperate and decided terms," redress for our wrongs (including Indian hostilities emanating from Florida), and, to force Spain's hand, he would recognize any established government in Spanish America. He preferred a war, if war should come, waged in the name of liberty, to one that might arise out of the seizure of East Florida, "a province which sooner or later we must certainly acquire."

He extolled the progress and enlightenment of the South Americans, and pictured the economic and political advantages that would accrue to the United States from an independent

---

[36] Cf. Adams, Memoirs, Vol. IV, p. 71.

[37] He told his constituents, June 7, 1820, that it "now appeared" that he and the Executive were in accord as to aims and differed only as to time and mode, rather than substance (Niles' Register, July 1, 1820). He could have taken this point of view, had he chosen to do so, three years before.

[38] Annals of Cong., 15th Cong., 1st sess., 1403f; Adams, Memoirs, Vol. IV, pp. 62–63, 66–67.

South America, guided by an American policy, and obeying "the laws of the system of the New World." Our trade and commerce would prosper. An independent Mexico would enhance the West's safety from foreign interference. The new states would stand with us, during future European wars, in maintaining and enforcing a liberal system of neutrality.[39]

There was an element of sardonic humor in demanding recognition for republics which had not even sent ministers to ask it, and in the days that followed, Forsyth, Lowndes and others upheld the wisdom of the Government's policy, and tore many of Clay's arguments to tatters. He came back at them savagely. Smith of Maryland was made acquainted with the fact that he cut a sorry figure in dealing with questions of public law. Lowndes lacked candor. Smyth of Virginia was informed that when he "has been a little longer in the House he will learn to respect its powers." The House was told that the Speaker hoped it would show no abject submission to the Executive pleasure. Nelson of Virginia protested against Clay's exclusive right to assume the character of a champion of liberty. "Sir," exclaimed the irate Kentuckian, "the galled jade winces." Nelson replied feebly that he would like to know what Clay meant by that.

In such jangling discord the debate terminated, and when the yeas and nays were taken on Clay's motion, it was defeated, forty-five to one hundred and fifteen.[40] Smarting under this rebuff, he refrained from taking any conspicuous part in debate for the remainder of the session.

Congress met again, on November 16, 1818, and again Clay was in an irascible mood.[41] Nothing that the Government did seemed to please him, and it was in thorough harmony with his previous course of procedure that he launched into an attack which brought a bitter and fateful enmity in its wake.

Spain had bound herself, by the treaty of 1795, to be a good neighbor, and not to allow her lands or ports to be used by enemies of the United States. The Spanish Government had

[39] *Ibid.*, 15th Cong., 1st sess., 1474–1500.
[40] *Ibid.*, 15th Cong., 1st sess., 1500–1646.
[41] *Ibid.*, 15th Cong., 2d sess., 360–366, 450f.

been too weak to keep this pledge. Florida's northern border had become a refuge for runaway slaves and hostile Indians who raided and plundered our territory. The United States Government's patience was exhausted by the spring of 1818, and Andrew Jackson was directed to pursue the hostile bands across the boundary to the limits of the Spanish posts.

Was he directed to do more? He asserted, later, that Monroe had approved his suggestion that all of East Florida be seized and held as an indemnity for Spanish outrages on the property of American citizens. Monroe denied it, and Jackson's most judicious biographer inclines to the opinion that the General's memory played him false.[42]

At any rate, the hero of New Orleans stormed into the Floridas, burning, destroying and hanging. He chased the Indians hither and yon; entered and occupied the Spanish town of St. Marks; captured and court-martialled two British subjects (Alexander Arbuthnot and Robert C. Ambrister) who had suspicious connections with the Indians; hanged one and shot the other, after refusing to accept the court martial's reconsideration and lighter sentence in the case of Ambrister; and occupied Pensacola in the face of Spanish resistance. Then, after presenting that town with a military guard, and the United States Government with several pretty international problems, he started home, May 29, 1818, the hero of the army and of the Southwest.[43]

When the news of this tornado reached Washington, it aroused a considerable commotion. The Spanish Minister, Don Luis de Onis, fairly danced with rage, and sent protest after protest to the State Department. President and Cabinet went into consultation. Monroe was anxious, irritable and undecided. Calhoun thought a military tribunal should deal with Jackson's conduct. Crawford was for stern action. Adams, who was apt to take a rather extreme view of American rights, alone upheld the General's course as only a *seeming* violation of orders. The

---

[42] J. S. Bassett, *The Life of Andrew Jackson* (N.Y., 1928), pp. 247–250, 276.

[43] Channing, *op. cit.*, Vol. V, p. 335; McMaster, *op. cit.*, Vol. IV, pp. 439f.

Government finally decided to surrender the Spanish towns, but, at the same time, to justify Jackson's action. This was done in various communications to the Spanish Government, especially in a brilliant though somewhat specious paper by Adams, in which Spain was virtually warned that she would have to restore order or get out of Florida.[44] The Executive Department was standing by Jackson. Would Congress do so?

Monroe's message of November 16, justifying what had been done in Florida and promising the documents, was sent to committees in both House and Senate. The House Committee on Military Affairs submitted a majority report censuring Jackson for the execution of Arbuthnot and Ambrister, and, January 18, 1819, the House went into Committee of the Whole on the subject. The debate raged for three weeks, and the friends of Crawford, who had a bone to pick with Jackson, joined with Clay and his henchmen in the attack.[45] Clay spoke on January 20.

The Kentuckian began with a labored disclaimer of unfriendliness toward either Jackson or Monroe. He felt, so he asserted, the greatest respect and kindness for the former. The latter he sought only to aid in the beneficent conduct of national concerns. He had differed with Monroe, and might again, but he never had and never would systematically oppose his administration or that of any other Chief Magistrate(!).

Then Clay launched into an examination of the causes of the Indian war. He denounced a treaty that Jackson had forced upon the Creeks in 1814, and it certainly merited denunciation, for its harsh terms had gone beyond all reason; he censured the treatment of Indian chiefs, who had been captured by a stratagem during the recent campaign and had been hung by way of retaliation. The execution of Arbuthnot and Ambrister was characterized as worse than the murder of the Duc d'Enghien, and the seizure of St. Marks as more inexcusable than the seizure of the Danish fleet at Copenhagen. It was implied that Jackson was ignorant of the laws of his country and

---

[44] *Amer. State Papers, For. Rel.,* Vol. IV, pp. 539–545.
[45] *Annals of Cong.,* 15th Cong., 2d sess., 11–18, 515–527, 583f.

of the obligations of humanity. The victor of New Orleans was absolved from harboring any designs inimical to the country's liberties, but — with references to Philip and Alexander, Caesar and Napoleon — Clay warned the House against giving a "fatal sanction" to military insubordination. Such sanction would mean "a triumph of the military over the civil authority — a triumph over the powers of this House — a triumph over the Constitution of the land. And he prayed most devoutly to Heaven, that it might not prove, in its ultimate effects and consequences, a triumph over the liberties of the people." [46]

This speech was promptly set upon by a host of critics, who succeeded in demonstrating that it was vulnerable at many points. The treaty of Fort Jackson, the seizure of St. Marks and Pensacola merited, it is true, the condemnation they received. But the hanging of the Indian chiefs was a form of retaliation generally practised in savage warfare. The execution of Arbuthnot and Ambrister was probably deserved, and it was significant that the British Government did not protest the penalty.[47] The veiled attack upon Jackson as a menace to liberty was unjust. And an identification of the Indian "prophets" with religious leaders demonstrated a rather astonishing ignorance of savage ways. Clay's sympathy for the Indians did him credit, but this oration was fundamentally the utterance of a factious and ambitious man, none too careful of his facts, and perhaps uncomfortably aware of the rising shadow of a rival for the presidency.

The resolutions that had grown out of the report censuring Jackson were decisively defeated by the House, but the contest meant far more than that. It had earned for Henry Clay the hatred of a man who never forgot and seldom forgave. And it was the prelude to a long series of bitter and agonizing clashes that were to dim the splendor of the Western Star.

There is good reason to believe that Clay's attitude toward the Administration was colored by what was now generally recognized as his desire for the presidency. The Kentuckians rallied to him on the South American question, and the *Ken-*

[46] *Ibid.*, 15th Cong., 2d sess., 631–655.

[47] Bassett, *op. cit.*, p. 259.

tucky Gazette and the *Kentucky Reporter* assumed a critical attitude toward Monroe and Adams. There were widespread reports that Clay was attempting to combine the whole Western country for his own election to succeed Monroe in 1824.[48] The Kentuckian's animosity toward Adams had been displayed more than once by 1819. It was to find sharp expression again and again during the next few years. His criticism of the foreign policy of the Executive was so virulent that, before the Sixteenth Congress met, a movement was started to displace the Kentuckian as Speaker. Monroe wisely advised against it, as foolish and calculated to strengthen Clay unduly in the West, and it was dropped.[49] Clay was elected almost unanimously, and before long found another opportunity to attack the Government's policy.

On February 22, 1819, a treaty had been signed between the United States and Spain, by which the latter ceded *both* the Floridas, and we assumed the claims of Spanish citizens against our Government to the extent of five million dollars. We also gave up any claims that we might have on Texas as a result of the Louisiana Purchase. Some critical comments which appeared in a Washington paper on the following day were supposed to have come from Clay, but on February 24 the treaty was unanimously approved by the Senate, and Monroe duly proclaimed our ratification. Then difficulties arose over land grants made by the King of Spain, and, on one pretext or another, Spanish ratification was delayed nearly two years, although this act was supposed to take place within six months. Considerable irritation over this delay manifested itself in the United States, but our Government was willing to take matters slowly, and continued to press for better neutrality legislation.

Such were the circumstances when Congress met in December, 1819, and again Clay rose in arms against Monroe and Adams. He had come to Washington, he wrote to John J. Crittenden, determined to go with the Administration on

[48] Hopkins, *op. et loc. cit.*, pp. 462–463, 466; Adams, *Memoirs*, Vol. IV, pp. 119–120, 229, 242–243; Monroe Papers, XVII, Worden Pope to Monroe, March 1, 1819; *National Intelligencer*, Sept. 4, Oct. 16, 1819.

[49] Adams, *Memoirs*, Vol. IV, pp. 174, 471.

Spanish affairs, but it was driving him into opposition. He was for renouncing the treaty, seizing Texas, and recognizing the patriots in South America.[50]

Clay repeated and elaborated upon these ideas in speech after speech before the Committee of the Whole. The conduct of the Spanish negotiations was denounced, the value of Texas and the necessity of its possession were enlarged upon. He offered resolutions denying the Government's right to alienate territory without the consent of Congress, and condemning the relinquishment of Texas. Opponents pointed out the shadowy nature of our claim to that region. This Clay denied, but the Committee rose without action.[51]

Defeated on this front, the Kentuckian shifted his ground, and, on May 10, called up another resolution which declared it expedient to provide an outfit and salary for such minister or ministers as the President might send to any of the independent governments of South America. This Clay supported in a bitter speech. He ignored his previous assertion that recognition was no violation of neutrality, and regretted that the United States had not recognized the provinces two years before, when they really needed assistance. The none too receptive ears of the House were regaled with glowing accounts of the high state of civilization of the provinces, and prophecies of gigantic favorable trade developments there.

What I would give [he exclaimed] could we appreciate the advantages which may be realized by our pursuing the course which I propose! It is in our power to create a system of which we shall be the center, and in which all South America will act with us. In respect to commerce, we should be most benefitted; this country would become the place of deposit of the commerce of the world. . . . We should become the center of a system which would constitute the rallying point of human wisdom against all the despotism of the Old World. . . . Our institutions now make us free; but how long shall we continue so,

[50] Crittenden Papers (Duke Univ.), Clay to Crittenden, Dec. 14, 1819 (copy), (Lib. of Cong.), II, Clay to Crittenden, Jan. 29, 1820. *Cf.* Clay Papers, Russell to Clay, Feb. 17, 1820; *Kentucky Argus*, July 9, 16, 1828, Clay to Kendall, Jan. 8, April 16, 1820.

[51] *Annals of Cong.*, 16th Cong., 1st sess., 1691, 1719–1731, 1781.

if we mould our opinions on those of Europe? Let us break these commercial and political fetters; let us no longer watch the nod of any European politician; let us become real and true Americans, and place ourselves at the head of the American System.

It was an eloquent effort and this time the response was more favorable. The resolution was reported to the House, and passed by a vote of eighty to seventy-five.[52]

Congress appeared to be growing tired of the continued delay in the Spanish negotiations,[53] and Jefferson, ardent expansionist that he was, wrote to Monroe that he was not sorry about Spain's failure to ratify and that Texas, Florida and probably Cuba would join us on the acknowledgment of their independence.[54] The Administration showed signs of nervousness. Adams told the French Minister that the time for recognition of some of the provinces was fast approaching, and the President's message to the second session was favorable to them, and would have been more so but for objections made by Calhoun and the Secretary of State.[55] Zealous efforts were made through the summer of 1820 to obtain Spanish ratification of the Florida treaty and this was finally received in October, with the objectionable land grants annulled. The Senate, almost unanimously, ratified the treaty again on February 19, 1821.

The treaty went through despite Clay's opposition. But recognition of the provinces was still deferred, and in the session of 1820–1821, Clay carried on the fight. A motion to appropriate an outfit and salary for any minister the President might send to any independent South American Government was made by him on February 9. It was defeated, seventy-nine to eighty-six, but on the following day, he submitted a resolution to the effect that the House participated with the people of the

---

[52] *Ibid.*, 16th Cong., 1st sess., 2223–2229.

[53] Adams, *Memoirs*, Vol. V, pp. 108–109. Adams felt that Clay's maneuvers were directed toward preventing ratification of the Spanish treaty, and thus discrediting Adams in the race for the presidency. He asserted that Clay's maneuvers, and various evidences of favor to the provinces given by Monroe to counteract the Clay program in Congress, were responsible for Spain's delay in ratification.

[54] *Cong. Globe*, 30th Cong., 2d sess., Appendix, 65.

[55] Adams, *Memoirs*, Vol. V, pp. 118, 111, 200.

United States in their sympathy for the South Americans; and that it was ready to support the President whenever he should think it expedient to recognize their governments. Both of these clauses passed. The first by a vote of one hundred and thirty-four to twelve, the second by a vote of eighty-seven to sixty-eight, and a committee, headed by the Speaker, was appointed to lay the resolution before the President.[56] With that victory, such as it was, Clay had to rest content for the time being.

The Kentuckian left Congress in the spring of 1821, on the plea of restoring his failing fortunes. He spoke twice in Lexington during the following summer, and each time he expressed his eagerness to see recognition achieved.

On one of these occasions he stated, in bolder form than ever before, his desire for an American System separate and distinct from Europe. He mentioned feelingly the reaction prevalent in the Old World, and the fact that we owed exemption from its baneful effects to distance and to the bravery of our countrymen. "But who can say," he continued, "that has observed the giddiness and intoxication of power, how long this exemption will continue?" It had seemed to him desirable "that a sort of counterpoise to the Holy Alliance should be formed in the two Americas in favor of national independence and liberty, to operate by the force of example and by moral influence; that here a rallying point and an asylum should exist for freemen and for freedom."

Bolivar and San Martin were winning victories in the provinces at the time when Clay spoke. Mexico was practically independent by the end of August. The revolutionists were proving their metal, and, the following March, Monroe sent a message to Congress recommending acknowledgment of the new states. The message that came to be known as the Monroe Doctrine was promulgated less than two years later.

How much significance can be attached to Clay's attitude toward our foreign policy during these years? There is plenty of

[56] *Annals of Cong.*, 16th Cong., 2d sess., 1081–1088.

evidence to show that it had a real effect in bolstering the morale of the revolutionists. His speeches were received by them with great favor. That of March 24, 1818, is said to have been translated into Spanish and read at the heads of different regiments. A book on South America and the revolution was dedicated to him by a Peruvian in 1819.[57] The revolutionary Mexican Government repeatedly sent him testimonials of its regard, and a certain Captain Thomson, returning from Mexico in June of 1822, reported that when Clay's name was mentioned there it was "like an electric fire," and that "if you were made President of the United States you could obtain anything you wanted to ask for." [58] The manifestations of respect and admiration accorded to Clay a century later by South Americans indicate the depth of his influence.[59]

Did he mold the American Government's policy to any marked degree? It is true that, as the exponent of a growing popular sympathy, he built up a real following in the West and in Congress, one that the Administration had to consider. His resolution of February 10, 1821, showed that the House favored recognition, and strengthened the hand of the Government for the action finally taken. Richard Rush asserted that Clay "led the way" to recognition.[60] But the stubborn fact remains that recognition did not come until almost a year after the Kentuckian had retired to private life, and then only after Florida had been acquired, England had begun to veer away from the Holy Alliance, and striking victories had ensured the success of the revolutionists. There is no proof that the Executive yielded to his arguments or his caviling. His repeated attacks made Adams morose and Monroe fretful, but any in-

---

[57] Hopkins, *op. et loc. cit.*, p. 466; Littell, *op. cit.*, p. 43; D. V. Pazos, *Letters on the United Provinces of South America* (N.Y., 1819).

[58] Clay Papers, III, B. O. Tyler to Clay, June 24, 1822. The Clay Papers contain many expressions of gratitude, particularly from Mexico.

[59] *Lexington* (Kentucky) *Herald*, May 8, 1921, May 8, 1927; S. P. Breckinridge, *Madeline McDowell Breckinridge* (Chicago, 1921), pp. 6–7; J. S. Rodriguez, *Discurso etc.* (Caracas, 1930), passim.

[60] Clay Papers, IX, Rush to Clay, June 23, 1827: ". . . the South Americans owe to you more than to any other man in either hemisphere their independence, you having led the way to our acknowledgment of it."

fluence he might have exerted over Monroe was neutralized
by the cool sanity of the Secretary of State.

Calhoun's comment was incisive. Clay, he said, reminded him
of a farmer who insisted that his neighbors sow their grain in
January. They refused, saying it was not yet time. He continued
each succeeding month and they declined until the proper time
arrived. When the crop turned out abundant and prosperous,
he claimed all the credit because he was the first who insisted
on its being sowed.[61]

Clay's headlong attempt at leadership did not resemble that
of a statesman half so much as it did that of some ambitious
pilgrim, feverishly urging his brethren to take a precipitous
short cut to the City of God. Weak in its impetuosity, its strained
conception of international law and its encroachment upon the
prerogatives of the State Department, it was of a nature to repel
rather than encourage action by the Government. In the last
analysis, the recognition of South American independence was
far more the result of the force of circumstance and the trend of
the Administration's policy than it was of the feverish activities
of Henry Clay.

Nor can it be claimed that he influenced the promulgation
of the famous message of December, 1823. The ideas which
the message contained had been floating about for many years,
and though Clay's declarations of 1820 and 1821 certainly foreshadowed it, there is not the faintest proof that Monroe was
influenced by the Kentuckian. The language of that document
was the language of Jefferson, Adams and Monroe.[62]

The nationalist program with which Clay had started in 1816
was only partially completed by 1823. Internal improvements
at national expense were still avoided by the National Government.[63] Industry still clamored for protection. Clay fought hard
for a new tariff bill in 1820, designed to make the United States
self-sufficient in food, clothing and means of defense. His

---

[61] *Ibid.*, VII, H. R. Warfield to Clay, May 5, 1826.

[62] Perkins, *op. cit.*, pp. 98–100; Gilman, *op. cit.*, pp. 162–170.

[63] Clay had by no means given them up. *Cf. Niles' Register*, Vol. XVIII,
p. 327.

speech, which showed clearly that he did not dream of manufacturing for foreign countries, contained two extraordinary arguments: first, that Europe's *permanent* inability to consume our products had been demonstrated by her failure to markedly increase consumption of our cotton, tobacco and breadstuffs; second, a pæan of praise to woman and child labor in factories. "Constant occupation," he said, "is the best security for innocence and virtue, and idleness is the parent of vice and crime." Labor exploitation was brushed aside, as arising out of "the nature of man." [64] The bill passed the House by a majority of thirteen, but was lost in the Senate by one vote.

Clay's course had been one of bitter opposition to the Administration and its policies, domestic and foreign. But in one other crisis of this period he played a rôle that demonstrated his love of the Union, and his desire to save it from the dangers of fratricidal strife. The factionist turned pacificator in the great struggle over the Missouri Compromises.

[64] *Annals of Cong.*, 16th Cong., 1st sess., 2034–2052.

CHAPTER VIII

THE BLACK SPECTER

IT was February, 1819, and Thomas W. Cobb, the eloquent and excitable member from Georgia, was raging against his Northern colleagues.

"If you persist," he exclaimed, "the Union will be dissolved" — and then, fixing his eyes upon James Tallmadge of New York: "You have kindled a fire which all the waters of the ocean cannot put out, which seas of blood can only extinguish."

Boldly, Tallmadge flung back the challenge. "If a dissolution of the Union must take place, let it be so! If civil war, which gentlemen so threaten, must come, I can only say, let it come!"[1]

The House was tense with excitement. The black specter of the Slavery Question was abroad in the land.

Missouri was the immediate cause of all this furor. The march of the pioneers had sent thousands of slaveholding settlers into the Louisiana Purchase Territory; and by 1817, these erstwhile natives of Virginia, North Carolina, Kentucky, and Tennessee were clamoring for admission as a state. Petition after petition was sent to Congress, and finally one was presented to the House by Clay which resulted in action. An enabling act was drafted, and on February 13, 1819, it was taken up in the Committee of the Whole. Tallmadge promptly moved an amendment prohibiting the further introduction of slaves, and freeing, at the age of twenty-five, all slave children born in the state. The fight was on.

The contentious clamor that filled the land had its origins in a few relatively simple conditions. Sectional rivalry, and a determination on the part of the South to preserve that political balance in the Senate which it had lost in the House, was one

[1] *Annals of Cong.*, 15th Cong., 2d sess., 1204.

factor. Moral animosity, which had developed in the North as slavery proved unprofitable there, jarred against an increasing, though still covert, admiration in the South for its peculiar institution. Slavery had been rooted there by the cotton gin, and this spawn of the Industrial Revolution was the real reason why Cobb and Tallmadge were shouting defiance at one another across the chamber of the House. Lastly, there was the conflict of interests between the Southerners, who demanded the right to take their slaves into the new territory, and the Northerners, who were determined that they would not compete with slave labor when they or their relatives and friends moved out into the West.

There had been no occasion for a clash, hitherto, for the Ohio River had been tacitly recognized as marking the division between the areas that were slave and free. The Northwest Territory had been organized on a free basis in 1787, and the territory south of the Ohio had developed economic interests similar to those of the Southern states which had ceded it to the Union. But the trans-Mississippi lands had no dividing line, and the South, now openly intent upon maintaining its political power, rallied to the defense of the slaveholders of Missouri, a defense all the more impassioned because slavery had always existed in the Louisiana Purchase.[2]

The House and Senate deadlocked over the Tallmadge amendment in the spring of 1819, and during the following summer excitement steadily rose throughout the country. The Sixteenth Congress met in December, 1819, with storm signals flying everywhere. There seemed to be no way out of the *impasse*.

Then, on December 30, a bill to admit the State of Maine was brought into the Committee of the Whole. It passed the House, but the Senate, where the South still held control, tied it to the unconditional admission of Missouri, and the debate waxed hot and heavy. The Missouri question became almost the only topic of conversation, and "civil war" and "disunion"

[2] *Cf.* Channing, *op. cit.*, Vol. V, pp. 323–324; J. A. Woodburn, "The Historical Significance of the Missouri Compromise," in *Amer. Hist. Assoc. Report*, 1893, pp. 252–253.

were words that became so commonplace as to be spoken "almost without emotion." [3]

The logic of the situation demanded a compromise. Senator Jesse B. Thomas, of Illinois, was a believer in slavery and a steadfast opponent of the Tallmadge amendment, but he was a moderate. On February 3, 1820, he proposed that Missouri be admitted as a slave state, but that the rest of the Louisiana Purchase north of 36° 30' should be forever free. Maine would be admitted at the same time. There were further long and bitter speeches, but the moderates on both sides rallied to this proposal. The Senate agreed to separate the Maine and Missouri bills; fourteen Northern members of the House helped to vote down the slavery restriction on Missouri by a margin of three votes, and on March 2 the Thomas amendment passed. The first stage of the Missouri struggle was over. [4]

Clay's part in this phase of the conflict is somewhat obscured by the fact that most of his speeches were not reported. But there is enough evidence to clarify his position, if one understands the Kentuckian's personal attitude toward slavery.

Clay always manifested an intense aversion to this "deepest stain upon the character of our country." It was "the greatest of human evils," one which redounded to our discredit in comparison with South America, where emancipation had taken place. [5] There is every indication that he was a kind and thoughtful master. Again and again he gave slaves their freedom in recognition of faithful service. [6] The happiest relations existed between him and the Dupuys, Aaron, his servant at Ghent, and Charles, who was Clay's valet in Washington for many years.

---

[3] Colton, *Correspondence*, Clay to Adam Beatty, Jan. 22, 1820; Adams, *Memoirs*, Vol. IV, pp. 525–526; Brown, *Missouri Compromises*, pp. 11–12, Wm. Plumer to his father, Feb. 20, 1820.

[4] *Cf*. Woodburn, *op. et loc. cit.*, pp. 263–265.

[5] Mallory, *op. cit.*, Vol. I, pp. 525, 527, Jan. 20, 1827. *Cf*. his speech of Dec. 17, 1829, in the *African Repository*, 68 vols. (Washington, 1826–1892), Vol. VI, pp. 1–25; *Annals of Cong.*, 16th Cong., 1st sess., 2228.

[6] Fayette County Court, Deed Book 6, p. 375; 11, p. 393; 18, p. 130. Henry Clay's will, dated Nov. 14, 1851, also recorded in this office at Lexington, Kentucky, in Will Book T, p. 474, July 12, 1852.

Furthermore, from 1816 on, he was a recognized leader in the American Colonization Society. This project for colonizing free Negroes in Africa was formally initiated in Washington, December 21, 1816, at a meeting over which Clay presided.[7] He was an active member, spoke in behalf of the society, aided in soliciting patronage, became one of its vice-presidents (as did Jackson, Crawford and other prominent Southerners), and, in 1836, was chosen president of the organization. He saw in this impractical plan a solution of the Negro problem, arguing, with his usual optimism, that it could and would eliminate the free-Negro question, and that, as the value of slaves was certain to continually diminish, more and more Negroes would be emancipated by their owners and be ready and eager to go to Liberia! [8] Events proved all of these arguments false, but he continued to maintain that the plan was the one feasible solution.

Such was the attitude toward slavery of Clay, the humanitarian. But, living with the institution, he tolerated and embraced it as a matter of practical business. His black property increased in amount as it increased in value. The man who had owned one Negro in 1799 had twelve in 1818. The number increased to fifty odd at various times thereafter, and in the year before his death he possessed thirty-three slaves.[9] He bought and sold Negroes and hired out his hands to other employers.[10] Property valued in thousands of dollars was worth a vigilant guard. Twice during his life, the Kentuckian went on record as earnestly favoring effective fugitive slave laws, and he was not averse to offering rewards for the return of his own runaway slaves.[11] In the autumn of 1832, in a private conversation the general tone of which deplored slavery, he estimated the profits of Kentucky slave breeding at between six and

[7] *National Intelligencer*, Dec. 31, 1816.

[8] *African Repository*, Vol. VI, pp. 9, 11, 21.

[9] Fayette County Tax Lists, passim; Clay's own list of taxable property, 1851, now in the possession of J. Winston Coleman, Jr., Lexington, Ky.

[10] Clay Papers, IV, memo. for Robert Scott, Nov. 10, 1823; XXV, Dec. 25, 1847.

[11] *Annals of Cong.*, 15th Cong., 1st sess., 828; *Cong. Globe*, 31st Cong., 1st sess., App. 115, 571, 612; *National Intelligencer*, Dec. 1, 1817.

seven per cent., and defended Negro trading on the ground that it carried vicious and incorrigible blacks to new country, where they might form better habits and propensities.[12]

An opponent of slavery in the abstract, Henry Clay accepted and utilized it as a concrete business proposition.

When Tallmadge offered his amendment against slavery in Missouri, the lanky Kentuckian's first reaction was that of the practical business man, and the Western politician standing for equality with the older states. The discussion in 1819 found him a vigorous champion of the Southern interest. He expounded volubly the old Jeffersonian argument of mitigation by diffusion, extolled the black slavery of Kentucky as contrasted with the "white slavery" of the North, and stood staunchly for states' rights, using the argument later made famous by William Pinkney's demand that Missouri should not be forced to come into the Union "shorn of her beams." [13] This was an outright defense of slavery extension, not merely love for states' rights; for at the same time, when an attempt was made to prohibit slavery in the new territory of Arkansas, Clay denounced the Free Soil members. He accused them of "Negrophobia," asked what the South had done that it should be proscribed, and demanded to know if the Free Soilers meant to coop up the slaveholders and prevent the spread of their population and wealth. More than that, his was the deciding vote in a successful attempt to recommit the Arkansas bill with instructions to strike out the restriction clause,[14] and Arkansas was organized with slavery. He aligned himself, by that casting vote, with those who demanded freedom to move their black chattels into the territories west of the Mississippi. He was, to all appearances, a leader of the Southern extremists.[15]

Outwardly, his position remained unchanged during the early part of the next session. No one knows who first suggested

[12] McDowell Collection, Diary of Henry Clay, Jr., Sept. 1832. He did not defend the *foreign* slave trade.

[13] *Annals of Cong.*, 15th Cong., 2d sess., 1166f. Most of his speeches were not reported, but his arguments appear from the direct answers of his opponents.

[14] *Ibid.*, 15th Cong., 2d sess., 1222f, 1272–1273.

[15] *Cf.* Adams, *Memoirs*, Vol. IV, p. 262.

combining Maine with Missouri, but Clay suggested it two
weeks before it took concrete form, by insisting that the admission of Maine depended upon slavery in Missouri. He emphasized states' rights in doing so, but slavery and the interests
of the South were the real points at issue.[16] He spoke for four
hours on February 8, against restriction on Missouri. He denounced New England "notions" on the subject very forcibly,
and with all his oratorical tricks — his mobile face and even his
body twisted "in the most dreadful scowls and contortions."
"If there is any passion he expresses in greater force than another it is contempt," wrote William Plumer, Jr.[17] The Southern hotheads threatened disunion, and Clay seemed to go along
with them — telling Adams that he was certain the Union
would be split apart within five years, threatening to go home
and raise troops to defend Missouri.[18]

But, as the climax of the first crisis approached in the winter
of 1820, and as the ominous threat of disunion loomed ever
nearer, Clay turned to compromise. Slavery in Missouri remained his *sine qua non*, but with Western interest salved by
admitting that state without restrictions that were abhorrent
to her, and with the actual and tacit recognition of slavery
south of 36°30′, Clay's patriotism and desire for national
leadership gained the upper hand. He probably felt that the
question of slavery north of the famous line was unimportant.
"No one was anxious [in 1820] to have slavery exist north of
that line, except in Missouri," he told the Senate in 1838.[19]
He was still willing to bluff in order to gain as much as he
could for the South, a fact that accounts for his threats and
dire forebodings,[20] but his letters written in January, 1820,

[16] *Annals of Cong.*, 16th Cong., 1st sess., 831–841; Woodburn, *op. et
loc. cit.*, p. 259.

[17] *Ibid.*, 16th Cong., 1st sess., 1170, 1426; Brown, *Missouri Compromises*, p. 8.

[18] Adams, *Memoirs*, Vol. IV, pp. 525–526; Brown, *Missouri Compromises*,
pp. 11–14.

[19] *Cong. Globe*, 25th Cong., 2d sess., App. 71.

[20] Two weeks before his alarming prophecy to Adams, he wrote to John
J. Crittenden that he felt the struggle would end in some middle-of-the-road
solution. — Crittenden Papers (Duke Univ.), Jan. 29, 1820.

show that he was fully alive to the sinister nature of the controversy, and deplored it.[21]

In that frame of mind, he turned to the Thomas amendment, and supported it. It is true that he did not speak on the subject, but when John Randolph denounced the Compromise, the Speaker's attitude was one of studied affront,[22] and he ensured the passage of the bill by a shrewd trick that made the eccentric Virginian boil with rage.

Randolph loathed the settlement because he felt that it was unfavorable to the South. He plastered the appellation "dough face" upon the Northerners whose votes helped it through the House, and on March 3, the morning after it had been accepted, he rose to move that the vote be reconsidered. Clay refused to allow his motion before the routine business of the morning was finished, and the House sustained this ruling. The Compromise bill was still in the Speaker's possession, but, while the House went through the procedure of receiving and referring petitions, he signed and sent it off post haste to the Senate. When Randolph was finally unleashed, Clay informed him that the bill had gone, and with it the opportunity for reconsideration.[23]

Clay had deliberately committed himself to the Compromise, and he exerted himself manfully to save it in the dramatic scenes of the second Missouri crisis.

He did not come to the second session of the Sixteenth Congress until January 16, 1821. Pressing business matters kept him away, and he resigned the Speakership, to which John W. Taylor of New York was chosen after a hard fight and twenty-two ballots.[24] When Clay finally arrived, he found the Missouri situation in a condition worse than the first.

The Missourians, stung by the attempted Congressional dictation, had chosen the members of their constitutional con-

[21] Colton, *Correspondence*, Clay to Beatty, Jan. 22, 1820; *Argus*, July 16, 1828, Clay to Kendall, Jan. 8, 1820.

[22] H. A. Garland, *The Life of John Randolph of Roanoke*, 2 vols. (N.Y., 1850), Vol. II, pp. 131–132, Randolph to Dr. Brockenbrough, Feb. 23, 1820.

[23] *Annals of Cong.*, 16th Cong., 1st sess., 1588–1590; Garland, *op. cit.*, Vol. II, pp. 128–130.

[24] *Ibid.*, 16th Cong., 2d sess., 434.

vention in a spirit of rage and resentment. Only one of the thirty-nine delegates was opposed to slavery, and the state constitution was framed with a clause making it the duty of the general assembly to exclude free Negroes and mulattoes from the state.[25] The instrument was then submitted to the National Legislature for approval, and Missouri was once more in the limelight.

The Free Soilers in Congress fell vigorously upon the offending clause, declaring it a violation of that part of the Constitution which guarantees the same privileges and immunities to all American citizens. The House was once more in turmoil, and attempt after attempt to obtain recognition of Missouri's statehood was voted down.

Her status was certainly anomalous. Congress had passed an enabling act. Under it the Missourians had formed a state constitution and a state government. They had voted as a state in the presidential contest of 1820, and they had chosen Senators and Congressmen. It would certainly seem that any debatable provisions in the state charter were matters for legal rather than legislative action, but the antislavery men were obdurate.

From December until the middle of January the House fumbled with the question, and passions rose. The Northerners were smug and the Southerners were angry. The latter were not very well organized, William Plumer noted, and their young hotheads urged them on. He thought they missed the guidance of Clay, "who, with all his violence & impetuosity, knew better how to control & direct his party, than any man they now have here." [26]

The situation had reached a dangerous impasse when Clay arrived. He looked over the ground and consulted with his friends. Then, on January 29, he moved that the House go into Committee of the Whole and take up a resolution that had been passed by the Senate, admitting Missouri. This resolution contained a proviso by which Congress washed its hands

[25] F. H. Hodder, "Sidelights on the Missouri Compromises," in *Amer. Hist. Assoc. Report*, 1909, pp. 155–156.
[26] Brown, *Missouri Compromises*, pp. 24–27.

of any responsibility for the free-Negro clause, leaving it a matter for court decision.

The debate continued for days. Both sides had the Missouri bull by the tail, and neither felt that it could safely let go. Clay took a leading part. He held that the true place for a verdict upon the constitutionality of Missouri's charter was the courts, and he stood for the Senate resolution.[27] His sympathy with Missouri was obvious, but his haughty arrogance was conspicuous by its absence.

He uses no threats, or abuse [wrote Plumer] but all is mild, humble, & persuasive — he begs, entreats, adjures, suplicates, & beseaches us to have mercy upon the people of Missouri — He is ready to vote for anything, & everything which we may propose, short of restriction, & he knows, such is his language, that we have too much justice, good sense, & good feeling to move again that odious question — The same tone is taken by his followers in general.[28]

Each side was afraid to accept the other's propositions. Amendment after amendment was rejected. Clay finally proposed that the original Senate resolution be submitted to a select committee of thirteen, and the weary House agreed.[29] This committee, with Clay as its chairman, discussed and wrangled for over a week. It agreed that no attempt should be made to restrict slavery in Missouri, but the clause debarring free Negroes continued to produce a marked diversity of opinion. Plumer reported that at one time a majority of the committee agreed to do nothing, and that the final report, which he considered "a very strange one," was agreed to by only seven out of the thirteen.[30] That report, based upon a resolution drawn up by Clay,[31] changed the Senate resolution in one important particular. It stated, as a fundamental condition of admission, that the state should never pass any law preventing

[27] *Annals of Cong.*, 16th Cong., 2d sess., 982, 1008.
[28] *Ibid.*, 16th Cong., 2d sess., 982f; Brown, *Missouri Compromises*, pp. 28–34. *Cf.* the letter from Wm. Brown (Feb. 14, 1821) published in the *Argus of Western America*, March 3, 1821.
[29] The Speaker appointed to this Committee only men selected by Clay. — *Cong. Globe*, 31st Cong., 1st sess., 510.
[30] Brown, *Missouri Compromises*, p. 34.
[31] *Cong. Globe*, 31st Cong., 1st sess., 125.

"any description of persons from coming to and settling in the said State, who now are or hereafter may become citizens of any of the States of this Union." The legislature of the state was to give its solemn assent to this condition. The report pleaded for compromise and the restoration of harmony.[32]

A heated debate over this report began on February 12. Clay struggled hard, but the majority was obdurate, and the resolution was defeated by three votes. On the following day, the House agreed to reconsider, and again Clay reasoned and remonstrated, entreating the members to accept the Compromise. But again the resolution was rejected, and by a majority of six. The *National Intelligencer* came out that day with high praise of the Kentuckian's efforts, but they appeared to have been in vain. The excitement was intense, and within twenty-four hours it exhibited itself in a wild burst of passion and fury.

The status of Missouri being still undetermined, it had been foreseen that trouble might arise over counting her electoral votes. Some days before, a joint committee of the House and Senate had been appointed to seek a way out of this difficulty. Clay was one of its moving spirits. Everyone knew that Monroe had been overwhelmingly re-elected, and on February 14, the very day of the count, Clay reported from the committee a plan for stating the result both with and without the electoral vote of Missouri.[33] The Senate had accepted this plan on the previous day. The House, amid great excitement and considerable opposition, agreed by a vote of ninety to sixty-seven. But the atmosphere was tense.

Clay then took the lead in perfecting the arrangements for the ceremony. On his motion, it was decided that a message be sent to the Senate, informing that body of the concurrence of the House, and of its readiness to proceed. He headed the committee bearing the message. He moved, and the House

[32] *Annals of Cong.*, 16th Cong., 2d sess., 1078–1080.
[33] Woodburn, *op. et loc. cit.*, p. 276, says he offered this on Feb. 4. This is an error, due to a misprint in the *Annals* (1147), which heads the day's proceedings "Wednesday, February 4," instead of Wednesday, February 14, as it should be. February 4 fell on Sunday, and there was no session of Congress on that day.

agreed, to receive the Senate standing and uncovered, and to give the Senators chairs on the right-hand side of the House chamber. On his motion, a committee of two, consisting of himself and Mark C. Hill of Massachusetts, was appointed to receive the Senate.

Soon thereafter that body made its appearance, the mild and courteous John Gaillard of South Carolina, president *pro tem*, walking at its head. It took the assigned seats, and then began the tedious procedure of reading the verifications and proclaiming the results. The afternoon waned, but everyone knew that a crisis was approaching, and the House was jammed with spectators.

At last Gaillard came to the Missouri vote. As he handed it to the tellers, Arthur Livermore of New Hampshire rose, and objected to its reception on the ground that Missouri was not a state. This was wildly seconded, and in an instant the House became a scene of tumult and confusion. High above the clamor a Senator's voice could be heard moving that the Senate withdraw. The question was put, and decided in the affirmative, and the members of the Upper House retired.

The Speaker of the House, John W. Taylor of New York, finally obtained a semblance of order, but John Floyd of Virginia, white with rage, moved that Missouri was a state and that her vote ought to be counted. Randolph rushed to his support, and proceeded to speak at length, until Clay, who had given way to him, obtained the floor and, "with great force and dignity," moved to lay the resolution on the table and invite the Senate back again. This was done, and the Upper House came back to the fetid atmosphere of a hall where the lamps and candles now cast their flickering shadows over the tense faces of the legislators, and the men and women in the crowded galleries.

All was not yet over. Missouri's vote was read and registered, but when Gaillard proceeded to announce the election of Monroe and Tompkins, with *and* without the vote of Missouri, Floyd and Randolph again interrupted, and inquired if that vote had been counted. Gaillard, distressed and nonplussed, said that he would answer no question. He could only declare the results. He began again, and Floyd, with menacing gestures and defiant shouts, again attempted to prevent the vote being declared. Cries of "Order! Order!" rose from all over the hall, drowning his voice. Randolph came to his support, and the chamber of the House was once more filled with sound and fury. Taylor ordered the objectors to take their seats. Floyd appealed. He was ordered down. Gaillard finished his proclamation. As he closed, Randolph was on his feet again. Amid renewed shouts of "Order!" he was commanded to sit down, but continued speaking. Then, for the second time that day, a motion to retire was made by one of the Senators. It was quickly carried, and, gathering what shreds of dignity they had left about them, that august body hurried in rather disorderly fashion out of the chamber — "glad, I believe," says Plumer, "to get out of a place where they were treated with so little ceremony or respect." [34]

Clay's part in all this had been marked by admirable dignity and restraint. "He kept his party down," wrote the member from New Hampshire, "& thus brought the election to a close in peace, if not in tranquility." [35] But the Missouri question was seemingly as far from settlement as ever.

It was during the discussions of this second crisis, as Clay recalled it in later years, that John Randolph approached him, during one of the evening sessions, and said, "How do you do, sir; I wish you would go with me to Kentucky." Clay understood him to mean that the South should withdraw from the Government at Washington. They talked for an hour about it on the following morning, and Randolph urged Clay to make no compromise. [36] But the Kentuckian held firmly to his course.

[34] Brown, *Missouri Compromises*, pp. 35f; *Annals of Cong.*, 16th Cong., 2d sess., 1154–1166; Woodburn, *op. et loc. cit.*, pp. 276–279; McMaster, *op. cit.*, Vol. IV, p. 599.

[35] Brown, *Missouri Compromises*, p. 38.

[36] *Cong. Globe*, 25th Cong., 2d sess., App. 71. This account is somewhat confusing, for in it Clay refers to himself as occupying the Speaker's chair on that evening. Perhaps Taylor had requested him to do so. Or the incident might have occurred during the first crisis and not the second, as Clay remembered.

On February 21, William Brown of Kentucky offered a
motion to repeal the first Compromise. He consented to postponement, at the suggestion of a Pennsylvania member, but
this action brought the situation to a crisis. The next day
word came of the ratification of the Florida treaty and it may
well be that the final consummation of this treaty, with its
abandonment of prospective slave territory in the Southwest,
considerably mollified the Free Soilers.[37] On that same day,
Clay moved a joint committee to consider the status of
Missouri.

The House accepted this by a vote of almost two to one,
and also accepted the Kentuckian's proposal that the twenty-
three House members be chosen by ballot. Clay picked his
own committee, drawing up the list of names and circulating
it through the House to be voted.[38]

The Senate chose a group of seven to sit on the committee,
and on Saturday, February 24, the deliberations of that body
began. They were continued over into Sunday. On the next
day, February 26, Clay introduced in the House the resolution
drawn up by the committee.

It was substantially the same as that of his previous committee of thirteen. The Missouri legislature must solemnly
agree that the state's constitution and laws should never be
used to deprive any citizen of any state of the privileges and
immunities to which he was entitled under the Federal Constitution. There was a brief, although sharp, final debate in
the House, but Clay skillfully pushed the measure through.[39]
It passed, eighty-seven to eighty-one, and two days later ran
the less formidable gantlet of the Senate by a vote of twenty-
eight to fourteen.[40]

The Missouri legislature made the required promise four

[37] Hodder, *op. et loc. cit.*, pp. 158–160. This is all the more probable
as the cause of agreement, because this final compromise really settled nothing.
Missouri proceeded to exclude free Negroes and mulattoes, and the Northerners
must have seen that she could.

[38] T. H. Benton, *Thirty Years' View*, 2 vols. (N.Y., 1863), Vol. I, p. 10;
Cong. Globe, 31st Cong., 1st sess., 125. The voting showed no great unanimity,
only seventeen members having a majority of the votes cast.

[39] Brown, *Missouri Compromises*, p. 43.

[40] *Annals of Cong.*, 16th Cong., 2d sess., 1240, 390.

months later, contemptuously adding that it had no power to bind the state,[41] and on August 10, 1821, a presidential proclamation admitted Missouri to the more or less happy family of the Union.

The Sixteenth Congress ended its stormy existence on March 3, 1821. It was Clay who in the evening session of that day proposed the vote of thanks to the Speaker. There was a joyous note in his brief remarks concerning the happy termination of the struggle; a note of warning, too, when he pointed to the moral of the drama.

"There are delicate subjects," he said, "exclusively appertaining to the several States, which cannot be touched but by them, without the greatest hazard to the public tranquillity. They resemble those secluded apartments in our respective domiciles, which are dedicated to family privacy, into which our nearest and best neighbors should not enter." He moved that they make the Speaker's office "the depository of our entire reconciliation," and when the House voted its thanks to Taylor, only one dissenting voice was heard.[42]

So ended this great contest over slavery. For the first time, the South had shown its belief that its destiny was tied up with the acquisition of more slave states. For the first time, the Northern section of the country had risen up against slavery.

It is easy enough to argue that, had the North held firm, had the slave power been definitely restricted then and there, the awful agony of future years might have been avoided. And certainly the situation remained ominous with possibilities, "a fire bell in the night" to the aged Jefferson. But the future lay then, as it does now, behind the veil. It is impossible to legislate always for the times to come, and the statesmen of a democracy, confronted by immediate and diverse popular desires, and forced to weigh the chances of imminent present, or possible future, discord and civil war, are impelled inevitably to legislate for their own time. Compromise was the answer, and for 1820 it was the statesmanlike solution.

[41] *Niles' Register*, Vol. XX, p. 388. The state later passed laws excluding Negroes and free mulattoes (Hodder, *op. et loc. cit.*, p. 161).
[42] *Annals of Cong.*, 16th Cong., 2d sess., 1295.

Clay had every right to feel that he had acquitted himself with credit. He had risen, in this struggle which threatened the Union, above the blind sectionalism that characterized the extremists on both sides, and his reputation grew as a result of his action. Contemporaries showered him with praise. Even Adams, who commented sourly upon one of the subsequent dinners given to Clay in Washington, remarked that the crisis had brought the Kentuckian's talents and influence into full display.[43] His enthusiastic constituents gave a public dinner in his honor when he returned to Lexington,[44] and from this time on, his admirers began to refer to him by the deserved title of "The Great Pacificator."

[43] Adams, *Memoirs*, Vol. V, pp. 330, 307. *Cf.* Brown, *Missouri Compromises*, p. 38, passim; *Argus of Western America*, March 3, 1821; Clay, *Works* (Fed. ed.), Vol. II, p. 263.

[44] *Kentucky Gazette*, May 24, 1821.

CHAPTER IX

FAMILY AND FORTUNE

THE rush and tumult of politics centered Clay's life at Washington during a major part of the Monroe administrations, but there were some months in every year when he could come back to the pleasant refuge of his home in Lexington.

"How changed the scene!" wrote Samuel R. Brown, who had visited Lexington in 1797, and again in 1816. The log cabins were gone, replaced by "costly brick mansions." The leathern pantaloons, hunting shirt and leggings of the pioneer were seen no more. Main Street, eighty feet wide, with footways twelve feet wide, was lined with fine brick houses and public buildings. The brick market house, set in the public square, was thronged on Wednesdays and Saturdays, and on the not infrequent occasions when an incorrigible slave was publicly flogged. The stores dispensed "prodigious quantities" of European goods to the inhabitants, who had "a healthy and sprightly appearance." Land was high. Good farms sold for one hundred dollars an acre, town lots at a much greater figure, and the fifty or sixty fine country estates near by had an air of opulence and elegance.

Timothy Flint found gambling and dissipation aplenty, and marked the persistent characteristic of boastfulness, but there was also a real interest in literature and art. *Niles' Register* averred that the inhabitants were "polished." Transylvania University set the tone, with its two hundred and eighty-two students, four less than Harvard, in 1821, and Lexington could boast with reason its title of the "Athens of the West." There, during the early 1820's, Matthew H. Jouett, "nothing but a damned sign painter," according to his disappointed father, was executing his brilliant and facile portraits. Constantine Rafinesque, able and eccentric naturalist, was teaching at Transylvania, under the presidency of genial Horace Holley. Jefferson Davis was a popular student at the University from 1821 to 1824, and Mary Todd and John C. Breckenridge were two of the town's promising children.[1]

In such surroundings, varied by trips to Washington, the Clay boys and girls grew up. There were seven of them at Ashland with merry, practical Mrs. Clay, while their father was in Europe. Theodore Wythe was the eldest, thirteen years old. Then they ranged down through Thomas Hart, Susan, Anne, Lucretia, and Henry Junior to the baby Eliza.

Mrs. Clay hired Amos Kendall, a lanky, critical New Englander, keen of wit but awkward of manner, as a teacher for the elder children, and he quickly discovered that they had good minds. They were all high-tempered, boyish rage sometimes rose to ferocious heights, but they were manageable, and Kendall became fond of them.[2] He left before Clay's return from abroad, but in May of 1816 he met the master at Ashland, and was "familiarly acquainted with him in half an hour."[3]

During the six years after Clay's return from Ghent, Laura, James Brown and John Morrison Clay were added to the family circle. Then the burden of childbearing came to an end for Mrs. Clay. But tragedy, that was to frown upon the family so often in future years, had already begun to rear its head. Laura died of whooping cough when three months old. This was in Washington, and Clay wept beside her as she lay in the arms of Margaret Bayard Smith. Some years later, fourteen-year-old Lucretia died at Ashland.[4]

The other children grew up and matured in the astonishingly

[1] S. R. Brown, *The Western Gazeteer* (Auburn, N.Y., 1817), pp. 91–95; *Niles' Register*, Vol. VI, p. 249, Vol. XX, p. 49, June 11, 1814, March 24, 1821; T. Flint, *Recollections of the Last Ten Years* (Boston, 1826), pp. 65f; W. H. Townsend, *Lincoln and His Wife's Home Town* (Indianapolis, 1929), pp. 24–25.

[2] A. Kendall, *Autobiography* (Boston, 1872), pp. 115–142. The above statements are based on the excerpts published in it from Kendall's journal. Kendall pays high tribute to the generosity and kindness of Mrs. Clay.

[3] *Ibid.*, p. 172.

[4] M. B. Smith, *op. cit.*, pp. 130, 299–303; *National Intelligencer*, July 4, 1823.

rapid way that children do. There are scattered references in the Clay papers to special schools for the girls, and most of the boys went to Transylvania when they reached the proper age. Theodore showed promise of eloquence, and was scheduled to deliver an oration at Lexington's Fourth of July celebration and barbecue in 1821. On April 22, 1822, Susan married Martin Duralde of New Orleans. She was seventeen years old.[5] Dashing James Erwin came up from Tennessee in the first part of October, 1823, with a letter bearing witness to his talents and respectability. He must have met sixteen-year-old Anne Clay before, or else it was a headlong courtship indeed, for, on October 21, they were married.[6] By marriage as well as by death the family circle was being depleted.

Clay was a generous and kindly father. Death and separation from his children were alike hard for him to bear. But there was always a solace in those who still surrounded him, and in his love for Ashland. The magnificent estate received a great deal of attention during these years. He bought twenty-five acres from two of his neighbors in 1816, and exchanged small plots with a third, rounding out his land. He transplanted dogwoods, hollies, redbuds, and other flowering and ornamental trees and shrubs from the southern Appalachians. Corn, hemp and other crops were raised, and Clay took a special interest in blooded stock of every kind. He purchased four thoroughbred Hereford cattle in England and had them shipped to Kentucky in 1817, the first to be sent there directly from abroad. His sheep were celebrated for their fine wool. His horses became famous, and he bred the dam of Woodpecker, one of the best Kentucky racers.[7] His correspondence for the period is full of references to agriculture, varying from the state of the weather, and farm prospects for the year, to a

[5] *Kentucky Gazette,* June 21, 1821. There is no mention of Theodore in the account of the celebration given in the same paper, July 5; *Kentucky Reporter,* April 29, 1822.

[6] Anderson Collection, N. Cannon to Clay, Oct. 4, 1823; *National Intelligencer,* Nov. 5, 1823.

[7] Draper Collection, 28CC81, Lewis Sanders to the *Albany Cultivator,* Dec. 1848; Clay Papers, II, G. Erving to Clay, Liverpool, Feb. 12, 1817; A. Beatty, *Essays on Practical Agriculture* (Maysville, Ky., 1844), p. 37.

new machine for dressing hemp and flax, and the plague of caterpillars in the spring of 1817.

Clay's interest in formal education had not diminished with the years, and after his return from Europe he had become again an active member of Transylvania's board of trustees. He drew up the will of his close friend, Colonel James Morrison, who died in 1823, and, although Morrison wished to make John Morrison Clay his residuary legatee, Clay persuaded him to give the money to the University instead. Morrison Hall, a fine example of the Greek Revival in American architecture, was built as the result of a twenty-thousand-dollar Morrison bequest.[8] The Kentuckian was made a Counsellor of the American Academy of Language and Belles Lettres in 1821, and the following year Transylvania gave him an LL.D.[9]

Clay's law practice had fallen into eclipse during his European journey, and it did not emerge for some time thereafter. He had engaged to look after Lafayette's land interests near New Orleans, and occasionally he took on other business, but such activity was not extensive, and he told a correspondent in October, 1817, that he had not considered himself a practitioner for several years.[10] Within a short time, however, financial difficulties forced him to return to his profession.

Gambling may have had something to do with his hardships. All sorts of rumors floated about Washington concerning his losses at the card table, and in the spring of 1820, Clay made what Adams promptly dubbed an "ingenuous" statement in Congress, about youthful indulgence in gambling that years and experience had determined him to abandon.[11] Times were hard in Kentucky during that period, and this may well have had a direct impact upon Clay's fortunes. But the great cause

[8] *Kentucky Reporter*, Sept. 22, 1827; *Kentucky Gazette*, April 12, 1879; H. R. Lynn, *Henry Clay and Transylvania University*, unpublished M. A. thesis (Univ. of Ky., 1930), pp. 15–16.

[9] *Kentucky Gazette*, May 3, 1821; Lynn, *op. cit.*, p. 41; McDowell Collection, passim; Flint, *op. cit.*, p. 77.

[10] Clay Papers, II, Lafayette to Clay, Oct. 26, 1815; Chas. Lanman, *Haphazard Personalities* (Boston, 1886), pp. 121–122, Clay to C. J. Lanman, Oct. 28, 1817.

[11] Adams, *Memoirs*, Vol. IV, p. 306, Vol. V, p. 59.

was a very heavy burden of debt which was suddenly thrust upon him, due to his openhearted willingness to endorse notes for his friends.

When his brother-in-law, Nathaniel Hart, died in 1811, Clay, as his endorser, had been forced to shoulder a considerable burden. That incident might have taught him caution, but he continued the practice. The crash came in 1820, through the failure of a friend for whom he had gone surety. Clay suddenly found himself owing a large amount, probably about forty thousand dollars, which was due principally to the Bank of the United States.[12] He had other debts as well, and though the tax lists valued his property in 1818 at seventy-five thousand, four hundred dollars, there was imminent danger of disaster. He announced his intention of leaving Congress, refused Adams' offer of a foreign diplomatic post,[13] and, establishing a system of rigid economy and a sinking fund, looked about for law cases.

Poor health dogged his footsteps more than once during the following years. In the fall of 1822 he was dangerously ill of a bilious fever that swept over his vicinity, and a report went around Louisville that he was dead. He was not at all well the following summer, and as late as September, he wrote to a friend that he was only then beginning "to feel that I see land, or rather that I may not get under it."[14] But he bent all his energies to the task of restoring his fortunes.

A part of his time was devoted to an unsuccessful championship of his state in a land dispute with Virginia,[15] but the Bank of the United States was his chief client.

[12] Harrison, "Reminiscences," in *Century Magazine*, Vol. XI (Dec. 1886), pp. 171–172. Adams, *Memoirs*, Vol. V, p. 58, mentions $25,000; *Cong. Deb.*, 23d Cong., 1st sess., 53, Clay's speech, Dec. 19, 1833.

[13] A Puritan's way of eliminating a dangerous rival for the presidency.

[14] *National Intelligencer*, Oct. 19, 23, 1822; Crittenden Papers, III, Clay to Crittenden, Sept. 13, 1823.

[15] For data on this dispute see *Niles' Register*, Vol. XXIV, p. 3, March 8, 1823, Vol. XXV, pp. 261, 275–276, Dec. 27, 1823, Jan. 3, 1824; Adams, *Memoirs*, Vol. VI, p. 138; *Kentucky Senate Journal*, 1823, pp. 15, 184. The Supreme Court handed down a decision, Feb. 27, 1823, completely quashing Kentucky's case. Clay told Adams that all the judges, save one, were superannuated.

That institution had been grossly mismanaged during its early years, and failure to check the paper issues and enormous loans of the Western branches had been attended with evil results. The Lexington branch had discounted one million, six hundred and nineteen thousand dollars, the Cincinnati branch one million, eight hundred thousand dollars in June of 1818 alone, and these discounts, comparable in size to those in Boston and New York, were characteristic of all the offices in the West.[16] When loans were as free as water they were as freely utilized, and the vaults of the Bank were loaded with the worthless paper of thousands of reckless borrowers. Contraction had begun in 1818, and vigorous and successful attempts thereat were made during the ensuing years, under Langdon Cheves's administration. These efforts were necessary to the life of the institution, and to the welfare of the national financial system, but they were a factor in precipitating the hard times that centered about 1819. It was then that the Bank began to acquire its reputation as a "monster."

The Bank had enlisted Clay's interest from its beginning in 1816. He had been active in the establishment of a branch at Lexington, and had advised his friends there as to the necessity of having a "decided majority" of Republicans upon its board of directors.[17] He had obtained five shares of stock, and, in January of 1818, had been chosen a director of the central institution.[18] This office had been refused, primarily, he as-

[16] Catterall, *op. cit.*, p. 34.

[17] Dreer Collection (Pa. Hist. Soc.), Clay to the Pres. of the Bank of the U.S., Jan. 3, 1817; Clay Papers, II, Clay to Thos. Bodley, Jan. 4, 1817. To exclude Federalists entirely, he told Bodley, would make the Bank "what it ought never to be, a party institution." But a decided majority of Republicans would seem to be almost as effective. Madison and Dallas did their best to make it a Republican institution.

[18] *Niles' Register*, Vol. XIII, p. 377, Jan. 31, 1818. *Ibid.*, Vol. XV, pp. 59–60, Sept. 19, 1818, carries an explicit statement from the *Aurora* that Clay had no stock at the time he was made a director, and had not sought the office. The first he heard of it was a letter announcing his appointment. Stock had been appropriated by somebody in order to qualify him, and the moment he received the appointment he declined it. This last statement is true, but Clay mentioned owning five shares of stock in the Bank as early as Dec. 12, 1817. It seemed to cause him no uneasiness and he continued to hold it until at least Dec. 13, 1819. — Etting Papers (Pa. Hist. Soc.), II,

serted, because of a desire to avoid suspicion of bias in any bank question that might come before the House. But the refusal had been heavily sugar-coated. "Altho' I thus decline any special connexion with the Bank," he wrote its president, "I shall continue to feel a lively interest in its prosperity. And I will with great pleasure from time to time, offer it any advice & afford it any aid, in my private character, that I can, and any too in my public station that may appear to me proper." [19]

The Bank continued its attentions, and Clay accepted them. His legal services were enlisted by it in 1819, and early in 1820 he became its counsel in the State of Ohio. On November 5 of that year, he accepted the superintendency of its legal business in both Ohio and Kentucky, and held that office for over four years. [20]

As the Bank's legal agent, Clay threw himself into the task of restoring its finances to a sound condition. His letters to Cheves and to Biddle during this period bear witness to his activity in the Kentucky and Ohio courts and in the Supreme Court at Washington, and to the strain entailed by these arduous exertions. He took to a successful conclusion in the Supreme Court the Bank's suit against Ohio for one hundred thousand dollars which the State had taken by force out of the branch at Chillicothe as payment of a state tax. He instituted suit against Richard M. Johnson of Kentucky, his brother John, and General John Payne, an action that involved about one hundred and thirty thousand dollars, and resulted in the Bank taking over all of their real estate that it could get in settlement. [21] The Bank's policy in general was to be as lenient as

Clay to William Jones, Dec. 12, 1817, III, Clay to Langdon Cheves, Dec. 13, 1819.

[19] Etting Papers, II, Clay to Wm. Jones, Feb. 4, 1818.

[20] In 1822, Clay sought an appointment for a brother in the New Orleans office of the Bank, and Cheves replied that he had put him in nomination. This was probably John Clay, who had gone to New Orleans about 1803, and had previously enlisted Clay's active support in an attempt to secure a variety of offices. — Clay Papers, III, Cheves to Clay, July 27, 1822. Cf. the Breckinridge Papers, XXIX, Clay to Breckinridge, Jan. 5, 1806, and the Sweet Collection, John Clay to Henry Clay, Dec. 1, 1808.

[21] Dreer Collection (Pa. Hist. Soc.), Clay to Cheves, Oct. 3, 1821.

possible, taking mortgages and accepting real estate on terms easy to the debtors. Clay encouraged this leniency,[22] but at the same time he acted vigorously in the Bank's interest, using all the resources of the law to obtain settlements. In the fall of 1822, on his way to Columbus to attend the federal court, he purposely went by Cincinnati in order to stimulate the zeal of the Bank's agents there. After the court session was over he wrote to Cheves that only three or four cases had been lost, and "I have the satisfaction to inform you, that we have obtained two hundred and eleven judgments, in cases issuing from the Cincinnati office alone, and that there were only about twenty causes continued." [23]

Clay received an ample reward for these services. The exact amount is not known, but a letter which he wrote to Cheves indicates that it was generous indeed. "The liberality of the allowance which has been made to me is such as to admit of my time, almost exclusively, being applied to its [the Bank's] service." And he told Adams that the Bank had given him the means of relieving his pecuniary embarrassments within four years.[24] He wrote to his brother-in-law, James Brown, in January, 1825, that he was no longer bowed down by debt, and that two years more of such prosperity would see him entirely free. Some years later the mortgages on his estate amounted only to ten thousand dollars, while the estimated value of the property was ten times that amount.[25] Clay had emerged, for the time being, from the mire of his financial difficulties. But this success was purchased at a considerable price.

Clay's connection with the Bank did not mean that he had

---

[22] *Ibid.*, Clay to Cheves, Sept. 13, 1822; Etting Papers, III, Clay to Cheves, Dec. 1821; Catterall, *op. cit.*, pp. 78, 84.

[23] Dreer Collection, Clay to Cheves, Sept. 13, 1822. *Cf.* the letters to Cheves in which he tells of complete success in sessions of the federal courts in Kentucky (Etting Papers, III, June 11, Dec. 3, 1821, and Catterall, *op. cit.*, p. 78).

[24] Etting Papers, III, Clay to Cheves, Feb. 27, Oct. 22, 1821, June 23, 1822; Adams, *Memoirs*, Vol. V, pp. 495–496.

[25] *National Intelligencer*, June 23, 1828, Clay to Robert Wickliffe, May 24, 1828.

become a tool of the institution. But it did mean that he resigned the Speakership in the Sixteenth Congress, and stayed away from the second session of that body two months in order to attend to the business of the Bank.[26] It meant also that on at least one occasion he exerted himself to put through Congress a bill in the Bank's interest.[27] It meant that he could lament the attacks upon it when it was foreclosing property right and left; that he was tied up very closely with the organization; and that, as its lawyer in a suit with the State of Ohio, he could assure it of being inspired with zeal for its cause "by considerations higher than any which can arise out of professional obligations."[28]

Such connections are regrettable in a public servant. They cloud the understanding, and render impossible an unbiased and impartial judgment where the interest involved is concerned. But Clay had this at least as his excuse. What he did was done openly, and the ethics of the time winked at, if they did not openly condone, the combination of law practice and legislative activity.

Politically, this connection was unfortunate. The Bank, in its legal proceedings, had acquired a large part of Cincinnati, and some fifty thousand acres of good farm lands in Kentucky and Ohio.[29] The former owners of this property loathed the institution with a mighty loathing, and the debtor class in Kentucky and throughout the West saw in it an ogre and a tyrant. The background was furnished for Benton to bawl in 1832: "All the flourishing cities of the West are mortgaged to this moneyed power. They may be devoured by it at any

[26] Etting Papers, III, Clay to Cheves, Nov. 5, 1820. Congress met on Nov. 13, 1820. Clay took his seat Jan. 16, 1821. The Missouri question had been raging for weeks.

[27] *Ibid.*, III, Clay to Cheves, Feb. 15, 1821. In this letter he sends a copy of a bill that has passed the Ohio legislature, adding: "The only provision which it contains, which it appears to me necessary that Congress should now legislate to obviate is that which denies the use of its jails; and I have submitted a proposition on that subject to the judiciary Comee." The "now" may or may not have been significant.

[28] Gratz Collection, Clay to Biddle, Jan. 28, 1823.

[29] Catterall, *op. cit.*, p. 67.

moment. They are in the jaws of the monster! A lump of butter in the mouth of a dog! One gulp, one swallow, and all is gone!" [30] Clay's intimate connection with "the monster" was destined to hurt his popularity in the West.

Nor was Clay's attitude toward the relief of debtors in Kentucky to be a benefit to him. That state was among those hardest hit by the depression. Reckless experiments in banking, land speculation and widespread borrowing paved the way for the terrible conditions in that state that were fully apparent by 1819. When the prices of land, crops and slaves fell drastically, and unemployment rose, feeling against the banks became bitter, a cry for help went up, and the state legislature began passing a series of "relief" laws. It attempted to tax the branches of the Bank of the United States, only to be prevented by the courts. It annulled the charters of the "Forty Thieves," as the forty-six independent banks were called. It passed laws forbidding imprisonment for debt, and a replevin law which prevented the execution of judgments against debtors for from one to two years. It established a Bank of the Commonwealth, giving it power to issue millions of paper money unbacked by specie. [31] Sound finance went overboard in response to popular demand, and a struggle began over the courts which quashed parts of this legislation. This battle between the "relief" and "anti-relief" parties was to convulse the state for years.

Clay did his best to steer clear of this maelstrom. Nevertheless, his attitude toward state finance was conservative, and, though he made no active opposition to the relief proposals, he regarded them with suspicion and disgust. [32] His friends were generally of the anti-relief persuasion, and by June of 1822, Amos Kendall was warning him that the relief party in the state was very jealous of him. [33] The full fruits of this were to be gathered in later years when George Bibb left him, and

[30] *Cong. Deb.*, 22d Cong., 1st sess., 1003.
[31] A. M. Stickles, *The Critical Court Struggle in Kentucky, 1819–1829* (Indiana University, 1929), pp. 5–25.
[32] Crittenden Papers, II, Clay to Crittenden, Jan. 29, 1820; *Cf.* Ritchie, *Reminiscences*, p. 3.
[33] Clay Papers, III, Kendall to Clay, June 20, 1822.

Richard M. Johnson, William T. Barry and other leaders went over into the Jackson camp.

Clay's conservative point of view on state finance, plus the memory of his Bank connections, was to be an important factor in separating him from the great and swelling democratic tide that carried Andrew Jackson into the presidency.

Chapter X

THE LURE OF THE PRESIDENT'S PALACE

While Clay was rebuilding his private fortunes, he kept an eye on the political situation. The fires of his ambition burned as brightly as ever, and when the question of returning to Congress came up in 1823, he sought the advice of friends as to the effect such a move might have upon his presidential aspirations. Their answers varying, his ardent nature and love of active leadership carried the day. He was elected to the Eighteenth Congress, and was again chosen Speaker of that body by an overwhelming majority. Once again the Western Star shone prominently in the political firmament.

The West, of which Clay could well regard himself as the leader, was now becoming a powerful factor in national politics. Its population was mounting into the millions and its membership in the House of Representatives rose accordingly.[1] With this increase in political power, the policies favored in that section became more and more significant.

None of those aims were more strongly urged than the demands for internal improvements with Federal aid, and for a protective tariff. The former, constantly reinforced by the practical lessons of difficulty in transportation, poverty, and state jealousies that prevented co-operation, continued to overshadow the Jeffersonian doctrines of private initiative and states' rights. The demand for protection, evident as early as 1810, had been increased by the hard times that had followed the war. During that period the foreign market proved utterly inadequate as an outlet for the West's surplus goods, and a great majority of the people became convinced that home markets were necessary, and that the development of domestic

[1] There were forty-seven Western representatives before the reapportionment of 1830.

manufacturing was essential to the re-establishment and maintenance of prosperity.[2] It was easy, too, for the patriotic West to believe that its interests were the national interests, and Clay, as he championed these ideals, threw about them the cloak of a nationalist fervor.

As was his wont, he took a prominent part in Congress. He stood stoutly against a bill for pensioning the mother of Oliver Hazard Perry, partly on the ground that it was folly to widen the pension list, partly because he was now discovering a distaste for heroes. "God knows we have had enough of them within the last twenty years — every man is now a hero," he exclaimed, and despite the sneer of eccentric George Kremer of Pennsylvania, he of the leopard coat, that Perry had "laid his bosom bare to every danger . . . while others staid at home, basking in the sunshine of Executive favor," the bill failed.[3]

Clay heartily approved the message, later famous as the Monroe Doctrine, which the President sent to the Eighteenth Congress. His liberal ardor envisioned a war against all Europe, if necessary, on behalf of South American independence, and he thought seriously of attempting to modify the naturalization law, and thus make the United States an asylum for all fugitives from oppression.[4]

When Webster offered a resolution defraying the expenses of an agent to Greece whenever the President might deem such an appointment expedient, Clay supported it in a ringing speech. The Greek revolt against Turkish oppression was enlisting considerable sympathy in the United States. The Kentuckian's excitable mind coupled this struggle for liberty with that in South America, and the perfidious Holy Alliance was wrapped about with scorching apostrophes. During the course of the debate he offered a resolve that the United States would not see "without serious disquietude" any forcible interposition of the allied powers on behalf of Spain in South America. He

[2] *Cf.* H. C. Hockett, *Western Influences on Political Parties to 1825* (Columbus, 1917), pp. 101f.

[3] *Annals of Cong.*, 18th Cong., 1st sess., 980–982.

[4] Adams, *Memoirs*, Vol. VI, pp. 224–225.

did not call this up for discussion, although he asserted that it, or something like it, must be adopted if our liberty was to be preserved, but there were several references to it in the debate about the Greeks. Randolph flayed both projects in his accustomed fashion, and Clay became very much excited. He evidently felt that an expression of sympathy for the Greeks would indicate our firm championship of liberty everywhere, and he dared the opponents of Webster's resolution to go home and tell their constituents that they had voted it down. This was bitterly resented by the opposition, and jibes and taunts flew thickly. Cooler counsels finally prevailed, the House refused to go a-tilting for the Greeks, and Clay did not call up his proposal about Latin America. The rancor and bitterness of his remarks scarcely helped his presidential prospects, and it was after this that Richard M. Johnson said that Clay "was the most imprudent man in the world." But liberty, as Clay knew, was a siren's song in the ears of the Western voters.[5]

There were two other songs with an even more seductive appeal for Westerners, and for many in the East as well, and in each case Clay's voice led the chorus.

On May 4, 1822, Monroe had vetoed, on constitutional grounds, a bill for repairing the Cumberland Road at national expense. Once again strict construction had thwarted Western ardor, but the Eighteenth Congress took up the question again, albeit in a rather gingerly fashion. A bill was introduced appropriating thirty thousand dollars for plans or surveys of such roads and canals as the President might consider to be of national importance from a commercial, military or postal point of view. It was so phrased as to involve no point of constitutionality, but when it came up for discussion in the House Committee of the Whole, Clay insisted upon discussing the broader aspects of the question.

Once more he threw down the gage of battle to the Ad-

<hr />

[5] *Annals of Cong.*, 18th Cong., 1st sess., 805–806, 1084f, 1104f, 1170–1178, 2763; E. W. Earle, "Early American Policy Concerning Ottoman Minorities," in *Political Science Quarterly*, Vol. XLII (Sept. 1927), pp. 353–356; Adams, *Memoirs*, Vol. VI, p. 241.

ministration. The public official who exceeded his powers was guilty of usurpation, but he was scarcely less culpable, asserted the Kentuckian, than one who neglected or refused to use the power that was his to promote public prosperity. If such a one stood in the way of promoting the public good "his treachery was greatly aggravated." Point by point Clay took up the old, familiar argument of incidental powers. The authority to *establish* post offices and post roads meant the authority "to fix, to make firm, to build." The power to regulate commerce postulated, in his opinion, the power to construct canals. The defense argument, the plea for Western equality with the East, the demand for a more perfect Union, were arrayed in all the gorgeous panoply of rhetorical display. He exclaimed: —

All the powers of this Government should be interpreted in reference to its first, its best, its greatest object, the Union of these states . . . can the federative objects of this Government be attained but by the application of federative resources? . . . We must reject, as wholly incompatible with their [the Fathers] enlightened and beneficent intentions, that construction of these powers which would resuscitate all the debility and inefficiency of the ancient confederacy.

Randolph answered in bitter fashion. He commented sourly upon Clay's stand for strict construction in 1811 and his position now. The broad interpretation of the Constitution, said Randolph, reminded him of the German whose name was Fyerstein. This gentleman had had his name anglicized to Firestone, got by translation from that to Flint, from Flint to Pierre-à-Fusil, and from that to Peter Gun! The Virginian sneered at lawyers as word shufflers, and at Clay's powers as a grammarian, philologer, and critic.

Clay seized upon the advantage to allude, in terms of pathos, to his own irenic nature and advancing age. With deep humility he acknowledged his defects. "I know my deficiencies," he said. "I was born to no proud patrimonial estate. From my father I inherited only infancy, ignorance and indigence. . . ." But the effect of this was somewhat marred when Randolph, turning to William Winston Seaton, said in a stage whisper:

"The gentleman might continue the alliteration, and add insolence." [6]

Mutual friends poured oil on the wounds engendered by such attacks, and the argument was over. The survey bill passed, and Monroe signed it. But the vote in the House, one hundred and fifteen to eighty-six, was significant. New England and New York (which had built its own Erie Canal), opposed the bill strenuously; the South disapproved by a majority of eleven votes; the West voted solidly for the bill. Sectional cleavage was plainly marked, but the measure had given Clay an effective opportunity for championing one of the most heartfelt interests of the trans-Appalachian region. Within a month another opportunity arose to curry favor with the West and the industrial East as well.

The tariff of 1824 is generally regarded as the first truly protective bill in our history. It was not a high tariff, after all the amendments were in, but it was urged as a measure for protection, not for revenue, and it did bolster the duties on iron, hemp, woolens and cottons, wool and cotton bagging. An analysis of the vote on its passage in the House shows the commercial and planting states decisively hostile, and the manufacturing and grain-growing states strongly in favor of the bill.[7] Webster and Hayne, strange bed-fellows in view of later years, marshaled the forces against it in the House and Senate. Clay was its outstanding exponent, and just as Webster's arguments remained a classic with free traders, so Clay's reasoning furnished a basis for the protectionist dialectics of the Middle Period.

The Kentuckian based his appeal upon the need for home markets. Stressing the gloomy economic condition of the country, he pointed out the failure of Europe to take the surplus of American agricultural produce since the war, and demanded the "genuine American System" of building up our own in-

[6] *Annals of Cong.*, 18th Cong., 1st sess., 990f, 1021–1041, 1296–1313; W. C. Bruce, *John Randolph of Roanoke, 1773–1833*, 2 vols. (N.Y., 1922), Vol. I, p. 451, note *a*.

[7] F. J. Turner, *Rise of the New West* (N.Y., 1906), p. 242; F. W. Taussig, *The Tariff History of the United States* (N.Y., 1923), pp. 74–78.

dustry, both as a market for our agricultural output and as a source of domestic wealth production.

He labored to prove that the bill was not a burden upon one section for the benefit of another. Duties were paid only voluntarily, he asserted, for consumers could avoid them by abstaining from the use of the foreign article, and either buying the rival American fabric or engaging themselves in its production (!). Protection would also mean better and cheaper American goods than the foreign articles that were then being imported.

One by one the arguments of the free traders were taken up and answered with consummate skill. Clay denied that the revenue would be seriously injured, pointing to an excise tax as always available. The bill would not compel capital and labor into manufacturing, but would open up new fields of business for all who chose to enter. These new enterprises would only be auxiliaries to agriculture, and we would always remain an agricultural people. It was nonsensical to expect that unprotected industry here could compete with protected foreign industry. We could put aside protection when we had perfected our industrial arts, but not before.

In closing, he dwelt upon the advantages that the bill would bring to all sections, even the South, through increased markets and cheaper manufactured goods, and its beneficial effects upon the unity and independence of the Nation as a whole. "The cause," he said, "is the cause of the country and it must and will prevail." [8]

There were specious elements in some of his arguments, and his gloomy picture of the country's economic status was undoubtedly overdrawn, but the speech was, on the whole, able and compelling, as is shown by the constant references to it during the remainder of the debate.

The supposed interests of the manufacturers and grain growers, the weight of Clay's arguments and the catch phrase "American System" produced a narrow victory. The bill passed the House on April 16 by a vote of one hundred and seven to

[8] *Annals of Cong.*, 18th Cong., 1st sess., 1961–2001.

one hundred and two. One month later it ran the gantlet of the Senate by a margin of four votes and Monroe signed it, May 25, 1824. Clay had won prestige among the protectionists by his attitude, and could hope for their support in the presidential campaign of that year.

The election of 1824 was fought out under conditions which were ripe for party division. The national program of the leaders who had been dominating the Republican Party since the War Hawk days was beginning to lose something of its appeal. Sectional interests, cleavages over the tariff and internal improvements were becoming important. Even more significant was the vigorous stirring of the democratic spirit. That impulse in American political life, so closely associated with the frontier, had received fresh impetus from the hard times of the early 1820's. Monetary troubles, business and bank failures, the bank exactions enforced under existing laws, the difficulty of obtaining relief, all bred suspicion and distrust of existing institutions, and a desire for more effective popular control. This rising democratic tempest manifested itself in a variety of ways, and the increasing antipathy for caucus nominations, the development of local parties, political conventions and appeals to the people were omens of the wrath to come.

Monroe had been re-elected without a contest in 1820, but his second term was not more than well under way when a veritable flock of candidates for the succession put in their appearance. They represented different sections of the country, but all had their eyes fixed upon the national crown.

Adams, able and acidulous, Monroe's Secretary of State, was the favorite son of New England. Calhoun, ambitious, brilliant to the point of rashness, a patriot with something of the air of an arch-conspirator about him,[9] shared the field as a Southern candidate with a third member of the Cabinet, William Harris Crawford, a burly Georgian whose love of political management was equaled only by a devotion to table luxuries which, men were soon to say, had brought on his earthly doom. Out of the West came the impetuous Clay, exerting all of his policy

[9] Poore, *Reminiscences*, Vol. I, p. 64.

and charm to win the prize that seemed within his grasp. Out of the West, too, came Andrew Jackson, a commanding figure, tall and erect, the fighter and the leader proclaimed by every line of that powerful face, sharp-eyed, firm of mouth and jaw, with the deep brow surmounted by a crown of rumpled hair.

The jealousy and strife of the Cabinet rivals and Congressional factions made Monroe's second term a wilderness of intrigue. The ambitious bickerings of Crawford and Calhoun rent the Cabinet, while their friends warred in the South to gain advantage. Confusion was only worse confounded when Clay returned to the House and Jackson came to the Senate of the Eighteenth Congress, both busily seeking favor, while making hollow pretenses of friendship toward one another.

Secretary Adams looked with bitterness and chagrin upon intrigues and equivocations which his principles constrained him to shun. His only recourse was to offer foreign posts to his chief rivals, but these were politely refused, and the Puritan's casuistry was unavailing.

The campaign was in full blast by 1822, with nominations by state legislatures and popular mass meetings becoming the order of the day. Calhoun was a prominent contender until, his hopes finally blasted by a Jackson swing in Pennsylvania, he centered his attention upon the vice-presidency. Crawford's chances began to diminish when, in the fall of 1823, he was smitten by a paralytic stroke which kept him in seclusion during the remainder of the campaign, and from which he never completely recovered, either in body or in mind. But he struggled on, pinning his faith upon Virginia, his native state, and New York, where the suave and immaculate Martin Van Buren, a past master in the art of political intrigue, was exerting all his influence in the Georgian's behalf. To the very end, Crawford's candidacy was a factor which the other aspirants had to take into account.

Jackson's rivals had not regarded "Old Hickory" at first as a serious menace. He was fifty-five years of age, and it was thought that he was not of rugged physique. Adams even advised his own followers to support the Tennesseean for the vice-presidency, "a station in which the General could hang no one, and in which he would need to quarrel with no one. . . . It would afford an easy and dignified retirement to his old age." [10] The members of the Tennessee legislature put Jackson in nomination July 20, 1822, but Clay believed that it had been done either to produce division in the West or as an empty compliment to the General.

The hopes and expectations of my friends in the West will be, *you may rely absolutely upon it,* completely realized in this quarter [Clay wrote to Porter]. In short, my dear Sir, without travelling over the whole ground, I think I may take upon myself to assert, with the greatest confidence, that all the Western states to the Gulph of Mexico, Alabama inclusive, will be cordially united in my support.[11]

But Jackson's campaign was skillfully conducted on a program calculated to appeal to all sections. He was portrayed as brave, but unassuming; the people's hero; a man who hated the undemocratic caucus system of nomination and worshiped at the shrine of popular rule. His adherents exalted him as the one great man of the people.

The General was undoubtedly possessed of bravery, a stately kind of courtesy, and shrewd political foresight, but his early career had scarcely measured up to the democratic ideal. A frontiersman, he typified the vices as well as the virtues of that region, and the former included living up to the letter of the law without too much regard for its spirit. He had engaged in land speculation, in his official capacity, in connection with the Chickasaw treaty of 1818, and his conduct during the negotiation of that treaty had been characterized by arrogance and shady dealing. In 1822–1823 he befriended Patrick Darby, a lawyer of very questionable reputation, and together they fought unsuccessfully to eliminate the Tennessee statute on limitations, which protected land occupiers of long standing from being evicted by absentee claimants. Already he had begun his long political warfare against William Carroll, who was the real father of the democratic movement in Tennessee

[10] Adams, *Memoirs,* Vol. VI, p. 333; Turner, *Rise of the New West,* p. 251.
[11] Porter Collection, Clay to Porter (confidential), Aug. 10, Oct. 22, 1822.

during the 1820's and 1830's. The Hero's closest advisers in his own state, William B. Lewis, John H. Eaton and John Overton, were interested in politics for reasons primarily selfish.[12] Old Hickory was an opportunist, thoroughly skillful at the game of playing safe. He congratulated Monroe on his veto of the Cumberland Road bill in 1822, but in 1824 he voted in the Senate for internal improvements. His stand on the tariff of that year classified him as a protectionist, but in April he qualified his position by announcing that he was for a "judicious" tariff, an utterance which made Clay shrug his shoulders, toss his head and explode, "Well, by ——, I am in favor of an injudicious tariff!"[13] Such tactics helped to make the military idol a formidable aspirant for the President's Palace.

Clay was unanimously nominated for President by the members of the Kentucky legislature on November 18, 1822. The Missouri assembly also chose him as its standardbearer, and on January 3, 1823, a partial caucus of the Ohio assembly gave him its approval.[14] His confidence in Western backing appeared to be well-founded. To hold this advantage and to gain support in the East, which he believed could be done by stressing his advocacy of the tariff and internal improvements, became the object of a voluminous correspondence that was carried on with friends in a majority of the states of the Union.

Adams had strength in the Northwest, and there is a con-

[12] Abernethy, *Frontier to Plantation*, pp. 241, 273–276, 262–266, 232–235. See also, by the same author, "Andrew Jackson and the Rise of Southwestern Democracy," in *Amer. Hist. Rev.*, Vol. XXXIII (Oct. 1927), pp. 64–77.

[13] Martin Van Buren, *The Autobiography of Martin Van Buren*, John C. Fitzpatrick, ed. (Wash., 1920), p. 240. *Cf.* Adams, *Memoirs*, Vol. VI, p. 258, and T. P. Abernethy, *The Formative Period in Alabama, 1815–1828* (Montgomery, 1922), pp. 106–107.

[14] *Niles' Register*, Vol. XXIII, pp. 245, 342; E. H. Roseboom, "Ohio in the Presidential Election of 1824," in *Ohio Arch. and Hist. Quart.*, Vol. XXV (April 1917), pp. 170–171. Thomas Hart Benton, Mrs. Clay's cousin, worked for Clay in Missouri. In Ohio the opponents of the caucus, over forty per cent of the assembly, withdrew. Clay received fifty votes, De Witt Clinton five, Adams one and Calhoun one.

siderable amount of circumstantial evidence to show that Clay took an active part in stirring up Western animosity against the New Englander. In the winter of 1821–1822, Clay intimated to Ninian Edwards that he intended to move against Adams on the Mississippi and Newfoundland fisheries question.[15] During the following summer, Jonathan Russell renewed the quarrel with Adams that had originated at Ghent over this question, and the dour Secretary of State confided to his diary that Clay was urging on his "jackal." [16] More than this, Amos Kendall, then a Clay man and editor of the influential *Argus of Western America* at Frankfort, was doing political writing for Clay in 1822 which was under cover, for Kendall suggested that, as his own hand was well known, the material should be copied before it was sent out.[17] Kendall asserted, later, that Clay had employed him to write a series of letters signed "Wayne," attacking Adams and accusing him of being hostile to the West and to internal improvements, and that Clay had these distributed in Ohio during 1822. Testimony was given under oath in the Kentucky legislature in 1828 that Clay had paid one hundred dollars to William Tanner, a printer, for the republication of certain letters by Kendall which attacked Adams on the Ghent negotiations, and this testimony was never refuted.[18]

But Adams was no mean opponent. Although morally certain that Clay was instigating the attack, he decided to direct his reply chiefly to Russell. *The Duplicate Letters, the Fisheries and the Mississippi* demolished that gentleman so completely and effectively that to "Jonathan Russell" a man passed into a proverb in New England. Clay was mentioned more than once in this rejoinder, but the Kentuckian evinced no desire to follow his erstwhile henchman into the abyss. He wrote to Russell, before reading the *Duplicate Letters*, that

[15] Adams, *Memoirs*, Vol. VI, p. 263.
[16] *Ibid.*, Vol. VI, p. 49.
[17] Clay Papers, III, Kendall to Clay, June 20, 1822.
[18] *Argus*, Feb. 20, July 9, 16, 1828; Adams, *Memoirs*, Vol. VI, p. 49; *United States Telegraph, Extra*, Vol. I, No. 1, transcript of proceedings before the Kentucky legislature, Jan. 31, Feb. 1, 1828.

Russell was undoubtedly in the right, but at the same time, requested his friend not to call upon him for support.[19] Feeling that Adams' strictures made some kind of response necessary, Clay published, toward the close of the year 1822, a letter in which he stated that he had found some errors of fact in Adams' book, and that he would lay his own narrative of the Ghent negotiations before the public at some "more propitious" time. Adams replied, signifying his readiness for any revelations that might be made. He had purposely spared Clay so far, he told Plumer, but the Kentuckian, too, was vulnerable, and if he "came out," he would receive as severe a dressing as had been given to Russell.[20]

Harry of the West was baffled. He disliked the way Adams had used him, he wrote to Porter, and felt justified in the public observations he had made, but, after reading Adams' book, he felt that Russell was in the wrong.[21] It is said that a friend asked Clay when he proposed to reopen the discussion. "Never!" he replied emphatically. "A man must be a born fool who voluntarily engages in a controversy with Mr. Adams on a question of fact. I doubt whether he was ever mistaken in his life. And then, if he happens to be in doubt about anything, he has his inevitable diary, in which he has recorded everything that has occurred since the adoption of the Federal Constitution."[22] Whether or not this tale is true, the quarrel was never renewed.

As the campaign developed, the bitterest charges and counter-charges were made by the partisans of all the candidates. Adams was accused of a whole category of sins, ranging from slavery-hating to slovenliness. The Crawfordites attacked Calhoun's record as Secretary of War and sought to drive him in disgrace from public life, while the latter's followers retorted in kind upon the Secretary of the Treasury. Jackson was branded a tyrant, a sinister figure, full of unbridled passions.

[19] Clay Papers, III, Clay to Russell, July 9, 1822; Porter Collection, Clay to Porter, Feb. —, 1823.

[20] Brown, *Missouri Compromises*, p. 81.

[21] Porter Collection, Clay to Porter, Feb. 4, 1823.

[22] "Recollections of an Old Stager," in *Harper's Magazine*, Vol. XLVII (July 1873), pp. 254–257.

Clay was denounced in the most violent manner. His private morals were questioned. He had been an enemy of Western prosperity when he opposed at Ghent the opening of the Mississippi to British trade. His advocacy of South American recognition had led us perilously close to the brink of war with the Holy Alliance. A coalition between Clay and Crawford was whispered on the street corners, and Clay's withdrawal from the race was industriously reported.[23]

At the same time, attempts at coalition were made on behalf of all the candidates. In Pennsylvania, Jackson rode to a brilliant victory in the state convention of March 6, 1824, and Calhoun was nominated for Vice-President, a conclusion that may have been prearranged. In many places throughout the South,

> John Quincy Adams,
> Who can write,
> And Andrew Jackson,
> Who can fight,

became the favorite ticket.[24] All kinds of attempts were made at combinations against Crawford, and Clay-Adams and Clay-Crawford combines were mooted. These schemes, primarily local in character, reflected the confusion of politics.

But whatever his supporters might do under the pressure of local political exigencies, the Kentuckian held himself resolutely aloof from bargains. One of his confidential letters to Porter expressed his attitude in clear though grandiloquent style.

There is one point on which I am extremely solicitous that my friends should uniformly be as explicit as I am firmly resolved, and that is, that I shall participate in no intrigues, enter into no arrangements, have no understandings with others formal or informal, make no pledges or promises. I am determined, if elected, to enter the office unmanacled, free to promote the interest of our Common country with the utmost

---

[23] Philo Jackson, *The Presidential Election* (Frankfort, 1824); Roseboom, *op. et loc. cit.*, pp. 196–200; *National Intelligencer*, May 3, 1824.
[24] McMaster, *op. cit.*, Vol. V, p. 68.

of my exertions, and at liberty to command the best & most faithful public servants. If not elected, cheerfully acquiescing in the better choice which, in that event, will have been made, I will have the satisfaction of preserving my hands unsullied, my heart uncorrupted & my conscience perfectly pure.[25]

The Kentuckian's weakness lay in the fact that, as primarily a Western candidate, he had to contend with a powerful foe in his own section. Also he had no military record and would adopt no democratic pose, factors which were gaining ground daily for Jackson. Clay's letters show his hope that, by appealing to nationalist sentiment, and championing the tariff and internal improvements, he could hold the West to his standard, get New York, and gain strength elsewhere. He did not comprehend the significance of the democratic movement which was making Jackson its idol. His optimism persuaded him that he was holding a solid block of Western states, even when the drift to Jackson was becoming apparent there,[26] and curiously enough, in the face of increasing popular opposition to caucus nominations, he did not come out against such action by the members of Congress. His position, and that of his friends, was rather one of aloofness, with an expressed willingness to participate if the caucus were generally attended. In such a case, he believed that he would be chosen, "for the friends of *all* the candidates would sooner unite on me than on any other." [27] But the Crawford rump caucus of February 14, 1824, attended by only sixty-six of the two hundred and sixteen Republicans in Congress, was "silly, not to say wicked."

[25] Porter Collection, Clay to Porter, Feb. 2, 1823 (confidential). He repeated this, in substance, in a letter to Porter written on the following day, and in a letter to J. S. Johnston, June 15, 1824. — J. S. Johnston Collection (Pa. Hist. Soc.), Clay to Johnston (confidential).

[26] Porter Collection, Clay to Porter, Jan. 31, 1824.

[27] *Ibid.*, Clay to Porter, Nov. 11, Dec. 24, 1823, Feb. 4, 1824. *Cf.* Adams, *Memoirs*, Vol. VI, p. 239. It has always been assumed that Clay's friends actively opposed a Congressional caucus, but Clay asserts that they did not. "They have constantly said secure a general attendance and we will go, but we will not go to a Cabal, to a factious assemblage." It was only when it became apparent that the Crawford forces would caucus alone that he characterized them as "desperate and despondent." — Clay to Porter, Feb. 4, 1824.

As a matter of fact, it was the fatal blow to the Georgian's wavering chances.

Almost until the very end, Clay kept his courage and his hopes. Crawford's friends tried to negotiate with the Kentuckian's supporters toward the close of January, 1824, and were repulsed. Clay felt, after the caucus fiasco, that the Georgian's followers, particularly in Virginia, would come over to the right side.[28] He longed for encouragement from New York, where for two years he had been trying to spur his friends to Herculean efforts. There was no satisfaction to be derived from Van Buren's Albany Regency, which was for Crawford. Adams, too, had powerful support there. But Clay hoped against hope that New York could be saved. The pressure was great, and about the first of April, 1824, he wrote to Porter the following "strictly confidential" letter: —

The affair of the Vice Presidency becomes one of much interest, as time elapses. My friends are desirous of running some one from your state. Mr. Thompson, yourself and Mr. Young have been thought of. Your unfortunate deafness forms an objection to you, and besides there is another place in which I think you can render more service to the public. Will you turn this matter over in your mind, and advise us? And I pray you to throw this note into the fire. What I have said in respect to yourself is more than I have ever said in relation to any other person whatever. I trust I need not apologize to you for saying it. *You* can never misconceive the *purity* of *my* motives.[29]

Porter remained noncommittal about the honor, and Nathan Sanford of New York was finally placed on the ticket with Clay.

As the fall wore on, the Kentuckian's hopes began to fade. Doggedly, he clung to the possibility of Crawford's withdrawal, which, he was confident, would give him Virginia. "My friends," he wrote to Porter, "are unalterably determined to persevere in support of me to the last," and at the beginning of September he still claimed to be confident of six

[28] Porter Collection, Clay to Porter, April 3, 1824; *Cf.* Adams, *Memoirs*, Vol. VI, p. 315, and J. S. Johnston Collection, Clay to Johnston, June 21, 1824.

[29] Porter Collection.

Western states, and to have "most encouraging intelligence" from Rhode Island, New Jersey, and part of Maryland. But the buoyant confidence of victory was gone, and in his letters there appeared now and then a querulous note, in complaints that he was not sufficiently before the public eye and had no newspaper support in the large cities.[30]

There was a last attempt by Crawford men at a coalition that would make Clay Vice-President. According to Adams and Plumer, Clay had sought that office in 1820. Now the Virginia Crawfordites played with the idea of nominating him without his consent. Van Buren, if not a party to the plot, at least knew of it. The plan fell through, even though the Kentuckian expressed to his friends a coy willingness to take the post, if it came to him by "public" demand and without seeking on his part. And he was obviously disappointed, after losing out in the election, that the plan had failed to fructify in Virginia.[31]

New York became at last the crucial point, and there political intrigue flourished hotly. The Regency stood stoutly for Crawford, and the Georgian appeared to be certain of the state. But Van Buren's organization made two blunders which heartened the opposition. The removal of De Witt Clinton from his office as Canal Commissioner, and the refusal to meet the demand that the electors be chosen by the people, aroused great popular indignation. When the legislature met to choose the presidential electors, a People's Party, sponsored by the friends of Adams and Clay, had already begun a vigorous campaign that was destined to defeat the Regency and make Clinton Governor. Crawford support in the legislature began to weaken.

The New York house and senate each chose an electoral ticket by majority vote. If the lists so chosen coincided, no

[30] Porter Collection, Clay to Porter, Sept. 2, 1824; J. S. Johnston Collection, Clay to Johnston, Aug. 31, Sept. 10, 19, Oct. 2, 1824.

[31] Van Buren Papers (Lib. of Cong., Mss. Div.), VI, Joseph Gales, Jr. to Van Buren, Oct. 17, 19, 1824, Asbury Dickins to Van Buren, Oct. 28, 1824; Colton, *Correspondence*, pp. 103, 107, Clay to Johnston, Sept. 10, 1824, Clay to Brooke, Dec. 5, 1824; Gallatin, *Writings*, Vol. II, pp. 297–300; Ambler, *op. cit.*, pp. 94–97.

further action was necessary, other than a formal declaration of the result.. If they differed, a joint ballot was required, confined to the names on the two lists. Crawford had a majority in the senate and the Crawford list was chosen there. The Adams men were most numerous in the house, although Crawford and Clay each had strong support. There, after several days of balloting and intriguing, the Crawford men finally voted for the Adams list, apparently believing that, in the joint ballot, the Clay men would go for Crawford rather than for Adams.[32] The joint ballot remained to be taken.

The Regency had put six "moderate" Clay men on the senate ticket, but this was not sufficient to bring Clay's supporters into alignment with the Crawfordites. Clay had given tacit consent to a coalition with Adams in the New York legislature, as early as September 1824,[33] and Porter, who was managing his campaign, told him that if a compromise were made it would probably be with the friends of Adams.[34]

At this juncture, another figure appeared upon the scene. Thurlow Weed, a Rochester editor, was just beginning to win his political spurs. Tall and robust, suave and genial, a shrewd judge of human nature, Weed united a capacity for inspiring confidence with a perfect readiness to play the political game with the weapons that were at hand. He was only twenty-six years old when he came to Albany that fall, to lobby for a Rochester bank charter, but he was a fervent Adams man and the friends of the New Englander welcomed him.

Weed was one of the principal figures in the frenzied negotiations that now ensued between the Adams and Clay leaders. The latter estimated that Clay must receive seven electoral votes in New York to keep him in the running if the election

[32] C. H. Rammelkamp, "The Campaign of 1824 in New York," in *Amer. Hist. Assoc. Report* (1904), pp. 177f; *Cf.* Van Buren Papers, VI, Van Buren to Crawford, Nov. 17, 1824 (draft).

[33] Porter Collection, Clay to Porter, Sept. 2, 1824. He wrote that he had heard of the plan of coalition with the Adams men, and a division of the electoral vote. He would not interfere, one way or the other, he said, but then, after doubting its practicality, added: "If your State shd. prefer either of two Candidates to a third, I do not know that it might not be for its interest to divide the vote between those two, as it could thereby certainly secure the election of one of them."

[34] Clay Papers, IV, Porter to Clay, Oct. 6, 1824.

went into the House of Representatives. These were guaranteed by the Adams men, and a split ticket was concocted for the joint ballot. The plan succeeded, and twenty-five Adams, seven Clay, and four Crawford electors were chosen.[35]

It looked like a fair bargain, and, had it held, Clay would have tied Crawford for third place in the electoral college, and without doubt his name would have gone before the House. But the evidence of trickery is strong, for when the electors met in December, Clay had lost three of his votes. The New York count stood: Adams twenty-six, Crawford five, Clay four, and Jackson one. The Adams group had not kept its word.

In vain did Weed seek to explain this away. His *Autobiography* states that the pledge of seven Clay votes was made conditional on Clay's carrying Louisiana, and that failure to do this absolved them. Louisiana did go for Jackson, which Clay explained by the failure of two of his supporters to reach the capital in time, the injury of two others who were overturned in a gig and unable to attend, and three who deserted on account of "false rumors." But the New York electors voted in ignorance of Louisiana's decision.[36]

The vote in the national election stood, finally: Jackson ninety-nine, Adams eighty-four, Crawford forty-one and Clay thirty-seven. The latter had carried only Kentucky, Missouri and Ohio. No candidate had a majority, and in consequence the election went to the House of Representatives, which was confined in its selection to the first three. Clay's hope of getting into the House was dashed to earth.[37]

---

[35] T. Weed, *Autobiography of Thurlow Weed*, 2 vols. (Boston, 1883), Vol. I, pp. 122–127; Rammelkamp, *op. et loc. cit.*, pp. 198–200; DeAlva S. Alexander, *A Political History of the State of New York*, 3 vols. (N.Y., 1906–1909), Vol. I, p. 337. *Cf.* Clay's letter to Francis Brooke, Nov. 17, 1824, in Colton, *Correspondence*, pp. 104–106.

[36] Weed, *Autobiography*, Vol. I, pp. 128–129; Porter Collection, Clay to Porter, Dec. 7, 26, 1824; *N.Y. American*, Dec. 8, 1824; Turner, *Rise of the New West*, p. 260. Weed himself admitted that seven New York votes for Clay could hardly have been found had Louisiana gone for the Kentuckian.

[37] E. Stanwood, *A History of the Presidency* (Boston, 1898), pp. 134–136. Clay stood third in the popular vote, but that was light and incomplete, six of the states electing by their legislatures. It gives no real indication of the popular will.

For the first time, a serious personal defeat had come to Harry of the West. The War of 1812 had been a bitter disillusionment, but, despite the meager results, it had not checked his climb to favor and preferment. For years he had held a prominent place in the nation's councils, and it was only natural that he should have begun to cherish visions of the highest public office in the land. And now, out of four candidates, including a man whose health was shattered beyond repair, he was the fourth and last. The first attempt to reach the glittering prize had failed. The first rebuff had been given to that blinding ambition which was to grow and grow, sending him, like some modern Tantalus, on the never-ending quest for a cup that would be forever dashed from his lips.

But to Clay, defeat, though always bitter, was never crushing, for he was not one to seek within himself the causes of disaster. The disappointment was hard to bear, but he assumed a brave demeanor. His mood was one of cheerful acquiescence, he told one friend, and he wrote to another that "I laugh off and bear with unaffected fortitude our defeat." His character, he felt, had been "elevated by the whole canvas." [38] Defeat had been due to "the discouragement of my friends — the power of the Atlantic press — the influence of governmental patronage — the fabrication of tales of my being withdrawn, propagated to date so as to accomplish their object before they could be contradicted. . . . I only wish," he concluded, "that I could have been spared such a painful duty as that will be of deciding between the persons who are presented to the choice of the H. of R." [39]

The duty was undoubtedly painful, but the consequences of performing it were to be productive of far greater agony.

[38] Porter Collection, Clay to Porter, Dec. 26, 1824; Colton, *Correspondence*, p. 107, Clay to Brooke, Dec. 5, 22, 1824.
[39] Porter Collection, Clay to Porter, Dec. 7, 1824.

CHAPTER XI

"THE JUDAS OF THE WEST"

CLAY came to Washington at the beginning of December, 1824, and took lodgings on Ninth Street. His wife remained at Ashland, pleading her long absence from society and the need for thrift against his wish for her company.[1] Lucretia might have been a real solace to him during that strife-ridden winter.

As Speaker, he welcomed Lafayette, who had been invited by the Government to visit the United States, and had made a triumphal tour of the country before Congress assembled. The nation's guest was formally received by the House at one o'clock on the afternoon of December 10. The Senators, and others specially invited, crowded the chamber as Clay greeted the famous man with a handsome tribute. Clay had carried on a correspondence with the sixty-seven-year-old liberal ever since the Ghent negotiations, and when the House adjourned he descended from the chair, and "most affectionately saluted the General. His example was followed by the members of the House, individually, and some time was spent in this agreeable manner before the General retired."[2]

Congress later voted Lafayette a gift of two hundred thousand dollars and a township of land, generosity that staggered even Clay.[3]

But the all important business of the session, the struggle that was to convulse Washington during the winter months, was the election of a President. Clay was the leader of the

---

[1] *National Intelligencer*, Dec. 4, 1824; Clay Papers, V, Clay to James Brown, Jan. 23, 1825.

[2] *Reg. of Deb.*, 18th Cong., 2d sess., 3–4. Lafayette visited Ashland that summer, and they kept up their correspondence until his death in 1834. For his visit to Ashland, see the *Kentucky Reporter*, May 23, 1825.

[3] Adams, *Memoirs*, Vol. VI, p. 440.

West in the House. Three Western states had given him their electoral votes, and it was generally felt that his influence would be the decisive factor in the choice.[4] Bargain and intrigue were in the air. The friends of all three candidates rushed to court the Kentuckian's favor and to insinuate attractive rewards, while his own friends appear to have been active in attempting to discover what he could obtain as a recompense for his support. Clay's situation was exceedingly delicate, but it was not without its humorous side.

My position in relation to the three returned candidates [he wrote to his friend, Francis Preston Blair] is singular enough and often to me very amusing — In the first place they all believe that my friends have the power of deciding the question and then that I have the power of controling my friends — acting upon this supposition, in the same hours, I am sometimes touched gently on the shoulders by a friend (for example) of Genl. Jackson who will thus address me — "My Dear Sir, all my dependence is upon you — don't disappoint us — you know our partiality was for you next to the Hero; and how much we want a Western President" — Immediately after a friend of Mr. Crawford will accost me — "the hopes of the Republican Party are concentrated on you — for Gods sake preserve it, if you had been returned, instead of Mr. Crawford every man of us would have supported you to the last hour — We consider him and you as the only genuine Republican candidates" — Next a friend of Mr. Adams comes "with tears in his eyes"[5] "Sir Mr. Adams has always had the greatest respect for you and admiration of your talents — There is no station to which you are not equal — most undoubtedly you were the second choice of New England and I pray you to consider seriously whether the public good and your own future interests do not point most distinctly to the choice which you ought to make"! How can one withstand all the disinterested homage and kindness. Really the friends of all three gentlemen are so very courteous and affectionate that I sometimes almost wish that it was in my power to accommodate each of them. . . .[6]

[4] Plumer wrote to his father, Dec. 16, 1824: "It is in fact very much in Clay's power to make the President." — Brown, *Missouri Compromises*, p. 123.

[5] A play upon Adams' affliction of watery eyes. — *Cf.* Adams, *Memoirs*, Vol. VI, p. 461.

[6] Collection of Mrs. Jouett Taylor Cannon, Clay to Blair, Jan. 8, 1825. This is a copy of the original, made by F. P. Blair. There is another copy

But behind such word play, the Kentuckian had devoted much serious thought to the choice that he had to make.

Crawford's personal condition, if nothing else, put him out of the running in Clay's mind. The Georgian's health had improved during the winter of 1823–1824, but in April he had suffered a relapse, the effects of which had badly limited his activities during the whole summer. Besides this, the Western leader could scarcely have voted for a man who represented Southern hostility to the tariff and internal improvements.[7]

Jackson's health, on the other hand, was good, and his views on the tariff and improvements could be interpreted as harmonizing with the views of the West. Such reasoning might well justify the Kentuckian in going for the candidate from the neighboring state of Tennessee.

Clay's previous relations with the Hero had been somewhat checkered. His acquaintance with Jackson had begun in the fall of 1815, at Washington. It was marked by cordiality on both sides, and Jackson promised to spend a week of the following summer at Ashland. He did not do so, writing a letter of regret. They next met in Washington, at the time when Clay was denouncing the General in the debate on the Seminole war. Clay called on the Hero, but the call was not returned.

Another meeting came in the following summer. Jackson accompanied Monroe on his Western tour, and the two men called on Mrs. Clay at Ashland and were given refreshments. Clay, meanwhile, was returning from a trip to Louisiana, and one July morning, after breakfast, as he was sitting at the door of a tavern in the little village of Lebanon, Kentucky, Jackson and his suite came up. As the General mounted the steps, Clay rose and spoke, but the salutation was barely returned.

in the Clay Papers which has some minor variations, the principal one being in the phrase "relation to the friends of the three returned candidates." Colton, *Correspondence*, pp. 108–109, agrees with the copy in the Clay Collection, which he probably used.

[7] *Ibid.*, Clay Papers, V, Porter to Clay, Jan. 14, 1825, X, Trimble to Watkins, Aug. 12, 1827; Brown, *Missouri Compromises*, p. 129; Porter Collection, Clay to Porter, Jan. 28, 1825. Clay seems to have agreed with Porter that Crawford tended toward an unsavory radicalism.

He went into the front room a few minutes later, but Jackson, who sat reading a newspaper, did not look up.[8]

They did not meet again until the session of 1823–1824, when Jackson was in the Senate and they were rivals for the presidency. Then some of the members from Tennessee undertook a reconciliation. They came to Clay, and explained that Jackson's brusqueness at Lebanon had been due to an ailment "which rendered necessary a quick retirement to the back yard." [9] The Kentuckian said that he saw nothing to prevent good relations and was assured that Jackson felt the same way. A dinner was arranged at Mrs. Claxton's, on Capitol Hill, where most of the Tennessee delegation boarded. The camaraderie about that festive board was doubtless somewhat hollow, but Jackson and Eaton took Clay home from this affair, and thereafter they dined with one another several times.[10] They exchanged calls, early in the following session, but met infrequently.[11] Amicable relations continued to exist, although the two men scarcely had become bosom companions. The embers of jealousy and dislike were smouldering, ready to burst into flame.

There were many reasons why Clay should not support Jackson. The Kentuckian was a shrewd and ambitious politician. He must have seen that there would be small advantage obtained from throwing his influence to his rival in the West. Adams, on the other hand, had no great personal popularity, and the growth of tariff sentiment in the North might well

[8] This account is based on Clay's letter to J. S. Johnston (Pa. Hist. Soc.), Oct. 6, 1827. Clay gave a sketch of his early relations with Jackson in a speech before the Senate, Feb. 19, 1838. In that he asserts that the reconciliation took place in the fall of 1824, but this is undoubtedly a mistake. See Mallory, *op. cit.*, Vol. II, pp. 316–317.

[9] Jackson said, in 1844, that he refused to shake hands with Clay at Lebanon because of Clay's speech on the Seminole war. — W. A. Butler, *A Retrospect of Forty Years* (N.Y., 1911), pp. 125–126.

[10] See Adams, *Memoirs*, Vol. VI, p. 258, for his account of Clay's presence at Jackson's birthday dinner, March 15, 1824.

[11] Clay remembered distinctly, however, that at a dinner given by the Russian Minister, December 24, 1824, he, Clay, had expressed the hope that the cause of internal improvements would flourish if Jackson were elected, and the latter had answered that it was merely a question of how much revenue could be appropriated to the object. — Clay to Johnston, Oct. 6, 1827.

mean that Clay could gain a powerful hold there by supporting New England's candidate. Such a move would augur well
for his chances in the succession.[12] There was also the question
of public policies. The Administration's recognition of the
South American republics and the famous warning to Europeans in December of 1823 had placed Adams in general harmony with Clay's ideas on foreign affairs: both men favored
internal improvements at national expense, and both were
agreed in principle upon protection. Finally, Adams had a long
and distinguished record of public service, and was an adminis-
trator of proven worth, while Jackson's record as Governor
of Florida Territory in 1821 cast grave doubts upon his fitness
for high public station.[13]

Clay did not openly state such considerations. His letter
justified the choice of Adams on the ground that he was the
lesser of two evils, and based objections to Jackson principally upon a general allegation of Jackson's lack of fitness,
and the perils inherent in stimulating martial ardor in a republic. There was danger, he wrote to Blair, in elevating a
military chieftain, "of whom I cannot believe that killing 2500
Englishmen at New Orleans qualifies for the various, difficult and complicated duties of the Chief Magistracy." [14]

There is excellent evidence to show that Clay intended to
vote for Adams, even before he left Kentucky. John J. Crittenden and Colonel James Davidson, the state treasurer of Kentucky, heard Clay assert that he could not vote for Jackson
in any event. This was in Kentucky, probably at Frankfort, in
the fall of 1824.[15] Clay told Francis P. Blair, about the same
time, that if the election went into the House, he should vote

[12] Porter wrote to Clay, analyzing the candidates to Adams' advantage,
and saying, among other things, that Adams' election now would be most
propitious to Clay's election "four years hence." Clay replied that he had
reached the same general conclusions about the candidates "by a similar
train of reasoning." — Clay Papers, V, Porter to Clay, Jan. 14, 1825;
Porter Collection, Clay to Porter, Jan. 28, 1825.

[13] Bassett, op. cit., pp. 294–318.

[14] Cannon Collection, Clay to Blair, Jan. 29, 1825. Copy by Blair.

[15] Crittenden Papers (Duke Univ.), Crittenden to Clay, Sept. 3, 1827;
Clay Papers, X, James Davidson to Clay, Oct. 20, 1827. See also Clay
Papers, XII, C. S. Todd to Clay, Feb. 18, 1828, and the National In-
telligencer, April 5, 1828, statement by Wm. Plumer, Jr.

for Adams in preference to Jackson, and Blair gave a statement to that effect after he had broken with Clay politically.[16]
The Kentuckian was in Washington by December 4, 1824.
Early in that month he told Thomas Hart Benton that he intended to vote for Adams, and during the latter part of December he made a similar statement to Lafayette.[17]

But later events appear to indicate that, though he had
crossed the Rubicon, he had not burned his bridges behind
him. Strong as his determination appears to have been, and
freely expressed in private, it was only natural to see how the
ground lay before committing himself directly to Adams.

All of the leaders had "friends," quasi-managers, who
bustled about in the interest of their favorites, and one of
Clay's intimates, who lodged in the same house with him,
acted in that capacity. This was the jovial Robert P. Letcher,
member of Congress from Kentucky. Letcher began coming to
Adams about the middle of December, telling him about political conditions in Kentucky and talking in general terms
about the approaching election. On December 17 he told Adams in some detail about the growing Jackson strength in
Kentucky, and the possibility of instructions from the legislature to vote for Jackson. Then he announced that Clay had expressed a wish to go in harmony with his own friends, which
Letcher interpreted as a wish that his friends should go in
harmony with him. Next he wanted to know Adams' attitude
toward Clay. Adams said he felt no hostility, and was assured
in turn that Clay had no hostile feelings toward him. Letcher
made no propositions and professed no authority from Clay,
but the drift of his talk, Adams noted, was "that Clay would
willingly support me if he could thereby serve himself, and
the substance of his *meaning* was, that if Clay's friends could
know that he would have a prominent share in the Adminis-

[16] Crittenden Papers, Crittenden to Clay, Nov. 15, 1827; Clay Papers,
XI, Blair to Clay, Dec. 31, 1827. *Cf.* Clay Papers, X, David Trimble to
Tobias Watkins, Aug. 12, 1827.

[17] *National Intelligencer*, Jan. 22, 1828; *Kentucky Reporter*, Feb. 6, 1828.
These publish Benton's letter which was written December 7 or 9, 1827.
Benton, *op. cit.*, Vol. I, p. 48; Clay Papers, X, Lafayette to Clay, Oct. 10,
1827, James Barbour to ———, Aug. 14, 1827.

tration, that might induce them to vote for me, even in the face of instructions." [18] Another conversation took place December 23, in which Letcher stressed the importance of Adams' being elected on the first House ballot, and seemed anxious to convince Adams that he might receive the Kentucky vote. Adams felt that Letcher was moving for Clay, and at the end of his notation concerning this conversation, he put the famous phrase *"Incedo super ignes."* Walking over fires was certainly fraught with danger. The New Englander was suspicious, and told Plumer that Clay's friends were trying to get the credit for President-making, with a view to putting Clay up as the next President. [19]

On New Year's Day, Letcher called again. He assured Adams that the Kentucky delegation would certainly vote for him, and spoke of the concern felt by some of its members over the lack of harmony between Clay and Adams. Would the latter have some conversation with Clay? Adams said that he would.

That night Adams and Clay sat beside one another, apparently on the best of terms, at a dinner given by the members of Congress for Lafayette. During the course of the meal, the Kentuckian whispered to Adams that he wanted to have a private and confidential conversation with him in a few days, and to this Adams agreed. It was a rather weighty straw, and William Plumer, Jr., one of Adams' confidants, wrote to his father that Ohio, Kentucky, Missouri and Maryland were lined up to go as Clay directed, and that he, Plumer, was certain that they were going for Adams. [20]

A week went by. Then, on the eve of his visit to Adams, Clay wrote the famous letter to Blair. In this, after the jocose comments on those who courted his favor, he dismissed Crawford on account of his health and Jackson because of the danger that lay in stimulating "the military spirit." The Kentuckian

[18] Adams, *Memoirs*, Vol. VI, pp. 446–447.
[19] *Ibid.*, Vol. VI, pp. 452–453; Brown, *Missouri Compromises*, pp. 123–124.
[20] Brown, *Missouri Compromises*, pp. 126–129. *Cf.* Jackson, *Correspondence*, Vol. III, p. 273, Jackson to John Coffee, Jan. 6, 1825.

would support Adams as "a choice of evils." He attached great weight to the fact that a majority of the Ohio delegation had a decided preference for the New Englander. For Kentucky to oppose him would only have the result of dividing "our friends," and even so Adams would probably be elected, for he was believed to be the second choice of three of the four Crawford states. "We are beginning," said Clay, "to think seriously of the choice which we must finally make. . . . I am inclined to think that nearly three fourths of our delegation have yielded to the influence of these views and will vote for Mr. Adams — My friends entertain the belief that their kind wishes towards me will in the end be more likely to be accomplished by so bestowing their votes." He had entreated them, however, to think only of the public good. "If I know myself, that alone has determined me." In conclusion, there was a request that the letter be shown only to Crittenden.[21]

Within twenty-four hours after this letter, so eloquent of its author's hopes and fears, had been dispatched to Blair, Clay paid his call on Adams. In a three-hour conversation they went over their past differences, their present views, and their expectations for the future. According to Adams, Clay gave the impression that, because of his recent candidacy, and because he wished to predispose his friends to an objective and impartial choice, he had so far maintained a neutral position. "He wished me, as far as I might think proper, to satisfy him with regard to some principles of great public importance, but without any personal considerations for himself." Then, presumably after Adams' reply, Clay stated that he would come out for Adams, although he wished to take his own time about it. Adams retailed this to Plumer, who wrote solemnly to his father: "I did not think it decorous to enquire more particularly — nor did Mr. Adams seem disposed to say anything further of what passed between them." [22]

[21] Blair, in reply to this letter, said: "I have no doubt that Adams is the safest choice, therefore the best." — Clay Papers, V, Blair to Clay, Jan. 24, 1825. Crittenden hoped that Jackson would be elected. — Crittenden Papers (Duke Univ.), Crittenden to Richard K. Call, Jan. 8, 1825.

[22] Adams, *Memoirs*, Vol. VI, pp. 464–465; Brown, *Missouri Compromises*, pp. 130–133.

The whole situation was calculated to arouse suspicion, but there is absolutely no reason to believe that any bargain had been struck which was more specific than an *entente cordiale*. Clay wrote to his brother-in-law, two weeks later: —

I can tell you nothing of the formation of the new Cabinet. I believe that, if I choose to go into it, I can enter in *any* situation that I may please. This opinion is formed from circumstances, not from assurances to which I should not listen, but which I should instantly check if attempted to be made. Feeling really great indifference about any office, resting upon the will of one man, I do not know that I should accept the first place in the Cabinet, if offered.[23]

If Clay was lying to this close and valued kinsman, it was with an unblushing effrontery that was entirely foreign to his character.

Meanwhile the Kentucky legislature was making an ominous demonstration. A number of powerful leaders in that state, including William T. Barry, John Rowan and George Bibb, had swung to Jackson's cause, and the movement had become so formidable that Jackson, who was watching events very closely, did not believe Clay could hold his influence over the delegation in Congress.[24] On January 7, a resolution was passed by the legislature, requesting the state's representatives in Congress to vote for Jackson, and in less than a week information of this reached Washington.[25] The Kentucky delegation was shaken, but rallied to its leader, who asserted that such instructions would only fix their determination to vote otherwise.[26]

[23] Clay Papers, V, Clay to Jas. Brown, Jan. 23, 1825. *Cf.* Colton, *Correspondence*, p. 113, Clay to Brooke, Feb. 4, 1825, where Clay's denial that he had been offered a Cabinet post is even more specific, and Weed, *op. cit.*, pp. 173–176, Albert H. Tracy to Weed, Jan. 23, 1825.

[24] Clay Papers, V, Kendall to Clay, Dec. 22, 1824; Jackson, *Correspondence*, Vol. III, p. 270, Jackson to John Coffee, Dec. 27, 1824.

[25] *Kentucky Senate Journal*, 1824, p. 113; Clay Papers, V, Barry to Clay, Jan. 10, 1825; Brown, *Missouri Compromises*, p. 132.

[26] Adams, *Memoirs*, Vol. VI, p. 469. Clay's position here is in marked contrast to the reverence he had expressed for instructions in 1816, and was to express again in 1839, when the Democratic Senators from North Carolina refused to obey instructions from the Whig legislature. In 1840, Clay asserted that he had obeyed the wishes of his *constituents* in voting for

Daily the atmosphere became more tense. The social amenities were preserved, but even the ladies organized their parties on an Adams, Jackson or Crawford basis.[27] Whispers of plots and intrigues floated everywhere.

On the twenty-first, one of the Missouri representatives, John Scott, came to Adams and spoke of his hope that Clay would be a member of the next Administration. Adams told him that, if elected by Western votes, he would naturally look to the West for much of the support that he should need. Scott went away, apparently satisfied, only to come back fearful lest what he had said might have the appearance of a bargain.[28] The Jacksonites, sensing the lay of the land, became desperate, and attempted a last minute coalition with the friends of Crawford, but this was doomed to failure. "They might as well think of turning the Capitol upside down as of persuading me to vote for Jackson," McLane of Delaware told Plumer.[29]

Meanwhile, the Ohio delegation had definitely made up its mind to go for Adams. There had been a drift in that state toward a coalition of Clay and Adams men since the Jackson press had become violent during the fall campaign, and the Ohio delegation's choice appears to have been made without the exertion of any real pressure by Clay himself.[30] On the morning of January 24, Plumer found the House buzzing like a hive. The Ohio and Kentucky members had just announced their intention of voting for Adams, and the odds had risen in his favor.

The news of this action roused the Jacksonites, and the followers of Crawford, to a fury of resentment. Their newspapers attacked Clay bitterly for having sold the West and

Adams, and that the Kentucky legislature had no right to meddle. But in February 1825, he had written: "My friends at a distance appear to be much divided, and give me advice of the most opposite character. Indeed I would not comply with their wishes unless, at the same time, I were to vote for all three of the candidates." — Mallory, *op. cit.*, Vol. II, pp. 351–352, 427; Gratz Collection, Clay to Wharton, Feb. 5, 1825.

[27] M. B. Smith, *op. cit.*, pp. 170–172.

[28] Adams, *Memoirs*, Vol. VI, pp. 473–474.

[29] Brown, *Missouri Compromises*, pp. 133–136.

[30] Roseboom, *op. et loc. cit.*, pp. 185, 202–204, 218–221. Roseboom demonstrates Ohio's satisfaction with the choice of Adams.

himself for the sake of the succession,[31] and on January 28, less than two weeks before the election, a specific charge of bargain was leveled against the Kentuckian by an ardent follower of Jackson.

This assault took the form of an insulting letter published in a Philadelphia paper, the *Columbian Observer*, by an anonymous member of the House from Pennsylvania. It alleged that the Clay men in Congress had offered to sell their votes to Jackson if Clay were made Secretary of State, and stated that, for the sake of office, Henry Clay had given his support to John Quincy Adams. The editor forwarded a copy of the paper to Clay.[32]

The charge appeared after Clay's thorough commitment to Adams. The day after this letter was published in Philadelphia, but probably before he had seen it, he sat with Adams for at least two hours, talking "with the utmost freedom of men and things." He knew perfectly well that some recognition would be offered to him for his support. He was aware that all kinds of charges were being made. But this public statement about the State Department as the prize provoked him into a fury of rash action.

On January 31, the *National Intelligencer* published a "card," signed "H. Clay." It pronounced the letter-writer "a base and infamous calumniator, a dastard and a liar" and promised, if he would reveal himself, to hold him responsible "to all the laws which govern and regulate the conduct of men of honor." On February 3, the *Intelligencer* published "another card," avowing the authorship of the letter, and offering to prove its charges. For the first and last time the eccentric simpleton, George Kremer, had assumed a prominent place in American history.

Clay precipitately abandoned his intention of fighting a duel, but, that same day, he asked the House for an investigation. Kremer announced that he "was willing to meet the inquiry and

---

[31] Adams, *Memoirs*, Vol. VI, p. 483; Cannon Collection, Clay to Blair, Jan. 29, 1825 (copy by Blair); Colton, *Correspondence*, pp. 113–114, Clay to Brooke, Feb. 4, 1825.

[32] The letter is reprinted in the *National Intelligencer*, Feb. 4, 1825.

abide the result," but when the committee chosen by the House asked for his evidence, he declined to appear. He seems to have been on the point of signing an apology to Clay, only to refuse at the last moment. His whole course was marked by evasion and contradiction; without a doubt, he was the cat's-paw of abler Jackson men.[33] It was the first skirmish in the great Clay-Jackson struggle, and Clay's precipitate action had put him at a disadvantage. His belligerent "card" was generally condemned, and an added touch of the ridiculous was given by the report in the New York papers that a duel had taken place, in which he had been killed.[34]

But now the charge of bargain was in the open, and ever fiercer raged the heated political discussions that warmed the bones of politicians during the frigid weather of early February. Bets were laid freely, with Adams as the favorite, and there were rumors that Jackson's standard would be raised in open rebellion, if, as his followers put it, the will of the people were thwarted.[35]

Election Day, February 9, came with a heavy snowfall, and Margaret Bayard Smith, looking out of her window that morning, noted it thankfully. The storm would keep the "lower citizens" from gathering together and committing some "foolish violence." Already an effigy of Mr. Adams, she knew, had been prepared.[36]

Promptly at noon the Senate filed into the hall of the lower House, whose members sat uncovered out of respect for the occasion. The electoral votes were read, and the President of the Senate rose and declared that there was no election, save

[33] Adams, *Memoirs*, Vol. VI, pp. 496–497; *Reg. of Deb.*, 18th Cong., 2d sess., 440–441, 486, 522–525; Clay Papers, X, Edward Ingersoll to Clay, Aug. 11, 1827; *National Intelligencer*, March 28–29, 1825; Parton, *op. cit.*, Vol. III, 102f; R. R. Stenberg, "Jackson, Buchanan and the 'Corrupt Bargain' Calumny," in *Pa. Magazine of Hist. and Biography*, Vol. LVIII (Jan. 1934), p. 64.

[34] Brown, *Missouri Compromises*, pp. 136–137; Kent Papers, Wm. Kent to Moss Kent, Feb. 8, 1825; *National Intelligencer*, Feb. 8, 1825.

[35] Willie P. Mangum Papers (Lib. of Cong., Mss. Div.), Mangum to Mrs. Mangum, Feb. 6, 1825; Kent Papers, Wm. Kent to Moss Kent, Feb. 8, 1825; Adams, *Memoirs*, Vol. VI, p. 483.

[36] M. B. Smith, *op. cit.*, p. 186.

for Calhoun, who had received one hundred and eighty-two votes for Vice-President. The Senate then retired, the roll of the House was called, the members seated themselves according to their respective delegations, and the balloting began.

At this point, Adams was certain of twelve states, at the most. He had the six New England states, together with Illinois, Missouri, Maryland, Louisiana, Kentucky and Ohio. There was a general expectation that there would be a number of ballots, and no one could predict the result.

Once again New York held the center of the stage. Her delegation stood seventeen for Adams, sixteen opposed, and one doubtful. The waverer was General Stephen Van Rensselaer, a fine old gentleman, tall and of commanding presence, sixty-nine years of age. He had been a Crawford man, but Adams had soothed his alarm about Federalist proscriptions, and when he reached the Capitol on the morning of the election, Clay had haled him into the Speaker's room, where, so the old man later told Van Buren, the Kentuckian and Webster had harrowed his mind by picturing the terrible consequences that might ensue if there were no election and had told him that it was in his power to cut the Gordian knot by voting for Adams on the first ballot. Van Rensselaer went to his seat in great mental distress, for McLane and other Crawfordites had in turn exerted themselves to counteract the impression that had just been made upon him. His agitation, evident to all in the chamber, increased as the ballot box was passed around. Just before it reached him, Van Rensselaer dropped his head upon the edge of his desk in a silent appeal for divine guidance, and as he took his hand from his eyes, "he saw on the floor directly below him a ticket bearing the name of John Quincy Adams." It was the answer to prayer. He picked it up, dropped it in the box, and Adams became the sixth President of the United States.[37] The battle was over,

---

[37] Adams, *Memoirs*, Vol. VI, pp. 493–494; Van Buren, *Autobiography*, pp. 150–152; M. B. Smith, *op. cit.*, pp. 191–193, 184–186; J. D. Hammond, *The History of Political Parties in the State of New York*, 3 vols. (Cooperstown, 1846–1848), Vol. II, pp. 190, 540; Alexander, *op. cit.*, Vol. I, pp. 341–343.

and for the moment the wearied adversaries rested on their arms.

Adams noted the result in his diary with the pious ejaculation, "May the blessing of God rest upon the event of this day!" He and his wife went to the President's drawing room that evening. It was crowded with guests. Clay smiled upon all alike as he walked about, a fashionable belle clinging to either arm. Jackson was there, surrounded by his admirers. He greeted Adams with composure, almost cordially, and appeared "altogether placid and courteous." [38]

But it was the calm before the storm.

Two days later, Adams told Monroe that he had decided to offer the Department of State to Clay, as due to his talents and his services to the West, and in recognition of the Western support he himself had received. This was done on February 12, and Clay took the matter under advisement. The Kentuckian considered the threatened opposition as of little moment.[39] He was walking into danger as delicately as King Agag had walked into the presence of Samuel.

Clay had begun consulting his friends about taking a place in the Cabinet before Adams was elected.[40] Their advice varied, but most of them appeared to favor such action. Adams' friends pressed the Kentuckian to accept, as did such supporters of Crawford as McLane of Delaware and Mangum of North Carolina.[41] There seemed to be equal danger of calumny, whether he said Yes or No. The pragmatic test appeared to be the only method of determining the wisdom of procedure, and it was to afford plenty of proof.

Clay accepted the office on February 20, 1825. Years later he made public recognition that in doing so he had committed a political mistake of the first magnitude.[42]

The Kentuckian had assured Adams that there would be little

---

[38] Adams, *Memoirs*, Vol. VI, pp. 501–502; M. B. Smith, *op. cit.*, pp. 182–183.

[39] Adams, *Memoirs*, Vol. VI, pp. 506–509.

[40] Clay Papers, V, W. Creighton to Clay, Feb. 14, 1825.

[41] Colton, *Correspondence*, Clay to Brooke, Feb. 18, 1825.

[42] Speech in Lexington, June 9, 1842. — Ms., Univ. of Chicago.

trouble from the Senate, but when the vote was taken on confirmation, March 7, fourteen out of forty-one were opposed. Jackson and Eaton of Tennessee, Holmes of Mississippi, Tazewell of Virginia, Berrien of Georgia, Branch of North Carolina were prominent on the list, and Adams recognized it for what it was, "the first act of the opposition." The die was cast, however, and that day he signed Clay's commission as Secretary of State. On March 8 the Kentuckian resigned his lucrative position as counsel for the Bank of the United States and entered upon the duties of his new office.[43]

Jackson's vote had symbolized his feelings. The General easily convinced himself that an infamous bargain had thwarted the people's will and his own ambition. A hard fighter and a good hater, his passionate nature was stirred to its depths by what he continued to the end of his life to assert was a sordid bargain. "So you see," he wrote to William B. Lewis, "the *Judas* of the West has closed the contract and will receive the thirty pieces of silver." And again, to Samuel Swartwout: "No midnight taper burnt by me; no secret conclaves were held, or cabals entered into, to persuade any to a violation of pledges given, or of instructions received. By me no plans were concerted to impair the principles of our Republican institutions, or to frustrate that fundimental one which maintains the supremacy of the people's will. . . ."[44] Theretofore he had been friendly to Adams, who had defended his conduct in the Florida expedition, but now all intercourse between them was at an end, and the Hero vowed vengeance upon the men who had thwarted his will.

Everywhere there was evidence that the battle lines were reforming with great rapidity. Feeling in Virginia rode high. Ritchie and his influential *Richmond Enquirer* accepted the Kremer charges as true and broke with Clay, Ritchie even suspending personal relations. The Jackson press bruited the most extravagant charges. "Expired at Washington, on the ninth of February," screamed one editorial, "of poison ad-

[43] Adams, *Memoirs*, Vol. VI, pp. 513, 525; Gratz Collection, Clay to Biddle, March 8, 1825.

[44] Jackson, *Correspondence*, Vol. III, pp. 276, 280, Feb. 14, 22, 1825.

ministered by the assassin hands of John Quincy Adams, the usurper, and Henry Clay, the virtue, liberty, and independence of the United States." [45] Worst of all was the effect in Kentucky, where the movements for Jackson and "relief" had already begun to fuse.

That state had been the battleground of a struggle over the question of legislative aid to debtors ever since 1819. The legislature had passed a variety of replevin laws which protected the property holdings of the distressed. In October, 1823, the state court of appeals had declared all these laws unconstitutional, and a wave of popular indignation had swept over the people. Democracy was being stifled by aristocratic judges, was the cry, and the division of Kentucky politics into relief and anti-relief factions had been accentuated. [46] The relief party had elected its Governor, Joseph Desha, and a sizable majority in each house of the legislature in the campaign of 1824. The new legislature had met in December of that year and had promptly proceeded to pass an act reorganizing the court of appeals.

Clay's point of view was known to be conservative, but he had managed to steer clear of the local struggle and both sides had supported him for President. When his chances vanished, a strong movement for Jackson sprang up in the state; the relief, "new court" party began to espouse that cause, and the relief legislature instructed the Kentucky delegation to go for Jackson. These instructions, as we have seen, were disregarded, Adams was elected, and Clay stood at his right hand. At the same time, it was widely reported in Kentucky not only that Clay was opposed to the formation of the new court (which was the truth), but that the question had been brought to bear on the presidential election and that Clay's position had been taken in concert with the old judges and their friends. Feeling ran high, and Kendall warned Clay of the resentment

---

[45] McMaster, *op. cit.*, Vol. V, p. 489. Calhoun privately expressed sentiments almost as extreme as these. He was determined upon opposition from the outset. — Calhoun to J. G. Swift, March 10, June 27, 1825, in *Amer. Hist. Rev.*, Jan. 1935, pp. 295–296.

[46] Stickles, *op. cit.*, pp. 21–42.

stirred up by this, urging that he avoid these local conten-
tions.[47]

The new court party leaders aligned themselves against
Clay. Rowan, Bibb and Barry had already raised the General's
standard. Before the year was out, Clay's close friend, Francis
Preston Blair, who had written to Clay as late as March 7, 1825,
that he hoped Jackson's prospects had been cut off forever,
went over to the opposition.[48] Kendall, a new court man, still
held for Clay, out of gratitude to Mrs. Clay, he said; but he
kept writing to the master of Ashland about his need for money,
either in the form of a loan or a lucrative salary. The Kentucky
situation was to grow worse during the ensuing years.

Clay's part in the election had been motivated by a combination of personal ambition and patriotic zeal. The alliance with
Adams, an attempted coalition of North and West on economic
grounds, seemed well calculated to advance his own interests.
At the same time, there is every reason to believe that he sincerely felt that such a combination, sponsoring his American
System, was for the best interests of the country. It was a conservative alignment, especially attractive to the men of property,
and, by its interest in national development, offering an appeal
to the people as a whole. But it had two fatal defects. It was
founded upon circumstances which could be twisted falsely into
an accusation of bargain and sale, and it took no account of the
rising democratic forces which had made Andrew Jackson their
leader. Those forces, riding on the crest of the General's popularity as a soldier and hero, took "the bargain" as their battle-
cry. They were destined to sweep the country in the next
campaign, and to force Clay into years of futile struggle against
the "military chieftain."

[47] Clay Papers, V, Kendall to Clay, Feb. 19, March 23, 1825.
[48] *Ibid.*, V, Blair to Clay, March 7, 1825; W. E. Smith, *The Francis
Preston Blair Family in Politics*, 2 vols. (N.Y., 1933), Vol. I, pp. 37–38.

Chapter XII

THE DIPLOMATIC RÔLE

From 1825 to 1829 John Quincy Adams and Henry Clay directed American foreign policy. It is impossible, generally speaking, to separate the parts they played in this, for they worked together with a surprising degree of cordiality, considering their past relations and personal dissimilarities. Differences of opinion did crop up, but these made no serious rifts, and both men bore testimony to the close co-operation that existed between them during Adams' term in the Executive Mansion.

Clay was not fitted by nature for his new rôle. Impetuous, high-spirited, loving the open forum and the clash of debate, his spirit drooped in the cool tombs that so frequently shroud the patient labors of diplomacy. He complained repeatedly to his friends about the long hours of toil and the drain upon his strength. His health suffered, and it was partly on this account that he left Washington during the summer months of each year. More than once he thought of resigning.

It might be inferred from this that his duties suffered from neglect, and it is true that occasionally there was lamentable delay in forwarding instructions, notably in the case of claims against France, and during the latter part of Poinsett's mission to Mexico. But, on the whole, he worked assiduously. The state papers written in his own hand are imposing, both in length and in number, and the lack of censure in Adams' diary is the best possible proof that Clay gave himself wholeheartedly to his tasks.

The major business of the department made these tasks heavy enough, but in addition to this there was a host of petty trials and tribulations. Mrs. Decatur appealed to him, because the servants of the Russian Minister, who had rented her house, were digging up the shrubbery. The French Minister, Baron de Mareuil, was a stickler for the fine points of etiquette and precedent, and. had to be handled with finesse. Letters of all kinds poured in, praising and warning against friends and enemies, and many of these, trivial though they were, Clay answered himself. One man asked the dismissal of a certain Dr. Thornton, connected with the State Department. Clay wrote a polite refusal, stating that he could not punish for private opinions. "If he has formed erroneous conceptions of the origin or merit of the Winged Gudgeon, that would not, I think, justify animadversion from me." [1]

Inventors sought to interest the Secretary in steam muskets, and cannon firing hundreds of shots a minute. Place seekers swarmed, asking favors that varied from diplomatic appointments to clerical positions.

> I am [wrote one of these individuals] one of the best dyers and best Bookkeepers in the US — I can draw in architecture, a specimen book of my drawings I have with me; my wife she assists me at this branch, I can draw in a scale, a Bank, an Episcopal Church, a goal, or penitentiary.

With all these accomplishments, this gentleman was willing to act as Clay's amanuensis. [2] Communications like this, sometimes amusing, often vexatious, took up a great deal of time.

During Clay's term of office, more treaties were negotiated than under any previous administration. They had to do mainly with claims and commerce, and were scarcely of epochal significance, but they bear witness to Clay's desire to broaden American trade and to strengthen the position of neutrals against British sea power. [3]

The main bulk of the negotiations with the European countries was confined to France and England. With the former the principal question concerned the adjustment of damage claims that had arisen out of the wars of the French Revolu-

---

[1] Domestic Papers (Dept. of State), XXI, Clay to Michael Withers, March 9, 1827.

[2] Clay Papers, XI, Isaac Rupell to Clay, Oct. 30, 1827.

[3] These treaties are given in Hunter Miller, *Treaties and Other International Acts of the United States of America* (Washington, 1931 —), Vol. III, pp. 195–484.

tion. Clay's brother-in-law, James Brown, had been Minister to France since 1823, and the negotiations were conducted through him. Fruitless efforts at collection had been made since 1816, and Clay became convinced, by the end of his first year in office, that vigorous measures should be taken. He was in favor of issuing letters of marque and reprisal, a drastic step, but Adams was cool to this idea, Brown advised against it, and no such action was taken.[4] Brown became convinced that it was useless to press the claims, but Clay eventually sent instructions to urge them upon Charles X.[5] The French remained evasive, however, and the close of Adams' administration saw the matter no further advanced toward a solution. Clay's idea as to the threat of reprisals was to take positive form under Jackson, with the Kentuckian in bitter opposition.

Negotiations with England were almost as disappointing. A variety of questions had been for years at issue between the two governments. The northwest and northeast boundaries, the navigation of the St. Lawrence, trade with the West Indies, property taken away by the British during the War of 1812, and other matters were discussed anew during this period. But of all these only one, the question of payment for property carried away during the war, was settled in a thoroughly satisfactory manner.[6] The other discussions accomplished nothing of great moment. Joint occupation of the Oregon Territory continued. The northeast boundary, between Maine and New Brunswick, a contentious question that necessitated tactful handling of Maine and her fiery Governor, Enoch Lincoln, was finally submitted to arbitration, but the award, given by the King of the Netherlands in 1836, was unsatisfactory to the United States. In vain the Government sought to obtain the right of free navigation of the St. Lawrence. Clay's contention that it was "a strait . . . connecting navigable seas . . . a free gift flowing from the bounty of heaven intended for all whose lots are cast upon its borders," and his rhapsodies about the

---

[4] Clay Papers, VI, Clay to Brown, Nov. 14, 1825, Brown to Clay, Dec. 24, 1825; Adams, *Memoirs*, Vol. VII, pp. 55–60.

[5] Instructions (Dept. of State), XI, Clay to Brown, May 28, 1827.

[6] Miller, *op. cit.*, Vol. III, p. 261. Great Britain agreed to pay $1,204,960.

"floating mass" of its waters which defied all authority until they reached "that ocean to which the presumptuous sway of no one has as yet been lawfully extended," had no effect upon the British Ministry.[7]

The worst trouble concerned the West India trade, which had been a bone of contention ever since the Revolution. During Monroe's administration, the liberal commercial ideas typified by William Huskisson had come into the ascendant in Great Britain, and had produced considerable modification of the British restrictions upon American commerce with those islands. Our Government, however, in a grasping attempt to force unheard-of trading privileges by commercial restrictions of its own, let slip the opportunity to meet these modifications by similar action in regard to American trade.

Clay had put himself on record as favoring the Government's policy, but he reached the opinion, early in 1825, that concessions were necessary and proper.[8] Adams did not share that viewpoint, apparently, until later, for instructions along these lines were not sent to the American Minister until June 19, 1826.[9] It was then too late. Before our change of front could be presented, the British Government, probably because of the wails of British shipowners, closed the West Indies to American shipping. George Canning, British Secretary for Foreign Affairs, refused to discuss the question further, despite an American offer to concede even more than Great Britain had formerly asked.

This was embarrassing to the United States, and Clay raged. The British, he felt, were clearly in the wrong, and Canning had taken grounds "which betray the scornful and jealous character of his nation."[10] On March 17, 1827, Adams proclaimed American ports closed to British ships coming from the principal British ports in the Western Hemisphere, and

---

[7] Instructions (Dept. of State), XI, Clay to Gallatin, June 19, 1826. Also in Clay Papers, Dispatches and Instructions, IV.

[8] *Annals of Cong.*, 14th Cong., 2d sess., 816–823, 16th Cong., 1st sess., 2047; Adams, *Memoirs*, Vol. VI, p. 540.

[9] *Amer. State Papers, Foreign Relations*, Vol. VI, pp. 247–249; Sir Charles Vaughan, "Papers," in *Amer. Hist. Rev.*, Vol. VII (April 1902), p. 507.

[10] Clay Papers, VII, Clay to Brown, Dec. 14, 1826.

thereafter no real approach to a settlement of the question was made until the time of Jackson. American delay was a real factor in producing the *impasse,* but for that it would appear that Adams rather than Clay should bear the blame.

All this contention had surprisingly little effect upon our trade with the British islands, which went merrily on by the indirect route of Canada and the West Indian ports of other nations; but American shipowners suffered to some extent, and the Government's failure to eliminate the British restrictions made excellent political capital for its opponents.[11]

Clay's instructions to our ministers in Latin America bear witness to the Administration's desire to extend its influence in the Western Hemisphere, and its jealousy of British prestige there. The Government strove to foster the development of commerce with the countries to the south, but the British generally won out in the race for trade.[12] Clay was also interested in stimulating political liberalism in that quarter of the world, and he informed our ministers and chargés d'affaires that they should explain the glorious nature of our political and social institutions to the Latin Americans.[13] At the same time, he warned against "improper interference in their public councils," but the tone of the instructions afforded an easy excuse for such action. John M. Forbes at Buenos Aires, Samuel Larned at

[11] This treatment of the controversy is based upon F. L. Benns, *The American Struggle for the British West India Carrying-Trade, 1815–1830* (Bloomington, Ind., 1923), pp. 107–162; *Amer. State Papers, Foreign Relations*, Vol. V, and Great Britain, Public Rec. Off., F.O., 5 (photostats); Vaughan, *op. et loc. cit.*, pp. 508–518.

The State Department tried to negotiate with Great Britain for the surrender of slaves who ran away to Canada, but Clay dropped the matter when our aid in suppressing the slave trade was demanded as a *quid pro quo.* This was done on the ground that the Senate had already manifested its opposition to a treaty involving suppression of the slave trade. — *Amer. State Papers, Foreign Relations*, Vol. V, p. 783; Clay Papers, Despatches and Instructions, I, Clay to King, May 10, 1825. T. E. Burton, "Henry Clay," in *The American Secretaries of State and Their Diplomacy*, 10 vols. (N.Y., 1927–1929), Vol. IV, pp. 125–126.

[12] J. F. Rippy, *Rivalry of the United States and Great Britain over Latin America (1808–1830)* (Baltimore, 1929), pp. 303f.

[13] Clay Papers, Despatches and Instructions, I, Clay to Forbes, April 14, 1825, Clay to Raguet, April 14, 1825.

Santiago, and Heman Allen at Valparaiso, not to mention others, spread propaganda about the political system of the northern republic, encouraged "by all proper means" the election of men favorable to democracy, and maneuvered against the ever present British influence. On one occasion, Larned even served on a Chilean constitutional committee, and appears to have had an important part in formulating a national charter.[14] This busybody diplomacy may have had some influence in preventing the triumph of the monarchical principle in South America, but it could not help breeding suspicion and dislike.[15] The statesmanship that encouraged such activities was at least questionable.

The island of Cuba was one focal point of our interest in Latin American affairs. Both Clay and Adams believed that the force of circumstances would eventually drop Cuba into the lap of the United States, but, for the time being, they wished simply to see it remain in Spanish hands. There was a possibility that this would not happen. The war between Spain and the new republics was still on, and Mexico and Colombia were considering expeditions against Cuba and Puerto Rico that, if undertaken, might have brought freedom for the islands or their annexation to a South American state. It was possible that Spain might decide to cede these remnants of her possessions to some powerful European country. The State Department acted vigorously. It brought pressure to bear, with considerable effect, to delay expeditions against the islands from South America, and it attempted to enlist Paris, London and St. Petersburg in an effort to push Spain toward peace by threatening her with the loss of Cuba. Russia, alone, appeared to fall in with this plan, and her co-operation was feeble. The Spaniards remained obdurate, even though Clay had hinted to Madrid that if the war continued and involved the islands, our interest in them might bring upon the United States "duties and obligations, the

[14] Samuel Larned Papers (Amer. Antiq. Soc.), Forbes to Larned, Dec. 8, 1825, Jan. 24, July 1, 1826; Allen to Larned, April 16, May 19, June 5, July 13, 15, 19, 28, Sept. 16, 1826; Larned to Clay, Nov. 10, 1826. The constitution that Larned helped to draw up was not adopted.
[15] Cf. Rippy, op. cit., pp. 146–148, 166–167, 175, passim.

performance of which, however painful it should be, they would not be at liberty to decline."[16]

The Administration was determined that the islands should not be ceded to any strong European power,[17] and when a French squadron appeared in the West Indies during the summer of 1825, the State Department showed marked signs of agitation. Clay felt that the occupation of Cuba by a French force would be just grounds for war, and even after the "menace" of the fleet disappeared, and Spain assured him that no cession was intended, he felt it necessary to inform France that the United States could not consent "under any contingency whatever" to the occupation of Cuba and Puerto Rico by any European power other than Spain.[18]

Such action indicated a disposition to maintain and even expand the principles set forth in Monroe's famous message of December, 1823, for it involved a principle of "no-transfer" that had not appeared in that warning to Europe. As a matter of fact, Clay and Adams had no intention of letting the "Monroe Doctrine" go to sleep. Brazil inquired if we would form an alliance to protect her against attack. Clay replied with a refusal of alliance, but indicated that the United States would regard such an attack upon the independent monarchy of Brazil as being, in general, subject to the same considerations as an assault upon the independent republics of South America. He took occasion to inform Mexico and other South American countries of our continued adherence to the pronouncement of 1823, and urged those countries to assert the same principles.[19] At the time of the French fleet scare, Mexico had appealed for action by the United States on the ground that Monroe's message bound us to such a course, and Clay sent to the Mexican

[16] Instructions (Dept. of State), X, 297f, Clay to Everett, April 27, 1825.

[17] Cf. Ibid., X, 225f, Clay to Poinsett, March 26, 1825; W. R. Manning, *Early Diplomatic Relations between the United States and Mexico* (Baltimore, 1916), pp. 105–165.

[18] Great Britain, Pub. Rec. Off., F.O. 5, Vol. 199, pt. 1, Vaughan to Canning, Sept. 30, 1825; Instructions (Dept. of State), X, p. 404, Clay to Brown, Oct. 25, 1825.

[19] Perkins, *op. cit.*, pp. 197–200; R. F. Arragon, *The Congress of Panama* (Ph.D. dissertation in Harvard Univ. Lib.), pp. 369–371.

Government a copy of his warning to France, as an indication that the United States had thus stood ready to redeem its "pledge." [20] Upholding the great principles of non-colonization and non-intervention by Europe in America was equally agreeable to Adams, who had played such an important part in their formulation, and to Clay, with his grand conception of an American System. Nevertheless, our southern neighbors continued to show a marked preference for English support.

Our relations with Mexico developed into anything but cordial co-operation. Clay's instructions to Joel Roberts Poinsett, Envoy Extraordinary and Minister Plenipotentiary to the Mexican Government, bore witness to the number of questions at issue. Poinsett was to obtain the complete opening of the Santa Fe Trail and conclude a commercial treaty. He was to get a demarcation of the boundary and, if possible, a considerable slice of Texas along with it. The instructions stressed our friendliness and disclaimed any desire for special favors. They emphasized the interest of the United States in democracy, and in the maintenance of the principles enunciated by Monroe in 1823. Finally, they informed Poinsett that he was to show "on all occasions" an "unobtrusive readiness" to explain the character of our political institutions. The mission, Clay felt, would "lay for the first time the foundation of an intercourse of amity, commerce, navigation, and neighborhood. . . ." [21]

These fond hopes were destined to be rudely blasted. Only a partial survey of the Santa Fe Trail could be agreed upon. Treaties regulating commerce and delimiting the boundary, though signed, had not been ratified by 1829, and the boundary treaty included no cession of territory. Poinsett was egged on by Clay and Adams, in 1827, to attempt to purchase over half of Texas for one million dollars, or considerably less for five hundred thousand, but he was quickly rebuffed. By 1829, Mexican resentment against him had risen to a high pitch and the Mexican Government demanded his recall.

There were various reasons for this fiasco. British influence

[20] Instructions (Dept. of State), X, p. 407, Clay to Poinsett, Nov. 9, 1825.
[21] Instructions (Dept. of State), X, pp. 225f, Clay to Poinsett, March 26, 1825.

was strong in Mexico. The American minister, by his own nature and by the character of his instructions, was bound to fight hard against British interference, and in doing so he aroused much hatred. He was also a vigorous advocate of federal democracy, and his connection with the York rite Masons (who represented the democratic struggle against aristocratic centralism), together with other interference in internal affairs, produced a great deal of bitterness and animosity.

It seems evident, however, that Poinsett was honestly trying to do his best for the Mexicans, as well as for his own country, and Clay and Adams must bear a goodly share of the blame for his failure. They knew about his enthusiastic liberalism. His earlier record as a Government agent in South America showed that he had no hesitation in exceeding the letter of his instructions.[22] Under these circumstances there was no excuse for Clay to incite him to action, as had been done by the instructions furnished at the beginning of his Mexican mission. They put upon Poinsett the obligation to stand for democracy, and virtually enjoined him to struggle against the English interference in Mexican affairs. Clay and Adams received information about his connections with Mexican politics, but no strictures upon his activities were sent to him by the State Department. In fact, Clay wrote in November, 1827, that the President approved his conduct. The Government's policy toward Mexico appears to have been as ill-advised as it was unsuccessful.[23]

Clay's desire to extend the sway of influence of the United States throughout the Western Hemisphere was never better displayed than in his enthusiasm over the Congress of Panama, a project that owed its origin to the South American liberator and patriot, Simon Bolivar.

Bolivar had long cherished a plan for ensuring liberty, peace and good relations to the South American states by bringing them together in a federation, and on December 7, 1824, in-

[22] Rippy, *op. cit.*, pp. 9–11; J. B. Lockey, *Pan Americanism* (N.Y., 1920), pp. 143–144.

[23] These judgments are based upon the Instructions (Dept. of State), X–XIII; Manning, *op. cit.*; J. F. Rippy, *Latin America in World Politics* (N.Y., 1928), pp. 68–87; J. H. Smith, "Poinsett's Career in Mexico," in *Amer. Antiq. Soc. Proc.*, Vol. XXIV (1914), pp. 77–92.

vitations were sent out to a meeting at Panama. Great Britain also received an invitation and the Liberator appears to have welcomed the prospect of British support for the undertaking.[24] Such a project of an American federation under the friendly aegis of British power was scarcely consonant with active participation by the great northern republic, and Bolivar had no wish for its interference. But Mexico and Colombia felt differently, and, in the spring of 1825, made inquiries as to whether the United States would come to Panama.

These communications warmed Clay's heart, for here was an opportunity to develop a great American confederation, guided by the United States. But his chief was not so enthusiastic. It is distinctly possible that both men published their views on the subject in April, 1825. At least an article, signed by Clay's old pen-name of "Scaevola," appeared in a Philadelphia paper, lauding American participation to the skies. It urged a confederation of all the American nations with an "Areopagus or Congress" that "should watch over the mutual relations of the confederated states, without interfering with their several, or internal regulations or governments — which should govern to a limited extent, the relations with foreign powers, of the whole, and of the several confederated states — and which should wield the whole force of the confederated states in defence of any member that may be attacked." Such a plan would secure to the United States "peace and power *abroad*, peace and happiness at home." This letter was reprinted in the *National Intelligencer*, together with a reply in the form of an editorial which denounced participation in any congress of nations whose decisions were to be *law* for this nation, and warned of danger to our independence from entangling alliances, although the writer was not opposed to a purely consultative conference.[25]

It is not certain that this reply was inspired or written by Adams, but it was in harmony with his point of view. That gentleman's diary for the period records Clay's enthusiasm for

---

[24] Lockey, *op. cit.*, pp. 387–390; Arragon, *op. cit.*, pp. 336–339.

[25] *National Intelligencer*, April 26, 1825. *Cf.*, *Reg. of Deb.* 19th Cong. 1st sess., 2360–2363, comment of Ingham of Pa.; Lockey, *op. cit.*, pp. 403f.

the Congress, adding as his own comment, that the project involved interests of great magnitude and was "a grain of mustard-seed." [26] Adams certainly saw possibilities in the plan, but he was more cautious and more cold-blooded than his Secretary of State, and it would have been out of keeping with his long demonstrated love for independent action had he espoused such a scheme as that proposed by "Scaevola."

Shortly after Clay told him of the inquiry about our participation, Adams instructed the Kentuckian to inform the ministers that, while we could not join in any deliberations regarding the war with Spain, such a conference might be useful in promoting harmony between the American powers and in settling disputed matters of public law and other questions of general interest to the Americas; and that, if the subjects to be discussed, the powers of the delegates, and the mode of organization and procedure could be agreed upon beforehand, the President would think that the United States should attend. [27]

Formal invitations came from Mexico and Colombia at the beginning of November, 1825, and Central America also requested our presence. By that time it had become apparent that we were not expected to join any confederacy that would limit our sovereignty in the slightest, and Adams was much more ready to accept. He told Congress, December 6, that he had done so, and three weeks later the names of Richard C. Anderson and John Sergeant, as delegates to the meeting at Panama, were laid before the Senate.

Clay was confident of the Senate's approval, and expected Sergeant to leave the United States by the middle of January. [28] But politics and stupidity now took a hand in the game. The Senate Foreign Relations Committee did not report until January 16, and then came out against the proposal. A long debate ensued, and the Committee's resolution, which stated that it was inexpedient to send ministers to Panama, was not

---

[26] Adams, *Memoirs*, Vol. VI, pp. 531, 536, 542, VII, 15–16.

[27] *Amer. State Papers, For. Rel.*, Vol. V, p. 835.

[28] Clay Papers, D. and I., III, Clay to Anderson, Nov. 25, 1825; Adams, *Memoirs*, Vol. VII, pp. 107, 112. Anderson was in Colombia as minister to that country.

voted upon until March 14, when it was defeated, nineteen to twenty-four. The delegates were then confirmed, but it was not until April 24 that the House passed the necessary appropriation by a vote of one hundred and thirty-four to sixty.

There was no good reason for this delay. Adams' message of December 26 had stated the Government's position with clarity. The Administration had no intention of abandoning its neutral position, or of contracting alliances, but sought better commercial relations, agreement upon the rights of neutrals, and a declaration from each country that it would resist colonization by any European power. We would seek to promote religious liberty, exert our influence to stop the war, and in general prove ourselves to be neighbors of benevolent interest.[29] But the opposition in Congress proceeded to call up all kinds of specters. Southern "statesmen" denounced the gathering as a menace to slavery, specifically because the Latin Americans meant to recognize the black Republic of Haiti and abolish the slave trade. Isolationists rose in wrath and Washington's Farewell Address was invoked with an almost religious zeal. States' rights men feared an increase of the National Government's power. South American meddling with Cuba and Puerto Rico was denounced, and Van Buren and other Northerners chose to regard the assembly as a menace to the sovereignty of the United States. Even the Administration's supporters were cool to the idea of having each American country adopt the non-colonization principle of Monroe, and thus make it a kind of Pan American public law.

Clay saw all this contention as primarily due to partisan opposition, and he was right.[30] There was undoubtedly some honest objection, especially by states' righters and slaveholders, but the leaders in the attack, men like Tazewell, Hayne and Van Buren, spent much of their time denouncing the avowed or implied objectives of the South Americans. The opposition confused these objectives with the Administration's motives for attending the Congress, and thus the aims of the Executive were deliberately distorted. It was feared that the success of the proj-

[29] *Amer. State Papers, For. Rel.*, Vol. V, p. 834.
[30] Porter Collection, Clay to Porter, Feb. 22, 1826 (confidential).

ect would make Clay and Adams popular, and distract public attention from the clamor that was being raised against them on other grounds.[31]

Clay's instructions to Anderson and Sergeant were dated May 8, 1826. He later asserted that they were "almost exclusively" his own work, drawn up "without consulting anybody particularly," and this was undoubtedly true.[32] But it should not be inferred from this that the ideas they contained were original with him, for Adams' message of March 15, 1826, requesting the appropriation for the mission, embraced practically all their principal points.[33] The delegates were to lay great stress upon the equality of the commercial privileges granted by any nation. They were told to make a bold stand along the old American line of neutrals' rights — clear definition of blockade and contraband, and the proposition that free ships make free goods. They were to throw their influence against any proposal to invade Cuba or Puerto Rico, and avoid any recognition of Haiti. On the other hand, a canal across the Isthmus of Panama, affected "by common means" and open to all the world upon "payment of a just compensation, or reasonable tolls" was a proper subject for consideration. The delegates were to exert themselves in favor of peace and the settlement of the boundary dispute between Mexico and Central America; they were to warn against establishing monarchies in order to curry European favor, and were to be ready at all times to explain our governmental theory and practice, and to extol "the manifold blessings which the people of the United States have enjoyed, and are continuing to enjoy, under them."

Such were to be our aims at Panama, but they were never broached before the assembled representatives of the nations. Sergeant was permitted to delay setting out until the fall, on account of his health and the torrid Isthmian climate, and Anderson was given permission to wait until that time, if he

[31] *Cf.* C. H. Smith, *The Washington Press in the Jacksonian Period*, p. 113. This excellent work was used while it was still in manuscript form. Also, Arragon, *op. cit.*, pp. 380f, 462f.

[32] Clay Papers, XXI, Clay to Walsh, April 25, 1836.

[33] Instructions (Dept. of State), XI, pp. 35–66, Clay to Anderson and Sergeant, May 8, 1826; Richardson, *op. cit.*, Vol. II, pp. 895–906.

preferred.[34] Anderson, however, left Bogotá on June 12, 1826, only to die en route to Panama. Had he lived, he could scarcely have reached the city before the delegates adjourned, July 15, to meet again at Tacubaya, near Mexico City. The Administration thought of appointing Monroe in Anderson's place, but Poinsett was finally selected.[35] Sergeant went to Mexico, but there was delay in convening the Congress, and after a few months he came back home. Thus ended the American effort at participation in a League of Nations project that was stillborn. Colombia was the only state willing to approve such agreements for mutual defense and arbitration as had been made at Panama.

Within a year, Clay began to manifest distrust of the man who had been responsible for calling the Panama meeting. Various agents of the United States in South America had become suspicious of the Liberator's intentions while the negotiations had been in progress, and had felt that the conference would be under English influence. Heman Allen and Samuel Larned, before they discovered that their own Government was to participate, had done their best to persuade Chile not to send delegates,[36] and the Larned Papers, as early as 1825 and 1826, show a deep distrust of Bolivar and his intentions. Such forebodings were communicated to Clay, and eventually had their effect. By March of 1827, the Kentuckian suspected Bolivar of ambitious designs which boded ill for the Congress. The South American wrote to Clay in 1827, expressing admiration and gratitude for his talents and his services to liberty. Almost a year later, Clay replied in rather frigid fashion. He was still hopeful that South America "would add new triumphs to the cause of human liberty," but he proceeded to expatiate upon his grave concern over reports of the Liberator's ambitious designs. Still, he was loath to abandon the belief that, in due time, Bolivar's conduct would be explained in satisfactory

[34] Instructions (Dept. of State), XI, pp. 69, 72, Clay to Sergeant, May 11, 1826, Clay to Anderson, May 19, 1826.

[35] Clay Papers, V, Clay to Brown, Oct. 8, 1826; Clay to Poinsett, Feb. 28, 1827.

[36] Larned Papers, Allen to Larned, April 5, 1826.

fashion. In closing, Clay expressed his hope that "preferring the true glory of our immortal Washington, to the ignoble fame of the destroyers of liberty, you have formed the patriotic resolution of ultimately placing the freedom of Colombia upon a firm and sure foundation. That your efforts, to that end, may be crowned with complete success, I most fervently pray." [37] Bolivar did not reply, and thus ended, on a faintly sour note, Henry Clay's Pan American Concerto.

In fact dissonance, rather than harmonious achievement, had characterized the orchestration of all this diplomacy. There had been some gains. One dispute with Great Britain had been settled and the arbitration of another had been agreed upon. A number of treaties involving claims and commerce had been signed. But the general handling of our relations with Latin America had produced resentment rather than material benefits, while French claims, West Indian trade, and the Congress of Panama venture had resulted only in furnishing campaign material for the opposition.

Intentions had been excellent. Save in regard to Texas, and there not vigorously, neither expansionist nor imperialist designs had been manifested, and the State Department had striven earnestly to propagate liberalism and democracy throughout the Western world. [38] But the meagerness of tangible achievement must have lain heavily upon the hearts of President and Secretary of State alike, a weight made doubly burdensome by the disastrous turn of domestic politics during these same four years.

[37] *Niles' Register*, Vol. XXXVIII, p. 173, April 24, 1830, Clay to Bolivar, Oct. 27, 1828. *Cf.* Clay Papers, VII, Clay to Larned, Jan. 1, 1829, and XVI, W. H. Harrison to Clay, April 11, 1830.

[38] Clay had even yearned to help the Greeks in their struggle for independence. G.B., Pub. Rec. Off., F.O. 5, Vol. 119, pt. 2, Vaughan to Canning, Oct. 31, 1825.

Chapter XIII

BLIFIL AND BLACK GEORGE

WHEN John Quincy Adams took the oath of office on March 4, 1825, he pleaded earnestly for complete and final political harmony. The appeal did honor to his idealism, but Shelley's luminous wings never beat more vainly against the void than did this adjuration against the ears of the politicians. Most of this gentry, Clay among them, had never really believed that the party system could be eliminated, and the bitterness engendered by the recent election, the rivalries of the leaders, sectional interests, conflicting political theories, and economic difficulties all combined in defeating the President's pious wish. Thus arose the political groupings that became known as the National Republicans, followers of Adams, Clay and Webster, and the Opposition (grouped under the banner of Jackson, Calhoun and Crawford) that was to eventually take the name of the Democratic Party.

These opposing camps contained many elements. Federalists, under the leadership of swarthy Daniel Webster, already the servant of the vested interests in Massachusetts, and Jeffersonian Democrats of the Clay stripe found themselves side by side in the National Republican ranks.[1] Many high tariff men looked to Clay for leadership. A strong Western element championed internal improvements at national expense. The party was con-

[1] In Clay's opinion, the principles of the National Republican Party merited full acceptance by the Federalists. He lamented the tendency of the Philadelphia Federalists to maintain their old name and discipline. "Is it for their interest," he wrote, "now that the causes which produced former divisions have ceased, to retain a *name* which can never benefit them? There are no parties now, in the Union at large, but those of the Administration and the Opposition; and old distinctions must in the sequel, be merged in these." — Peters Mss. (Pa. Hist. Soc.), Clay to R. Peters, Jr., Oct. 16, 1826 (private and confidential). *Cf.* Van Buren, *Autobiography*, p. 193.

servative, by and large, favored a vigorous national government, and sought to establish its predominance by an alliance of East and West.

The Opposition was decidedly heterogeneous. There were Southerners, hating the tariff and fearing that a strong central government would endanger slavery; Northern high tariff men, who distrusted Adams or disliked Clay; states' rights advocates and strict constructionists, moved to wrath by Adams' woefully inept championship of a vast system of internal improvements at national expense; democrats and demagogues who championed the downtrodden, demanded a government free from corruption, and cried out against aristocratical successions. The Opposition had a liberal tint, but the group, as a whole, required careful handling. Clear-cut principles were dangerous to it, so it fell back upon shibboleths. "Corruption," "Democracy," and "Jackson" became its watchwords. The Hero refused to commit himself on constructive policies, and the party gathered its strength upon a platform that consisted mainly of veneration of Old Hickory and hatred of Henry Clay and John Quincy Adams.[2]

The Kentuckian had taken office in 1825 with hopes that were characteristically sanguine. To be sure, he felt that the Cabinet might have "more talent with less harmony,"[3] but he looked forward to a successful Administration. Never was a man more bitterly disappointed.

Adams was cold, reserved, and lacking in personal magnetism. He never succeeded in gaining a hold upon the popular imagination, nor, though he entertained religiously, was he an adept at exerting influence through social intercourse. His devotion to internal improvements, a stand so pronounced that even Clay was taken aback,[4] roused a fury of resentment. A moderate program might have attained its objective, for there was powerful support in the West and in most of the middle

---

[2] Cf. the interesting article by Isabel T. Kelsay, "The Presidential Campaign of 1828," in East Tenn. Hist. Soc. Pub., Vol. V (Jan. 1933), pp. 69–80.

[3] Porter Collection, Clay to Porter, April 23, 1825.

[4] Adams, Memoirs, Vol. VII, pp. 59–61, 191.

Atlantic states. But this extremism roused the specter of national tyranny and intensified a growing desire among the states to do their improving after their own fashion. Unwittingly, the President accelerated this movement, and though a sum of over two million dollars was appropriated, his pet project of a great system of national roads and canals went down in ruin.[5]

The Administration was avowedly for a protective policy, and this was unpopular in the South. The lack of achievement in foreign policy, particularly in regard to the West India trade, created a good deal of dissatisfaction throughout the Union.

Under such circumstances, a good party machine would have been invaluable, but Adams stood staunchly by the merit system. Complaints came in early, and they increased in volume as the months went by. Many Administration supporters became lukewarm or were alienated by this course of action. The President could scarcely be called a success as a party leader.

Clay's reaction to these aspects of the Administration took a variety of forms. His nature was at the opposite pole from that of the President. Warm-hearted and impulsive, naturally hospitable, he made friends easily among the people, and the Clay home in Washington became a social center. Evening parties and dances featured the life of the capital, and the Clays took a lively part in these functions, especially after they moved into the spacious Decatur house in the spring of 1827.[6] Their furnishings were enhanced from time to time with purchases made for them by Nancy Hart Brown, wife of the Minister to France. Parisian china, branched candlesticks, bracelets, velvets, embroidered handkerchiefs, marabou feathers that would wash like linen, all lent an air of elegance to the frequent entertainments in the Clay home.[7] Balls and dinner parties were given in profusion, and this social round kept up for four years. Wrote Margaret Bayard Smith in the winter of 1828: —

[5] *Cf.* Van Buren, *Autobiography*, p. 195.
[6] McDowell Collection, Clay to Henry Clay, Jr., April 2, 1827; Sweet Collection, Clay to Jas. Brown, May 30, 1827.
[7] Clay Papers, VIII, Mrs. Brown to Mrs. Clay, Feb. 13, July 30, Sept. 12, 1827.

. . . Mrs. C. . . . is overwhelmed with company, besides a very large dining company every week and a drawing room every other week. She says when Mr. C. dines at home, he never dines alone but always has a social company in a family dinner, which however is really the trouble of a large one. She is obliged to go to other people's parties, sick or well, for fear of giving offence, a thing more carefully avoided now than ever. . . .[8]

In such surroundings, Clay's nature expanded and he was at his best. Men owned his brilliance and women his charm. "You never fail to meet some handsome ladies — wherever you go," wrote Eliza Johnston. "I do think you have enough to do without observing the Ladies so particularly."[9] But, such semi-serious chiding aside, these social activities were a real asset to the Government.

Clay differed from Adams also in his attitude toward patronage. The Kentuckian was not a spoilsman in the extreme sense of the word. At the beginning of the Administration he stood for moderation, urging the President to avoid both "political persecution and the appearance of pusillanimity." Bitter and repeated attacks upon his patronage distribution in the State Department only succeeded in demonstrating a few instances when the public printing had been shifted on political grounds.[10] On the other hand, he urged dismissals where hostility was evident, as in the case of the Postmaster-General, John McLean, and believed it salutary to make the Administration's power felt upon occasion. Like Webster, he had a lively sense of patronage and newspaper values in the political game.[11]

There was logic in this desire to separate the sheep from the goats. With men prominent in the Administration opposed to its policies, friends hanging their heads over appointments, and

[8] M. B. Smith, op. cit., pp. 212–213. Cf. Clay Papers, VIII, Clay to James Brown, Dec. 14, 1826; J. O. Harrison Papers, family letters; Colton, Correspondence, p. 186.

[9] Clay Papers, XII, E. Johnston [to Clay], July 14, 1828.

[10] Cf. C. H. Smith, op. cit. (ms.), pp. 114f.

[11] Adams, Memoirs, Vol. VI, pp. 545–547, Vol. VII, p. 349; Clay Papers, VI, Wm. Carroll to Clay, Nov. 25, 1825; Peters Mss., XII, Misc., Clay to Peters, Oct. 16, 1826 (private and confidential); Webster Papers (Lib. of Cong.), II, Clay to Webster, April 14, 1827.

Vice-President Calhoun "up to the hub with the opposition," [12]
the fires of enthusiasm had little chance of making headway.
But the President held stoutly to his course, only weakening a
little, under pressure, at the end.

Clay wished to identify the National Republican Party with
his American System policy of high tariff and internal improvements. He was most anxious, he wrote to Webster, that internal
improvements should be supported in New England, and that
the West and Pennsylvania should be made aware of that
support. He hoped that Webster would be able to sustain the
cause. "You have your equivalents in other forms, if not in that
of I. Improvements. We must keep the two interests of D. M.
[domestic manufactures] & I. I. allied, and both lend to the
support of that other great & not less important interest of
navigation." Six months later he was pleading with the New
York leaders to realize the dangers to the American System in
a Jackson victory.[13] He appears to have urged the Harrisburg
meeting of high protection enthusiasts in the summer of 1827,
the direct precursor of the tariff of 1828.[14] It was obviously
Clay's desire to make the tariff a leading issue in the campaign,
but the Tariff of Abominations, as the South termed it, was
framed with the Jackson men in control of the House.

Drawn up by an Opposition Committee on Manufactures,
this bill was designed solely for political effect. It was protective,
but the duty it imposed on woolen goods was considerably
lower than that demanded by the manufacturers, while the
tariffs on raw materials necessary to New England, such as
high grade hemp, coarse wool and molasses, were energetically
boosted. All the Jackson men were to vote together in preventing amendments. The New Englanders, it was supposed,
would be unable to accept it, and in the final vote the Southerners would join with them in defeating the bill. In this way
the Jacksonites in the North would get credit as friends of pro-

[12] Crittenden Papers, Clay to Crittenden, March 10, 1826.
[13] Webster Papers, II, Clay to Webster, June 7, 1827; Porter Collection,
Clay to Porter, Jan. 14, 1828 (private and confidential).
[14] *Quarterly Journal of Economics*, Vol. II (July 1888), pp. 490–491.
Clay to B. W. Crowninshield, March 18, 1827.

tection, while the Administration's party would bear the blame for the defeat of the measure.

Clay saw the plot, and was especially incensed by the blow it dealt to the woolen manufacturers. "A viler cheat was never attempted on an intelligent people than the bill reported by the Committee," he wrote to Porter, adding that no one believed there was any prospect of passing a proper bill on the subject.[15] The House did lower somewhat the duty on raw wool, the only change of moment that was made in that body. It was a slight sop, but Clay, determined to brave all for protection, now advised that the measure be passed.[16] Whether or not this advice had weight, the House passed the bill, and in the Senate, after a slight advance of the duty on woolens, enough New England Senators swung for it to pass the measure. The Tariff of Abominations, a thoroughly bad bill, had gone through under the whip of political exigency, and the South flamed with wrath. But the Jackson men from the Middle and Western states had voted for it, and the National Republicans could not make an effective issue in the campaign.

Checkmated on internal improvements by Adams' excess of zeal, thwarted in gaining prestige through participation in the Panama Congress, deprived of the tariff issue by the tactics of the Opposition, the Administration was doing little more than ride out a succession of storms. Nor was this barren record the only blow to the sanguine hopes of the Secretary of State. He had to watch with bitterness and chagrin the gradual defection of his own state from his leadership.

The Kentucky struggle over relief had reached alarming proportions from the point of view of Clay's prestige. The conflict was not only depriving him of vital support among the voters, it was pushing one of the ablest of writers and subtlest of politicians into the Jackson camp. The old court, anti-relief

---

[15] Porter Collection, Clay to Porter, March 1, 24, 1828; Mrs. Chapman Coleman, *The Life of John J. Crittenden*, 2 vols. (Philadelphia, 1871), Vol. II, pp. 66–67.

[16] Porter Collection, Clay to Porter, April 12, 1828. It is possible that he felt it would be better to pass it in the House, allowing the Senate to defeat it, but he gave no indication that this was his idea. In his speeches later that year, he defended the tariff. It was thoroughly acceptable to the West.

party captured the Kentucky assembly in the 1825 elections, and, with the legislature deadlocked, the old and new courts of appeals challenged each other's jurisdiction. Feeling ran high. It was exacerbated by the pro-relief editorials in the *Frankfort Argus*, editorials written by Amos Kendall.

Clay's sympathies were obviously on the side of the anti-relief party,[17] and he felt, apparently, that to remove Kendall to Washington would be a diplomatic stroke. Letters relative to a Government position began passing between them early in 1825. The editor was on the lookout for money. His pen was for sale, and Clay was willing to buy it, at a moderate price. Kendall wanted a Government job, not too laborious, with liberal compensation attached, that would leave him free "to sport my pen as I pleased. . . . Employed in the administration, I should certainly not write against it, and I should take some pride in vindicating you from the aspersions with which your enemies would overwhelm you." [18] He had no particular fondness for Jackson, he asserted, and would as soon support Adams as the Hero. But the position that was offered paid only one thousand dollars, and Kendall, who wanted fifteen hundred dollars, refused.[19]

Kendall hesitated to come out on national politics, alleging his gratitude for Mrs. Clay's kindness. He told Governor Desha (a relief and Jackson man) that he disliked both Adams and Jackson. Desha asserted, five years later, basing his statement upon his journal, that his own threat of setting up a vigorous pro-Jackson paper as a rival to the *Argus* was what finally converted Kendall to the Jackson cause.[20] Whether because of pressure from his friends, or in the hope of driving a

[17] *Argus*, July 9, 16, 1828, Clay to Kendall, Oct. 18, 1825; Crittenden Papers, III, Clay to Crittenden, March 10, 1826; Crittenden Papers (Duke Univ.), Crittenden to Clay, Nov. 25, 1826; Clay Papers, VI, XI, Blair to Clay, Jan. 11, 1826, Nov. 14, 1827.
[18] Clay Papers, V, Kendall to Clay, April 28, 1825.
[19] *Ibid.*, Kendall to Clay, Oct. 4, 1825; Joseph Desha Papers (Lib. of Cong.), Desha to Kendall, May 6, 1831; Kendall to Desha, June 2, 1831; *Argus*, May 28, 1828.
[20] Desha Papers, Desha to Kendall, May 6, 1831. Blair also claimed credit for Kendall's change of position. — W. E. Smith, *Blair Family*, Vol. I, p. 38.

better bargain with the Administration, the editor finally plumped for Jackson, and began attacking Adams, an attack which did not include the Secretary of State.[21] Clay, thereupon, took the Government printing, amounting to something over one hundred dollars a year, away from the *Argus* and gave it to a rival paper, chiefly on the ground that he could not countenance the line drawn by the *Argus* between Adams and himself.[22] The *Argus* screamed in fury, and from January, 1827 on, Henry Clay had no more bitter opponent and Andrew Jackson no more devoted champion than Amos Kendall.[23]

The anti-relief men were victorious, and, in December, 1826, the new court of appeals was abolished by the legislature. The struggle over relief had ended, but plenty of bitterness remained. The relief party had polled a heavy vote, and tens of thousands of voters were rallied by its leaders into the camp of General Jackson. During the following summers, when Clay visited Kentucky, he exerted to the utmost his powers of persuasion and charm, but the state was no longer safe for the Administration.[24] The heritage of the relief quarrel, Jackson's personal popularity, the blast of "bargain and sale" charges, did their work. The supporters of Clay and Adams were defeated in the election of 1827. The National Republicans elected Thomas Metcalfe Governor the following year, by eight hundred votes, but the Jackson candidate for Lieutenant-Governor was elected and both houses of the legislature had Jackson majorities. The stage was set for a humiliating defeat in the national election. Kentucky had drifted, for the time being, into the arms of the Hero.

But, hard as it was to watch the fickle behavior of the state he loved, the continual cry of "bargain and sale" inflicted keener torture. Shortly after the election of 1825, Kremer restated his assertion that Clay's support of Adams had been

---

[21] *Argus*, Oct. 4, 1826, *et seq.*

[22] Crittenden Papers, Clay to Crittenden, Dec. 12, 1826 (copy).

[23] *Argus*, Jan. 10, 1827, *et seq.*

[24] *Cf.* Stickles, *op. cit.*, pp. 108–113. Adams and Clay looked for advice, and gave positions chiefly to the anti-relief men.

rewarded by the State Department. The Kentuckian replied at length in an "address" to his constituents, defending his course and denouncing Kremer and his friends. This was well received. Chief Justice Marshall, Joseph Story, President Horace Holley of Transylvania University, John Tyler of Virginia, and many others commended the "address," expressing their confidence in his integrity. Harvard University conferred an LL.D. upon the Kentuckian that fall, in recognition of his attainments, character and standing.[25] Clay was convinced that his triumph over his assailants had been "complete and signal," but by the beginning of the New Year "rumbling thunders" were indicating an approaching "tug of war," [26] and within three months his ordeal had begun in earnest.

On March 27, 1826, the *United States' Telegraph*, a Jackson paper published in Washington, came out with a full-page editorial on "Bargain, Management and Intrigue." Three days later, John Randolph rose in the Senate and delivered a most extraordinary philippic. In the midst of a wealth of Latin quotations, allusions that verged upon the indecent, irrelevant excursions into European history, denunciations of broad construction, and insinuations that the invitations to Panama had been forged in the State Department, he pilloried Clay and Adams for corruption.

"Let Judas have his thirty pieces of silver!" exclaimed the mad Virginian. They might "go to buy a Potter's field, in which to inter this miserable Constitution of ours, crucified between two gentlemen, suffering for 'conscience sake,' under the burthen of the two first offices of this Government." He referred to the alliance "between Old Massachusetts and Kentucky — between the frost of January, and young blythe, buxom, and blooming May — the eldest daughter of Virginia — young Kentucky — not so young, however, as not to make a prudent match, and sell her charms for their full value." And finally, after Hayne had tried vainly to stop him, came a vicious attack upon Adams, and the mocking confession, "I was de-

[25] Clay Papers, V, President J. T. Kirkland to Clay, Sept. 22, 1825.

[26] *Ibid.*, V, Clay to James Brown, May 9, 1825; Gratz Collection, Buchanan to Wm. Morris, Jan. 15, 1826.

feated, horse, foot, and dragoons — cut up — and clean broke
down — by the coalition of Blifil and Black George — by the
combination, unheard of till then, of the Puritan with the
black-leg." [27]

Randolph's eccentricities had been displayed many times before, but never to more spectacular advantage. He was almost
fifty-three, and already his genius had, on several occasions,
reached, if it had not passed, the border line of insanity. But
now he had turned the knife of his sarcasm in a spirit already
deeply wounded, and Clay could think of nothing but of vindicating himself upon the field of honor.

The Kentuckian's attitude toward dueling was much like his
position on slavery: a combination of theoretical dislike and
practical tolerance. Two-and-a-half years before, he had done
his best to prevent an encounter between two prominent citizens
of his own state. But the practice was an evil, he felt, too deep
for legal correction; one that could be eliminated only by chang-
ing public opinion. "I fear," he had written to Porter in 1813,
"in spite of all the efforts of Legislation, we shall go on to fight,
in single combat, and go on to condemn the practice." [28] He had
not the moral courage to abandon the code of "the duello,"
despite the fact that he deplored it. He dismissed from consideration his wife, who was still grieving desolately over the
recent death of two of their daughters, Eliza Clay and Susan
Duralde.[29] Even the thought of Randolph's mental condition
did not deter the irate Kentuckian. Rage held him helpless, and
the challenge was delivered by his second, General Jesup, on
the morning of April Fool's Day.

Jesup, and Colonel Tatnall, Randolph's second, together
with Thomas Hart Benton, succeeded in delaying the duel for
a week by bringing up nice points of honor, but it was eventually
arranged that the meeting should take place just across the

[27] *Reg. of Deb.*, 19th Cong., 1st sess., II, 393, 395–399, 401.

[28] Crittenden Papers, III, Clay to Crittenden, Sept. 13, 1823; Porter
Collection, Clay to Porter, Dec. 24, 1813.

[29] Twelve-year-old Eliza had died of a fever at Lebanon, Ohio, on the
way to Washington with her parents, and Mrs. Duralde (Susan Hart Clay),
died in New Orleans of yellow fever in September 1825, less than a month
after the death of Eliza.

Potomac from Georgetown,[30] on the afternoon of Saturday, April 8, at half-past four. The weapons were pistols, the distance ten paces. Firing was to begin upon the word, and end as soon as the words "one, two, three, stop" had been rapidly uttered.

The night before the duel, Benton called upon the Clays. He was Mrs. Clay's cousin, but politics had estranged him from Clay and he now wished to make a declaration of his unaltered personal esteem. He found a tranquil family scene, little John Morrison Clay asleep on the sofa, Lucretia sitting near by, sorrowful in spirit over the family bereavements and completely unaware of what was planned for the morrow. After the rest had left the room, Benton's assurance of friendship was cordially received, and the two men parted at midnight.

The next day at noon, with the duel only four-and-one-half hours away, Benton went to Randolph's lodgings and told him of this peaceful scene in the Clay home, thinking to strengthen a determination not to fire at Clay which had already been expressed by the Virginian. The latter, engaged in making codicils to his will, said quietly, "I shall do nothing to disturb the sleep of the child or the repose of the mother," and went on with his writing, only to break out into a wild rage a little later because the bank had not sent him the gold pieces that he wanted as souvenirs for his friends.

Just as the sun was setting behind the Virginia hills, the party assembled at the dueling ground, Benton tagging along behind. Clay was in deadly earnest. He had protested against too short a time for firing on the ground that, unaccustomed to the use of a pistol, he might not be able to fire within the limit, and Randolph, who had told one of his seconds the night before that he might change his mind about returning the shot, "if I see the devil in Clay's eye," had become uncertain as to what his own course of action would be.

Tatnall, Randolph's second, won the choice of position, and this gave Jesup the word. As he was explaining the procedure to Randolph, the latter's pistol, which had been set on the hair

[30] A sign marks the spot to-day, on the Virginia side within fifty yards of the old Chain Bridge.

trigger, was accidentally discharged. Clay immediately called out that it was an accident, another pistol was furnished, and they took their places, Clay with his usual lounging grace, his tall figure garbed in customary dress, while Randolph's thin, erect and meager form was partially concealed in the voluminous folds of his white dressing-gown.

At the word, each man fired, and missed. Randolph's shot, aimed low, hit a stump almost directly behind Clay, and the latter's bullet kicked up the gravel behind Randolph — after having passed, according to one witness, through Randolph's clothes. Benton offered mediation, but Clay waved it away, saying, "This is child's play!" and Randolph also asked another fire. Again the Kentuckian's bullet punctured his adversary's gown; but this time Randolph fired in the air, and exclaiming, "I do not fire at you, Mr. Clay," advanced with extended hand. Honor, strangely enough, had now been satisfied. Clay met him halfway, and in a voice choked with emotion exclaimed: "I trust in God, my dear sir, you are untouched: after what has occurred I would not have harmed you for a thousand worlds." Randolph remarked, "You owe me a coat, Mr. Clay," and the latter replied, "I am glad the debt is no greater." Then everyone went back to Washington.[31]

Clay suffered no qualms of conscience as to this affair. "My regrets," he wrote to a clerical friend, "are limited to the countenance which a pernicious practice may receive from one example, and to the apparent violation of religious obligation. I must however say that my present feelings are in a state of composure and satisfaction, which I should not have enjoyed, if the occasion had not occurred. We are strange beings!" His friends, however, were much alarmed. There were rumors that a duel with McDuffie of South Carolina was imminent. A story got about in Kentucky that Clay and Calhoun had fought and

---

[31] This account is based upon that in the *National Intelligencer*, April 10, 1826; Benton, *Thirty Years' View*, Vol. I, pp. 70–77; Van Buren, *op. cit.*, pp. 204–207; Clay Papers, VI, Jesup to Clay, April 1, 1826, and Extracts from a Private Journal, April 9, 1826; Colton, *Correspondence*, pp. 145–147; Garland, *John Randolph*, Vol. II, pp. 258–260. The only material discrepancies are in the varied accounts of the remarks of the principals, but all agree as to the spirit of those remarks.

that the latter had been killed. "In your situation," wrote Crittenden, "you have more occasion to consult your discretion, than your courage," and James Brown told Clay bluntly that he should not quarrel with Randolph, that "unfortunate man. . . . You may drive a ball through his body, but you can never drive a *fixed idea* from his brain. . . . If you can keep your temper and the affairs of the Country go on smoothly Mr. Adams will be sure of being reelected. Everything which can be done will be done to provoke him and you as you are both suspected of a little infirmity of temper." [32]

But the duel did not put a stop to clamor about intrigue, and Brown's certainty of political success was based upon hope, rather than upon the actual state of affairs.

A tremendous campaign for "democracy" was burgeoning throughout the Union, with Jackson as the standardbearer. The Tennessee legislature nominated him in October, 1825, and he promptly resigned from the Senate with a speech which favored a single presidential term and the prohibition of Government offices to Congressmen. Old Hickory's first Cabinet was to hold five members of Congress out of six appointments, and it was to be scarcely necessary to draft him for re-election in 1832, but now he was only the would-be guardian of democracy and he could go far, since it was only in theory. Gradually, with Crawford out of the picture, the Jackson-Calhoun-Van Buren alliance took shape, a league that was due in no small part to the skillful guidance of the Red Fox of Kinderhook. This opposition showed its power in the debate on the Panama Congress. It demonstrated its vindictive malevolence and a shrewd

[32] Crittenden Papers (Duke Univ.), Crittenden to Clay, April 27, 1826, III, Clay to Crittenden, May 11, 1826; Clay Papers, VI, Clay to the Rev. Mr. Bascom, April 10, 1826, Brown to Clay, May 10, 23, 1826.

Randolph went to Europe that summer, and the stories of his antics on shipboard were weird in the extreme. At table, with ladies present, he made such remarks as "I wonder if there was ever a young lady who did not long for the pains and perils of childbirth?" He hated internal improvements — "damn the steamboats, I wish they were all blown up. I wish there was not a single turnpike road in Virginia." He offered to shoot all of his Negroes if everybody else would shoot theirs — he could shoot all of his in two hours, etc., etc. — Clay Papers, VII, Christopher Hughes to Clay, Aug. 18, 1826, Thos. Hulme to Clay, Aug. 24, 1826.

understanding of human frailty in the continued clamor over "bargain and sale" that filled the Jackson press.

That political soldier of fortune, Duff Green, became editor of the *United States' Telegraph* in the spring of 1826; and shortly thereafter, he announced that he could prove corruption in the preceding election.[33] Clay spoke at Lewisburg, Virginia, in August, laboriously clearing himself, but Green published a series of five articles in November which, without being too definite, attempted to prove that Clay had supported Adams out of self-interest. The following spring a letter was published, written by Carter Beverly of Virginia, according to which Jackson had stated that he had been approached by Clay's friends with an offer to make him President if he would promise not to make Adams Secretary of State. Clay challenged the truth of Beverly's statement. The latter called on Jackson to back him up. Old Hickory came out, June 6, 1827, with the assertion that he had been approached by a Congressman who, he supposed, came from Clay, with the offer mentioned. Jackson further stated that he had declined to mention his choice for the State Department, and that two days later Clay had come out for Adams. Clay replied, in the *Kentucky Reporter*, July 4, with a blanket denial and a demand for evidence, which was renewed in an able speech at Lexington, a week later. Jackson rehearsed the whole sorry mess in a long public letter, and named James Buchanan of Pennsylvania as the Congressman who had approached him.

Buchanan now entered the ring, but as a most reluctant second. He had not come to Jackson as a Clay emissary, and he said so, lamely trying, at the same time, to shield the General.[34] "How General Jackson could have believed I came to him as an emissary from Mr. Clay or his friends to make a corrupt bargain with him on their behalf I am at a loss to understand," wrote the wretched Pennsylvanian to his friend Ingham.[35]

[33] *U. S. Telegraph*, June 5, 1826.
[34] *Lancaster* (Pa.) *Journal*, Aug. 8, 1827.
[35] G. T. Curtis, *Life of James Buchanan*, 2 vols. (N.Y., 1883), Vol. I, p. 51.

Clay and his friends were delighted with Buchanan's letter, and the Kentuckian determined to follow it up with a convincing proof of his innocence. For two-and-one-half years, he had been writhing under the odious indictment. Now he would end it for good and all. He had collected a large number of letters from Congressmen who had voted for Adams, and from other people as well,[36] and, in December, he published his *Address to the Public*.[37] It contained a mass of evidence to the effect that he had not used improper influence, and that he had decided to vote for Adams before coming to Washington. This was spread broadcast in pamphlet form, and followed by later publications.

But the charge would not down, and a false step on the part of Clay's friends in the Kentucky senate gave it fresh currency. That body was in session when Clay's pamphlet came out, and his supporters moved a resolution declaring him exonerated. The opposition called for evidence, and a four-day investigation ensued. From the sworn testimony, three major facts appeared. Clay had paid to have Kendall's letters against Adams printed in 1823; David White, Congressman from Kentucky, had voted for Adams because he was assured that it would help make Clay Secretary of State; and Blair had in his possession a letter — the letter of January 8, 1825 — in which Clay had commented upon his position in regard to the rival candidates.[38]

The hunt then changed its cry, and the Jackson press of Kentucky, headed by the *Argus*, demanded that this letter be published. Finally, at the request of the Administration Central Committee of Kentucky, Clay agreed to allow that body to show to any individual who asked it the parts of the Blair letter that dealt with the last election. Blair supplied the Committee with copies and Kendall saw them. During the summer of 1828, he published excerpts from the letter, with viciously misleading

---

[36] One enthusiastic soul proposed that Clay write him a letter, dated Nov. 1824, as if in answer to inquiries concerning his vote, saying that he intended to vote for Adams. Clay wrote on the back: "I was shocked by the proposal in this letter, & need not say that it was impossible to comply with it." — Clay Papers, XI, G. M. C. to Clay, Oct. 22, 1827.

[37] *Ibid.*, XI, 1891f.

[38] *U.S. Telegraph, Extra*, Vol. 1, no. 1.

commentaries,[39] and the clamor over "bargain and sale" was at fever heat during the last months of the campaign.[40]

This was not the only personal attack that developed. By 1828, a host of other charges were being circulated. Adams was living in splendor at the President's Palace. He had purchased a billiard table and a set of chessmen from a Congressional appropriation for Executive Mansion furnishings! He had received "immense sums of money out of the public purse" and while abroad had not only "admired the structure of kingly governments," but had used the public money to speculate in Russian stocks.[41] Isaac Hill, editor of the scurrilous *New Hampshire Patriot*, published a story asserting that, to gain influence at the Russian Court, Adams had attempted to prostitute a beautiful American girl to the Emperor Alexander.[42] Clay was accused of cheating two carpenters out of their wages, of kidnapping a free Negro in Pennsylvania and taking him to Kentucky, of treasonable connections with Aaron Burr and a design to separate the West from the Union.[43] Jefferson was reported to have had a very low opinion of the Kentuckian as a political leader. It was insinuated that Clay had embezzled twenty thousand dollars, a legacy left to Transylvania University by Colonel James Morrison.[44] "Adams, Clay and

---

[39] *Argus*, July 16, Aug. 13, 20, 1828. See particularly the issue of Aug. 20, with parallel columns from the letter and Clay's address at Lexington, June 29, 1827. Kendall quoted the letter from memory, for his quotations, though substantially exact, are by no means literally correct.

[40] There is an excellent study of the whole controversy in C. H. Smith, *op. cit.*

[41] *Argus*, Aug. 20, 1828. The stories of the billiard table and extravagance had great effect. — Clay Papers, VIII, F. Johnson to Clay, April 8, 1827.

[42] Adams, *Memoirs*, Vol. VII, pp. 415–416.

[43] Clay Papers, XII, W. W. Worsley to Clay, March 30, 1828; Miscellaneous Collection (N. Y. Pub. Lib.), Clay to Joseph Gales, Oct. 20, 1828; *Argus*, Sept. 24, 1828; *National Intelligencer*, Oct. 18, 1828.

[44] *Kentucky Reporter*, Sept. 22, 1827, March 19, June 18, 1828; Lynn, *op. cit.*, pp. 26–37. The charge was false, and the Transylvania trustees retained full confidence in Clay as the executor of Morrison's estate.

Clay asserted in May, 1828, that his financial affairs were in excellent shape, but within a month he was trying hard to obtain a loan in Philadelphia, and that summer he proposed that the trustees leave the $20,000

Company" — ran a toast drunk in South Carolina. "Would to God they were like Jonah in the whale's belly; the whale to the devil; the devil in hell; and the door locked, key lost, and not a son of Vulcan within a million of miles to make another." [45]

This storm of calumny was retorted to with interest by the friends of the Administration. Jackson was portrayed as a military butcher of the first order. Handbills were scattered over the country, black with representations of coffins and containing a dreadful account in verse of Jackson's execution of six militiamen.

> Oh! Did you hear the plaintive cry
> Borne on the southern breeze?
> Saw you John Harris earnest pray
> For mercy, on his knees? [46]

Jackson was accused of participation in land frauds, of willful lying, of blasphemy. The charge of conspiracy with Burr was hurled back at him, and Clay lent himself to an attempt at obtaining incriminating papers from Mrs. Blennerhassett. [47]

Worst of all was the attack upon Mrs. Jackson. The General had married her while she was still Mrs. Lewis Robards, believing that Robards had obtained a divorce. Technically, they had lived in adultery until the divorce was obtained, when a second marriage had been promptly performed. Charles Hammond, in Ohio, spread the scandal in his *Truth's Advocate and Monthly Anti-Jackson Expositor*, and anonymous pamphleteers took it up. "General Jackson and Mrs. Robards . . . voluntarily, and for the gratification of their own appetites, placed themselves in a situation to render it necessary that Mrs. Robards should be convicted of desertion and adultery, in respect to Robards. . . . Those indifferent to the character of the President's wife and those who conceive that a fallen

legacy in his hands, on the security of a six per cent. mortgage. The trustees accepted his proposal. — *National Intelligencer*, June 23, 1828; Transylvania Archives, 1828-U-46, Clay to John Bradford, Aug. 16, 1828.

[45] *National Intelligencer*, Oct. 6, 1828.

[46] Kelsay, *op. et loc. cit.*, pp. 74–79.

[47] Clay Papers, XII, Porter to Clay, March 26, 1828; Porter Collection, Clay to Porter, April 2, 1828.

female may be restored by subsequent good conduct, may conscientiously give General Jackson their support." [48]

There is no evidence that Clay was responsible for this vicious attack upon Rachel Jackson. He said, according to Hammond, "that the affair ought not to be brought before the public." [49] But Jackson's bitterness over these onslaughts embraced all of his opponents. "They suppose," he wrote to R. K. Call, "when the election is over, all things will die away — *but not so,* — I look forward to the first of December, next, with much anxiety as a day of retribution." [50]

For a long time Clay held to the belief that the Administration would be vindicated in the election. In December 1826, he forecast Adams' re-election "by a majority of at least two-thirds." [51] The tariff and internal improvements, he believed, would hold in line the West, New England, and Pennsylvania. But by the close of 1827 Kentucky was showing an ominous coolness, the news from New York and Pennsylvania was most disquieting, and Mrs. Clay began to talk of going back to Kentucky within a year as though that were a certainty. [52]

Clay's health, which had given him much anxiety ever since he had entered the State Department, was very bad in the spring of 1828. There was nothing organically wrong, the great Doctor Philip Physick assured him, but his heavy labors, the constant flood of persecution, and family troubles had drained his strength and lowered his spirits to such an extent that he himself believed that death was near. [53] He thought seriously of resigning from the State Department, and did absent himself from its labors as much as possible. But he did his best, by his correspondence and occasional speeches, to stem the im-

---

[48] *View of General Jackson's Domestic Relations* (Amer. Antiq. Soc.), pp. 8–9.

[49] Clay Papers, VIII, Hammond to J. H. Eaton, Jan. 27, 1827 (copy).

[50] *The Collector*, Vol. XIX (Dec. 1905), p. 17, Jackson to Call, May 18, 1828. *Cf. Va. Mag. of Hist.*, Vol. XXIX (April 1921), pp. 191–192, Jackson to Call, Aug. 16, 1828.

[51] Clay Papers, VIII, Clay to Brown, Dec. 14, 1826. *Cf.* Clay to Brown, March 27, 1827.

[52] M. B. Smith, *op. cit.*, pp. 211–212.

[53] Adams, *Memoirs*, Vol. VII, pp. 517–521.

pending flood. That deluge, if it came, might be interpreted as a sign of Divine displeasure, he told an audience in Baltimore, and added, "I would humbly prostrate myself before Him, and implore His mercy, to visit our favored land with War, with pestilence, with famine, with any scourge other than military rule, or a blind and heedless enthusiasm for military renown." [54] He had dramatized the conflict into a struggle between good and evil powers, an histrionic conception to which he clung during the whole Jackson era.

Doggedly his optimism put aside the discouraging reports that came in from every quarter. He wrote to James Brown, in May, that Adams would win, and as late as October he was still hoping for the best, although his confidence had visibly abated and he despaired of Pennsylvania and Virginia.[55] But at the end he faced reality. "General Jackson, without doubt, will be elected," he wrote to his son Henry Junior, then a student at West Point. "He will obtain the votes of Kentucky and Ohio, and perhaps of Indiana also. I consider the question as decided." [56]

And Jackson won. Demos spoke in unmistakable accents at the polls, and the West, the South (save Delaware and Maryland), New York and Pennsylvania carried the General to a decisive victory. The charges of corruption, aristocracy and extravagance, the propaganda against centralization and for truly popular rule, had done their work. Individualistic, suspicious of wealth and class privileges, devoted to the belief that the people are their own best guides, the American democracy had rebuked the National Republicans, and put its trust in the Military Chieftain. Was something worse than "war, pestilence and famine" about to sweep across the land?

[54] Mallory, op. cit., Vol. I, pp. 555–557.
[55] Sweet Collection, Clay to Brown, May 17, Oct. 11, 1828. "Whatever may be the result, the tariff will be maintained," he wrote in October.
[56] McDowell Collection, Clay to Henry Clay, Jr., Nov. 14, 1828.

CHAPTER XIV

RETIREMENT — NOT REST

CLAY's life in Washington, during the last months of the defeated Administration, was made up of both sweet and bitter elements. His party had been badly worsted, but there were a number of pleasant aspects to both private and public affairs in which he could take comfort. He had been instrumental in the selection of a new President for Transylvania University, Dr. Alvah Woods of Brown, and felt that the prospects of the institution were decidedly hopeful.[1] Henry Junior, an earnest, able youth, though much inclined to distrust his own ability, was at West Point, where he was making an excellent record. Henry Clay watched over this promising offspring with solicitude and pride.

And now, my dear Son [he wrote, in the same letter that conveyed his certainty of political defeat], you are one of my greatest comforts. Indeed there is no object in life about which I have so much solicitude as your success in your studies, which I believe to be so intimately connected with your welfare and future usefulness. I entreat you therefore, by your love for me, and by your own good, to persevere, and do as you have done.[2]

All through that winter, the reports from "the Point" furnished a comforting solace to the statesman.

The prospect of temporary relief from the ordeal of political battle was also inviting to the battered leader. To retire for a short time at Ashland, giving the Jackson party an opportunity to split up into its discordant elements, and then

---

[1] Letters in Transylvania Archives; McDowell Collection, Clay to Henry Clay, Jr., Oct. 21, 1828. President Horace Holley had resigned, supposedly on account of religious differences early in 1827.

[2] McDowell Collection, Clay to Henry Clay, Jr., Nov. 14, 1828.

return to Congress as the great leader of a triumphant opposition, was by no means an unpleasing possibility. Clay was already beginning to envisage himself as a successful presidential candidate in 1832. There were times when his buoyancy of temper was in the ascendant, and Margaret Bayard Smith commented repeatedly upon his high spirits and good humor.[3]

But despondency was not a stranger to him during that winter season. A major political defeat is scarcely inspiring and, after all, the political future was mantled with uncertainty. Other troubles, too, weighed heavily upon the Kentuckian.

Family misfortunes, preluded by the loss of Susan and Eliza three years before, were now crowding thick and fast. Clay's own health was not good that winter. Mrs. Clay's sister, Nancy Brown, belle of the embassies in Paris, was slowly fading away. Worst of all was the anxiety caused by two of his sons. Theodore, the eldest, had received a head injury when a young boy and, according to family tradition, this was responsible for growing fits of moroseness and wild behavior that were a constant source of worry to his parents. Thomas Hart Clay, the second son, a youth of brilliant parts who in later years became a prominent citizen of Kentucky, was at this time prone to intemperate excesses, and apparently had no fixed aim in life. He spent some time in a Philadelphia jail, during the winter of 1828–1829, while his father and mother were keeping up the social whirl that attended the close of the Administration.[4]

It was not strange that Clay was unable to sleep for weeks without the aid of soporifics, nor that at times his home had a funereal air.[5] That house was filled with the anguish that had prompted the appeal to his third son, two years before: —

[3] Clay Papers, XIV, Clay to Niles, Nov. 25, 1828, Brown to Clay, Dec. 12, 1828, Clay to Brooke, Jan. 10, 1829; Webster Papers, II, Clay to Webster, Nov. 30, 1828; Adams, *Memoirs*, Vol. VIII, p. 86; M. B. Smith, *op. cit.*, pp. 246, 248–250, 285–287, 299–304.

[4] Clay Papers, XIV, T. J. Wharton to Clay, March 6, 1829; M. B. Smith, *op. cit.*, pp. 259, 277, 303.

[5] M. B. Smith, *op. cit.*, pp. 256–258, 271, 277–281.

If you too disappoint my anxious hopes a Constitution, never good, and now almost exhausted, would sink beneath the pressure. You bear my name. You are my son, and the hopes of all of us are turned with anxiety upon you.[6]

Jackson was inaugurated March 4, taking the oath on the east portico of the Capitol before an immense throng, and then throwing the Executive Mansion open to the roaring, glass-smashing, china-breaking mob of humanity that had gathered to celebrate the advent of the people's President. The old General, bowed down with grief over the recent death of his wife, entered upon his new duties with a heavy heart, but perhaps there was some solace in the reflection that the "day of retribution" had at last arrived.

Meanwhile, the members of the former Administration were making preparations for leaving the city. Clay was given a farewell dinner by his friends, at which he warned of the danger of military tyranny. His own attitude toward the new government was plainly indicated. He would make "no pledges, no promises, no threats, and I must add, I have no confidence." At the end, he proposed a toast: "Let us never despair of the American Republic." [7] After this final burst of shell fire there was little left save the business of departure. The Clays auctioned their household goods, realizing over three thousand dollars.[8] On March 12, the Kentuckian took leave of the Adams family, manifesting "some sensibility at parting," [9] and the next day the Clays left Washington for the long trip home. They arrived at Ashland on April 16, and Clay at once set about improving the house and grounds, which had been rented during their absence and were out of repair.[10]

Clay's constituents would have sent him to the Kentucky legislature or back to the House of Representatives at Washington, but he decided to concentrate mainly upon regaining

---

[6] McDowell Collection, Clay to Henry Clay, Jr., April 2, 1827.

[7] Clay Papers, XIV, March 7, 1829 (draft).

[8] *Ibid.*, XIV, 2448, 2483 (auction lists). Furnishings brought $2,886.37; Madeira and champagne, $405.

[9] Adams, *Memoirs*, Vol. VIII, p. 110.

[10] McDowell Collection, Clay to Henry Clay, Jr., April 19, 1829.

his health and improving his estate. Devotion to the law was not essential, and, although he was not a stranger to the courts, his interests centered chiefly about Ashland.[11]

There were, of course, the trials and tribulations common to large families. Clay's mother, stepfather and brother John died within two weeks of one another as the year 1829 drew to its close, and Nancy Brown passed away less than a year later.[12] Thomas still found himself unable to settle down, and Theodore's ailment developed into violent insanity by 1831.[13] Mrs. Clay was still a gracious hostess to the guests brought to Ashland by her husband, but she was griefstricken by the tragedies that seemed to have become an inevitable part of her lot, and seldom took any part in the social activities of her home town.

On the other hand, there were many pleasant aspects of this retirement. Public dinners and other honors were showered upon "the Great Hal," as his Kentucky friends called him. There were business and pleasure trips that sometimes had a decided political tinge, to Cincinnati and Columbus, to the southern part of Kentucky, and with the family in the summertime to Olympian Springs. Several months in the winter of 1830 and 1831 were spent in New Orleans, and Clay would have purchased a plantation near that city, in partnership with his son-in-law, James Erwin, had not the seller backed out at the last moment.[14]

At Ashland, the master repaired the mill and moved it to a more favorable location. He built a conical icehouse, one of the two that still remain on the estate. Over one hundred acres of land adjoining Ashland were purchased, and the live-

---

[11] Colton, *Correspondence*, pp. 232–233; *National Intelligencer*, July 21, 1829; *Niles' Register*, Vol. XXXVIII, p. 327, June 26, 1830.

[12] McDowell Collection, Clay to Henry Clay, Jr., Dec. 23, 1829; Clay Papers, Brown to Clay, Oct. 28, 1830.

[13] Commonwealth of Ky. *vs.* Theodore W. Clay (lunacy). Fayette Circuit Court, file 746. June 10, 1831. When Theodore's condition was most alarming, Clay could still write to Peter B. Porter a touching letter on the death of Porter's wife, urging the New Yorker to visit Ashland, that they might "mingle in your sorrows, and do all that the sincerest friendship, on the part of Mrs. Clay and myself, could prompt to mitigate them." — Porter Collection, Clay to Porter, Aug. 22, 1831.

[14] Clay Papers, XVI, Clay to Brown, April 17, 1830.

stock was augmented, especially by the acquisition of fifty pure-blood merino sheep that came from western Pennsylvania. The assessed valuation of his property increased in the tax lists from fifty-one thousand, five hundred dollars in 1829 to seventy-two thousand, two hundred and fifty in 1831, exclusive, as the records quaintly state, of "Studs, Jack Asses and Billiard Tables." [15]

"The Western Hotspur" wrote to his friends that farming was weaning him away from politics, and, though political reports were most encouraging, he confided to Henry Junior: —

I am getting so much attached to the pursuits of my farm — I consider life as so uncertain, and public affairs so full of vexation, that I have become more indifferent than I ever expected to be in regard to public life.[16]

In the spring of 1831, James Erwin purchased the General Trotter farm, between Ashland and Lexington, and brought his wife and growing family there for a part of each year. Anne Erwin, the Clays' one remaining daughter, was intelligent and sprightly and her father was very happy over this renewal of close associations. A few months later, Henry Junior graduated with the second honor at West Point. (The time was not far distant when he was to abandon the military profession, under what he believed was persecution by Jackson, and take up the law, a step that his father encouraged and to which he himself had been inclined for several years.[17]) Despite sorrow and tragedy, these years of retirement brought also real happiness to Henry Clay.

But though domestic matters engrossed much of his attention, the President's Palace still held its lure,[18] and, through

---

[15] Fayette County Tax Lists, 1829–1831.

[16] Clay Papers, XVI, Clay to Brown, April 17, 1830; Colton, *Correspondence*, pp. 260–261, Clay to Brooke, April 19, 1830; McDowell Collection, Clay to Henry Clay, Jr., May 24, 1830.

[17] McDowell Collection, Henry Clay, Jr.'s Diary. Young Clay had been recommended for the Engineers by the faculty, but Jackson refused to make the appointment.

[18] This may well have been in Clay's mind when he rejected Adams' offer of a place on the Supreme Court. — Wm. H. Smith, *Charles Hammond* (Chicago Hist. Soc., 1885), p. 56.

a voluminous correspondence and occasional speeches, Clay gradually laid plans for leading his defeated party to victory in 1832. There was little question of his leadership, for Adams, who had borne the brunt of the disaster, was determined for the time being upon a retirement as complete as that of "a nun taking the veil." [19]

The Kentuckian's plan of campaign developed along simple lines. It combined a loud defense of protection and internal improvements with critical scrutiny of the Administration's policies. Clay mistakenly underrated Jackson's ability as a leader, and felt confident that the people would tire of "Jackson thraldom," the compound of "imbecility, tyranny and hypocrisy which now disgraces our Metropolis." [20]

Clay's first onslaught came at a public dinner in Lexington, May 16, 1829, in the form of a denunciation of Old Hickory's spoils system, and his appointment of Congressmen to political offices.[21] The President was vulnerable on both counts, for his opportunism, to use no harsher term, had never been displayed to better advantage. His condemnation of Congressional appointments in 1825 had been based on high moral grounds, but his record in 1829 stamped this earlier effusion as either vindictively partisan or insincere. In 1798, again on high moral grounds, he had condemned using office for partisan purposes, and in 1816 he had urged Monroe to disregard party in the selection of his Cabinet and appoint only "the most honest, possessing capacity, virtue, and firmness." [22] But in 1829 he gave a powerful impulse to the trend toward the spoils system that had been checked by John Quincy Adams. It is true that a bureaucracy, with its attendant evils, had been developing in the National Government. The people probably expected a general office turnover, and Jackson may have believed, naïvely, that any American was capable of filling any vacancy. But the

---

[19] Adams, *Memoirs,* Vol VIII, p. 107.

[20] J. B. Harrison Papers, 1812–1888, Clay to Harrison, June 2, 1829.

[21] *Niles' Register,* Vol. XXXVI, pp. 399–405, Aug. 15, 1829; Mallory, *op. cit.,* Vol. I, pp. 568–585; Cf. Watterston Papers, Clay to Watterston, July 21, 1829.

[22] Jackson, *Correspondence,* Vol. I, pp. 42–44, Vol. II, pp. 261–262, 263–265, 272–273. Cf. Van Buren, *Autobiography,* pp. 233–239.

"day of retribution" had come, and the hundreds of dismissals and new appointments that swept his opponents out of the paying offices under his control in the North and West were based primarily upon politics, personal prejudice and a charitable inclination to relieve the needy "outs." [23] The remedy was worse than the disease.

On the other hand, Clay's onslaught was based in part upon political expediency, rather than devotion to the highest principles of a merit system. He had recognized the value of appointing supporters to office, and had chafed under Adams' policy in this regard. It is not unfair to believe that there was an element of baffled rage in the Kentuckian's attack upon a practice that was building up the political power of a victorious rival.

Jackson's Indian policy gave Clay an opportunity for further criticism. The President was determined to support Georgia in her attempt to seize the lands of the Cherokees. His first message recommended that Congress set aside a great reservation in the Far West to which the Indians might go, and a bill was passed accordingly by a strictly party vote. Adams had upheld the Cherokees and the National Republicans opposed Jackson's project. The Cherokees had treaty rights, if Indian treaties really constituted rights. Clay sympathized with the red men and denounced Jackson's attitude as disgraceful to the country. He headed an attack in Kentucky, based upon national honor and the expense of removal, and suggested that a similar movement be inaugurated in other parts of the country and in Congress.[24] Jackson lost popularity among the Methodists and Quakers because he would not shield their missionaries from Georgia's interference, but his course of procedure failed to give the opposition any real political advantage.

The Kentuckian's ire was also roused by the President's

[23] Jackson, *Correspondence*, Vol. IV, p. 33; W. T. Barry, "Letters," in *William and Mary Quart.*, Vol. XIII (April 1905), pp. 236–244, Barry to his daughter, June 11, 1829; C. R. Fish, *The Civil Service and the Patronage* (N.Y., 1905), pp. 117–126, 132.

[24] Colton, *Correspondence*, pp. 273–274, 278, Clay to Everett, June 16, 1830, Clay to Johnston, June 14, 1830.

stand in regard to certain internal improvements. Jackson had vacillated on the question of improvements at national expense during his earlier career, but as President he came to some extent under the influence of his Secretary of State, Martin Van Buren, who was an opponent of that policy.[25] Both men were anxious to strike at their great rival. On May 27, 1830, the President vetoed a bill for subscription to the stock of a company that was to construct a road from Maysville to Lexington, Kentucky. It was a highway wholly within the boundary of a state, Clay's state, and so was pounced upon by Van Buren as a local measure. Jackson's veto message dwelt particularly upon constitutionality, the necessity for governmental economy, and his cherished project of extinguishing the national debt. It was inconsistent, certainly, for Old Hickory signed a good many internal improvement bills, some of them fully as local as the Maysville road,[26] but it made excellent political capital.

The veto was a double-barreled attack upon the Kentuckian. It struck at one of the main supports of his American System, and it was a blow at a vigorous movement for improving Kentucky's transportation system that he had been pushing ever since his return to Lexington.[27] The Maysville road was one of Clay's pet projects, and he promptly began fostering a vigorous attack upon the President's action. He gave his hearty approval to indignation meetings in Kentucky, and encouraged movements throughout the West and East for censuring the veto

[25] See Van Buren, *Autobiography*, pp. 312, 320f. New York had constructed the Erie Canal, and had no desire to see Federal funds used to aid Pennsylvania in building a rival system.

[26] See the table compiled by John G. Van Deusen, *The Economic Bases of Disunion in South Carolina* (N.Y., 1928), p. 128.

[27] McDowell Collection, Clay to Henry Clay, Jr., Dec. 2, 1829; Mallory, *op. cit.*, Vol. I, p. 582; H. A. Smith, *op. cit.*, pp. 27–32. Clay was a leader in promoting the Lexington and Ohio railroad, incorporated in January 1830. His friends subscribed $10,000 worth of stock in his name while he was in New Orleans. He felt the financial strain of his subscription, but was a zealous sponsor of the railroad. See Account Book of the Louisville and Frankfort R.R. (Univ. of Ky. Lib.); *Niles' Register*, Vol. XL, p. 181, May 14, 1831; *Kentucky Legislature Reports*, Dec. 1840, p. 349; T. D. Clark, "The Lexington and Ohio Railroad," in *Reg. of the Ky. State Hist. Soc.*, Jan. 1933, pp. 9–28.

and demanding a constitutional amendment that would permit
a simple majority of both Houses of Congress to pass a bill
over the President's veto.[28] Clay believed that Jackson had
sealed his fate in the West, and many Jackson men wore dole-
ful faces, but the General's arguments and popularity carried
the day. Pennsylvania, as crucial a state as any, held firm in
his support, and the West's passionate devotion to him was not
seriously impaired.

Regardless of Jackson's motives, this veto marked the beginning of the end for the long struggle over nationally constructed roads and canals. The nation, turning back to the
Jeffersonian ideal of a limited central government in judging
this question, and already becoming accustomed to ambitious
improvement programs by the states, had lost its enthusiasm
for one of the most grandiose concepts of the American System.

Clay was also engaged in making his position clear on the
tariff and nullification. South Carolina's resentment had flamed
high over the "tariff of abominations." Talk of nullification
and dissolution of the Union was rife, and Calhoun became
one of the leaders in this energetic protest. Webster's reply
to Hayne, and Jackson's defiance to Calhoun,— "Our .Federal
Union — it must be preserved," — were indications of a common nationalist stand with which Clay was in full sympathy.
On March 13, 1830, he spoke at Natchez, Mississippi, denying that disunion was imminent, and urging, with specious
logic, that the tariff was a national necessity which had raised
the price of Southern cotton and lowered the cost to the South
of manufactured goods.[29] He praised Webster's reply to Hayne,
denounced nullification, and lent his approval to popular meetings in Kentucky where similar action was taken. No state had
a right to withdraw from the Union (he asserted at Columbus,

---

[28] Porter Collection, Clay to Porter, June 13, 1830; Colton, *Correspondence*,
pp. 273–278.

[29] Mallory, *op. cit.*, Vol. I, pp. 586–589. This tariff argument was enlarged
and expounded in a speech at Cincinnati, Aug. 3, 1830. — *Ibid.*, Vol. I, pp.
593–597. Clay had been fearful of disunion, however, as early as Dec. 1828.
— Adams, *Memoirs*, Vol. VIII, pp. 87–88.

Ohio) without the common consent of the other members; and he suggested in semiserious vein that it might be politic to let South Carolina go. She would soon be begging for readmittance.[30]

The Government debt was being rapidly extinguished, and by the latter part of 1831 Clay was willing to reduce or eliminate tariffs on noncompetitive goods, in order to avoid creating a surplus, but he was still determined to retain "unimpaired" the principle of protection. With a strange obstinacy, he asserted that such reductions ought to satisfy all but the Southern extremists.[31]

Clay's program had now been formulated by a vigorous attack upon Jacksonian policies in regard to spoils, the Indian question, arbitrary executive power, and internal improvements, an equally vigorous championship of protection, upon which the President had taken no decided stand, and, rivaling Old Hickory, a forthright opposition to nullification. Meanwhile, he fostered the development of newspaper attacks upon the Administration,[32] and awaited the inevitable nomination, the imminence of which began to appear from the action of state conventions and mass meetings by the fall of 1830.

The general outlook, however, was not promising. It became more and more evident that Jackson's vetoes (for other improvement bills had suffered also) had popular support. His Administration scored a victory when Van Buren, as Secretary of State, placated the British by a frank acknowledgment of

[30] Mallory, *op. cit.*, Vol. I, pp. 603–604. Clay at Cincinnati, Aug. 3, 1830. Madison complimented Clay for his attack on nullification, with its "hideous aspect and fatal tendency." He specially commended Clay's argument that the Virginia and Kentucky Resolutions furnished no precedent for South Carolina's threatened action. — Clay Papers, XVI, Madison to Clay, Oct. 9, 1830.

[31] J. B. Harrison Papers, Clay to Harrison, July 24, 1831; Colton, *Correspondence*, pp. 314–317, Clay to Brooke, Oct. 4, 1831. At this time, Clay found no authority in the Constitution for distributing any surplus among the states.

[32] Watterston Papers, Clay to Watterston, July 21, 1829; Porter Collection, Clay to Porter, Nov. 22, 1829; Philip R. Fendall Papers (Amer. Antiq. Soc.), Memo., Feb. 1, 1830, and *ibid.* (Duke Univ.), Clay to Fendall, April 30, 1830.

our previous diplomatic mistakes, and secured the reopening of the West Indian trade in the fall of 1830. The National Republicans had no issue in their opposition to nullification. The elections of 1830 proved to be disappointing not only in such Eastern states as New York and Maine, but in Kentucky and Ohio as well. The Western elections in 1831 filled Clay with disappointment and mortification.[33] Worst of all, perhaps, a third party was springing up that tended to split the opposition to Jackson in the East. This party arose out of the Antimasonic movement.

In September 1826, a stone-mason named William Morgan, who had written a book exposing the secrets of the Masonic order, had been abducted in Canandaigua, New York, and taken to the Niagara frontier, where all trace of him disappeared. The Masons had previously made determined efforts to prevent the publication of his book, and the excitement which these attempts had occasioned in western New York grew by leaps and bounds with his mysterious exit from the scene. This febrile state of mind promptly produced an influence upon politics. In 1828, the Antimasonic Party in New York elected four senators and seventeen assemblymen, thus demonstrating its potential strength.

Thurlow Weed, convinced that the old National Republican leadership was incapable of combating Jacksonian democracy, saw an opportunity in the Antimasonic furor. He and another rising New York politician, William Henry Seward, began to mould it into what they hoped would become a great national party, taking over the National Republican program, and opposing Jackson and Van Buren.[34] Weed, Seward, Francis Granger and others were forging to the front as the most important anti-Jackson leaders in New York State. Granger, Antimason candidate for Governor in New York, was defeated in 1830, but membership in the assembly was increased. Meanwhile, September 11, 1830, a national Antimason convention was held at Philadelphia, eleven states being represented.

---

[33] Johnston Collection, Clay to Johnston, Aug. 20, 1831.
[34] Chas. McCarthy, "The Antimasonic Party," in *Amer. Hist. Assoc. Report* (1902), Vol. I, pp. 375–397.

This meeting paved the way for a nominating convention, which was to meet at Baltimore, September 26, 1831.

Clay had become inactive in the Masonic order in November 1824, apparently because he had been rebuffed in attempting to form a General Grand Lodge for the United States two years before.[35] He did not, however, scoff at the fraternity, and during the first years of the excitement took little notice of it, save to regard Antimasonry as a delusion.[36] But as the movement grew in power, the Kentuckian's stand on Masonry became more and more important, and by the spring of 1830, Porter was beseeching him to write a letter that could be confidentially shown, expressing his real views. Clay replied at some length. He had never been, he said, a "bright" Mason, had never attached much importance to the order. He had never differentiated in public or private life between Masons and non-Masons, and he believed that, practically, Masonry did neither good nor harm. Still his sense of honor forbade him to either renounce or denounce it, and, as he did not think that this explanation of his attitude would do any good, he requested Porter not to use it.[37]

By the latter part of 1830, Clay had perceived the real object of Weed and his followers. They were, he wrote, "in the pursuit of power . . . without regard to the means of acquiring it." He was still hopeful, however, that the new party would join with the National Republicans in raising the Clay standard. He advised conciliation, and suggested the possibility of supporting the Antimason nominee for Governor in 1832, in return for support of himself for President.[38]

By the spring of 1831, however, conditions had become worse. Richard Rush sent word from Pennsylvania that the

[35] Coleman, *Masonry in the Bluegrass*, pp. 92–93.

[36] Porter Collection, Clay to Porter, March 24, 1828. In the campaign of 1828, Jackson papers charged him with fomenting Antimasonic excitement, and also with being one of the authors of Morgan's fate(!). — *National Intelligencer*, March 18, April 16, 1828.

[37] Clay Papers, XVI, Porter to Clay, May 23, 1830; Porter Collection, Clay to Porter, June 13, 1830.

[38] Colton, *Correspondence*, pp. 288–291, Clay to John Bailhache, Nov. 24, 1830.

Antimason state convention had resolved that Clay would not be nominated at Baltimore if he were still a Mason, and besought Clay to shake off the institution "like a dewdrop from the Lion's mane." [39] The Antimasons, developing a formidable strength in Pennsylvania and New England as well as in New York, had become such an important factor that Calhoun's supporter, Duff Green of the *Telegraph,* was casting sheep's-eyes in their direction.[40] Still Clay persisted in refusing to come out against Masonry. He believed that the National Government could take no action in regard to the order, that an Antimasonic nomination would be still-born, and that the party might yet be won to the National Republican fold.[41]

Two weeks before the Antimasonic convention was to meet at Baltimore, a bold attempt was made to install Clay in its good graces. Peter B. Porter and William B. Rochester, both close friends of Clay and prominently connected with his interests in New York State, published in a Buffalo paper their stand on Masonry. Porter stated that he had withdrawn from the order long ago, because its pomp and pageantry were distasteful to him, and because of a conviction that it had outlived its usefulness. He believed that it was proved that Morgan had been murdered by Masons. In order to prevent similar occurrences, and to propitiate those who believed that Freemasonry authorized crimes, the lodges should surrender their charters. Rochester's letter concurred with these sentiments. Then the two men made a joint statement. They hesitated to say anything about Clay's opinion on the subject, but they would do so, since he had never in his conversations imposed any restraint upon them. His sentiments, they asserted, "correspond with, and have in fact, corroborated those entertained by us. That he has neither made, nor authorized any publick annunciation of those opinions, is not surprising to those who are familiar with the characteristic delicacy of his feelings,

[39] Clay Papers, XVII, Rush to Clay, June 3, 1831; Rush to Edward Ingersoll, June 9, 1831.

[40] Weed Papers, D. Russell to Weed, Sept. 13, 1831.

[41] Johnston Collection, Clay to Johnston, July 23, Aug. 30, 1831; Colton, *Correspondence,* pp. 303–304, Clay to Brooke, June 23, 1831.

which would forbid his doing any act that might be construed into an effort on his part, to advance his well-earned popularity by indirect means." Porter wrote to Clay, September 15, that the step had been a bold one, but that, in his opinion, it would be justified by its effect in the Northern and Middle states.[42]

But this effort was destined to fail, despite the fact that, aside from Masonry, the political principles of the New York Antimasons were those of Clay. Weed may have honestly tried at an earlier date to tie the fortunes of his new party to the Kentuckian, but by the fall of 1830, so the New York politician's *Autobiography* asserts, he had become convinced of Clay's opposition to political Antimasonry.[43] At any rate, the Antimasonic leaders were adamant in the determination not to nominate him. They sounded Rush, but he declined. Adams was approached, but, though willing, he was reluctant, expressing a distaste for hurting Clay's chances of election.[44] John McLean was offered the honor, but refused. So, evidently, did John Marshall. William Wirt was the final candidate, but his letter of acceptance, received before the convention adjourned, stated that he had once been a Mason, dropping out only through loss of interest, that he refused to lead in a general proscription of Masons, that he did not believe Masonic implication in the Morgan case characterized the whole order, and that in view of these circumstances, he wished to give the convention an opportunity to change its nomination.[45] He remained the standard-bearer. But the Antimasonic leaders certainly might have discovered, had they cared to do so, that his position was not essentially different from that of Clay.

The New York election of 1831 gave the Antimasons nearly thirty members in the legislature, the National Republicans

---

[42] *Buffalo Journal and General Advertiser*, Sept. 14, 1831; Porter Collection, Porter to Clay, Sept. 15, 1831 (copy).

[43] Weed, *Autobiography*, pp. 350–354; McCarthy, *op. et loc. cit.*, pp. 395, 410.

[44] Adams, *Memoirs*, Vol. VIII, pp. 400–401, 403, 412–413; W. H. Seward, *Autobiography of William H. Seward*, F. W. Seward, ed. (N.Y., 1877), pp. 205–206.

[45] *Niles' Register*, Vol. XLI, pp. 83–85, Oct. 1, 1831. *Cf.* Gammon, *op. cit.*, pp. 44–52.

six.[46] But the former party had expected much better results than it obtained, and its leaders regarded the outcome as extremely disappointing. The reason, Seward wrote to Weed, was that the Clay men, who in 1830 had either voted with them or remained neutral, had given their support to the Jackson ticket. It was a plot, he charged, designed to break down Antimasonry and compel the withdrawal of Wirt in favor of Clay, at the same time compelling "Mr. Calhoun's friends to come to the standard of the Kentucky chief." But all was not lost. There would be three presidential tickets in the field in New York, and the break-up of the Clay-Jackson coalition would benefit the Antimasons. He added: —

Be the result of the Presidential Election what it may (and now I think that under the circumstances there can be no doubt of the success of General Jackson) there is an end to this unfortunate controversy between the Rival Chieftains. Whether Jackson or Clay be elected the merits and claims of both are determined, the old interests, the inveterate prejudices, and the blind devotion of both Parties will be broken up and then will succeed the season when men will look upon Anti Masonry first with curiosity next with interest increasing to solicitude, then favor, and then regret for having left it to stand knocking and unanswered so long at their door.[47]

The time was not far distant when the National Republicans and the Antimasons were to be merged in the Whig Party, but the rivalry between Clay on the one hand, and Weed and Seward on the other, for leadership in that organization had begun in 1830 and 1831.

Under circumstances so depressing that friends gave way to gloom, and Clay himself thought for a moment of giving up the struggle,[48] the Kentuckian finally decided to carry the fight into the enemy's camp, and re-enter the United States

[46] J. D. Hammond, op. cit., Vol. II, p. 397.

[47] Weed Papers, Seward to Weed, Nov. 14, 1831. Cf. Kent Papers, VI, Wm. Kent to Moss Kent, Nov. 19, 1831. "The tempest of Jacksonism has again gone over us," Kent wrote, but added that his dread and disgust of the Antimasons was such "that I really upon the whole prefer the 'regular' party to them."

[48] Johnston Collection, Clay to Johnston, Aug. 20, 1831.

Senate. His friends importuned him to do so,[49] John J. Critten-den, to the vexation of his brother and daughter, willingly gave way that Clay might be chosen,[50] and, in the face of a ferocious Jackson press attack, Clay was elected by a small majority of the Kentucky legislature and came to Washington at the beginning of December, 1831.

Clay had been acknowledged for some time the inevitable candidate of the National Republicans, and the local nominations were climaxed by a National Republican convention at Baltimore, December 12–16, 1831, when he was chosen by acclamation, with John Sergeant as his running mate.[51] It had been certain for almost a year that Jackson would run again,[52] and now the "Rival Chieftains" stood face to face, both eager for a fight in which there was little question of giving or receiving quarter.

[49] Webster urged him to come, saying that it would be an arduous session, with attacks on the tariff and the Constitution itself. "Everything is to be debated as if nothing had ever been settled." — Clay Papers, XVII, Webster to Clay, Oct. 5, 1831.

[50] Clay Papers, XVII, W. W. Worsley to Clay, Oct. 22, 1831; Crittenden Papers (Duke Univ.), Crittenden to Ann Mary Butler Coleman, Nov. 18, 1831.

[51] See Gammon, op. cit., pp. 66–71, for an account of this nomination. The era of national political conventions, foreshadowed by the Federalists in 1808 and 1812, was just beginning.

[52] Niles' Register, Vol. XXXIX, p. 385, Vol. XL, p. 127; Washington Globe, Jan. 22, 1831.

Chapter XV

ARMAGEDDON IN 1832

CLAY came back to Washington bowed down by family afflictions, and filled with gloomy forebodings as to the political future. But he put on a brave front, joked with his friends, asked Adams, who had come back into the House, how it felt to be a boy again, and gave at least the appearance of health and animation.[1]

The Capital to which he now returned as a legislator was slowly growing, but it still remained a city of magnificent distances, with straggling houses and cows pasturing on the Commons. It was a focus for all quarters of the Union, where aristocratic Southerners moved cheek by jowl with uncouth Western and stiff Northern representatives. Society, gay and often dissipated, frequented Boulanger's Restaurant on G Street, marveled at Calvin Edson, "the living skeleton," and patronized the theater when Junius Brutus Booth or Henry Finn came to town. Politics was an all-absorbing topic of conversation that winter, and the giants of the Senate were to furnish ample materials for discussion.

The Senate was notable. There sat Calhoun, its president — a slender figure, whose kindly nature was in part belied by his piercing eyes and the sternness of mouth and brow. This leader of the Nullification Movement had committed the unforgivable sin of criticizing Old Hickory's conduct in Florida fourteen years before, and was now spewed out by Jackson for the sake of patriotism and Van Buren. The ruddy, good-humored Preston, and the pompous Benton, "swelling amid his piles of papers and books," sat near by. Opposite them

[1] M. B. Smith, *op. cit.*, pp. 324–325; *Constitutional Whig*, Dec. 20, 1831; Adams, *Memoirs*, Vol. VIII, p. 443; Colton, *Correspondence*, p. 321, Clay to Brooke, Dec. 9, 1831.

Clay, with his weatherbeaten, homely face, and white hair combed straight back from his temples, lounged in his seat. And the gravity of Frelinghuysen, the majestic brow and deep-set eyes of Webster, lent an air of solemnity to an opposition eager to exploit the slightest weakness of the party in power.

The Kentuckian was a dominant figure in debate that winter. An impatient listener, he was wont to sit at indifferent ease, reading, or eating sticks of striped peppermint candy, a procedure varied by occasional restless wanderings over to the snuffbox that stood on the table of the Senate.[2] But when he spoke, his telling arguments and effective gestures and his marvelous voice compelled the attention of his listeners. He spoke frequently, for party strife was bitter, and the White House, as it was then beginning to be called, was at stake.

January saw skirmishing begin all along the line. One of these encounters ended that same month with a boomerang victory for the Clay forces: The Senate rejected Van Buren as Minister to England.

The Red Fox of Kinderhook had resigned his position as Secretary of State in 1831, when Jackson's first Cabinet had been broken up in the conflict over pretty Peggy Eaton and the strife between the Calhoun and anti-Calhoun factions in the Democratic Party. In June of that year, Jackson had given the London mission to the New Yorker, too late for the Senate to act upon the appointment. Now it was January, 1832, and his confirmation was at the mercy of his foes.

Some of the Clayites doubted the expediency of rejection, but folly urged them on, and four Calhoun men co-operated. The latter charged Van Buren with plotting the disruption of the Cabinet. Clay, Webster, and their followers denounced him as a spoilsman, and thundered against his instructions to McLane in 1829. These instructions, in regard to the West India trade, had suggested telling the British Government that the preceding Administration had been in error, that its policy had been rejected by the people, and that the present Administration would not revive the claims that had been made.[3] Clay's characteriza-

---

[2] Poore, *Reminiscences*, Vol. I, pp. 143–144.
[3] *Executive Documents*, 21st Cong., 2d sess., No. 24, p. 64f.

tion of this as "prostrating and degrading the American eagle before the British lion" was a bit far-fetched, but his argument that the withdrawal of former demands should have been based upon the ground of concession and not upon criticism of the previous American policy was undoubtedly correct.[4]

Van Buren's nomination was rejected by the casting vote of Calhoun, and the opposition prided itself upon having delivered a just rebuke. Clay had held from the first that the move would be both just and expedient, and after the deed was done he asserted to his friends that it had been an excellent political stroke. Calhoun exclaimed in Benton's hearing: "It will kill him dead, sir, kill him dead. He will never kick, sir, never kick." But Jackson was a shrewder prophet. As he foretold, the martyr's crown well became the "Little Magician," and the short-sighted tactics of his opponents paved Van Buren's way to the White House.[5]

Meanwhile the Kentuckian had become involved in a tremendous struggle over the tariff and the public lands, two of the most important questions of the day. The sections were markedly divided on these issues. The North Atlantic states were very desirous of a high tariff to guard their manufactures, and high-priced public lands which would help to ensure a goodly supply of cheap labor. The seaboard South was vehemently low-tariff, and the West was equally eager for cheap land, its desire for that commodity surpassing its zeal for internal improvements. A West-South alliance had been in existence since 1830, with Benton and Hayne the leaders in an effort to be mutually agreeable by supporting tariff reduction and a generous land policy.[6]

[4] *Cong. Deb.*, 22d Cong., 1st sess., Sen. Exec. Proceedings, 1320–1325. It was, at this time, in reply to a denunciation of proscription by Clay that Marcy observed that American politicians "see nothing wrong in the rule that to the victor belong the spoils of the enemy."

[5] Porter Collection, Clay to Porter, Jan. 14, March 10, 1832; Colton, *Correspondence*, pp. 326–327, Clay to Brooke, Feb. 21, 1832; Benton, *Thirty Years' View*, Vol. I, p. 219; Jackson, *Correspondence*, Vol. IV, p. 401, Jackson to Coffee, Jan. 21, 1832; Gammon, *op. cit.*, pp. 94–95.

[6] R. G. Wellington, "The Tariff and Public Lands from 1828 to 1833," in the *Amer. Hist. Assoc. Report* (1911), Vol. I, pp. 179–183.

The Administration, which, until now, had taken no decided stand on either the tariff or the public lands, began to clarify its position during the winter of 1832 with a distinct trend toward the policy favored by the West-South alliance.[7]

What was Clay to do?

First came a sop to the West and South, in an inspired article in John H. Pleasant's *Constitutional Whig* of Richmond. This statement made it clearly apparent that the Kentuckian favored using the proceeds of the public lands as a resource for internal improvements, with the Western states receiving "a more liberal application of this fund." On the other hand, it asserted that he was tender of the rights of the states; that he opposed using tariff revenue for roads and canals; and that he was "disposed to limit the amount of [tariff or tax] Revenue to the necessities merely of the Government, and to apply accidental excesses only to Internal Improvements." Those who favored states' rights and opposed Federal encroachment, the article continued, had nothing to fear from this attitude.[8]

In this manner appeared Clay's bid for support in the South and West. The latter would receive special benefits from the sale of public lands; the former should understand that he stood for a revenue tariff with incidental protection, and had no intention of destroying the rights of the states. The plan assumed that the West was as eager for internal improvements as it was for low-priced lands, and that the South would accept protection if it were "incidental."[9] Therein lay two great errors.

Clay was determined to maintain the protective policy, the pillar of his strength in the North, and toward the close of December he laid down a tariff position for his followers. The

---

[7] *Cong. Deb.*, 22d Cong., 1st sess., 625; Schouler, *Hist. of the U.S.*, Vol. IV, p. 66; J. A. Hamilton, *Reminiscences of James A. Hamilton* (N.Y., 1869), p. 243; Chas. C. Johnston to J. B. Floyd, Dec. 16, 1831, in *William and Mary Quarterly*, Vol. I, ser. 2 (July 1921), pp. 201–206.

[8] *Constitutional Whig*, Nov. 29, 1831; Colton, *Correspondence*, pp. 314–317, Clay to Brooke, Oct. 4, 1831; Adams, *Memoirs*, Vol. VIII, p. 441.

[9] Clay told Adams, December 26, that Southern discontent in regard to protection was almost entirely "imaginary or fictitious." — Adams, *Memoirs*, Vol. VIII, p. 443.

revenue was to be reduced immediately, by removing the duties from noncompetitive goods, and by making a few protective duties absolutely prohibitive. He had no patience with the Administration's desire to extinguish the public debt by March 4, 1833. To preserve and strengthen the American System, he "would defy the South, the President and the devil." [10] He brought this plan before the Senate two weeks later in the form of a resolution, and a vigorous debate ensued.

The Kentuckian spoke before a crowded Senate on January 11, 1832, outlining his ideas. He would avoid a surplus, which it would be unwise and unconstitutional to distribute among the states, by abolishing all duties on noncompetitive articles, save silks and wines, and by reducing those. The duties might be radically raised in a few instances, thus cutting off imports, and he mentioned distilled spirits in this connection. He denounced Secretary of the Treasury McLane for desiring a general reduction of duties that would destroy protection, and pleaded for amicable adjustment along the lines of his own plan. [11]

Hayne, Smith of Maryland, and others attacked the protective policy. Mahlon Dickerson of New Jersey, a Jackson man but a staunch protectionist and chairman of the Committee on Manufactures of which Clay was a member, supported the Kentuckian's resolution. At the beginning of February, Clay again took the floor, and spoke for the better part of three days, glorifying the blessings of protection for North, West and South in a speech remarkable for its bitterness and violence. His ardor drove him to denounce his opponents as free-traders who were inviting us to adopt "the British colonial system," and to defend — as he had done in 1820 — the labor of women and children in the factories. He flung his shafts of sarcasm at Calhoun, a tariff proponent in 1816, and denounced Gallatin, who had written against the tariff, as an alien, arrogantly ordering him to go first to his native Europe and inculcate her sovereigns with the Utopian doctrines of

[10] Adams, *Memoirs*, Vol. VIII, pp. 444–448. *Cf. Cong. Deb.*, 22d Cong., 1st sess., 15–16.
[11] *Cong. Deb.*, 22d Cong., 1st sess., 66f.

free trade. If it could be proved that protection pressed "immoderately" anywhere, he would be glad to see modification made. But adequate protection would have to be maintained. With this were mingled glowing denunciations of the spoils system and a solemn warning to South Carolina against Nullification and disunion.[12]

When Clay had finished, the venerable Samuel Smith of Maryland arose. He had been President pro tem at the beginning of the session and he took exception to assertions by the Kentuckian that he had been a leader in the spoils hunt, and unfair to the friends of protection in the appointment of committees. Smith pointed out that he had stood for protection in 1795, and again in 1816. His remarks were conciliatory, but the Kentuckian retorted that all they meant was that the ancient Marylander had once been a friend of manufactures and had now abandoned them. This was the way, Clay sneered, that

> Old politicians chew on wisdom past,
> And totter on in business to the last.

At this, Smith rose in high dudgeon. "Totter, sir?" he exclaimed. "I totter! Though some twenty years older than the gentleman, I can yet stand firm, and am yet able to correct his errors. I could take a view of the gentleman's course which would show how inconsistent he has been."

"Take it, sir, take it. I dare you," shouted Clay.

Cries of "Order" arose. Smith declined the challenge, saying that he "would not so far disregard what is due to the dignity of the Senate," and adjournment ended the scene.[13]

Storm and strife marked the days that followed this exchange. The Administration Senators vigorously attacked the Western Hotspur. Hill of New Hampshire and Grundy of Tennessee defended Gallatin. Mangum of North Carolina pleaded for a moderation of protection, and denounced the glowing picture of female and child labor in the factories. But Clay had support from New England and the Northwest, and

[12] *Ibid.*, 22d Cong., 1st sess., 256–295.
[13] *Ibid.*, 22d Cong., 1st sess., 296–297.

his resolution was adopted. It was sent to the Committee on Manufactures, which reported a bill along the general lines of his plan, although it made some reductions on protected articles, notably wool.[14] This bill was still highly protective, however, and Clay gave it his support. But despite his efforts, it had been laid on the table when the real tariff of 1832, sponsored by Adams' House Committee on Manufactures, came up to the Senate.

The Adams bill swept away the vicious minimum valuation system on woolens, for an ad valorem duty. Cheap wool was admitted duty free, and other protective duties were distinctly lowered. It brought the tariff back to the general level of 1824, clearing it of some of its worst evils, even though the reductions still came mostly among noncompetitive articles.

Clay had no love for this measure. He strove hard to get amendments increasing many of the duties, and succeeded in some cases, notably in the case of cotton bagging, sugar, wool and woolens. But, in conference, the House disagreed to many of these, and the Senate receded, much to the Kentuckian's disgust. He finally gave in because, as he explained, it was still protective, the reductions being mainly on unprotected goods, but he voted steadily against receding from the amendments.[15] The protectionists, in general, found the bill acceptable. It passed, July 12, and Jackson signed it two days later.

Meanwhile, the public land policy had confronted the Kentuckian with a very thorny situation. The younger Western states had become dissatisfied with the price of a dollar and a quarter an acre that had been fixed in 1820, and, under Benton's leadership, were clamoring for cheap lands. The Administration began to show itself amenable to the general principle involved in this demand. McLane's Treasury report,

---

[14] Crittenden Papers (Duke Univ.), Crittenden to Clay, Feb. 23, 1832; Wm. L. Marcy Papers (Lib. of Cong.), Marcy to B. Brown, May 6, 1832.

[15] He had written to Hezekiah Niles, before the Senate amendments were rejected by the House, that they were "essential," and that he and other protectionists had tried to restore the woolen minimum system. — Clay Papers, XIX, Clay to Niles, July 8, 1832.

December, 1831, suggested that the lands be disposed of at
"a fair price" to the states wherein they lay, the proceeds to
be divided up among all the states.[16] Clay opposed this vigorously, fearing a destruction of land revenues that would in
turn destroy his plan for internal improvements. But when the
Senate took up the question, it thrust the Great Hal upon
the horns of a dilemma.

The West-South alliance wished to tie together a lowering
of the tariff and cheaper land prices. Administration Senators
desired to embarrass Clay. As a result, the Committee on
Manufactures, while it was engaged in dealing with the tariff,
was ordered to report on the propriety of reducing the price of
public lands.[17] There was a sinister meaning in Benton's remark at the time, that "the West has a powerful representative
on that Committee; and whatever is done, she is entitled to
know why and wherefore."[18]

Clay saw the trap. The committee report would be attributed
to him. If it favored the demand of the new states, the old
would be dissatisfied; if it favored the old states, the new would
rise in wrath. An impartial measure might satisfy no one. But
he stripped off his coat and went to work.[19]

The result, Clay's land bill, became a credo for the Whig
platforms of succeeding years. Its basis, the use of public land
sales for internal improvements, had been urged by Gallatin
in 1808, and adopted by the Kentuckian at least as early as
October, 1831.[20] His report for the Committee opposed any
considerable price reduction, and argued against ceding the
lands to the states in which they lay. The bill which he introduced at the same time provided that ten per cent. of the
land revenue should go to the states in which the land lay, and

[16] *Cong. Deb.*, 22d Cong., 1st sess., App., 29–30.

[17] Wellington, *op. et loc. cit.*, p. 183; Colton, *Correspondence*, pp. 330–
331, Clay to Brooke, March 28, 1832.

[18] *Cong. Deb.*, 22d Cong., 1st sess., 634.

[19] *Ibid.*, 22d Cong., 1st sess., 1097; 24th Cong., 1st sess., 52; Mallory,
op. cit., Vol. II, pp. 446–447.

[20] *Amer. State Papers, Misc.* (Washington, 1834), Vol. I, p. 741, Gallatin's report to the Senate on roads and canals, April 4, 1808; Colton, *Correspondence*, pp. 314–317, Clay to Brooke, Oct. 4, 1831.

that the rest of this revenue should be divided among all the states in proportion to their representation in Congress. This should be applied to education, internal improvements, the colonization of free blacks, or the reduction of state debts, as the states might see fit.[21]

The intent of the plan was to keep public land prices high, thus protecting other land values and the labor supply of the Eastern industrialists. Furthermore, by distributing the proceeds of public land sales, it left to the tariff the burden of meeting the expenses of government. The North Atlantic states and the Old West were pleased. But Clay was mistaken in believing that the bonus offered by the plan would conciliate the New West. That section joined with the South in referring his report to the Committee on Public Lands, and that Committee reported in favor of lowering and graduating land prices, and recommended a fifteen per cent. distribution from sales to the new states alone.[22] The issue was plain.

At the crucial moment, some misunderstanding arose between the leaders of the South and West in the Senate and their coalition fell apart. The proposal to graduate land prices failed by four votes, July 2, and, on the following day, Clay's land bill passed by a vote of twenty-six to eighteen. In the House, however, there were enough Administration men and Southern and Western opponents to obtain postponement until the following session.[23]

Clay felt that his land bill would be a powerful support to his presidential aspirations.[24] It was, of course, a consistent part of his American System, and the national values of that program were supposed to be its chief drawing card. But the protection he championed set one section of the country against another, and his land scheme ignored the justice of a graduated price for lands of varying value, ran counter to the desires of the New West, and closed the door of opportunity to the masses of

[21] *Cong. Deb.*, 22d Cong., 1st sess., App., 112–117.

[22] *Ibid.*, 22d Cong., 1st sess., App., 126.

[23] *Ibid.*, 22d Cong., 1st sess., 2853; Wellington, *op. et loc. cit.*, pp. 183–184.

[24] Porter Collection, Clay to Porter, April 26, 1832.

the poor.[25] In reality, although he would not have admitted it, his policies were more Eastern than national. Conservative, and favorable to the immediate interests of the wealthy, they opposed the desires of the American democracy.

Never was this more clearly demonstrated than in the struggle over the paramount political question of 1832, the recharter of the Bank of the United States.

Nicholas Biddle, handsome, cultured, able and somewhat arrogant, an excellent example of Eastern conservatism, had administered the Bank with great ability for the preceding nine years. He had striven sedulously to give it that stability and power which alone could make it useful to the country, and seems to have made a real effort to keep the institution free from dabblings in political corruption. By the time Jackson's regime got under way, the Bank had acquired a whip hand over the American financial system, and by doing so had largely eliminated depreciated state bank-notes and had established a sound and uniform currency for the United States.

But the Bank was not an unmixed blessing. It concentrated enormous financial power in the hands of a few capitalists. Errors of judgment, short-sighted desires for immediate gain, could, through its instrumentality, create great hardship in the country. And in it there was always a potential menace to political freedom. As the struggle for recharter developed, the Bank spent over forty-two thousand dollars in three years for campaign purposes and for propaganda, under the leadership of a man who had declared repeatedly that it should be kept out of politics. Even though no bribery, save perhaps in the case of one or two newspaper editors, could honestly be charged against it, the possibilities of corruption were enormous. So thought Andrew Jackson.

[25] By the later 1820's, labor was beginning to contend for free access to the public domain in order to ameliorate the condition of the workers. Few laborers had sufficient capital to buy land. — R. G. Wellington, *The Political and Sectional Influence of the Public Lands, 1828–1842* (Cambridge, 1914), pp. 7–8. See also Norman Ware, *The Industrial Worker, 1840–1860* (Boston, 1924), pp. 36, 180–186.

Old Hickory's acquaintance with the complexities of finance was most superficial, and in consequence, he disliked and feared what he did not understand. He had no love for either banks or paper money, and this attitude was intensified after 1828, by the suspicion that the Bank of the United States had used its influence against him, and by Biddle's rather incautious attempt to protect the institution against possible attacks.[26] Despite the fact that many of his friends and political supporters favored the Bank, Jackson does not seem to have been seriously swayed from his hostility toward it at any time,[27] even though he and his supporters had no constructive plan for replacing the financial balance which was threatened by their animosity.

Clay had continued to maintain a lively interest in the Bank's welfare, an interest stimulated, perhaps, by the institution's assistance to Kentucky road-building.[28] He corresponded with Biddle, and gave him advice from time to time. In 1830 the Kentuckian believed that application for recharter should not be made until shortly before the date of expiration, which was 1836. He based this stand upon his conviction that Jackson was hostile and would welcome the injection of the issue into the campaign of 1832.[29] Biddle agreed with this point of view, and expressed appreciation of Clay's advice,[30] but a year later both men had changed their minds.

Although Jackson's hostility to the Bank was unwavering, he was not anxious to act until after the election. He hoped for a smashing victory at the polls, and also, as a part of his plan for paying off the national debt by March 4, 1833, he was considering selling the Government's seventy thousand shares of stock back to the Bank. A fight would depreciate the value of

[26] Nicholas Biddle Papers (Lib. of Cong., Mss. Div.), XXI, XXXI, Biddle Memo., c. Nov. 1829, C. J. Ingersoll to Biddle, Feb. 2, 1832; Gammon, op. cit., pp. 105–117; Bassett, op. cit., pp. 589, 601; Catterall, op. cit., p. 183.

[27] Gammon, op. cit., pp. 124–130. Cf., however, Biddle Papers, XXI, M. L. Bevan to Biddle, Oct. 21, 1829.

[28] Dreer Collection, Clay to Biddle, Jan. 2, 1830.

[29] Biddle Papers, XXIII, Clay to Biddle, June 14, Sept. 11, 1830. Cf. Mallory, op. cit., Vol. I, pp. 592–593.

[30] Clay Papers, XVII, Biddle to Clay, Nov. 3, 1830.

these shares.[31] Hence, in December, 1831, he took a comparatively mild attitude toward the institution, and it was rumored that there would be an end to strife between him and the Bank, at least for the time being.

The Kentuckian must have heard these reports. He was anxious for a good issue in the campaign, and apparently he began to feel that the Bank would offer one. He seems to have reasoned that, if the National Republicans espoused its cause, and it applied for a recharter, Jackson would be placed in a dilemma. To accept a bill for recharter, after his repeated evidences of hostility to the institution, would give his opponents an opportunity to claim credit for the victory. To veto such a bill would gain the President little or nothing in the West (so Clay believed) and would almost certainly result in the defection of Pennsylvania from the Democratic ranks. Peter B. Porter stated the situation with brutal frankness when he wrote to Clay that Jackson "would rather see a shoat enter the palace than such a Bill; and if it does not cause his political, I am not sure that it will not, his physical death." [32] Clay began urging Biddle to action during the latter part of November 1831, and the National Republican convention that nominated the Kentuckian denounced Jackson as the enemy of the Bank.[33]

Biddle was an independent man, who acted for the Bank's interests as he saw them, without regard to politics. The advice of his special agent in Washington, Thomas Cadwalader, was probably the deciding factor with him. But the knowledge that Webster, Clay and company were pushing hard for action, and that they might abandon the Bank's cause, if it did not act immediately, must have had considerable weight.[34] Despite the opposition of the Bank's Democratic friends, Biddle decided

[31] Gammon, *op. cit.*, p. 124.

[32] Hamilton, *Reminiscences*, p. 243; Biddle Papers, XXIX, Samuel Smith to Biddle, Dec. 17, 1831; Porter Collection, Porter to Clay, Feb. 25, 1832 (copy).

[33] *Niles' Register*, Vol. XLI, pp. 310–311, Dec. 24, 1831.

[34] Biddle Papers, XXIX, Correspondence of Samuel Smith, Webster, Thos. Cadwalader, etc., with Biddle, Dec. 17–26, 1831. *Cf.* Weed, *Autobiography*, pp. 373–375.

to make the move, and thus threw the issue squarely into the political arena.

Jackson's devoted followers tried desperately to procrastinate, but Clay and Webster forced the bill through, and there were enough Bank men among the Democrats to ensure passage in both Senate and House.[35] It passed the latter body on July 3. The House had fixed July 9 for adjournment, but on that day, Clay and Webster moved delay, thus avoiding a pocket veto and forcing Jackson to express himself. The next day the veto message came.

Jackson was faced with a battle for his political life, and he knew full well that this was the case. "The bank is trying to kill me, *but* I will kill it!" he told Van Buren,[36] and the veto message was certainly framed with that end in view. Its indictment of the Bank on economic grounds was superficial and misleading. In attacking its constitutionality, Jackson made the indefensible statement that "each public officer who takes an oath to support the Constitution swears that he will support it as he understands it, and not as it is understood by others." But the strength of the veto lay in its appeal to class hatred, sectional jealousy and prejudice against foreigners. Its observations about handing over millions of dollars "out of the savings of the American people" to wealthy Easterners, its excoriation of financial dictatorship and monopoly, its denunciation of an institution that was not "purely American" — these were arguments that had a profound appeal. And, when Jackson declared that it was the duty of government to avoid acts that would "make the rich richer and the potent more powerful," he was calling with prescient political instinct to the masses who had elected him in 1828.[37]

[35] The bill passed the Senate by a vote of 28 to 20, the House by 107 to 85. It is interesting that Senator Willie P. Mangum of North Carolina, an Administration man who regarded the continuance of the Bank "as of almost indispensable necessity," voted against it — Mangum Papers, IV, Mangum (to Wm. Gaston), Jan. 19, 1832; *Cong. Deb.*, 22d Cong., 1st sess., 1073.

[36] Van Buren, *Autobiography*, p. 625.

[37] Richardson, *op. cit.*, Vol. II, pp. 576–591; Catterall, *op. cit.*, pp. 239–240. With happy malice, the veto message used against Clay his own argument on the constitutionality of the Bank in 1811.

Biddle was delighted with the veto. "It has all the fury," he wrote to Clay, "of a chained panther biting the bars of his cage." [38] Webster and Clay denounced the President's action in a storm of rhetoric that rocked the walls of the Senate chamber. The Bank could not wind up its affairs in so short a time without serious menace to the nation's welfare. The institution was a benefit to the West. Foreign stockholders were an aid in building up American prosperity. The President's attitude toward the Constitution was truly alarming. If accepted, it would lead inevitably to "general nullification, and end in the complete subversion of the government."

Benton rose in defense of Jackson, denounced the Bank, and characterized Clay's attack as wanting in courtesy and decorum. The Kentuckian took this as personal, and retorted savagely. Benton was twitted with the statement that when "some Senators" rose to speak, "the galleries are quickly emptied, with whatever else the Senate chamber may then be filled." Clay would take no instruction in courtesy and etiquette from Benton. The Kentuckian professed himself at a loss in determining to which of the Missourian's opinions of Jackson one ought to conform. Caustic allusion was made to a fight between Jackson and the Benton brothers that had taken place several years before. Certainly, Clay sneered, "I never complained of the President beating a brother of mine after he was prostrated and lying apparently lifeless. The member from Missouri needs no more specific indications of the transaction to which allusion is now made." Benton flung back taunt for taunt. It was true that he had fought with Jackson, but three months afterward they were good friends and had been so ever since. There had never been between *them* any question of an "adjourned veracity remaining on the public mind. No sir! If such were the case, there would have been a separation between us, wider than the gulf which separates heaven from hell!" So one aspersion brought another until, somewhat belatedly, the chair forced a restoration of order. Then the question was put on the passage of the Bank bill over the veto, and, by a

[38] Clay Papers, XIX, Biddle to Clay, Aug. 1, 1832 (private).

vote of twenty-two for and nineteen against, the bill failed to pass. It was Friday, July 13, 1832, and a black day for Henry Clay.[39]

The National Republicans tried to push several issues in the campaign. The Young Men's National Republican Convention, called by the Democrats "Clay's Infant School," had met in Washington, May 7, 1832, and had drawn up resolutions advocating a high tariff, internal improvements, and the maintenance of the Supreme Court's authority.[40] Executive usurpation and the spoils system had been denounced at the same time.[41] These points were utilized to the utmost in campaign speeches and pamphlets. It was upon the Bank veto, however, that the Clay forces pinned their hopes. Biddle called it a "manifesto of anarchy," and believed that it would be a signal aid in overthrowing "these miserable people."[42] The National Republicans vied with the Democrats in circulating it throughout the country and praise and denunciation of the Bank became the great theme of the closing months of the campaign.

Clay maintained throughout an air of optimism. He felt that the Democratic nomination of Van Buren for Vice-President was a fatal blow to "Jacksonism."[43] He was certain that the congressional session had been a sequence "of glorious triumphs for the Country and our cause," and that the Bank veto would "finish the work."[44] As late as August he believed that New York and Pennsylvania would repudiate the Administration. Even the election of Democratic Governors in Kentucky and Ohio failed appreciably to dampen his enthusiasm.[45] The

[39] *Cong. Deb.*, 22d Cong., 1st sess., 1221–1296.

[40] Jackson had refused to execute a Supreme Court decision which was unfavorable to Georgia in her quarrel with the Cherokees. He is reported to have said: "John Marshall has made his decision. Now let him enforce it." — Bassett, *op. cit.*, pp. 688–692.

[41] Gammon, *op. cit.*, pp. 168–169, for these resolutions.

[42] Clay Papers, XIX, Biddle to Clay, Aug. 1, 1832 (private).

[43] Cannon Collection, Clay to Edmund H. Taylor, May 26, 1832.

[44] Clay Papers, XIX, Clay to Niles, July 8, 1832.

[45] McDowell Collection, Clay to Henry Clay, Jr., Aug. 5, 1832; Washburn Papers, IV, Clay to John Holmes, Aug. 27, 1832; Sweet Collection, Clay to Jas. Brown, Oct. 23, 1832; Johnston Collection, Clay to Johnston, Oct. 6, 1832.

Antimasonic Movement gave, Clay felt, an opportunity to lessen Jackson's strength, and he urged a conciliatory attitude toward the followers of Wirt. This course was pursued in Pennsylvania, where the Clay electoral ticket was eventually withdrawn, and in New York it was carried so far that, with the Kentuckian's direct approbation, a coalition was established by which the National Republicans put up no state ticket, and the two parties chose a half-and-half electoral ticket of Clay and Wirt men. That ticket, it was understood, would cast its vote for the man most likely to win.[46]

But despite the fact that thousands of conservatives believed with the Kentuckian that Jackson had "put a pick axe at the base of every pillar that supports every department and every valuable institution in the Country,"[47] the fight was a losing one. In vain the National Republicans told the country that Jackson's veto would bring back "Rags!!" for money; that the "miserable old man" was merely the tool of "political gamblers and bankrupts," a "Usurper" and a "Tyrant."[48] What was this compared to "the monster"? "A whole party," shrilled the *Globe*, "have put on the badge of mammon, and have taken his mark on their forehead . . . harnessed and toiling in the yoke of a monied institution contending perpetually in that sordid cause, as if the things that make the true glory and happiness of a nation had no existence." "A monied institution," warned the *New York Evening Post*, "has thrown its capital of thirty millions, into the arena of political strife. . . . The Saviour of the world was betrayed for thirty pieces of silver . . . and the interests of the Union may be betrayed for thirty millions of dollars." Such diatribes found a ready response among the masses.

Nor was this all. In many states the Antimasonic Movement undoubtedly sapped Clay's strength far more than that of

[46] Seward, *Autobiography*, pp. 99–100; Gratz Collection, Clay to Ambrose Spencer, May 12, 1832 — although Clay's letters to Porter show that at first he had some doubts as to the feasibility of the plan. See especially the letter dated May 3, 1832.

[47] Gratz Collection, Clay to Ambrose Spencer, May 12, 1832.

[48] Anon., *Facts for the People; a Retrospect of Andrew Jackson's Administration* (1832).

Jackson, and even where the Antimasons and the Clay men co-operated all was not harmony. Weed and Seward gave the coalition ticket their vigorous support, at least in the open, but full co-operation could scarcely be expected in a state where, as late as May 1832, Seward was trying to awaken the benighted "from the charms of Clayism." [49] Ambrose Spencer, whose son John was one of the pillars of Antimasonry, professed to be a good Clay man, but toward the close of the campaign he wrote to Chancellor Kent (a staunch Clayite who headed the electoral ticket) arguing that New York must go for Wirt to save the day, and begging Kent, if he intended to vote for Wirt, to write a letter saying so to John Spencer at Canandaigua. This letter was to be shown about. Kent refused to act, and four days later, received another communication from Spencer, saying he was glad Kent had not complied, as a certain vague Van Buren plot had now fallen through. The whole incident reeked of trickery.[50] After the election was over, Clay was informed that New York had been lost because the Antimasons in the Middle and Eastern parts of the state deserted their own ticket.[51]

The verdict of the people was a smashing defeat for Clay. The Kentuckian carried his home state,[52] Maryland and Delaware, and three states in New England, — Massachusetts, Rhode Island and Connecticut, — for a total of forty-nine electoral votes. Vermont alone supported Wirt, and South Carolina threw her vote away upon John Floyd. Jackson carried the rest. He received two hundred and nineteen votes in the electoral college, a popular majority of approximately one

[49] Weed Papers, Seward to Weed, Auburn, May 10, 1832. After the New York coalition had been established, and before a similar arrangement had been made in Ohio, Seward was supposed to go to the latter state to effect the bargain. He was the only one who could do it, Porter felt, but Seward was taken sick and did not go. — Clay Papers, XX, Porter to Clay, Aug. 30, 1832.

[50] Kent Papers, VI, A. Spencer to Kent, Oct. 27, 1832 (profoundly confidential); same to same, Oct. 31, 1832.

[51] Clay Papers, XX, R. W. Stoddard, Nov. 12, 1832; Porter Collection, Porter to Clay, Nov. 22, 1832 (copy).

[52] Kendall wrote to Van Buren, Nov. 10, 1832, that Clay's leading friends in Kentucky had abandoned private business and given up their time to electioneering. — Van Buren Papers, XVII.

hundred thousand, and his party had a majority of forty in the new House of Representatives. Seldom have a man's policies and popularity been more strikingly upheld by the American people than was the case with Old Hickory in 1832. "It will be," Chancellor Kent had written to Webster, on the eve of the election, "the great battle of *Armageddon* between the Genius of Liberty and the spirits of darkness. . . . If we fail, then, indeed we may hang our harps upon the willows or on the witch-elm that shades Saint Fillan's Spring." [53]

The willows were doubtless plentifully adorned during those dark November days.

[53] Kent Papers, Kent to Webster, Oct. 31, 1832 (confidential).

CHAPTER XVI

COMPROMISE AGAIN

THE disastrous outcome of the election of 1832, and the evident disruption of the National Republicans, were bitter pills for Clay. He offered to give up his place in the Senate to John J. Crittenden and apparently regretted the latter's refusal. As late as January 3, 1833, the chastened Hotspur was still toying with the idea of resignation.[1] But the affairs of the country were rapidly approaching a crisis of the first magnitude, and after coming to Washington, the Kentuckian turned resolutely to political affairs.

The center of interest that winter was the South Carolinian revolt against the tariff. Indignation had waxed in the Palmetto state as the years had gone by after 1828 without any mitigation of protection, and by the fall of 1832 Calhoun had placed himself at the head of a powerful demand for direct action against the tariff burden. By December of that year, South Carolina had taken drastic action. The state had thrown away its vote in the presidential election, and had chosen a belligerent legislature. That body had summoned a state convention, which convention had met and passed an Ordinance of Nullification, on November 24, declaring null and void, as from February 1, 1833, the tariffs of 1828 and 1832. The Ordinance added that any attempt to coerce the state would be just cause for secession, and that, if such action were taken, the people of South Carolina would organize a separate and independent government of their own. Governor Hamilton asked the legislature for troops, and the Unionists in the state, powerless to stem the tide, appealed to the President for aid.

Jackson's message to Congress, December 4, 1832, men-

[1] McDowell Collection, Clay to Henry Clay, Jr., Jan. 3, 1833.

tioned the situation "in one quarter of the United States," but
its tone was so moderate that Clay regarded it as "ultra on the
side of State rights." [2] Six days later, however, the President's Proclamation to the people of South Carolina fell like
a thunderbolt. There was, it is true, a note of fatherly admoni-
tion to the citizens of his native state, but it warned in stern
and unmistakable fashion against any attempt to break up the
Union. The Nullifiers were told that the Constitution formed
a government, not a league; that their action made a "miserable mockery" of valid national legislation; and that to claim
for any state the right to secede was to say that the United
States was not a nation. "Disunion by armed force is *treason*.
Are you really ready to incur its guilt?" were words that could
not be mistaken. [3]

But the state was unrepentant. Robert Y. Hayne, the newly
elected Governor, issued at the legislature's request a counter-
proclamation warning the people to pay no attention to the
President and to be ready to defend their liberties. Active military preparations were being made. Calhoun resigned as Vice-
President, and was promptly elected to the United States
Senate to fill Hayne's seat, and champion the cause in Washington.

On January 16, 1833, Jackson asked Congress for increased
powers so that he might execute the laws in South Carolina,
and five days later the Senate Judiciary Committee reported the
"Force" or "Bloody Bill" giving the President ample authority to enforce the laws wherever they might be endangered.
Debate began on January 28, and feeling was intense. States'
rights men broke from the Jackson ranks. Patriotic members
of the opposition rallied to Old Hickory, and Webster announced that he would support the bill.

Meanwhile, the friends of the Administration had thrust
out what could well be regarded as an olive branch. On December 27, Verplanck of New York, chairman of the House
Ways and Means Committee, had reported a new tariff bill

---

[2] Richardson, *op. cit.*, Vol. III, p. 1162; Colton, *Correspondence*, p. 345,
Clay to Brooke, Dec. 12, 1832.
[3] Richardson, *op. cit.*, Vol. III, pp. 1203–1219.

which made large immediate reductions and proposed to lower duties approximately fifty per cent. by 1834. Northern protectionists considered this remedy worse than the disease; their resentment flamed high, and the bill had been held up in the House. Clay's attitude, still undeclared, became hourly more important, and John Tyler wrote to Governor Floyd of Virginia that only the Kentuckian could settle the tariff imbroglio.[4]

Clay had left Kentucky for the East, believing that he would be unable to perform "any useful public service." There is nothing to indicate that he was seriously considering any pacificatory gesture toward South Carolina at that time. Nor had he any intention of wielding a whip against that rebellious state. A movement against Nullification had appeared at Louisville which, he believed, had been inspired from Washington, "but I can see no advantage," he wrote, "in our taking part in proceedings agt. S. Carolina heresy, whilst that of Georgia and the President remains triumphant."[5] But after sensing the temper of affairs in Washington and Philadelphia, he had become convinced that a compromise was not only feasible, but necessary.[6]

His first plan, drawn up in Philadelphia, where he stayed during a major part of December, provided for the retention of existing duties until March 3, 1840, when a tariff for revenue only should take its place.[7] Then the Verplanck bill was introduced, and Clay became apprehensive of its passage. He consulted with various members of Congress, and with Northern manufacturers, and undoubtedly benefited by suggestions from Tyler and eventually from Calhoun.[8] Still the Kentuckian

[4] Tyler Mss., I, Tyler to Floyd, Jan. 16, 1833.

[5] Crittenden Papers, IV, Clay to Crittenden, Nov. 28, 1834; McDowell Collection, Clay to Henry Clay, Jr., Nov. 24, 1832.

[6] Benton, *Thirty Years' View*, Vol. I, p. 342, asserts that Letcher suggested the idea of compromise to Clay.

[7] G. T. Curtis, *Life of Daniel Webster*, 2 vols. (N.Y., 1870), Vol. I, pp. 434–435. A copy of this plan, in Clay's handwriting, was put in Webster's hands by a third person. Such a proposal would scarcely have appeased the South.

[8] John Floyd Mss. (Lib. of Cong.), Tyler to Floyd, Jan. 10, 1833; *Cong. Globe*, 24th Cong., 2d sess., 969–970, 26th Cong., 1st sess., 96–97, 31st

hesitated, fearful of the storm of opposition that would develop if he offered any tariff plan. But the final form of the compromise was taking shape in his mind, and toward the close of January the introduction of the "Force Bill" pushed him toward a decision.

Clay supported the "Force Bill" reluctantly, but openly.[9] In his opinion, Jackson had "marked out two victims So. Carolina and the Tariff and the only question with him is which shall be first immolated."[10] Tyler solicited the Kentuckian's aid from the floor of the Senate, echoing the cry of Buckner of Missouri, three weeks before.[11] John Randolph, nearing the end of his long and stormy journey, stumped his district in Virginia against Jackson's proclamation, and was reported as saying that Clay alone could save the Union. John M. Clayton of Delaware, an ardent protectionist, told the Kentuckian that it would not do to let Jackson hang those fine fellows in the South Carolina delegation.[12] Clay held a number of conferences with Congressional leaders. It is distinctly possible that some states' rights men gave promises to support Clay's bill for distributing the proceeds of the public lands. At length even Calhoun, fearful and jealous of Old Hickory's power, sought and obtained Clay's pledge of assistance. Harry of the West had "stepped across the Potomac," and West and South began to act in unison.[13]

Cong., 1st sess., App. 1413. Clay denied, in 1837, that he had had an interview with any Southern Senator prior to the introduction of the bill, but Tyler's letter to Floyd, which mentions an interview with Clay, and gives the essential elements of the compromise plan finally introduced, destroys the value of this statement.

[9] He voted repeatedly against its postponement, and though not present on the evening that it passed, he asserted on the floor of the Senate during the ensuing days that he favored the bill, and would have voted for it, had he been present. His health was his excuse for absence.

[10] Porter Collection, Clay to Porter, Jan. 29, 1833.

Mangum believed that war upon South Carolina was imminent. — Mangum Papers, V, Mangum to his wife, Feb. 2, 1833.

[11] Cong. Deb., 22d Cong., 2d sess., 377–387.

[12] Garland, op. cit., Vol. II, pp. 361–362; Clayton Papers, I, Clay to Clayton, Aug. 22, 1844.

[13] Curtis, Webster, Vol. I, p. 444; Adams, Memoirs, Vol. VIII, pp. 524–525; R. G. Wellington, op. cit., pp. 44–47. It is possible that Clay accepted

The tariff measure which Clay introduced on February 12, 1833, was very different from his December draft. It provided that, beginning January 1, 1834, all duties in the tariff of 1832 that were over twenty per cent. should be gradually reduced at two-year intervals until 1840. Then two sharp reductions were to take place, and on July 1, 1842, the duties were to stand at a uniform rate of twenty per cent. Badly drafted, the violent reductions between 1840 and 1842 were highly objectionable, but the bill gave, so Clay asserted, adequate protection for at least nine years. It would preserve the manufacturers and restore harmony. It would prevent the danger of a civil war, with other Southern states coming to the aid of South Carolina. It would separate the tariff from politics. And, as he said repeatedly, it could be repealed at any time that the country demanded it.[14]

The bill did not pass the Senate easily. Calhoun loathed the principle of home valuation which Clay introduced as an amendment and the latter thought at one time that the measure would be lost on this account.[15] Webster opposed the whole measure bitterly, terming it destructive and ineffectual. "It will not be all requiem and lullaby when this bill shall be passed." [16] The great Daniel, now a welcome guest at the Palace, was fighting Jackson's fight for the "Bloody Bill," and he and Clay crossed swords more than once in the debate.

But while the giants contended in the Senate, the Compromise had gone through the House "like a hurricane," [17] and, with that victory, it became evident that the end was near. On March 1, the new tariff passed the Senate, twenty-nine to sixteen. The "Force Bill" went through also, and Jackson signed both measures on the following day. Ten days later the South

modifications in his original tariff plan as a part of his bargain with the Southern Senators. *Cf.*, however, Colton, *Correspondence*, pp. 360–363, Clay to Brooke, May 30, 1833.

[14] *Cong. Deb.*, 22d Cong., 2d sess., 462–486, 718–742.

[15] Clayton, who was very instrumental in pushing the bill through, was strenuous for this principle, and it seems to have been the determining factor in the continuance of his support. *Cf.* Benton, *Thirty Years' View*, Vol. I, pp. 343–344.

[16] *Cong. Deb.*, 22d Cong., 2d sess., 727f.

[17] Adams, *Memoirs*, Vol. VIII, p. 527.

Carolinians nullified the "Force Bill," but, since they now graciously agreed not to maintain tariff nullification, the danger of collision passed away.

The Compromise marked another stage in the destruction of the American System. Jackson had already sapped and mined internal improvements and the Bank. Now Clay himself was yielding to a modification of protection. Why did he do so?

The Kentuckian gave his reasons to Porter, shortly after the Compromise was introduced. His opinions in regard to the American System were, he averred, unchanged. But, fearing its total sacrifice by the destruction of protection, he had brought forward a measure that would "protect the manufacturers for the present and gain time, with its chapter of accidents for them," and at the same time would —

> preserve the Union, prevent Civil war, and save us from the danger of entrusting to And^w Jackson large armies &c. . . . In short my desire and my efforts are to obtain stability and present security to our manufacturers, with the belief that when reason and good feeling once more return all will be done hereafter for them that they will require.[18]

These reasons, patriotic and otherwise, were undoubtedly sincere, even the fear of Jackson, for Clay, to his own satisfaction, had long since dramatized Old Hickory into a figure closely resembling the Prince of Darkness. But it cannot be doubted that there were other reasons as well. The Compromise mitigated the threat to his own popularity which had appeared in National Republican approval of the President's patriotism. It gave the Kentuckian an opportunity to assert predominance over Webster, a troublesome rival for leadership. It was a means of capitalizing the growing resentment against Jackson of Southern states' rights men, such as Tyler, Bibb and Tazewell,[19] and finally, it gave an opportunity for a deal by which Clay's land bill could be passed through Congress with the aid of Southern votes.

[18] Porter Collection, Clay to Porter, Feb. 16, 1833.
[19] *Cf.* E. M. Carroll, *Origins of the Whig Party* (Durham, 1925), pp. 73–77, and A. C. Cole, *The Whig Party in the South* (Washington, 1913), pp. 17–18. Clay urged Tyler's re-election to the Senate.

There were, however, some rather troublesome flies in the ointment. Webster was decidedly ruffled,[20] and good relations between him and Clay were not fully resumed until the end of the year. A breach had been made in the protective wall. Any combination between Clay and the exponents of states' rights was bound to be unstable, at best. And Jackson, who had come out in December, 1832, for reducing the price of Western lands and helping the settlers to become freeholders as soon as possible, left Clay's land bill unsigned, to be returned with a veto to the next session of Congress.

A reconciliation between Clay and John Randolph took place that winter. Feeble and wan, the Virginian came to Washington and visited the Senate. Clay was speaking. "Raise me up," commanded his old rival, "I want to hear that voice again." When Clay had finished, he went over to Randolph and the two men shook hands cordially. They never met again, and within a few months Randolph had passed away. His heart warmed to the Kentuckian toward the last, but the long years of enmity had left traces that could not be lightly forgotten, and he was buried with his face to the West, men said, so that he might still keep an eye on Henry Clay.[21]

Clay returned to Ashland in the early part of April, and busied himself with caring for his farm, and enjoying family life. Henry Junior had married Julia Prather of Louisville the preceding fall. He had given up a legal career in New Orleans because of his health, and his father took the responsibility in the spring of 1833 of helping the youthful bridegroom to select and pay for a farm in the neighborhood of Lexington. Julia was in Louisville for her accouchement in July, and the news of Henry III's arrival brought a letter of congratulation from his grandfather.

We most cordially felicitate you and our dear Julia on her safe delivery, and, not on that happy event merely, but that your first born should be a son! And then, if we are to credit your account of him, so "noble a boy.". . . Tell Julia to make haste and get able to bring

[20] Biddle Papers, XXXIX, Clay to Biddle, March 4, 1833.
[21] Colton, *Correspondence*, Clay to Brooke, March 11, 1833; Clay Papers, J. W. P. to Clay, May 31, 1833; Bruce, *John Randolph*, Vol. II, pp. 36, 47.

her prize here that we, as well as her Louisville friends, may have the satisfaction of seeing and caressing it. In regard to its name, I shall certainly feel flattered if mine is given to it, although I presume I should have to share the compliment with another.[22]

But the great event of the summer was the cholera, which ravaged Lexington during the month of June. The plague had wasted various parts of the United States during the preceding year, but nowhere had its ravages been more severe than they were in the Bluegrass country. At its beginning in Lexington, over fifty people died within three days, and panic reigned. Many fled as the deaths increased and the town, Clay wrote to Porter on June 16, wore "a frightful gloom. All the stores and shops are closed, the presses stopt, and no one moving in the streets except those concerned with the dead or the sick." The Erwin family at the Woodlands became alarmed and came over to Ashland. "I have endeavored to rally them," Clay wrote to Julia, "and they passed a very good night and have all risen this morning quite cheerful." By July 2, the deaths in Lexington were estimated at nearly five hundred, and the pestilence had spread into near-by towns. Paris and Lancaster were stricken, and "the whole village of Lancaster horse foot and dragoon, with few exceptions, marched off. In one instance the entire family deserted their house, leaving its head dead and unburied." Ashland and the Woodlands miraculously escaped, and by the middle of July the disease had disappeared from Lexington, but it had been a fearful experience and the anxiety and responsibility it entailed induced Clay to postpone until the fall a northern trip that he had planned to begin in July.[23]

That fall, the Kentuckian and his wife went on a journey that extended from Philadelphia through New York to Boston, then across Massachusetts to Albany and down into New Jersey

[22] McDowell Collection, Clay to Julia Prather Clay, April 14, 1833; Clay to Henry Clay, Jr., June 7, July 23, 1833.

[23] This account is based upon letters in the McDowell, Porter and Sweet Collections. The cholera prevented a visit to Kentucky by Webster, who had come out to Ohio that summer. He had been invited to visit Ashland if he came, and a real conciliation was delayed until the end of the year.

before they finally reached Washington. Jackson had visited New England the preceding June. He had found it an exhausting ordeal, and the Clays had the same experience. Mrs. Clay kept out of the limelight as much as possible, but receptions, dinners, and huge crowds pressed upon her husband at every turn. Webster's friends held aloof in Boston; Adams commented sourly upon this "peddling for popularity"; but on the whole, New England responded in a fashion that seemed to belie earlier reports of affections weaned away by the tariff of 1833. Clay looked upon the trip as a tremendous success. The strain had been great, he had received so many valuable presents that he sometimes felt ashamed to accept them, but he returned to the battle in Washington convinced that commercial New England was still loyal to him.[24]

Each summer called Clay back to Ashland, and, even in the press of the political struggle at Washington, domestic matters, grave or gay, formed a vital part of his life. The pure blood stock in which he took such pride was steadily increased. Horses and sheep were added from time to time. More than a dozen expensive jacks and jennies were imported from Spain and France, and Durham and Devon cattle were obtained in England. The cost of building up his herds was compensated in part by the high prices received for the progeny. In 1835, he sold a cow with her day-old calf for five hundred dollars, and a nine-months-old bull calf for two hundred dollars. Three years later, he sold another cow for two thousand dollars, which was more, as he confessed to Joshua Giddings, than any cow was ever worth.[25] When one of his prize bulls, Orizimbo, died, Clay was not entirely jocular in announcing

[24] McDowell Collection, Clay to Henry Clay, Jr., Nov. 24, Dec. 1, 1833; Porter Collection, Clay to Porter, Dec. 26, 1833; *Niles' Register*, Vol. XLV, passim. See the interesting description of Clay's visit to Worcester, Mass., in "Christopher Columbus Baldwin's Diary" (John Nelson, ed.), in *Americana*, Vol. XXVIII (July 1934), pp. 336–337. Baldwin wrote that Clay was "rapid in conversation, full of anecdote, and swears most insufferably. But this last quality is common to all Kentuckians."

[25] Giddings Papers (Ohio State Hist. and Arch. Soc.), I, Giddings to one of his daughters, Jan. 1 [1839].

the event to the United States Senate as "a great loss, public and private."

The Kentuckian continued to act as financial backer for Henry Junior, and also for Thomas, who settled down at the Mansfield farm and became much interested in the manufacture of hemp. The Clays gave one hundred and twenty-five acres of bluegrass land to their one remaining daughter, Anne Clay Erwin, in the fall of 1833.[26] James was guided through a period of indecision, which finally ended with the adoption of a legal career, and the father and mother watched anxiously over their youngest boy, John, whose health was none too good, and who exhibited signs of waywardness. These family responsibilities meant considerable expense and, although his finances appear to have been in fairly good condition, Clay had found it necessary, by 1836, to borrow twenty thousand dollars, a sum lent to him by John Jacob Astor.[27]

Disease and death added heavy burdens to Clay's life during this period. His eldest son, Theodore, was brought from the asylum for occasional visits to Ashland, but his condition did not improve. In the winter and spring of 1834, Mrs. Clay suffered from a serious stomach disorder, and her husband almost despaired of her life. Dr. Physick prescribed for her, and she recovered, although it may be considered doubtful if the learned man's favorite remedy for sour stomach, "fresh hickory ashes and soot" diluted with water "to prevent it from excoriating the mouth," [28] did as much for her as a rest at the Virginia Springs, near Warrenton.

James Brown, always a wise counselor and a devoted friend, died in Philadelphia, April 7, 1835. This was a severe loss, but it was eclipsed that fall by a tragedy far more difficult for the Kentuckian to bear. Anne Clay Erwin died in childbirth, and her father was nearly prostrated by grief. The letter containing the tragic news came at a moment when he was feeling merry

[26] Henry and Lucretia Clay to Anne B. Erwin, Fayette County Court, Deed Book 9, p. 188, September 10, 1833.
[27] McDowell Collection, Clay to Henry Clay, Jr., Feb. 19, 1835; Clay Papers, XXI, interest receipt from Astor, Oct. 7, 1836.
[28] Clay Papers, XX, Physick to Clay, April 19, 1834.

and lighthearted, and a friend who was present witnessed the shock that it gave, and heard the bereaved man exclaim, "Every tie to life is broken!" Some two weeks later he wrote a desolate letter to Margaret Bayard Smith.

From no friend could condolence, on the occasion of my recent heavy affliction, have come more welcomely; but dear Madam all the efforts of friendship or of my own mind have but little effect on a heart wounded as mine is. My daughter was so good, so dutiful, so affectionate; her taste and sympathies and amusements were so identical with my own; she was so interwoven with every plan and prospect of passing the remnant of my days, that I feel I have sustained a loss which can never be repaired. Henceforward, there is nothing before me in this world but duties.

My poor wife has suffered beyond expression; but she has in affliction a resourse — a great resourse — which I have not. . . .[29]

Four years later, Henry Junior's wife died shortly after giving birth to a son. Her husband had been devotedly attached to her, and this tragedy was a blow so heavy that he surrendered himself to melancholy, haunted by "the idea that my wife and sister are calling me to a place of more perfect rest." Something of this he wrote to his father, and the reply deserves to be remembered.

My Dear Son

I received last night your letter communicating the afflicting intelligence of the death of your dear wife my poor daughter Julia. It was so sudden and appalling, and so unexpected to me that it overwhelmed me with sorrow and grief. I scarcely slept last night, and have risen hardly able yet to realize the loss which we have sustained. The manner of her death resembles so much that of my lamented Anne!

Yes, my dear Son, I do condole and sympathize with you, from the bottom of my soul. But I hope that you will not forget that she has left you tender & responsible duties to perform towards the children of your mutual love and affection. These will require all your care, and I hope that you will command the fortitude requisite to the fulfillment of your duties to them.

[29] M. B. Smith, *op. cit.*, p. 375. There is an equally touching letter in the Clay Papers, XXI, Clay to the Rev. Stansbury, Dec. 19, 1835.

How one after another are the objects which fastened me to this life passing away and leaving me with scarcely any wish but that I may soon follow them! Whatever might be my desire that must be my fate. During the short remnant of my life, I too shall need your kindness and affectionate attention. I beg, therefore, on my account, as well as that of my dear grand children you will take care of yourself.

Had you not better yet make your trip to N.O. and proceed from thence by the way of Augusta and Charleston to this place? [30]

Like Abraham Lincoln, who loved and honored him, Henry Clay possessed a great warmth of affection. And, like the Great Emancipator, he was a man of sorrows.

[30] McDowell Collection, Diary of Henry, Jr., entry of Feb. 20, 1840; Clay to Henry Clay, Jr., Feb. 20, 1840; Clay to Lucretia Clay, Feb. 21, 1840.

CHAPTER XVII

THE STRUGGLE WITH JACKSONISM

OUT of the wrack of political hatreds and ambitions, jealousy, fear of Jackson and a modicum of principles, the Whig Party took shape in the winter and spring of 1834. Whether it was Philip Hone, the New York merchant, or another, who first christened it is a matter of little moment.[1] Derived from British politics, the name had never entirely disappeared from American political nomenclature. To those who rallied under its standard in 1834, it symbolized the struggle against the tyranny of King Andrew. His vetoes, his use of the patronage and contempt for the Supreme Court, the claim that he was co-equal with Congress in representing the will of the people, and his "right" to uphold the Constitution as he understood it, were denounced over and over again. This ogre and his Tory followers would have to be thrust out of power, if American institutions were to be saved from the curse of despotism. Old Hickory was a tyrant, a knave, a despot, bent upon the subjugation of the country to his will and already planning, with fiendish ingenuity, the elevation of his successor to the throne.[2] "I felt," wrote Clay in 1836, "that I was struggling for the Country, for its civil liberty, its institutions, its property, its virtue."[3]

[1] Philip Hone, *Diary*, 2 vols. (N.Y., 1927), Vol. I, p. xii, Vol. II, p. 629; D. R. Fox, *The Decline of Aristocracy in the Politics of New York* (N.Y., 1919), p. 367; Carroll, *op. cit.*, p. 123. Clay's first use of the term as designating the new party opposed to Jackson came in a speech before the Senate, April 14, 1834. Ten days later, Henry Clay, Jr. wrote to Crittenden, suggesting that the name "Whig" be adopted in Kentucky and that they call their opponents "Tories." — *Cong. Deb.*, 23d Cong., 1st sess., 1313; Crittenden Papers (Duke Univ.), Henry Clay, Jr. to Crittenden, April 24, 1834 (copy).

[2] Clay Papers, XX, Erastus Root to Clay, Jan. 12, 1834. It is one of many expressing similar sentiments.

[3] *Ibid.*, XXI, Clay to R. Walsh, April 25, 1836.

The old National Republicans marched foremost in the ranks. Webster came back, albeit reluctantly, to co-operation with Clay, his flirtation with Jackson ended by the latter's continued hostility to the Bank. Calhoun, believing that his states' rights group would be the nucleus of the new party, co-operated closely, avowing himself a Whig.[4] Gradually, the Antimasons swelled the ranks.[5] An amorphous group of pro and anti tariff men, pro and anti Bank men, pro and anti Internal Improvements men, pro and anti Nullifiers, conservative in tenor but not daring to proclaim conservatism, the Whigs could unite upon no general policy save fulminations against "Executive Power" and a demand for the overthrow of the Administration. To marshal such a group, scarcely worthy of the name of "party," was a difficult task. But it held together in the assault upon "Old Andy," and the Western Hotspur, dashing in attack, assumed the leadership.

The onslaught in the spring of 1834 centered upon Jackson's continued hostility to the Bank, a hostility strikingly evinced by his removal of Government deposits from that institution in the fall of 1833 to a number of specifically designated "pet banks."[6] This was a move which should have been made very slowly and with the Bank's co-operation. Jackson was competently advised that it would produce a panic by forcing the Bank to reduce its discounts in proportion. But Kendall and Blair had urged him on, and he had convinced himself not only that the Government moneys were not safe, but that, if left in the Bank's vaults, they would be used to bribe members of Congress to pass a recharter over his veto.[7] Two Secretaries of the Treasury, who refused to do his bidding, had been sent flying, and finally Roger B. Taney, a consistent Bank enemy, had executed the decree.

The removal of the deposits fostered wildcat banking, in-

---

[4] Carroll, *op. cit.*, pp. 33–34.

[5] McCarthy, *op. et loc. cit.*, pp. 424–426, 458f, 525, 530.

[6] They were not arbitrarily removed, but no further deposits were made in the Bank of the U.S., and the money in that institution was quickly paid out to meet Government expenses.

[7] Catterall, *op. cit.*, pp. 287, 290–294.

flation, and the development of a paper surplus.[8] It also contributed to immediate financial stringency. The Bank had previously begun reducing accommodations, in view of the attacks upon it. As these developed, it naturally strove to protect its credit. But, undoubtedly with a view to forcing Jackson into retreat, Biddle reduced discounts and exchange far in excess of any possible need.[9] A goodly share of the severe sufferings of that winter must be laid at the Bank's door, and they illustrate its dangerous potentialities.

In the midst of this excitement, with the wailings of the Whig press resounding through the land, the Clays ended their Eastern trip and rented a small furnished house near Gadsby's Hotel in Washington.[10] Once settled there, Clay lost no time in organizing his line of battle.

The House of Representatives was anti-Bank by some twenty votes, but the Clay-Calhoun-Webster group controlled the Senate by a narrow majority. That body took the appointment of committees away from the president pro tem; and Webster headed the Committee on Finance, his retainer from the Bank undoubtedly "refreshed," as he demanded.[11] The Democrats were fearful, and the opposition exhibited signs of confidence. But Clay's control over the Senate was, in reality, far from certain. Webster had shown signs of wavering from the Kentuckian's leadership, and the latter had to call up all his reinforcements. "If you are here," he wrote to Clayton, "I believe we shall be safe, even if there be defection. For God's sake then come to us. And do not let anything keep you away." [12]

On December 10, Clay began to develop his attack. He offered a resolution requesting Jackson to lay before the Senate a condemnation of the Bank which Old Hickory had

[8] E. G. Bourne, *The History of the Surplus Revenue of 1837* (N.Y., 1885), pp. 13–17.

[9] Catterall, *op. cit.*, pp. 299–329.

[10] Sweet Collection, Clay to Brown, Dec. 10, 1833. Clay felt that there was need of economy for him. Henry, Jr. was drawing heavily on his father's credit in order to establish himself as a farmer in Kentucky.

[11] Biddle Papers, XLIII, Webster to Biddle, Dec. 21, 1833.

[12] Clayton Papers, I, Clay to Clayton, Dec. 12, 1833.

read to his Cabinet. This Jackson properly refused, standing upon his prerogative.[13] The President had won the first skirmish, but the Kentuckian plunged ahead. He attacked William T. Barry for his inefficient management of the Post Office Department, and began a denunciation of Taney that continued intermittently throughout the session.[14]

Toward the close of December Clay launched his great attempt to obtain a formal condemnation of the President. The Kentuckian moved a resolution which declared that Jackson, by his arbitrary dismissal of Treasury Secretaries, and by his appointment of a man who would remove the deposits, had assumed a control over the Treasury not granted by the Constitution or the laws, and dangerous to popular liberty. This was coupled with another which asserted that the reasons assigned for removing the deposits were "unsatisfactory and insufficient." [15]

The case for this attempt at censure rested upon the ground that the Constitution, and the Fathers, had meant to lodge the power of the purse in the hands of Congress, and that the Secretary of the Treasury was responsible to that body and not to the President. It is true that the law creating the Treasury Department did not call it an "Executive Department." It is also true that the Secretary was ordered to make reports to Congress, not to the President. But there was nothing to forbid the appointment of the Secretary by the Chief Executive, and such appointments had been uniformly made. Furthermore, the law expressly recognized the President's right to remove the Secretary from office,[16] and the Bank's charter gave the Secretary permission to withdraw the deposits from the Bank at his discretion.[17] Jackson had delayed sending Taney's appointment to the Senate for confirmation, and this afforded just reason for criticism, but the legal and Constitutional

---

[13] *Cong. Deb.*, 23d Cong., 1st sess., 23–37.
[14] Clay later made a personal apology to Taney. — Samuel Tyler, *Memoir of Roger Brooke Taney* (Baltimore, 1872), p. 317.
[15] *Cong. Deb.*, 23d Cong., 1st sess., 58.
[16] *The Public Statutes at Large* (Boston, 1845), Vol. I, pp. 65–67.
[17] Catterall, *op. cit.*, p. 487.

grounds for attacking appointments or removals were decidedly weak. The President had not touched Congressional prerogatives.

But the Kentuckian's political warfare was scarcely based upon objective considerations. He told the Senate, in a three-day speech supporting his resolutions, that "we are in the midst of a revolution, hitherto bloodless, but rapidly tending towards a total change of the pure republican character of the Government, and to the concentration of the power in the hands of one man." He foresaw "an elective monarchy" by 1837, in the person of a Chief Executive armed with the purse and the sword. Old Hickory's actions were compared to Caesar's assaults upon the Roman treasury. Jackson had "proclaimed an open, palpable, and daring usurpation." The argument even went so far as to consider the Bank and the Treasury as one and the same. It was only when Clay assailed the deposit removals as economically unwise, and criticized the selection of "pet banks" as depositories, that he succeeded in making out a strong case.

The debate which was thus opened ran on for three months, the longest single debate in either House since the Government had been organized. Webster and Calhoun supported Clay's onslaught. Forsyth, Benton and others did their best to repel it. In its course, the President's actions and motives were subjected to a merciless castigation, and the Kentuckian even questioned the President's power to remove any Government official without the consent of the Senate, and disparaged the Chief Executive's right to have a Cabinet, or to negotiate treaties or send ministers abroad until the Senate's consent had been obtained.[18] Such divagations showed the state of mind into which the Whigs were lashing themselves.

While the argument was proceeding over Clay's resolution of censure, another bitterly partisan struggle developed in the Senate and throughout the country on the question of public distress. The Bank's contraction of credit was being felt severely, and the hard times produced a violent outburst

[18] *Cong. Deb.*, 23d Cong., 1st sess., 1172–1177.

of partisan rage. Democratic mass meetings denounced the "aristocratic" Senate and blamed the "monstrous" Bank for all the trouble. Whig strongholds bemoaned the President's "tyranny" and declared that the Bank, if left alone, would be the salvation of the country.

Objectivity had vanished. Tyrone Power, the Irish actor, found worthy citizens in Pittsburgh blaming the lack of street lights on the removal of the deposits, and a zealous Whig in Cincinnati wrote to Jackson: "Damn your old soul, remove them deposites back again, and recharter the bank, or you will certainly be shot in less than two weeks and that by myself!!!" [19]

Hundreds of petitions, many of them couched in intemperate language, flooded into the Senate. The signatures were not always trustworthy, a profusion of John Does and Richard Roes, to say nothing of more eminent names appearing in unexpected places, indicating partisan zeal rather than discretion. But these documents were in a measure a reflection of public opinion, and the majority of them came from pro-Bank localities. Clay and the other Whig leaders played them up to full advantage, presenting them with accompanying speeches that depicted the country's direful plight. "Everything was falling," Clay declared, "everything was going down, down; and everything would be still lower unless some remedy should be applied." The question, he asserted, was "a question between the will of one man and that of twelve millions of people. It is a question between power — ruthless, inexorable power — on the one hand, and the strong deep-felt sufferings of a vast community, on the other." Fervently he expressed the hope that the memorials would soften Jackson's heart and induce him to restore the deposits. [20]

The Democrats listened unmoved to such tragic admonitions, and on one occasion, Clay overreached himself, giving Van Buren an opportunity for a neat counterthrust. On March 7, the Kentuckian addressed a moving appeal to the Vice-

[19] Tyrone Power, *Impressions of America*, 2 vols. (Philadelphia, 1836), Vol. I, pp. 197–198; *Niles' Register*, Vol. XLVII, p. 409, Feb. 14, 1835.
[20] *Cong. Deb.*, 23d Cong., 1st sess., 223, 718.

President, imploring him to intercede with Jackson and save the land from ruin.

"You can, if you will, induce him to change his course. . . . Go to him and tell him, without exaggeration, but in the language of truth and sincerity, the actual condition of his bleeding country," the "heart-rending wretchedness" of the unemployed, the "tears of helpless widows" and of "unclad and unfed orphans."

Tell him to guard himself against the possibility of an odious comparison with that worst of the Roman Emperors who, contemplating with indifference the conflagration of the mistress of the world, regaled himself during the terrific scene in the throng of his dancing courtiers. . . . Tell him that he has been abused, deceived, betrayed, by the wicked counsels of unprincipled men around him. . . . Entreat him to pause and to reflect that there is a point beyond which human endurance cannot go, and let him not drive this brave, generous, and patriotic people to madness and despair.

This eloquence drew sobs from the ladies in the galleries, and Van Buren received it with an air of respectful innocence. But when Clay had finished, the Red Fox called a Senator to the chair, walked down the aisle to the Kentuckian's seat, asked for a pinch of snuff, inhaled it, and walked away.[21] It was Clay's belief that his method of attack would bring the country to thorough disapproval of the President's "usurpation," and its "evil consequences." Then, and only then, the time would be ripe to move for a recharter of the Bank.[22] Accordingly, he incited movements for drawing up the distress memorials, and petitions for restoration of the deposits, and looked with favor upon the Bank's contraction of its credit. His hopes were pinned upon the country's distress. Success in

[21] *Ibid.*, 23d Cong., 1st sess., 829–832; *Lexington Intelligencer*, March 21, 1834, quoting the *United States' Telegraph*; Benton, *Thirty Years' View*, Vol. I, p. 420.

[22] *Cong. Deb.*, 23d Cong., 1st sess., 478; Biddle Papers, XXXIX, Clay to Biddle, March 4, 1833, XLV, Clay to Biddle, Feb. 2, 1834; Miscellaneous Papers (N.Y. Public Lib.), Clay to Joseph Gales, Jr., March 24, 1834. Clay strenuously opposed plans laid by Webster and Calhoun for recharter bills, and rendered those plans nugatory.

the House, he wrote to Henry Junior, "will depend upon the extent of the re-actions among the people. . . . The distress in the Eastern Cities is intense. I am glad it has not reached you; but it will before next fall."

Three weeks later, he wrote: —

The deposite question remains undecided. We have thought that we do not lose by delay. Great excitement prevails in the Eastern Cities, and strong impression has been undoubtedly made on members of the House.

And on February 19: —

Whether the Admin. will be able to retain its present small majority there [in the House] depends upon the continuation of the existing distress and the expression of public opinion. I still hope for ultimate success.[23]

But Jackson's spirit flamed higher in the face of disapproval. "Go to the monster," "go to Nicholas Biddle," he stormed at the committees which went to see him; "I will not bow down to the golden calf." And as the General showed an intrepid face to the foe, his party rallied about him.

As a matter of fact, distress produced an effect upon the country exactly the opposite of that anticipated by Clay. Public opinion sharpened, not against Jackson, but against the Bank and its policy. Erstwhile friendly newspapers began to criticize it. The Democratic Party in Pennsylvania, which had been faithful to the institution, executed a *volte-face*. At the close of March, in response to pressure from New York and Pennsylvania business men, Biddle announced a cessation of contraction, a move which convinced thousands of people that his previous policy had been inexcusable. On April 4, resolutions passed the House against recharter and restoration of the deposits, and for an investigation of the Bank. Once again, Clay had betrayed his inability to understand the force of the democratic movement which had swept Jackson into power.

[23] McDowell Collection, Clay to Henry Clay, Jr., Jan. 23, Feb. 11, 19, 1834.

The Kentuckian's resolution of censure, stating in its final form that the President had "assumed upon himself authority and power not conferred by the constitution and laws, but in derogation of both," passed the Senate, twenty-six to twenty, with the support of Webster, Calhoun and Tyler. Stung by this action, the President sent an indignant Protest, which warned the country against a senatorial oligarchy. The Senate refused to enter this upon its journal, and Clay, in a bitter and insulting speech, asserted that the Administration was expiring in agony, and declared that if a phrenologist examined Jackson's head, he would find "the organ of destructiveness prominently developed. Except an enormous fabric of Executive power, the President has built up nothing. . . . He goes for destruction, universal destruction. . . ." [24]

The House did not think so. "I have never seen party spirit in the House more shameless," wrote Clay, with unconscious humor,[25] but, shameless or not, it stood behind the President as the struggle became even more fierce than it had been before. Clay introduced a joint resolution for the restoration of the deposits. It passed the Senate, but died in the House. A House bill to regulate public deposits in the state banks was tabled by the upper chamber. Benton moved to expunge the vote of censure from the journal. This was voted down, and the Senate proceeded to reject a long list of important nominations, including Taney, which had been sent in by Jackson.[26] The session ended with the Whigs attacking the terrible abuses that did exist in the Post Office Department,[27] while the Administration, alarmed by the inflation which its destruction of the Bank was stimulating, made a vain attempt to force paper money out of circulation by Congressional and state action.

The Whigs, under Clay's leadership, had gambled upon forcing Jackson to restore the deposits, and they had lost. The Democrats were victorious in the elections of 1834, and the Bank disappeared as an issue. In the following session, Clay

[24] *Cong. Deb.*, 23d Cong., 1st sess., 1564.
[25] Crittenden Papers, IV, Clay to Crittenden, April 8, 1834.
[26] *Senate Executive Journal*, Vol. IV, pp. 397–398, 403, 410f.
[27] *Cong. Deb.*, 23d Cong., 1st sess., 2113–2116, App. 215–242.

admitted that it was doomed and that any attempt at recharter had become impracticable. That its demolition was a gross error from the standpoint of sound finance cannot be disputed. Webster and Clay stood on solid ground as they continued to point out the dangerous results of removing this balance wheel — the development of wildcat banking, the inelasticity of the currency, the increasing chaos of paper issues and of exchange. But demagoguery, Jackson's ignorance and hatred, state bank jealousy, and a popular fear of the institution that was in part justified by the very fact that it possessed such great power, had produced the overthrow of the Bank. Had it not been for the violent partisanship displayed on both sides, the best answer to the problem might have emerged in the retention of the Bank with more effective Government control.

Clay had been successful only in obtaining the Senate's vote censuring the President, and even that triumph turned to ashes. Every year an attempt was made to expunge, and in January of 1837 a Democratic majority stood triumphantly behind a resolution which directed the Secretary of the Senate to bring the Journal into the chamber, draw black lines about the offending words, and write across them: "Expunged by order of the Senate, this —— day of ——, in the year of our Lord, 1837."

Benton gloried in his triumph. "Solitary and alone . . . I put this ball in motion," he roared, and the Whigs answered him with impotent rage. "It is not in the power of your black lines to touch us," cried Preston of South Carolina. "Remove us. Turn us out. Expel us from the Senate. Would to God you could. Call in the praetorian guard. Take us — apprehend us. March us off." Webster, in stately, measured language, protested the unconstitutionality of defacing the journal, and Clay, in flaming speech, stressed this same argument, and denounced the President as a tyrant.

He has swept over the Government, during the last eight years, like a tropical tornado. Every department exhibits traces of the ravages of the storm. . . . What object of his ambition is unsatisfied? When disabled from age any longer to hold the sceptre of power, he designates his successor, and transmits it to his favorite! What more does he want? Must we blot, deface, and mutilate, the records of the country, to punish the presumptuousness of expressing an opinion contrary to his own? . . . Black lines! Black lines! . . .

But Benton, eager for his pound of flesh, moved that the resolution be carried out. The Whig Senators withdrew. The Secretary of the Senate came forward and did as he was bid, while loud and repeated hisses broke from the gallery.[28] Thus vanished in humiliation the Senate's great rebuke to Jackson's bank policy.

There were other humiliations for Harry of the West during Jackson's last years of office, and chief among them was the fate of his land bill. From 1833 on, the public lands question was linked, not with the tariff, which was regarded as almost sacred, but with the general financial situation. Clay continued to press his plan for keeping up land prices and distributing the proceeds of sales to the states, with special consideration for those states where the land lay. In this way, he urged, all parts of the Union would benefit, the dangerous surplus would be distributed, and the states would receive funds for internal improvements. The Administration continued its stand for the settlers and the new Western states. The result was a deadlock. The price of lands remained at a dollar twenty-five an acre and no further steps were taken toward pre-emption, but neither did Clay's distribution bills, which he introduced repeatedly, go through. The whole question had become a political football, and the income from the public lands became a major factor in distending the Treasury surplus.

This surplus was primarily paper, not specie. It consisted largely of bank credits. The speculators bought land and paid for it with bank notes. These went into the deposit banks,[29] and were again lent out to the speculators. Thus a vicious circle was formed, and thus was stimulated an inflation of bank credits and prices that paved the way for the panic of 1837.

[28] *Ibid.*, 24th Cong., 2d sess., 429f, 440f.
[29] There were 29 of these, Jan. 1, 1835; 33, Dec. 1, 1835; 89, Nov. 1, 1836. — D. R. Dewey, *Financial History of the United States* (N.Y., 1931), p. 210.

Clay's project for the distribution of land sales was not an effective remedy for this evil situation. The plan would have disposed of the surplus, but its benefits in that direction would have been counterbalanced by its stimulus to speculation and inflation on the part of the states. Price graduation and restriction of land sales to actual settlers would have lowered drastically the Government's income from land, and would have acted as a check upon both the surplus and the inflation. This would have been more businesslike, as well as more democratic in its implications. But Clay hung doggedly to his own proposal, nothing constructive was accomplished, and paper continued to pile up in the Treasury.

The surplus was handled very badly. It reached thirty-six million in 1836, and this readily available treasure aroused the cupidity of the states to a pitch that swept away what little judgment both parties possessed. In June, 1836, Congress passed, by rousing majorities, a bill which distributed all the surplus above five million among the states, in proportion to their representation in Congress. Jackson, who had been both for and against such action since he became President, appears to have helped it through the House.[30] Clay and the Whigs, desirous of removing this fund from the Administration's control, supported the measure vigorously in the Senate, although the Kentuckian had previously opposed surplus distribution. Parts of the bill attempted to check the extravagant note issues of the "pet banks," but Congressional enthusiasm centered on the distribution feature. Whigs and Democrats alike shared the blame for this evil measure, which was in effect a monkey wrench thrown into the nation's financial machinery, dislocating capital, spurring the states to extravagance, encouraging speculation. It was political juggling, pork barrel legislation with even less sound sense behind it than had Clay's distribution land bill, but Jackson signed it, probably with the idea of helping Van Buren's presidential campaign.[31]

[30] Jackson, *Correspondence*, Vol. V, p. 409, R. M. Johnson to Jackson, June 21, 1836; Bourne, *Surplus Revenue*, p. 23.

[31] Jackson became openly critical of the measure after the election of 1836 was over. — Richardson, *op. cit.*, Vol. III, pp. 1459–1464; Bassett, *op. cit.*, pp. 696–697.

The bill distributing the surplus was far from halting the vicious financial evils which had now beset the country. Jackson finally awoke to the true significance of the enormous public land sales [32] and determined to check inflation, and protect the Treasury and the settlers from the effects of land speculation. His remedy was the Specie Circular of July 11, 1836, which limited payments for the public lands to gold and silver. This drastic step had a very real effect in overthrowing a financial structure that had become decidedly topheavy. The measure spread distrust in the banks, and created a tremendous demand for specie, forcing that commodity out of the East into the West. It helped the speculators in a fashion, for the settlers had great difficulty in obtaining specie, and the restriction practically limited the land supply to that already purchased from the Government. The circular rocked the money market, just as the banks were getting ready for the surplus distribution, and money became very tight.[33] About all that can be said for it is that it was a belated attempt to protect the interests of the West, and an emphatic warning that all was not well in the financial world.

The Whigs denounced the measure and attempted to force its repeal. On December 14, 1836, Ewing of Ohio offered a joint resolution to that effect, and Clay supported this, pointing out the evil consequences of Jackson's act and prophesying the coming storm. He offered, as a suggestion, that the Government be obligated to accept, in payment of its debts, bank notes which had a par value at the place where payment was made.[34] This was constructive, for such a move would have mitigated the severity of the circular. The joint resolution went down to defeat, but feeling against Jackson's remedy was strong, and a bill designating and limiting the funds receivable for revenue, which, in accordance with Clay's proposal, included provision for the reception of the notes of specie-paying

[32] Compare his messages to Congress in 1835 and 1836. — Richardson, *op. cit.*, Vol. III, p. 1381, Vol. IV, p. 1468.

[33] Dewey, *op. cit.*, p. 229; R. C. McGrane, *The Panic of 1837* (Chicago, 1924), pp. 61–63, 92–93.

[34] *Cong. Deb.*, 24th Cong., 2d sess., 373–374.

banks, passed the Senate and the House. The President and the Attorney-General, however, found the measure too vague and too much in conflict with existing laws, and it was disposed of by a pocket veto.[35]

Jackson's policies were formulated and adopted in the midst of such desperate and bitter controversy that political expediency often had a most unfortunate weight with both parties. In that warfare the Whigs represented, on the whole, the conservative point of view of the solid and substantial elements in the population, while the Democrats showed greater responsiveness to the moods and desires of the masses. If one sets this consideration apart, however, and examines the financial ideas of Jackson and of Clay primarily on the ground of soundness and wisdom, the Kentuckian has the better of the argument.

The President was not equipped to deal intelligently with financial problems. His action in regard to the Bank, the surplus and the Specie Circular produced vicious results, paving the way for the depression which was soon to overwhelm the country. Clay's program was by no means perfect. His land proposal would have encouraged inflation and speculation. His acceptance of surplus distribution was motivated apparently by political considerations rather than sane financial judgment. But in upholding the Bank and opposing the Specie Circular, he stood for sound finance and against two of Old Hickory's worst mistakes. Had Clay prevailed in his struggle against "Jacksonism," the American financial system of the 1830's would have rested upon decidedly safer foundations.

Clay's one major victory over Jackson was gained in connection with the French crisis of 1834–1835. On July 4, 1831, a treaty had been signed at Paris by which France had agreed to pay twenty-five million francs for outrages committed upon American commerce during the Napoleonic wars. Ratifications had been exchanged at Washington, February 2, 1832, and the payments, in six annual installments, were supposed to begin one year after that date. Louis Philippe was anxious to carry out this agreement, but the French Chambers were unwilling to make the necessary appropriations. Jackson waited almost two

[35] Richardson, op. cit., Vol. IV, pp. 1501–1507.

years, his anger mounting the while, and then launched a startling attack upon our recalcitrant debtor.[36]

The President reviewed the history of the case in his message to Congress, December 1, 1834. He noted the repeated but unfruitful manifestations of good intentions by the French Government, noted too, that our Minister, Livingston, had received "positive assurances" that, at the next session of the Chambers, the King and his Cabinet would press the appropriation. If Congress wished to wait, said Old Hickory, well and good, but if Congress were in a sceptical frame of mind, the question arose as to the measures that should be pursued.

Then came the belligerent tone. The President revealed his conviction that the United States should insist upon "prompt execution" of the treaty, and, in case it be refused, or longer delayed, take redress into their own hands. He recommended that a provisional law be passed, authorizing the seizure of French property to the amount of the debt, in case the ensuing session of the Chambers refused to put through the appropriation bill. This, he said, was necessary to preserve our "national rights and honor," and France should consider it as such, and not as a menace.[37]

This fulmination was considered to be so important that express riders scurried out of the Capital with it, covering the distance to New York, as Philip Hone sourly noted, at a reported cost of seven hundred dollars.[38] Immediately there was great alarm in the commercial world, with real apprehensions of war. French public opinion was mightily aroused and the French Minister was recalled from Washington. Livingston wrote from Paris of the unfavorable reception of the message and indicated his belief that Congressional delay, or a proposal of mere commercial restrictions, would be the best way now to get the appropriations through the Chambers.[39]

---

[36] Livingston, Minister to France, had suggested a firm tone in the annual message, but that suggestion seems to have been unnecessary — Richardson, *op. cit.*, Vol. III, p. 1349; Bassett, *op. cit.*, pp. 667–668.

[37] Richardson, *op. cit.*, Vol. III, pp. 1319–1326.

[38] Hone, *Diary*, Vol. I, p. 143.

[39] *Cong. Deb.*, 23d Cong., 2d sess., App., 164–165. Later despatches indicated his belief that it would pass without such action.

Clay had not been averse to reprisals against France when he was Secretary of State, but now he viewed the situation with alarm. Political considerations probably influenced him. He was greatly depressed by the discordant nature of the Whig Party, and longed for some stimulus to unity. It may be that he saw this stimulus in opposing Jackson's French policy. But he seems also to have been sincerely alarmed about the possibility of war.

The most engrossing subject of the Session [he wrote to Henry Junior] is likely to be the President's Message relative to our French affairs. His rashness, in advising a war-like measure, without waiting for the decision of the French chambers at their approaching Session, seems to be generally condemned. It is apprehended that, if his message reaches France, as is probable, before any appropriation is made, the Chamber of Deputies will refuse the appropriation, in consequence of the threat which the Message contains. In that event, our difficulties will be greatly increased. Irritation begets irritation, and I should not be surprised if, in the sequel, two gallant nations, hitherto entertaining for each other the greatest respect, shall be found unexpectedly engaged in War.

The Senate has placed me at the head of the Com^{ee} of F. Affairs — the most responsible situation of the Session. I shall endcavor to discharge my duty, but I confess I have less heart than ever to exert myself in public business.[40]

On January 6, 1835, Clay reported for the Committee on Foreign Relations a resolution "That it is inexpedient at this time to pass any law vesting in the President authority for making reprisals upon French property . . . ," and accompanied this by a report which was thoroughly fair and devoid of partisan animus. He asserted our just claim to the indemnity, and the necessity of protecting American rights in general, but he also mentioned the difficulties confronted by Louis Philippe's Government. He brought out the milder parts of Jackson's message, but indicated that it might easily be misunderstood, and that reprisals would probably be regarded as an act of war.

[40] McDowell Collection, Clay to Henry Clay, Jr., undated, but either Dec. 1834, or Jan. 1835.

He urged confidence in the honor and good faith of France, and speedy action by Congress in making known its position.[41]

With his consent, discussion was postponed until Wednesday, January 14, when he spoke again defending the report, rehearsing his arguments, and urging the value of a stand by Congress soothing to the French spirit. The discussion on both sides of the Senate was thoroughly amicable. All seemed to recognize his honest intent, and Clay accepted an amendment to the resolution which eliminated any direct reference to the President. The report was then adopted without a dissenting vote.[42] On March 3, Clay again reported for the Committee on Foreign Affairs, and again advised delay.

Meanwhile, with the short session approaching its close, the House Democrats and John Quincy Adams expressed approval of a firmer stand. There, after vigorous debate, the House Committee on Foreign Affairs was discharged from further consideration of Jackson's comments upon France, but the House unanimously approved preparations for any possible emergency arising out of the question,[43] and passed a fortifications bill which appropriated three million dollars for the President's use in defending the country, provided it became necessary to use it before the next session of Congress.

When this came up to the Senate, a storm of opposition developed. Webster and Calhoun hoped the Senate would disagree. B. W. Leigh of Virginia averred that to pass such a bill would be almost equivalent to saying "that the President should be made Consul for life, or Emperor of the American people." Wright and Buchanan painted the horror of a French attack upon our defenseless shores, but Calhoun retorted that there was about as much danger of the Capitol being swallowed by an earthquake before Congress met again. Clay protested against the appropriation. The bill, he said, was a blank check which gave the President unnecessary powers. France showed no bellicose intentions, and he "deprecated a preparation for war, or which might lead to war, at this time, as calculated to

[41] *Cong. Deb.*, 23d Cong., 2d sess., 104, App., 208–219.
[42] The vote was 45 to 0.
[43] *Cong. Deb.*, 23d Cong., 2d sess., 1634.

keep up excitement abroad, and prevent an early settlement of our claims. This proposition partook much of the character of the President's message; that unfortunate message, he might say; for it had produced a good deal of unpleasantness, and put in jeopardy the peace of the country." He hoped it would be rejected.

The House proposal was voted down on party lines. The House insisted, but the Senate voted to adhere to its disagreement. A conference ensued, and an agreement was reached for an appropriation of three hundred thousand dollars for fortifications, and five hundred thousand dollars for the Navy. But when, at two A.M. on the morning of March 4, the report of this reached the House, that body had begun dispersing and there was no quorum. The bill had been lost.[44]

In April, 1835, the French Chambers passed the necessary appropriation, with a proviso that it should not be paid until some satisfactory explanation should be given of Jackson's language. The President was determined not to yield, Livingston came home, and finally the American legation in Paris was closed. Early in the following winter, Jackson drew up another bellicose message to Congress, a message which his advisers succeeded in softening. As a result, its language was comparatively restrained, and it included a denial of any intention to menace or insult France. British mediation in January, 1836, further smoothed the path, the French professed themselves satisfied, and payments began in the spring of 1836.

Historians have always divided on the merits of this question. Was Jackson's attitude inexcusably harsh, or did it simply show France and Europe that they could not trifle with us? Did Clay and the Whigs stand on the very threshold of disloyalty or did they smooth the pathway of negotiation?

Old Hickory's message of December, 1834, was certainly rash and provocative. The United States had an excellent moral case against France, the force of which could only be weakened by threats. Reprisals, if adopted, would have meant a long step on the road to an expensive war, and would have enhanced neither the honor nor the character of the United States. On

[44] Benton, *Thirty Years' View*, Vol. I, p. 556.

the other hand, the President's action may have heightened foreign respect for American rights.

The Whig position was doubtless motivated in part by political enmity. There is some ground for the criticism that Congressional action in order to ameliorate the effect of the message was an unwarrantable intrusion upon the Executive's conduct of foreign affairs. The Whigs have been accused of leaving the nation "naked to the foe." [45] But the fact remains that the Whig stand, whatever its motives, served as an emollient. Clay's report was spread abroad in France. It showed that the United States was not bent on war, and thus it helped to keep open the pathway of negotiation. Madison praised it, and pointed out that France could take the ground that the treaty was not binding on her, "appealing for the fact to the structure of her government, which all nations treating with her are presumed and bound to understand." [46] The passage of the three-million-dollar defense appropriation would likewise have exacerbated French feeling. France had shown no disposition to resort to arms, and passage on the ground of preparedness might very easily have been interpreted by that country as a bellicose step that would have to be met in kind. The question really simmers down to this: If one believes in sabre-rattling diplomacy, the Whigs should be condemned; if not, they should be praised.

As in the French imbroglio, Clay displayed evidences of a pacificatory spirit in connection with the Texas question. The American inhabitants of that territory broke away from Mexico during the latter part of the Jackson Administration. A Mexican attempt to crush their rebellion failed in the spring of 1836, and in July of that year Texas asked annexation to the United States. [47]

By that time, Mexican feeling against the United States was rising to a high pitch. American citizens and American supplies had aided the Texans, and General Gaines had advanced into Texas on the ground of protecting the United States against Indian attacks. Jackson had made two attempts to purchase

---

[45] C. G. Bowers, *The Party Battles of the Jackson Period* (Boston, 1922), p. 405.

[46] Clay Papers, XXI, Madison to Clay, Jan. 31, 1835.

[47] J. H. Smith, *The Annexation of Texas* (N.Y., 1911), p. 20.

Texas, and after the battle of San Jacinto, in April, 1836, he became a cautious advocate of recognition, with a view to eventual annexation.[48]

But evidence was not lacking that Texas might produce serious trouble within the United States itself. Southerners were anxious for the acquisition of this new territory, and Northern antislaveryites were beginning to raise a hue and cry against annexation. The situation was pregnant with all kinds of dangerous possibilities.

On Wednesday, May 4, 1836, Benton reported from the Committee on Military Affairs a bill authorizing the President to accept the services of volunteers for frontier defense, and Preston of South Carolina spoke in alarming terms of danger on the Southwestern Border. Clay scouted the need for this force. There was no danger of invasion, he said, and "he must see a very different state of things from any that had as yet presented itself, before he should be willing to interrupt the pacific relations of the Government, and precipitate it into a war with Mexico."[49] The bill failed, as did another, for increasing the army, which was introduced in June and against which Clay spoke.[50]

On May 23, Walker of Mississippi moved reference of a petition for recognizing Texan independence to the Committee on Foreign Relations, and Calhoun announced himself in favor of recognition and of annexation as well. Some four weeks later, Clay made a unanimous report for the Committee, a report recommending the recognition of Texas "whenever satisfactory information shall be received that it has in successful operation a civil Government, capable of performing the duties and fulfilling the obligations of an independent Power." But the speech that accompanied this report was not that of an annexationist. It decried haste, and stressed the lack of adequate information. It was not very important, the Kentuckian said, that the recommendation be acted upon immediately. The resolution based upon this report passed, July 1, by a vote of thirty-nine to nothing, but Clay repeatedly urged the necessity

[48] Ibid., p. 27.
[49] Cong. Deb., 24th Cong., 1st sess., 1385–1388.
[50] Ibid., 24th Cong., 1st sess., 1746.

for delay in recognition on the ground of lack of information.

His attitude remained the same at the next session. When Walker moved recognition, Clay still urged delay. He did announce that he would vote yea, in conformity with his actions in regard to the South American states. There would remain, however, he said, "the grave and important question of annexation; on which he would at present express no opinion. They were entirely distinct questions; and a vote on the one would not commit any man on the other." When the resolution to recognize passed on the evening of March 1, Clay's vote was not recorded.

At the same time, February, 1837, Jackson was taking a very belligerent attitude toward Mexico because of the non-payment of American claims. He would have one more attempt made at collection from the deck of an American warship off the coast of Mexico. If that failed, he urged reprisals, backed by the Navy. The Senate Foreign Relations Committee, with Buchanan as chairman, made a report earnestly commending one more attempt at peaceful settlement, which should be followed, in case of its failure, by prompt consideration of further measures. Clay was still a member of the committee, and announced his support of its stand. But he criticized the report on the ground that it made out too strong a case against Mexico.

There was a reluctant spirit manifested in all this. Where was that expansionist fever, for which the Kentuckian had been once so famous? Advancing years — for he was now almost sixty — may have moderated his ardor for an aggressive foreign policy. But recognition was a step toward annexation. The latter would stir up afresh the fierce slavery quarrel that had first reared its ugly head in 1820, and, just as the Van Buren supporters recognized that such a step might bring disastrous political consequences, so Clay may have seen the whole movement as an omen sinister to the Union and full of difficulties for the party of which he was an acknowledged leader.[51]

----

[51] There is no doubt that annexation was recognized as a move which would be weighty with the gravest possibilities. See the somber warning given by Southard of New Jersey, in July 1836. — *Cong. Deb.*, 24th Cong., 1st sess., 1915.

Clay continued to manifest great alarm over the encroachments of Executive power, repeatedly attacking Jackson's "tyranny." In March of 1834, he had told Van Buren that continued popular support of the Administration would justify fears for the end of free government and the establishment of a despotism. He asked, in a public speech in 1835: —

Can it be doubted that, if the President's bed had been fruitful instead of barren, the same means which are now employed, with his concurrence and approbation, to ensure the election of his favorite [Van Buren], would have been directed to the elevation of his own son? [52]

But the Kentuckian, like the rest of the Whigs, shied away from too concrete an attempt to limit the President's power, and the basis for his attacks, as well as those of others in his party, was obviously practical politics rather than any well-defined theory of Congressional government.[53]

Clay had shown great tenderness for the prerogatives of Congress during his warfare with the Monroe Administration, and he reverted to this attitude during the Jackson regime. He would have liked to find grounds for impeaching the President in the vetoes and in the dismissals from office, but men with whom he consulted discouraged him,[54] and he never attempted to utilize that sovereign remedy. In March, 1834, Clay introduced resolutions in the Senate declaring that Congress had the right to prescribe the tenure of offices created by law; that arbitrary removals from such offices by the President were not authorized by the Constitution; that the Judiciary Committee should inquire into the expediency of providing by law for the concurrence of the Senate in removals; and that the Committee on Post Offices and Post Roads should make a similar inquiry in regard to a law providing for the concurrence of the Senate in the appointment of deputy postmasters.[55] In his supporting

[52] Clay Papers, XX, Clay to Brooke, March 23, 1834 (copy); *Lexington Observer & Reporter*, July 15, 1835.
[53] Carroll, *op. cit.*, pp. 178–187.
[54] Clay Papers, XX, Madison to Clay, June–, 1833, Tazewell to Clay, Feb. 19, 1834.
[55] *Cong. Deb.*, 23d Cong., 1st sess., 834–836.

speech, he asserted his belief that the Executive's arbitrary removals were unconstitutional, as well as dangerous. These resolutions were printed and made the order of the day for April 7; but on that date, because of absences and "other reasons," Clay moved their postponement for two weeks. This was done, but on April 21 the President's Protest against the vote of censure was under discussion and the resolutions were not called up. During the following session, Clay introduced a project making necessary the Senate's consent for removals from all offices to which appointments were made with the advice and consent of that body. But again he did not press the issue.[56]

The Kentuckian was disappointed by the Whig Party's reluctance to accept him as its standard-bearer in 1836. To be sure, he repeatedly stated his unwillingness to run unless the party could unite upon him, but this stand was coupled with a very critical attitude toward the availability of other possible candidates.[57] He was warned, early in 1833, that he must not expect the nomination, but almost two years later, despite a lack of encouragement, he was clinging to the last hope.[58] There were, however, too many obstacles in the path. His smashing defeat in 1832, the tariff of 1833 and his relations with Calhoun which had made the Kentuckian unpopular with the New England Whigs, anti-tariff and states' rights elements among the Whigs of the South, anti-Bank sentiment in Virginia, all these factors lessened his availability. He gave up the struggle reluctantly, and on December 26, 1835, it was authoritatively announced that the Kentuckian would not be a candidate.[59]

[56] *Ibid.*, 23d Cong., 2d sess., 523.

[57] Porter Collection, Clay to Porter, April 11, 1834; Colton, *Correspondence*, pp. 392–395, Clay to ——, July 14, 1835.

[58] *Ohio Hist. and Philosophical Society Pub.*, V:2:75, Oran Follett to Clay, Jan. 10, 1833; *Buffalo Hist. Society Pub.*, Vol. XI, pp. 156–158, Fillmore to Weed, Dec. 28, 1834. *Cf.* John Floyd Mss., Duff Green to Tyler, Nov. 20, 1833, and Mangum Papers, VII, Letcher to Mangum, Dec. 2, 1835. Clay had stated in December, 1833, that he intended "to open and push a vigorous campaign," but he may have meant by that simply a campaign against Jacksonism. — Colton, *Correspondence*, Clay to Brooke, Dec. 16, 1833.

[59] *Niles' Register*, Vol. XLIX, p. 283, Dec. 26, 1835.

Divided by their differences, unable to present a national platform or unite upon a single candidate, the Whigs fell back upon the project of running strong leaders in different sections of the country. Webster was the choice of Massachusetts. The Tennessee Whigs nominated Hugh L. White, as strict a constructionist and anti-Bank man as could be found in the land. Pennsylvania raised the flag of William Henry Harrison. But Whig divisions were fatal, and Martin Van Buren, Jackson's designated successor, won a fairly decisive victory. The only comfort for the opposition was Harrison's strength in the Western and Middle Atlantic states, a showing which made him a logical candidate for 1840.[60]

Clay had found political life full of hardships during Jackson's terms of office. Many of his letters in 1835 and 1836 reflect a spirit of deep depression. In a letter on family affairs, written in February of 1835, occurred a single sentence bearing on his public life: "I am truly sick of Congress."

In December of 1836, he wrote again: —

I feel less interest than ever in public affairs. Indeed I should be very happy if I were not restrained by a sense of duty from returning home. There alone, if anywhere, I must look for repose and tranquility, during the residue of my life.

Kentucky re-elected him to the Senate in 1837, and he accepted, but it was with a heavy heart. This decision, he wrote to Letcher, had cost him "the most painful sacrifices of feeling," and, smarting under the recent passage of the expunging resolution, he added: "The Senate is no longer a place for any decent man."[61]

The political tide was, in truth, still running strongly against

[60] Clay backed Francis Granger for Vice-President in Ohio, and L. G. Tyler lays stress on this as showing Clay's desire to prevent Whig unanimity on John Tyler for Vice-President, a unanimity which might have resulted in Tyler's victory over the rather unpopular Democratic candidate, Richard M. Johnson. This is possible, but there is no satisfactory proof. — L. G. Tyler, *Letters and Times of the Tylers*, 3 vols. (Richmond, 1884–1896), Vol. I, pp. 519–520.

[61] McDowell Collection, Clay to Henry Clay, Jr., Feb. 19, 1835, Dec. 16. 1836; Crittenden Papers (Duke Univ.), Clay to Letcher, Jan. 17, 1837.

him. The Bank was gone. His land bill had been defeated. Internal improvements had been checked, and the tariff was being slowly lowered. For eight long years the White House, in such tantalizing proximity to the Capitol, had been triumphantly held by his most bitter enemy, and that enemy had chosen his own successor. But hope remained, and Clay's head was not yet bowed.

On March 4, 1837, — a beautiful, springlike day, — Martin Van Buren made his triumphal progress at high noon down Pennsylvania Avenue. Tom Ritchie had come up from Richmond to see the inaugural ceremony, and, as he went into the Senate chamber, he came face to face with Harry of the West. All personal relations between the two men had ceased in 1825, and Ritchie had been unsparing in his attacks; but perhaps there was a sudden memory of happy days in Richmond, long ago, when a gangling boy with a big mouth had declaimed about the glories of the French Revolution and liberty and setting out boldly for the as yet uncharted shores of political freedom. Their hands met, and Ritchie remarked that time had dealt very gently with the Kentuckian. Clay smiled and lifted up his hands. "Ah! I will keep the Old Fellow off as long as I can," he replied; "and suiting the action to the word, he threw both his arms forward, as if keeping off Time and his fatal scythe." [62]

[62] Ritchie, *Reminiscences*, p. 4.

CHAPTER XVIII

THE TILT WITH VAN BUREN

VAN BUREN had scarcely taken office when the panic of 1837 burst upon the country. It had been brought on primarily by Jackson's financial policy, the mad speculation and over-confidence of the early 1830's, and a depression in England which drastically lowered the price of cotton and increased specie export from the United States. Failures began in March, and by May the banking system was in chaos. Specie payments were generally suspended, and the Government found itself not only unable to accept bank notes offered in revenue payments, but without any banks where it could lawfully deposit its receipts. Under these circumstances, with laborers walking the streets, bankruptcies of everyday occurrence, business stagnating, and the currency going from bad to worse, Van Buren reluctantly called a special session of Congress.

Clay was convinced that the distress was a result of Democratic policies, and that it was up to the Democrats, not the Whigs, to furnish a program of relief.[1] His chief aim was to establish an active opposition, for he believed that a National Bank must be the core of any constructive relief, and as yet he saw no prospect of its establishment.[2]

The Red Fox, in his message of September 4, attributed the hard times primarily to undue business expansion, distribution of the surplus and the drain of gold abroad. He refused to consider re-establishing a National Bank, was opposed to keeping up the deposit system, and proposed that the Treasury keep its own money in its own hands, the so-called Sub-Treasury

[1] Sweet Collection, Clay to A. W. Stow, April 26, 1837; *The Collector*, Vol. XXII (May 1909), pp. 75–76, Clay to W. Thompson, July 9, 1837.

[2] *The Collector*, Vol. XXII (May 1909), pp. 75–76, Clay to Thompson, July 9, 1837; Gratz Collection, Clay to M. L. Davis, July 3, 1837 (confidential).

or Independent Treasury plan. The Specie Circular was stamped
with the President's approval. He urged that the transaction
of Government business should be put on a specie basis, asked
the passage of a uniform bankruptcy law, and recommended
that the fourth installment of the surplus (three quarters of it
had been distributed) should be kept, and that Treasury notes
should be issued to tide the Government over the depression.
Clay pronounced this program barren, and saw nothing in it to
justify the extra session.[3] It was apparent from the start that he
would fight the Administration's proposals.

The Democrats passed bills authorizing ten million dollars
in Treasury notes, and postponing indefinitely the payment of
the fourth installment of the surplus. Both measures were necessary, but Clay opposed them. He favored distribution, even
though there was no money to distribute, and castigated the
Treasury notes as an issue of paper money which put the
Government into competition with all the banks of the country.
Such a stand scarcely rose above blind partisanship.

The great measure of the special session, however, was the
Sub-Treasury bill. The idea which underlay this bill was
neither revolutionary nor destructive. It consisted simply of
keeping the public money in the mints, post offices and customs
houses of the country until it was paid out. This plan was part
and parcel of the Democratic "hard money" policy, which derived from a fear of inflation and a desire to profit politically
from popular distrust of banks. The Democrats sought to
divorce the Government from all direct connection with banking, and, by legislation, to establish a sound currency of gold
and silver.

Clay held that it was as impossible to divorce the Government from banks as from the people, and that a metallic currency would crush the debtor class beneath it and dangerously
strengthen the National Government. He ascribed the panic to
the destruction of the Bank of the United States and to the
hard money program and, by inference, he made these responsi-

[3] *Cong. Deb.*, 25th Cong., 1st sess., 1–3; Richardson, *op. cit.*, Vol. IV,
pp. 1541–1563.

ble for the European depression as well. The Kentuckian, like the Whigs in general, was most solicitous for the state banks and would have kept the Government deposits in them until popular demand should force the restoration of a National Bank.[4] This he would re-establish with every practical safeguard against its use of "improper" influence. The bank would then exercise a salutary control over all bank note issues and thus produce a sound paper currency.[5]

Such a program had merit and, carefully worked out, would probably have been better for the country than the Democratic plan. But it is only just to add that the Democratic policy had the great virtue of severing the Government from banks which relied chiefly upon Government support to maintain the soundness of their issues; that it bolstered the Government's credit; and that the attack upon paper money was in itself a check upon wildcat issues.

The Democrats controlled the Senate in the special session and voiced their opposition to a National Bank in no uncertain terms. They passed the Sub-Treasury bill in the Senate, but the House voted it down, due to a combination of Whigs and conservative Democrats, and a long struggle began.

The Sub-Treasury plan was again recommended by Van Buren in his December message to Congress. A Democratic split, Rives of Virginia heading a group of conservatives favorable to the state banks and opposed to a purely specie policy, gave Clay some encouragement, and after Silas Wright reported the Sub-Treasury bill out of the Senate Committee on Finance, January 16, 1838, the Kentuckian denounced it repeatedly. He declared with the utmost solemnity "that all the calamities of war with the most potent power on earth would be a blessing compared with the consequences of this measure." By a feat of mental legerdemain, he proved that it was dangerous both because it centralized power and because, on account of its failure

---

[4] *Cong. Globe*, 25th Cong., 2d sess., App. 456; Mallory, *op. cit.*, Vol. II, p. 394. David Kinley, *The Independent Treasury of the United States* (N.Y., 1893), pp. 37, 39–40, points out that this would have cost the Government terrible losses in 1839, when another bank collapse came.

[5] *Cong. Deb.*, 25th Cong., 1st sess., 251–269; *Cong. Globe*, 25th Cong., 2d sess., 396–397.

to establish a uniform currency, it promoted disunion.[6] On February 19, he spoke for four hours and one half, denouncing the bill. He maintained that Jackson had deliberately plotted the establishment of a Government Bank, to be administered and controlled by the Executive Department; that the deliberate destruction of both the Bank of the United States and the state banks was a part of this plan; and that Van Buren was carrying out this nefarious scheme. Obviously a political attempt to solidify the financial powers of the country behind the Whig Party, this exposition really dignified beyond merit Jackson's haphazard financial policy. In addition, Clay attempted to prove that Treasury drafts would circulate as currency, driving the issues of the state banks out of circulation, establishing a perfect union of the purse and the sword, and utterly prostrating the states to the Federal Government.[7]

The speech contained a bitter attack upon Calhoun, who had come out for the Sub-Treasury bill. The South Carolinian's Whiggery had been based upon his hatred of Jackson and his hope of dominating the Whig Party. This latter had been impossible, and he had come to see that to remain in an uneasy coalition with Clay and Webster would probably mean his own political annihilation. The Democrats, furthermore, had begun a systematic campaign to show that they respected states' rights and had a strong sympathy for minorities.[8] Calhoun's support of the bill signalized his return to the Democratic fold, and the clash between him and Clay which followed hard upon Clay's speech marked the resumption of warfare between the two men.

Despite the vigorous opposition of Clay and Webster, the bill again passed the Senate, March 26, 1838, by a vote of twenty-seven to twenty-five, but the House stood firm once more and the session ended in another stalemate.

---

[6] *Cong. Globe*, 25th Cong., 2d sess., 151–152. Clay was working hand in glove with Biddle. — N. Biddle, *The Correspondence of Nicholas Biddle*, R. C. McGrane, ed., pp. 299–301.

[7] Mallory, *op. cit.*, Vol. II, pp. 310–349.

[8] Cole, *op. cit.*, pp. 45–48. *Cf.* J. C. Calhoun, "Correspondence of John C. Calhoun," in *Amer. Hist. Assoc. Report* (1899), Vol. II, pp. 409, 435, 449.

Clay continued to fight hard against the pertinacity of the Little Magician. The Kentuckian and Webster led a successful attempt that spring to rescind the Specie Circular. This was a laudable victory over the Administration's hard money policy, although it was marred by a barren altercation among the friends of the two chieftains as to which should have credit for the authorship of the resolution.[9] But the struggle between the bank and the Sub-Treasury forces was not to have so successful an issue. Clay took pains to explain that he did not approve of an attempt to establish a National Bank until it was clearly demanded by the people. He moved "to detach the Whig cause from Mr. Biddle's bank," stating that he would not recharter the old institution.[10] But he harped upon the necessity of a National Bank until Niles of Connecticut sourly remarked that Clay reminded him of an old Negro fiddler, very proud of his skill and always displaying it, who could play only one tune, "Pea Straw." Most of the Senators, said Niles, were getting tired of the old Bank tune of "Pea Straw, Pea Straw."[11]

The Kentuckian was not alone in his advocacy of a Bank, however. All through the bitter years of the Van Buren Administration, the Whig Party identified itself with the banking interests in bitter opposition to Van Buren's financial policy. Repeatedly, in state elections, its leaders voiced their desire for a National Bank, while they excoriated their opponents as anti-Bank radicals and agrarians, who were attacking the fundamental rights of property.[12] Such tactics did not prevent the Democrats' obtaining a majority for the Sub-Treasury in both Houses of the Twenty-sixth Congress; and, despite a last bitter attack by the Kentuckian and his supporters, the bill went

[9] *Cong. Globe*, 25th Cong., 2d sess., 344–419, App. 294–296; Porter Collection, Clay to Porter, June 9, 1838; *Buffalo Hist. Soc. Pub.*, Vol. XI, pp. 168–169, Fillmore to Weed, May 30, 1838.
[10] Porter Collection, Clay to Porter, May 28, 1838; *Cong. Globe*, 25th Cong., 2d sess., 396–397. Buchanan asserted, May 21, 1838, that Clay had created a distinct issue between the two parties in posing a National Bank against the Independent Treasury.
[11] *Ibid.*, 25th Cong., 2d sess., 420.
[12] McGrane, *Panic of 1837*, pp. 149–176.

through, just as the extraordinary presidential campaign of 1840 was swinging into full blast.

While the Sub-Treasury battle was raging, another contest had developed over the public lands. Van Buren had had no clearly defined policy on the public domain up to December, 1837. But he had soon found that he could not pass his Independent Treasury bill without giving way to the New West in the matter of a liberal land program.[13] Hence developed, mainly under Benton's leadership in the Senate, a proposal to graduate the price of public lands and another project for securing pre-emption rights to squatters who had settled before purchasing. A majority of the Whigs, and the East in general, averse as ever to cheap lands, opposed these measures.

Clay was in the van of the battle. He held true to his land policy, denouncing pre-emption as "fraudulent, heartless, scandalous, abominable speculation" that despoiled the Government of its land,[14] and terming graduation economically wasteful, unfair to the old states and conducive to speculation.[15] Both measures passed the Senate, however, April 13, 1838, although graduation was defeated in the House.[16] Again, in January, 1839, he did his best to defeat a graduation bill that passed the Senate only to die in the lower chamber, and a year later, he quarreled bitterly with Calhoun over the latter's proposal to cede the lands to the states in which they lay.[17]

By 1840, the West held the balance of power between the parties, and the Whigs had begun maneuvering for Western support by stirring up a movement for the indirect assumption of state debts through the distribution of public land sales which could be used for the payment of those debts. This was nothing but Clay's old distribution plan in a thin disguise, and was certainly as vulnerable as the Democratic proposal to re-

[13] Wellington, *op. cit.*, pp. 66–70.

[14] *Cong. Globe*, 25th Cong., 2d sess., 130f, App., 129–143.

[15] *Ibid.*, 25th Cong., 2d sess., 293, App., 563–564.

[16] Clay actually favored *increasing* the price of public lands — Clay Papers, XXII, Clay to John B. Dillon, July 28, 1838.

[17] *Cong. Globe*, 26th Cong., 1st sess., 96–97, 202–203. Calhoun's bill failed. He was evidently trying to reap political profit from the Western demand for cheap land.

duce land prices. Benton exposed its weak points. It was unfair to the non-indebted states; it established a dangerous precedent, encouraging state extravagance; and, by fostering the spirit of distribution, it laid the basis for new and excessive tariff duties. But it found favor in Clay's sight, and he vigorously opposed resolutions denouncing the plan.[18]

The Whigs and the East prevented the passage of any graduation bill, but the Democrats succeeded in getting through the session of 1840, which passed the Sub-Treasury bill, another pre-emption act that extended the previous measure for two years. This ended the great land squabble until after the election.

Clay's defense of the moneyed interests makes it not at all surprising that he became very much excited when, in February, 1840, Benton and William Allen of Ohio denounced a monopoly in the salt trade and the resulting cost of that commodity to the people. Allen's attack upon the salt monopoly, said Clay, was "disorganizing and revolutionary . . . All this about monopoly was but a new form of attacking the rights of property. A man may not use his property in what form he pleases, even if sanctioned by the laws of the community in which he lives, without being denounced as a monopolist. . . . We are told that the object is to effect a repeal of the duty on salt — a repeal of this miserable duty of six cents a bushel! And how will that prevent the manufacturer from getting, what every man has a right to get, the highest price for his productions? But, sir, the whole tenor of the gentleman's remarks were in conformity with that agrarian spirit, which I regret to be compelled to say has of late years been so prevalent, and which is rapidly increasing." The state legislature, he held, was the proper place to obtain redress against a company which violated its charter, and "he protested against the doctrines of the speech of the Senator from Ohio, as detestable in their nature and abominable in their consequences."[19]

---

[18] Wellington, *op. cit.*, pp. 75–81; *Cong. Globe*, 26th Cong., 1st sess., 123–124, 243–245. The proposal was dropped during the campaign.

[19] *Cong. Globe*, 26th Cong., 1st sess., App., 178. Clay held that national regulation of corporations was undesirable. The states, he said, were "much

Henry Clay had a warm and generous nature, and a real passion for justice, as he understood the term. He sympathized with foreign authors whose works were pirated in America, and helped to initiate a movement for adequate copyright laws. He had a keen sense of the hardships suffered by the Indians as a result of Jackson's policies, and frequently protested against the treatment accorded to the red man. His sympathy was readily extended to individual cases of poverty and oppression. But his economic philosophy, whether consciously or not, favored the rich and the able at the expense of the masses. The democratic spirit of the Middle Period, typified by the increasing recognition of the common man, found Clay intent upon furthering the interests of the businessmen and the financiers.

more competent than Congress is to exercise all necessary and proper jurisdiction over corporations . . . the assumption of a jurisdiction over them by Congress would be incalculably dangerous, alarming, and mischievous." This statement was made in connection with his opposition to a compulsory clause in a general bankruptcy bill. — *Ibid.*, 26th Cong., 1st sess., App., 316–318.

Chapter XIX

BLACK GOLD AND POLITICS

While Clay was fighting his battles against Jackson and Van Buren, the "reprieve," which Thomas Jefferson had seen in the Compromise of 1820, came to an end.

There were two great underlying reasons for the revival of the slavery controversy. Cotton culture by means of slave labor was expanding steadily in the South, and that section had become convinced that slavery was an essential part of her economic system. The apologetic Southern attitude of the earlier part of the century was rapidly being replaced by an open defense of the "peculiar institution," and writers such as the influential Thomas R. Dew of William and Mary College were upholding slavery upon moral as well as upon economic grounds.[1]

Then, too, as the 1830's wore on, the South became more and more aware of its heavy economic dependence upon the North. The necessary capital for Southern business was concentrated mainly in the great Northern cities; Southern cotton was carried to Europe in Northern bottoms, and goods for Southern consumption came chiefly from Northern markets. The Yankees were getting a lion's share of the Government aid for public works. The embers of the tariff controversy still smoldered, for no one could tell with certainty what might be done to the tariff after 1842.[2] Resentment over this state of economic tutelage was increasing.

But the most direct cause of strife between the sections was a growing Northern demand for the complete eradication of

[1] T. R. Dew, *Review of the Debate in the Virginia Legislature of 1831 and 1832* (Richmond, 1832), pp. 28–38, passim.

[2] See the study by John G. Van Deusen, *Economic Bases of Disunion in South Carolina* (N.Y., 1928), pp. 56–58, 120f, 185f, 336.

slavery. Already in evidence before 1830, Abolitionism received a powerful impetus from the Great Revival of that year, a benevolent and converting mania which laid the basis for an ensuing fervor in moral reform. The Abolitionist Movement found its prime movers in men like the brothers Tappan, Theodore Dwight Weld, and H. B. Stanton, all prominently connected with the religious revival. It found its "figurehead of fanaticism" in William Lloyd Garrison, a free-lance journalist and reformer with a mighty hatred of slavery, and during the early 1830's it sprouted newspapers like the *Liberator* and organizations such as the American, New England and New York City Antislavery Societies.[3] All of its leaders urged emancipation. Many, like Garrison, demanded immediate freedom for the Negroes, and, as the propaganda from the societies flooded through the mails and Antislavery petitions deluged Congress, resentment grew apace below Mason and Dixon's line.

By 1837, the South, led by the ultra defenders of slavery, had taken vigorous action against its tormentors. Fearing the effects of propaganda upon the blacks, convinced that a minor slave insurrection in Virginia in 1831, headed by one Nat Turner, had been caused by incendiary publications, various Southern states, with the connivance of the Postmaster-General, Amos Kendall, attempted to stamp out the circulation of such literature within their borders. Such action was of course construed by the Abolitionists as a direct violation of the liberty of the press, an argument that could rally to its support the innate respect of Americans for the Constitution.

An attack upon the right of petition was more serious still. Petitions denouncing the horrors of slavery in general, and demanding its abolition in the District of Columbia and in the territories, were bitterly detested by the Southern Congressmen. The great body of sentiment in the North was still hostile or indifferent to Abolitionism, and Southern leadership in the House established, in 1836, a "gag rule" which prevented even the reception of such petitions. No such rule was passed in the

[3] G. H. Barnes, *The Antislavery Impulse, 1830–1844* (N.Y., 1933), pp. 1–16, 33, 58, 107.

Senate; but, by consistently ordering that a motion to receive be laid on the table, the upper chamber also prevented the reception of petitions in any real parliamentary sense. John Quincy Adams, who was by no means an Abolitionist, led a crusade in the House against this violation of a Constitutional right. Other leaders took up the cry. The "gag rule" stirred up great indignation, and had no small effect in augmenting the number of what was to become the Antislavery host.

Like all the leaders of his time, Clay was forced into the maelstrom of this controversy, and his attitude toward slavery, the Abolitionists, and the Southern ultras manifested a singular combination of moral idealism and political maneuvering.

His dislike of slavery had not abated with the years. In 1829 he had asserted that Kentucky's failure to establish gradual emancipation had retarded her economic development. In 1833, speaking in the Senate, he had denounced slavery as "the darkest spot in the map of our country," and called it "this great evil." Three years later, he told the Kentucky Colonization Society that he considered slavery "a curse to the master; a wrong, a grievous wrong to the slave." In April, 1837, he wrote to a friend in Louisville that slavery was "fraught with great mischiefs to both races, to say nothing of the injustice it inflicts upon one of them." [4]

But, at the same time, as has been pointed out before, he was a slaveholder, living in a country which had a heavy Negro population, and, willy-nilly, he was enmeshed in the toils of the peculiar institution.

When, in 1829, "black Lotty" instituted suit in Washington for her freedom, Clay contested the suit, had her thrown into jail, and forced her back into his employ. In 1830, he assisted a Mrs. Warfield of Lexington in the attempted recovery of a slave who had run away to the North. [5]

---

[4] *African Repository*, Vol. VI, p. 6; *Cong. Deb.*, 22d Cong., 2d sess., 75; *National Intelligencer*, Sept. 10, 1836; Sweet Collection, Clay to Stow, April 26, 1837.

[5] Porter Collection, Clay to Porter, Sept. 28, 1830; Fendall Papers (Duke Univ.), Clay to Fendall, Sept. 10, 1830, approving Fendall's order to the marshall to imprison Lotty. "Her husband and children are here," wrote Clay. "Her refusal therefore to return home, when requested by me to do so through

As a friend of the business interests, he could appreciate Henry Junior's report from London, in 1835, that agitation of the slavery question would weaken American credit in Europe.[6] As a political leader, the Kentuckian dreaded the blight that a sectional controversy might cast upon his presidential hopes. And as a patriot, he dreaded the threat of disunion latent in every slavery controversy.

Colonization was his one solution of the question, and he sought repeatedly to demonstrate that it was logical and practical. He had delivered an elaborate argument before the Kentucky Colonization Society in 1829, seeking to prove that the natural increase of the white labor supply in the United States would lower the wages of labor and thus cause a decrease in the value of slaves; that in consequence of increasing competition from white labor, slaves would diminish in number, become more and more miserable, and be tempted more and more to crime. He anticipated frequent insurrections among the blacks, and lauded colonization as the only answer to the question.[7] He continued to argue that colonization of free Negroes would set an example that the Southern states might be stimulated to follow in getting rid of their slaves.[8]

Thomas R. Dew tore the whole proposal to shreds in 1832, demonstrating its ghastly expense and utter impracticability,[9] but the Kentuckian clung doggedly to the plan.[10] Why did he do so?

you, was unnatural towards them as it was disobedient to me. She has been her own mistress, upwards of 18 months, since I left her at Washington, in consequence of the groundless suit which she was prompted to bring against me for her freedom; and as that suit has been decided against her, and as her conduct has created insubordination among her relatives here, I think it high time to put a stop to it, which can be best done by her return to her duty. How shall I get her, is the question? . . . In the meantime, be pleased to let her remain in jail and inform me what is necessary for me to do to meet the charges."

[6] McDowell Collection, Henry Clay, Jr. to Clay, Dec. 20, 1835.

[7] *African Repository*, Vol. VI, pp. 8–12, 21.

[8] Mallory, *op. cit.*, Vol. I, p. 525; *Cong. Deb.*, 22d Cong., 1st sess., 644, 22d Cong., 2d sess., 75.

[9] Dew, *op. cit.*, pp. 47f, 69f.

[10] *Cong. Deb.*, 24th Cong., 1st sess., 1901; Sweet Collection, Clay to Stow, April 26, 1837; *Lexington Intelligencer*, Jan. 5, 1838.

It is evident that by the 1830's he was reduced to seeking a very painless remedy for slavery. He was no longer the eager emancipationist of 1799. In 1831, his friends in Kentucky refused to take any part in a plan for gradual emancipation, and two years later he showed himself to be distinctly cool to such a movement, alleging the expense of compensation, public sentiment against a Constitutional amendment, and that if such a step were taken in Kentucky, "while slavery existed in other slave states, a great deal would remain to be done." [11] In 1836, and again in 1838, he expressed the same view. He saw that the spirit of the times in Europe and America was turning against slavery, and preferred reliance upon the slow formation of public opinion to any more hasty action.[12] Colonization, then, was in his opinion the only practical remedy for a chronic disease. It was voluntary for the free blacks and exerted no pressure upon the slaveowners; it would operate very slowly; and, by removing the free Negroes, it would "render the slaves more docile, manageable, and useful." [13] A more innocuous program for dealing with slavery could not well be imagined, but Clay had to have such a program, for political reasons, if for nothing else. It was a compromise between his humanitarianism and his sense of the practical, and he held on to it desperately, feeble reed though it was.

But direct questions involving slavery were continually forcing him upon perilous grounds during the 1830's, as the growing tumult raised by the Abolitionists caused him increasing apprehension and concern. For that group he had only aversion. They were, he felt, engaged in unwarrantable meddling with a Southern institution, and were forcing slavery into politics, where it did not belong.[14] They had no direct interest, and their interference was "rash and impolitic." [15] Nevertheless, he could

[11] A. E. Martin, *op. cit.*, p. 69; *Ky. Hist. Soc. Register*, Vol. IV (May 1906), pp. 71–72, Clay to Dr. Berry, June 15, 1833.

[12] *Ky. Hist. Soc. Register*, Vol. IV (May 1906), Clay to Berry, June 15, 1833; Sweet Collection, Clay to Stow, April 26, 1837.

[13] *National Intelligencer*, Sept. 10, 1836.

[14] *Cong. Deb.*, 24th Cong., 1st sess., 779.

[15] Sweet Collection, Clay to Stow, April 26, 1837; *Cf.* Clay Papers, XXI, Lewis Tappan to Clay, June 22, July 20, 1835.

not afford, as a national leader, to become an extreme opponent of the movement.

On June 8, 1836, he spoke on a bill introduced by Calhoun which would have prohibited the circulation of antislavery publications through the mails. Clay opposed it as totally unnecessary and uncalled-for by public sentiment, and on the high ground of its unconstitutionality. Here he shared honors with Webster, who had made an able argument for freedom of speech and of the press a few minutes before, and the defeat of the bill was a proper rebuke to the Senator from South Carolina.[16]

The question of petitions asking the abolition of slavery in the District of Columbia and in the Florida Territory was a more complicated one. The antislavery ground here was cleverly chosen, for it involved the right of petition and asked for action only where Congress had paramount authority. Southern Senators in general fulminated against these petitions as initial moves in a wholesale attack upon slavery, and sought to prevent all discussion of slavery in the Senate, but Clay's attitude was both wary and judicious. He regarded the Southern ultras as "quite as mischievous as the abolitionists," [17] for he saw the danger involved in denying the right of petition. He defended discussion of the burning question, and took ground, in December, 1837, for receiving and referring such petitions. At the same time, he made it clear that he would by no means grant them, and maintained this position during the controversy that followed.[18]

On December 27, 1837, Calhoun offered a set of resolutions which were designed to clarify the Southern position and to force support from the Van Buren Democrats, with whom the South Carolinian and his followers were now politically aligned.[19] These resolutions, "as abstract as a metaphysical mind can well devise," according to Clay, outlined Calhoun's compact theory of the Federal Government, and the relation of that Government to the slavery problem. They asserted that

[16] *Cong. Deb.*, 24th Cong., 1st sess., 1728–1729.
[17] Porter Collection, Clay to Porter, Dec. 24, 1837 (confidential).
[18] *Cong. Globe*, 25th Cong., 2d sess., 34–39, App., 58.
[19] Meigs, *op. cit.*, Vol. II, p. 155.

the Union was a compact of the states; that the latter had exclusive control over their domestic institutions; and that the Government at Washington was in duty bound to safeguard that control. The fifth of these resolutions stated that "intermeddling" by Congress, the states, or their citizens on moral grounds to abolish slavery in the District or in any of the territories would be direct and dangerous attacks upon the interests of the slave states. The sixth carried the point still further by claiming that the Union rested upon equality of rights among the states, and that to refuse to "strengthen" the Southern and Western states, or to refuse to increase their limits or population by the annexation of new territory or states, on the ground that slavery was immoral or sinful, would be contrary to the equality of rights guaranteed by the Constitution and would, in effect, disfranchise the slaveholding states.[20]

Here, then, was the extreme Southern position. The Senate was asked to go on record as opposing any kind of interference with slavery anywhere, and as virtually recommending the annexation of Texas or any other territory which the South might judge necessary for the maintenance of its political power.

Clay found Calhoun's last two resolutions unacceptable. He felt that Calhoun was attempting "to revive and rally the states' rights party," thus advancing his own political interests, while at the same time undermining the Kentuckian by forcing him to take definite ground for or against the extreme pro-slavery view.[21] These resolutions, Clay asserted, would increase rather than allay the excitement over abolition; and dragging in the question of Texas, for so everyone would understand it, was "peculiarly unfortunate." The Abolitionists, left to stand alone, would go down before the sentiment of Union. But if the Senate should persist in giving them new allies by its action on petitions, and "if we should also unhappily place in their hands an additional instrument, by unnecessarily coupling the annexation of Texas with the subject of abolition in the same series of resolutions, then indeed there will be too much reason to

[20] *Cong. Globe*, 25th Cong., 2d sess., 55.
[21] *Ibid.*, 25th Cong., 2d sess., App., 57; Colton, *Correspondence*, Clay to Brooke, Jan. 13, 1838.

apprehend that the North, at no distant day, will be united as one man."

His own confidence, said Clay, was placed in the Union.

We allow ourselves to speak too frequently, and with too much levity, of a separation of this Union. It is a terrible word, to which our ears should not be familiarized. I desire to see, in continued safety and prosperity *this* Union, and no other Union. I go for this Union as it is, one and indivisible, without diminution. I will neither voluntarily leave it, nor be driven out of it by force. . . . I am opposed to all separate confederacies and to all sectional conventions. No state of actual danger exists to render them expedient, or to justify deliberation about them. This Union, this Government, has done nothing, nothing whatever, to excite the smallest alarm. It will do nothing; but if it should; if, contrary to all human probability, the rights and the security of the slaveholding states shall be assailed by any authoritative act emanating from this Capitol, a state of things for resistance, forcible resistance, will then occur. It will be time enough then to act. . . . And, sir, when that fatal day shall come, if it ever do come, when the slaveholding states have to defend, by force, their rights, the state whose servant I am will rush to battle, as she always has done, with her accustomed ardor, and with gallantry unsurpassed by that of any other state.[22]

Clay then offered a series of resolutions which he had prepared. They declared that Congress had no jurisdiction over slavery within the states, and approved the instant rejection of any petitions for its abolition, as beyond the Constitutional power of Congress. They censured the Abolitionists' activities, and opposed any attempt by Congress to eliminate slavery from the District or from Florida. They asserted that Congress had no power to interfere with the interstate slave trade. At the same time, they virtually guaranteed the right of petition against slavery within the District.

These resolutions were not at all to Calhoun's liking. He wished to meet the antislavery agitation "at the frontier." "If we yield an inch, we are gone," he exclaimed. But Clay's milder attitude toward abolition in the District and Florida

[22] *Cong. Globe*, 25th Cong., 2d sess., App., 58.

prevailed over that of Calhoun in the resolutions which finally passed, and Calhoun's attempt to recommend territorial annexations was laid on the table.[23]

The Kentuckian's attempt to pour oil on troubled waters had been undertaken partly out of patriotism, but also with a very real desire to advance his own interests. He felt that Abolitionism was still a minor force in the North, and that condemnation of it would not redound against him there, while respect for the right of petition would inure to his advantage. So far as the South was concerned, Clay felt too that he had lost nothing. Calhoun had attempted to trap him, but had failed. "I have borne myself," Clay wrote triumphantly to Porter, "in such a manner as to lose nothing neither at the South nor at the North. And I will equally disappoint him as to Texas." [24]

Clay was certainly averse to any radical step in the direction of annexing Texas. Definitely opposed to war for such a purpose, he asserted also that, even if that territory became independent and established peace with Mexico, he would not "concur in incorporating Texas in this Confederacy, against the decided wishes of a large portion of it." In his opinion, it was "better to harmonize what we have, than to introduce a new element of discord into our political partnership, against the consent of existing members of the concern." This was a position which, he believed, would be his political salvation, and when, in April of 1838, Walker of Mississippi urged that a squadron be sent to demand "instantaneous redress" for Mexican insults and spoliations, Clay was among the foremost in counseling caution and delay.[25]

The Kentuckian's middle-of-the-road position exposed him to attacks from extremists on both sides. He probably felt that his position with the Northern business interests was secure; and his desire for Southern support, plus the belief that the Abolitionists' program constituted a growing menace to the Union, led him into a further condemnation of that antislavery

---

[23] *Ibid.*, 25th Cong., 2d sess., 55, 98, App., 60–70, 98.
[24] Porter Collection, Clay to Porter, Jan. 10, 1838.
[25] *Ibid.*, Clay to Porter, Jan. 26, 1838 (confidential); *Cong. Globe*, 25th Cong., 2d sess., 299, 300–301.

group in February, 1839.[26] He stated his opposition to tampering with slavery in the District and Florida, or with the interstate slave trade. He drew the aegis of the Constitution over slavery, denying the right of the Central Government to meddle with it where established, and denounced the Abolitionists for stirring up dangerous hatreds over a matter that was none of their concern. Abolition, put in practice, would mean racial collision or race war. It would be unjust economically, unless the free states raised the one billion, two hundred million dollars necessary to compensate the slave owners. Already it had thrown back the cause of emancipation half a century, destroying the hopes of such a gradual movement in states like Kentucky and stimulating rigorous treatment of the blacks throughout the South. Slavery was "an exception resulting from a stern and inexorable necessity — to the general liberty of the United States." Abolitionism could be accomplished only by subverting the Union, "and beneath the ruins of the Union would be buried, sooner or later, the liberty of both races." [27]

Joshua Giddings, a rising Whig Congressman from Ohio, had been trying to bring about conciliation there between Clay's friends and the Abolitionists. This speech put him in an awkward position and he wrote to Clay, asking if Congress could not abolish slavery in the District solely on the ground of benevolence. A few days later Clay came over to the House and the two men had a short conversation in the lobby. The Kentuckian said that his speech was a sufficient answer to Giddings' note. Then, reports Giddings, the conversation became dull, and "with a cold invitation to call & see him, he left me." [28] But Clay continued to uphold the right of petition, and when, a few days later, Calhoun spun out his logic to prove

[26] It scarcely seems probable that the remark "I had rather be right than be President," attributed to him by Preston of South Carolina, in connection with this attack, afforded a complete exposition of his motives. — *Niles' Register*, Vol. LVI, pp. 54–55, March 23, 1839; *National Intelligencer*, March 30, 1839.

[27] Mallory, *op. cit.*, Vol. II, pp. 355–375. *Cf.* his position as stated in May 1839, *National Intelligencer*, Aug. 14, 1839.

[28] Giddings Papers, "Diary of Three Months, etc.," pp. 88–91. *Cf.* Clay Papers, XXII, Clay to A. Spencer, Feb. 25, 1839.

that petition had been superseded by general suffrage and instructions, and had been transformed from a shield against wrongs into a sword with which to attack the rights of others, Clay rose once more in its defense as a fundamental guarantee of liberty.[29]

Clay's position on these immediate questions was sound and statesmanlike. But there is little to show that he appreciated the significance of the South's economic discontent. His political program, in general, championed the economic interests that the South was growing to fear and hate. His strength in the North rested upon those interests and it is, therefore, not surprising that he overlooked, or at least chose to disregard, one of the main causes for the bitterness of the slavery controversy.

[29] *Cong. Globe*, 26th Cong., 1st sess., 187, 191.

CHAPTER XX

THE ELUSIVE SCEPTER

AT the very beginning of Van Buren's administration, Clay
pictured himself as the Little Magician's opponent in 1840.
A yearning for the nomination manifested itself in letters to his
friends, and as the summer of 1837 wore on, he discovered
prospects of being "again forced into the Presidential arena." [1]
He professed a devotion to the national welfare and a regard
for party superior to his own ambition, but his satisfaction
over evidences of support from various quarters of the Union
was unconcealed, and a rumor spread through Washington in
December that he had gone to the White House "to examine
the premises, and to satisfy himself whether they would be
likely to be in a tenantable condition about three years hence." [2]
The Kentuckian's public policies felt the impact of his hopes
and aspirations. The tariff he professed to regard as settled by
the Compromise of 1833. Internal improvements were still
in favor, but now that the states had taken them in hand so
well the Federal Government had little left to do, save to
render aid by distributing the proceeds from land sales. A
National Bank, although he believed it essential, should wait
for a clear manifestation of popular desire. Clay was no longer
ready to defy the South, the President, and the Devil for his
American System.

His attempt at a judicious stand on Abolitionism formed
another aspect of his program. Still another was the attempt to
conciliate the Democratic Conservatives, led by Rives of Virginia, and Tallmadge of New York, who broke with Van
Buren over the Sub-Treasury. The Kentuckian supported
Rives at the expense of the logical Whig candidate, Tyler, for
United States Senator, and urged New York Whigs to treat

[1] Colton, *Correspondence*, p. 418, Clay to G. D. Prentice, Aug. 14, 1837.
[2] *Cong. Globe*, 25th Cong., 2d sess., 54.

the Tallmadge group very tenderly. Finally, his stand on relations with Great Britain was doubtless influenced by considerations of party and personal interest.

Late in 1837, during a minor rebellion in Canada, a party of British soldiers crossed the Niagara River, seized the *Caroline*, an American-owned ship which was running guns to the insurgents, and, after one American had been killed, fired the vessel and cast it loose to drift over the Falls. The frontier blazed with wrath, and the Government sent General Winfield Scott and other military leaders into northwestern New York to preserve order. Clay approved measures for restraining the excitement on the frontier, but when, less than two weeks after the event, Van Buren laid before Congress such scanty evidence as the Government possessed in regard to the *Caroline* affair, the Kentuckian denounced the British action as "a most unparalleled outrage." He did not really believe that war would come, "he should as much as any man, deplore a war; but, looking to the vast resources of our country, the valor of our citizens, and our achievements in former times, he would not fear the result. If it should be war with Great Britain, he would deeply deplore it; but in this cause it would be a just war, and he would be ready to meet it." Such hasty comment was doubtless due in part to the old dislike of Great Britain, but its vote-gathering potentialities, especially in New York State, are obvious.[3]

Clay's attitude toward the Maine boundary question, a problem which had led by 1838 to the armed difficulties known as the "Aroostook War," is susceptible to a similar explanation. It is obvious from his remarks on the subject that he realized the necessity of restraining the belligerent citizens of Maine, pending an attempted settlement by negotiation, but he rose to the defense of Maine's title to all the territory in question, and announced that if American rights could not be secured by negotiation, he would favor a "just war."[4]

The Kentuckian's strength was formidable, and, as early as

---

[3] *Ibid.*, 25th Cong., 2d sess., 79–87.
[4] *Ibid.*, 25th Cong., 2d sess., 496–497; 3d sess., 222–229, App., 210f, 308f; 26th Cong., 1st sess., 126–127, 322–324.

December, 1837, he felt certain that he was the people's choice.[5] He had powerful support among the Northern business interests. The Southern Whigs and the Conservatives became increasingly favorable to his candidacy, and by 1839 Clay could reckon confidently upon their support. But in the North and West, Abolitionists, Antimasonic elements, cheap land advocates, and the friends of Webster and Harrison constituted a diverse opposition that caused the veteran candidate considerable anxiety.

This was shown by Clay's hesitation over the method to be used in the direct pursuit of the nomination. At first he deplored early attempts to bring out candidates, and discouraged such efforts; but, evidently concerned over a movement on the part of Webster's friends, he wrote to a supporter in July, 1837, that a candidate should be agreed upon at the next session of Congress.[6] In August, 1837, he came out for a National Convention; but by January, although still feeling that it ought not to be opposed, his mind dwelt upon fears that the Whigs of the South and Southwest might not attend, and that the contest for delegates might engender bad feelings.[7] Then he expressed an anxiety to see his supporters swing into action, although his letters continued to betray a mixture of eagerness for a declaration in his favor by the New York legislature and a desire to avoid such a step if it would endanger the Whig cause in the state by creating division there.

The Kentucky legislature came out for Clay in January, 1838; Rhode Island and Maryland soon followed, and a host of local meetings endorsed his name. He heard, and believed, that the Massachusetts Abolitionists were for him. "If I am to judge," he wrote to Henry Junior, "from information which daily, almost hourly, reaches me, there is everywhere an irresistible current setting in towards me." [8] In May, the

---

[5] Porter Collection, Clay to Porter, Nov. 24, Dec. 24, 1837.

[6] Gratz Collection, Clay to M. L. Davis, July 3, 1837 (confidential); *The Collector*, Vol. XXII (May 1909), pp. 15–16, Clay to W. Thompson, July 9, 1837.

[7] Porter Collection, Clay to Porter, Jan. 5, 1838 (confidential).

[8] *Ibid.*, Clay to Porter, March 13, 1838; McDowell Collection, Clay to Henry Clay, Jr., March 2, 1838.

Whigs in Congress fixed place and date of the National Convention as Harrisburg, December 4, 1839, and although Clay apparently took no active part in this proceeding, he felt perfectly confident of his selection as the candidate.[9]

Meanwhile, Webster and his friends had been active. Movements in his favor had begun in New York City, early in 1837, and that spring the "godlike Daniel" made a Western tour which elicited much enthusiasm, even, as Philip Hone confided to his diary, in "General Jackson's own dunghill."[10] Webster told Weed and J. Watson Webb that he would cordially support Clay if that gentleman were nominated, but there was no cordiality lost between the two men, even though they appeared together, on apparently good terms, at Lexington and Louisville. As 1838 wore away, the *Atlas* of Boston, generally regarded as a Webster organ, came out for Harrison, and, although Webster was not behind this move, Clay began to suspect him of throwing his strength to the Ohioan, a suspicion which deepened during the ensuing months. Relations became strained, and the followings of the two leaders assumed the appearance of personal factions.

Webster went to England in the spring of 1839, and his name was withdrawn from the contest early in July; but mutual distrust and dislike continued to prevail, and in the sequel his friends worked valiantly against Clay's nomination.[11]

Harrison, meanwhile, had shown signs of decided strength,

[9] "You will have seen," he wrote to Mangum, "that the Nat. Convention is fixed for Dec^r., 1839 at Harrisburg. I understand that the day was made so distant in conformity with the urgent desire of members from N. York, Vermont, Pennsa. and Ohio." — Mangum Papers, VIII, Clay to Mangum, May 31, 1838 (confidential). *Cf.* Anderson Collection, Clay to Lucretia Clay, May 27, 1838; Porter Collection, Clay to Porter, May 28, 1838.

[10] Hone, *Diary*, Vol. I, p. 264.

[11] Porter Collection, Porter to Clay (copy), Jan. 7, 1837, Clay to Porter, June 3, 1838, Feb. 24, 1839; Clay Papers, XXI, Webb to Clay, Sept. 29, 1837; Mangum Papers, VIII, Clay to Mangum, May 31, 1838 (confidential); Weed Papers, C. F. Mitchell to Weed, June 1, 1838; Adams, *Memoirs*, Vol. X, pp. 43, 77; McDowell Collection, Clay to Henry Clay, Jr., Jan. 18, 1839. David Ogden, a friend and supporter of Webster, told Porter in May of 1839 that he had urged Webster to withdraw his name, and that, if this were done, most of Webster's friends would come out for Clay. The actual result of Webster's withdrawal was very different.

especially in the West. An Ohio Whig state convention had declared for him in July, 1837. Some of his supporters kept asserting that he would run, whether or not he was nominated by the National Convention. The Antimasonic Whigs in Pennsylvania, with Thaddeus Stevens as a moving spirit, rallied steadily to him. In December, 1838, an Antimasonic convention, attended by delegates from several states, met near Philadelphia, and nominated Harrison for President and Webster for Vice-President. The Clay Whigs in Pennsylvania fought hard against this movement, called a convention of their own the following June, and nominated the Kentuckian. But, eventually, a Harrison delegation represented Pennsylvania at the National Convention.[12] Early in 1839, Webster had come to the conclusion that the Whigs' only chance was with Harrison.[13] The General's military record, the strong showing that he had made in the states north of the Ohio in 1836, and the fact that he had no strenuous, or at least no widely known convictions on political policies, made him attractive as a candidate for the amorphous Whig Party.

As has so often happened in American politics, New York was a state of critical importance. Her attitude hinged largely upon the decision of Thurlow Weed, the "Dictator" of the Whig Party there, and William Henry Seward, his protégé and close ally. Weed professed to favor Clay early in 1837,[14] but the force of circumstances moved him irresistibly away from the Kentuckian. Harmony was an important consideration to the practical New Yorker, and he regarded Clay as a stumbling block in the path to that desired objective. Antimasonic feeling against the Kentuckian was still strong, Fillmore and Granger strenuously opposing his candidacy. The Abolitionists became more and more violent against Prince Hal, and the New

[12] Porter Collection, Porter to Clay, March 8, 1838 (copy); L. Hurst, "National Party Politics, 1837–1840," in *Ind. Univ. Studies*, Vol. XII (June–Dec. 1925), pp. 121, 145–146; D. B. Goebel, *William Henry Harrison* (Indianapolis, 1926), pp. 326–335; Mueller, *op. cit.*, pp. 56–60.

[13] Webster, *Correspondence*, Vol. II, p. 45, Webster to Jaudon, March 29, 1839.

[14] Porter Collection, Porter to Clay, Jan. 7, 1837 (copy); Weed, "Recollections of Horace Greeley," in *The Galaxy*, Vol. XV (March 1873), p. 373.

York leaders regarded that group as very important.[15] Webster's friends, and Harrison's, likewise, were active in the state. The Democrats were constantly assailing Clay as a pro-Bank man, and Weed had no desire to revive that old issue. Fillmore, surveying the scene in Washington during May, 1838, wrote to Weed that the zeal of Clay and his followers knew no bounds, and that their efforts were dangerous in the extreme. He believed that Harrison could carry every state that would go for Clay, and Pennsylvania also, and retailed information from Indiana that Clay's opposition to the pre-emption law would blast his chances in all the new states. Fillmore argued that the Abolitionists would hold the balance of power in seven states, and urged the nomination of Harrison.[16]

Both Weed and Seward deprecated premature movements for the nomination, probably because they wanted to prevent a Clay boom. They were seriously considering Harrison as a candidate, and early in 1838 Weed went down to New York and succeeded in choking off a Clay demonstration that had been planned there.[17] It is not strange that the New York legislature refused to avow a preference for the Kentuckian.

Seward was elected Governor of New York in the fall of 1838, and Clay, who had been so depressed by the adverse results of earlier fall elections that he had thought of giving up the race, was filled with optimism and energy by this Whig victory. He began urging his friends, particularly in Virginia and New York, to push legislative action in favor of himself. Although professing confidence that New York was for him,

[15] Weed Papers, Seward to Weed, Nov. 15, 1837. "The Abolition question," wrote Seward, "is to succeed the Bank issue. Our experience of the latter may well enough teach us what we have to expect in the former. Can we not be wise for once, and suffer popular error to have its course — when we know that the consequence will be a voluntary return to principles which we in vain endeavour to press upon their consideration when they are heated by the arts of demagogues."
[16] Weed Papers, Fillmore to Weed, May 26, 1838.
[17] Ibid., Seward to Weed, Nov. 5, 1837, A. Worden to Seward, May 23, 1838; Albany Argus, June 2, 4, 1838; Seward, Autobiography, p. 348; T. W. Barnes, Memoir of Thurlow Weed (Boston, 1884), pp. 56–58. Both Seward and Worden heartily favored stopping the New York Clay meeting.

he wrote to Porter in a somewhat apprehensive tone about the state, stressing the "great danger" to the Whig cause that would be cleared away by an expression of preference. Fillmore and other New York Congressmen, he wrote, "while they are free to avow their own preference for me, profess to be apprehensive about my election." How was western New York? "Is there any prospect of action at Albany? How is Weed, Seward &c? Do they stand unmoved by any recent events?" [18] Porter replied, rather weakly, that he had so much confidence in Clay's nomination that he had not felt it necessary or expedient to urge a particular candidate in New York. Rather, his efforts had been exerted to maintain the principle of harmony. Fillmore and others were office-seeking Antimasons, but they were clever and Clay should keep on good terms with them.[19]

The anti-Clay movement continued to be fostered in New York state. According to Henry A. Wise of Virginia, Clay's opponents used a method called the "triangular correspondence." Three professed friends of Clay in different districts would write to one another, each man telling the others to do all that was possible for Clay in their districts, as his own was against the Kentuckian. The letters were intended to discourage Clay's real friends, so that he would be cast aside for either Harrison or Scott, and Harrison would be nominated.[20]

Scott began to figure prominently as a candidate early in 1839. His handling of the border situation after the *Caroline* affair had made him very popular in western New York, and rumors of his candidacy became more and more common, although he assured Clay that he was not seeking the nomination.[21]

Weed's position, however, remained ambiguous. Porter continued to believe as late as May, 1839, that the "Dictator" and Seward were favorable to Clay, but that spring Weed told

[18] Porter Collection, Clay to Porter, Dec. 27, 1838; McDowell Collection, Clay to Henry Clay, Jr., Jan. 18, 1839.

[19] Porter Collection, Porter to Clay (copy), Jan. 20, 1839.

[20] H. A. Wise, *Seven Decades of the Union* (Philadelphia, 1872), pp. 165-166.

[21] T. H. Clay, *op. cit.*, p. 266, note 1.

Webster that New York was going to choose a Scott delegation to keep the state away from Clay, and that it looked to him as though Harrison would be the nominee.[22] The New York boss moved carefully and not even Seward knew his full intent.[23] He was weighing chances, apparently ready to swing finally to either Harrison or Scott on the ground of availability. By the end of July the rumor was abroad that Scott was to be taken up in New York in place of Clay, and Weed's paper, the *Albany Evening Journal*, broke ground in that direction.[24]

It was high time for Prince Hal to make a dramatic move, and though he had refused to make a Northern tour, the year before, on the ground that it would be electioneering in a manner unworthy of the office,[25] he determined to come up into the enemy's country in the early fall of 1839. A desire to avoid public appearances was professed, and he brought his son James with him, but the tour was burdened with public dinners, crowds and speeches.[26] At Buffalo, he made his position clear. He would withdraw, if necessary, in the interest of harmony and party success. He looked forward to honorable retirement.

No veteran soldier, covered with scars and wounds inflicted in many severe battles and hard campaigns, ever received his discharge with more pleasure than I should mine. But I think that, like him, without presumption, I am entitled to an honorable discharge.[27]

[22] Schurz, *op. cit.*, Vol. II, pp. 175–176; Porter Collection, Porter to Clay, May 26, 1839 (copy); T. W. Barnes, *op. cit.*, p. 76.

[23] Weed Papers, Seward to Weed, May 20, 1839. Seward wrote: "I have read what you say about the Presidential candidates with an earnest desire to know more than it is prudent to ask."

In July, a prominent Connecticut politician wrote to Weed, saying that he had learned in New York that only Scott could carry the state. Clay was Connecticut's favorite, but if matters stood so in New York, "We wish to know it, in order that the way may be prepared for bringing Connt. on to the same ground." — Charles L. Porter to Weed, July 8, 1839.

[24] *National Intelligencer*, Aug. 3, 1839; T. Weed, "Recollections of Horace Greeley," in *The Galaxy*, Vol. XV (March 1873), p. 373.

[25] Porter Collection, Clay to Porter, June 3, 1838.

[26] Clay's route lay from Buffalo through central New York, up to Montreal and Quebec, then down to Saratoga Springs and finally to New York City.

[27] *National Intelligencer*, July 26, 1839.

Clay visited Seward's home in Auburn, although Seward was not there. Then after some three weeks of progress through central New York and Canada and a tumultuous reception at Burlington, Vermont, the Kentuckian came to Saratoga Springs, where he stayed several days and was royally entertained.

The famous watering place was crowded by dandies, office seekers, fortune hunters, fashionables and statesmen. Seward had been there just before Clay arrived on August 9. Weed was there; and Scott, "the rising sun," — wrote Philip Hone, — "shone among us to-day." [28]

The placid and courteous Van Buren stopped, as did Clay, at the United States Hotel. "I hope I do not obstruct your way," said the Red Fox to the Kentuckian, who was endeavoring to pass by him in the grand saloon. "Not here, certainly," was the reply. [29]

Hone bears witness to the extraordinary enthusiasm with which Clay was received at Saratoga, and Clay wrote home that it had been "most enthusiastic and gratifying." [30] He had told Seward, who had seen him in northern New York a few days before, that the demonstrations everywhere had convinced him that he was well with the people. He was convinced by the manner of "A. H. T." [Albert H. Tracy] and "F. G." [Francis Granger] that their feelings were changed toward him. "I told him," Seward wrote to Weed, "that all was right toward him except the feelings of the Abolitionists and the fears as they truly exist predicated upon the supposed hostility of that class," but Clay replied that such fears were groundless, and that many Abolitionists had come to him, confessing their principles "but declaring their preference for and devotion to him." Clay asked Seward to meet him at Saratoga, or elsewhere. "This of course," wrote Seward, "I cannot do — He knows not that I cannot go purposely to meet him — nor does he know that my movements are as much embarrassed with demonstrations as his own." [31]

[28] Hone, *Diary*, Vol. I, p. 412.
[29] *Ibid.*, Vol. I, pp. 415–416.
[30] Anderson Collection, Clay to Mrs. Clay, Aug. 12, 1839.
[31] Weed Papers, Seward to Weed, Aug. 15, 1839.

The New York group would have none of him, but they had to treat him gently. Greeley, who had given Clay up only reluctantly, was urged to meet him at Saratoga and gain his consent to wait until 1844; but the New York editor had no heart for his task and got no farther than Albany.[32] Weed took up the burden, and talked with Clay at Saratoga. He evidently brought up the Bank as an argument, and also the necessity of combining all the elements of the opposition to Van Buren, but Clay waved these objections aside as inconsequential and refused to withdraw, although he again stated that he would abide by the result of the Convention.[33] Although it cannot be proved, it is distinctly possible that either Weed or Seward suggested that he withdraw in favor of Scott,[34] but if so, this was seed sown upon unreceptive soil.

The early fall elections of 1839 showed Democratic victories, and the Kentuckian seems to have had some fear that his candidacy was the cause.[35] But his conviction of his popularity and his belief that withdrawal would harm rather than help the Whigs were so firmly imbedded, that he remained fixed in his determination to leave the issue "to the people and to Providence," by way of the Harrisburg Convention.[36]

The movement for Scott, meanwhile, had assumed consider-

[32] Weed, "Recollections of Horace Greeley," in *The Galaxy*, Vol. XV (March 1873), p. 373.

[33] Weed, *Autobiography*, p. 480. Some days later, Seward wrote to Weed that "the letter to Clay was sent with some modifications — Is that what makes you silent — I trust it was right although your silence and Mr. Secretarys [sic] suggestions which came too late make me think it doubtful." — Weed Papers, Seward to Weed, Aug. 25, 1839. I have been unable to find this letter.

[34] *Niles' Register*, Vol. LVII, pp. 250–251, Dec. 14, 1839, Clay's letter to the Kentucky delegates to the Harrisburg Convention, Nov. 20, 1839. This mentions requests he had received to withdraw in favor of Harrison, and other requests "by various respectable and intelligent citizens of New York, directly and indirectly recommending me to decline the contest in behalf of another eminent citizen, who has been distinguished in both the military and civil service of the United States."

[35] Clay Papers, XXII, Allen A. Hall to Clay, Nashville, Sept. 23, 1839.

[36] Porter Collection, Clay to Porter, Sept. 27, 1839; Sweet Collection, Clay to Nathan Sargent, Oct. 25, 1839; Weed Papers, P. Potter to Weed, Nov. 29, 1839; *Niles' Register*, Vol. LVII, pp. 250–251, Dec. 14, 1839.

able proportions. Aided by Weed's open declaration, and by some of Webster's friends, particularly his close confidant, Edward Curtis of New York, a shrewd and able politician who was violently opposed to Clay, it succeeded in capturing a majority of the state's delegates to Harrisburg.[37] Ogden Hoffman and Moses H. Grinnell, New York Congressmen, made a special trip to Baltimore and Washington where they "went the whole figure for Scott," with "good effect." The South, Curtis wrote to Weed, must not be alarmed by the Abolitionist argument against Clay. Else it would never go for Scott. "I pray you to remember this in the counsels you give to our friends who are to perform *inside* of the Convention." [38]

The Clay forces tried valiantly to beat back the attack, and at least threw some measure of panic into the Scott ranks.

I tell you again [Curtis wrote from New York to Weed], we shall be swamped without the most *energetic* efforts. Seward must write a *frank* full letter to Mr. Clay, & that too forthwith. He told me he would write his views to some other person & give the letter to you to use. But it is better, fairer, more manly to send the letter to Mr. Clay himself, & *forthwith*. The delegates are coming in here and they think the City is the world & Noah & Selden are raising hell with them. Come down and stand here until you go South. I believe we are ruined and damned.[39]

Violent efforts against Clay were made constantly at Washington, and as the delegates gathered at Harrisburg his opponents found the North Carolina Congressmen "far more reasonable than had been supposed." Practically all the New York Congressmen, some of whom Clay had believed were his friends, agreed that he could not carry the state. Charles F. Mitchell, who had stood out for the Kentuckian almost to the last, told him of this, and Clay accepted it calmly, saying that

[37] Weed Papers, Curtis to Weed, Oct. 1, 1839; Clay Papers, XXII, Willis Hall to Clay, Nov. 20, 1839. Hall wrote to Clay that, to prevent a Scott delegate going from the Albany district, the Clay men would probably unite with the Harrison men and send Solomon Van Rensselaer. He was certain that Harrison would not be thought of at Harrisburg.

[38] Weed Papers, Curtis to Weed, Nov. 18, 1839.

[39] *Ibid.*, Curtis to Weed, *n.d.*

he would tell the Kentucky delegation that he wished the strongest man nominated and promising hearty support.[40]

The one principle which seems to have guided Weed in his machinations was availability, and he was sure that Clay did not have that qualification. Weed's power in New York was great, and the Scott delegation from that state was prepared to go for Harrison if circumstances made that General the better choice.[41] In New York City the "Dictator" conferred with two delegates from New Hampshire who were devoted friends of Webster, and before they reached Harrisburg, an agreement had been made to act together.[42]

It is, of course, possible that Weed had simply been using Scott as a stalking horse to get Clay out of the way, but it seems more likely that he went to Harrisburg ready to take either General, as circumstances might dictate. Certainly, the story of a coalition between Weed and Webster's friends to force the hero of Tippecanoe upon the Convention is more than doubtful. Some of Webster's supporters were for Harrison. Others were for Scott. Edward Curtis, who was so influential with Webster that he had withdrawn Webster's name from the race for the nomination and then informed "the godlike Daniel" of the fact, remained a loyal Scott supporter to the end.[43]

On the day that the Convention met, Clay wrote to Porter from Washington that he anticipated Scott's nomination. A majority of the New York delegation had been "brought

---

[40] *Buffalo Hist. Soc. Pub.*, Vol. XI, p. 194, Fillmore to Weed, Dec. 2, 1839; Granger Papers, Granger to Weed, Nov. 1839; Weed Papers, Curtis to Weed, Dec. 2, 1839.

[41] H. Greeley, *Recollections of a Busy Life* (N.Y., 1868), pp. 130–131; Weed, "Recollections, etc.," in *The Galaxy*, Vol. XV (March 1873), p. 373.

[42] Weed, *Autobiography*, Vol. I, p. 481. These delegates went for Harrison on the first ballot.

[43] Wise, *op. cit.*, p. 166; Porter Collection, Porter to Clay, Jan. 28, 1841 (copy); Weed Papers, Curtis to Weed, Dec. 15, 1839. Curtis wrote in this letter, a week after the Convention was over, that he was still full of "Scottism," but "I have rather concluded that, on the *pis aller* principle, I may have been wrong, & that Scott was a *stouter* adversary of Clay & Harrison than he ought to have been, for success. *No matter*. My dear friend, you have done wisely, & all is well."

over," he asserted, at Albany and New York, and the New York Congressmen had nearly all gone in the same direction, despite the fact that both delegations declared that nine tenths of their constituents were for him [Clay]. Only the firmness of his friends, and the reported quarrels between the factions of the two Generals at Harrisburg, could prevent Scott's nomination. "They think," Clay wrote bitterly, "that it is easier to carry nine to one than one to nine! The contingency ought to be very certain in which such odds as nine to one is staked." [44]

The anti-Clay men found fertile soil to work in, at Harrisburg, for the two hundred and fifty-four delegates who gathered there from twenty-two states were ferociously anxious for a bountiful political harvest. Clay had most of the Southern delegates, and some support from the East. Harrison had Ohio, Indiana, and considerable strength in the Middle states. Of the New York delegation, twenty were for Scott, ten for Clay and two for Harrison. Scott also had support in New Jersey and Vermont. Most of the New England delegates were uninstructed. Clay had a plurality of votes, but this was counterbalanced by the fact that a good many of them were from states that the Whigs could scarcely hope to carry.

A plan to neutralize the Kentuckian's predominance was promptly adopted. A motion was jammed through that established a kind of unit rule. Each state delegation appointed a committee of three as its representative. These committees met together, learned the views of the delegations, and reported back to their own. Then each state delegation balloted, a majority vote being accepted as the vote of the state. The committees then met, compared the results, and again reported to their delegations. This process was repeated until there was a majority for a candidate, when the result was put before the Convention as a whole for its acceptance or rejection. [45]

This system was supported by Clay's opponents, and smacks of Weed's political strategy. It militated against Clay, depriving him of the advantage to be gained from his plurality; but an effort made to secure its reversal, after its significance

[44] Porter Collection, Clay to Porter, Dec. 4, 1839.
[45] Stanwood, *op. cit.*, pp. 194–195.

was fully apparent, proved unavailing. The work of his enemies had already been effective.

The first ballot by states gave Clay 103, Harrison 91, and Scott 57.[46] After several ballots, Connecticut transferred her vote from Clay to Scott, and Michigan went for Scott, making his vote 68 and reducing Clay to 95. On the final ballot, late on the third day of the Convention, New York, Michigan and Vermont changed from Scott and Illinois shifted from Clay, all going for Harrison, who thus received a majority.[47]

The Vice-President was another question, and an important one, for many of Prince Hal's friends were angry and aggrieved. There is conflicting evidence as to just what happened, but it appears that several of Clay's close supporters — Crittenden, Tallmadge, Mangum, Leigh and others — were proposed, but declined the honor before an actual ballot could be taken. The nomination was finally given to John Tyler, a states' rights strict constructionist, vice-presidential candidate in 1836, and popular with the Southern Whigs. Tyler had worked for Clay before and during the Convention. Rumor had it that he cried when Clay was defeated. It was felt that the choice would heal the wounds engendered by Clay's defeat, and would help to make up a balanced ticket.[48]

From the point of view of expediency, the nominations were good. Harrison had a military record and no pronounced views, other than a decided willingness to be the Whig candidate. The New West had no reason to dislike him, as it had in the case of Clay. The Antimasons favored him, and he had not offended the Abolitionists. Webster's friends, and the great man himself, preferred "Old Tip" to Harry of the West. Beside this man from Ohio ran a Virginian who appealed strongly to the conservative Whig interests of the South, where Harrison lacked popularity. They were both "available" for a party that had no platform and only divergent principles. No one thought

[46] *National Intelligencer*, Dec. 13, 1839. Stanwood, *op. cit.*, p. 195, gives the Harrison vote as 94.

[47] *National Intelligencer*, Dec. 13, 1839.

[48] *Niles' Register*, Vol. LVI, pp. 275–276, June 29, 1839, Vol. LXI, pp. 232–233, Dec. 11, 1841; Weed, *Autobiography*, Vol. I, p. 482; Greeley, *Recollections*, p. 131.

of Tyler's possible accession to the throne, and attention was concentrated upon Harrison, the standard-bearer of a Whig democracy.

Clay had been certain that he was the popular choice, and naturally felt that he had been deprived of the nomination by intrigue. According to Wise, he gave way to passion upon hearing the news, swearing violently, striding up and down the parlor of his boarding house, and exclaiming "My friends are not worth the powder and shot it would take to kill them!" [49] Wise's statements, unsupported, are open to suspicion, but if the Kentuckian did let his anger slip the leash, he atoned for it thereafter. Both publicly and privately, he gave his immediate support to the ticket. [50]

"Clay is a truly noble fellow," Weed wrote to Francis Granger, and Harrison thanked the Kentuckian "for the magnanimity of your conduct," and gave assurance that he would "highly appreciate any advice or suggestions you may think proper to give me pending the canvass. Indeed it is my sincere wish that our correspondence should be as free and unreserved as it once was." [51] Throughout the extraordinary campaign that was to follow, Clay worked zealously for the Whig ticket.

The Whigs borrowed the Democratic appeal to the masses in 1840. Seizing upon a Democratic sneer about Harrison's proper place being in a log cabin with a barrel of hard cider and a pension, they pictured the General's commodious dwelling at North Bend, Ohio, as being just such a humble abode. The log cabin became the spurious symbol of a spurious Whig democracy. Webster glorified it. All over the country, the log cabin, the coonskin, the barrel of hard cider, and simple farmer Harrison, "the Cincinnatus of the West," became the positive part of the Whig campaign. Van Buren, on the other hand, was pictured as a man who wore corsets, put cologne on his

---

[49] Wise, *op. cit.*, pp. 170–172.

[50] *Lexington Observer & Reporter*, Jan. 1, 1840; Granger Papers, Granger to Weed, Dec. 9, 1839; McDowell Collection, Clay to Henry Clay, Jr., Dec. 14, 1839, Feb. 22, 1840; *Niles' Register*, Vol. LVIII, p. 158, May 9, 1840.

[51] Barnes, *Memoir*, p. 86, Weed to Granger, Feb. 20, 1840; Gratz Collection, Harrison to Clay, Jan. 15, 1840.

whiskers, slept on French beds, rode in a British coach, and ate with golden spoons from silver plates when he sat down to dine in the White House. He was the symbol of executive usurpation, tyranny and bloated aristocracy. As to real issues, there were no clear-cut ones. Each side tried to use the slavery question to the detriment of the other. The Whigs avoided the Bank issue, despite Democratic attempts to fasten it upon them. The Democrats tried unsuccessfully to portray the Whigs as Federalists. The Whigs championed distribution of land sales in the East, and avoided a definite land policy in the West, simply picturing Harrison as the West's great friend.

It was a campaign replete with blatant demagoguery, and Clay had small liking for that part of it.

I lament the necessity, real or imaginary [he wrote to Crittenden], which has been supposed to exist, of appealing to the feelings and passions of our Countrymen, rather than to their reasons and their judgments, to secure his [Harrison's] election. The best, and only, justification of this course is to be found, in the practice, which was resorted to, in the instance of the election of Genl. Jackson. But that does not prevent my regret that either party should have ever been induced to employ such means.[52]

The Kentuckian was convinced that he was still the leader of his party. Doubtful of Harrison's ability to avoid snares set by "artful men,"[53] and eager to announce a creed for the Whigs "without committing anybody," he consulted with Clayton and one or two other friends, and then proceeded to an exposition of principles. On June 27, 1840, at Taylorsville, in Hanover County, Virginia, after carefully stating that he had no authority to announce the purposes of the nominee, he laid down a program for the Whig Party. According to this, the Executive was to be strictly limited, either by legislation or constitutional amendment. He should be restricted to a single term, the veto power should be limited; the power of dismissal and appointment should be curtailed; and the Treasury Department should be put under the exclusive control of Congress. As to national

[52] Crittenden Papers (Duke Univ.), Clay to Crittenden, July 31, 1840.
[53] *Ibid.*

finances, the currency must be made stable and uniform, either by the adoption of a system of state banks for Government deposits, or by a new Bank of the United States. He believed that a National Bank was necessary, but asserted that the choice between the two methods was a question of expediency, and that "public opinion ought to have a controlling influence." Protection should be maintained on the basis of the tariff of 1833. Economy should be practiced. The construction of roads and canals should be left to the states, which would be aided by the distribution of the fourth installment of the surplus [!] and by the passage of his land bill. Lastly, Congress should keep hands off all slave property rights.[54]

Here was a program which Clay outlined as being, in general, acceptable to his "political friends." And Harrison, though he was vague on many points, agreed in general with Clay's stand on slavery, finance and the limitation of Executive power.[55]

The election resulted in a decisive Whig victory. To be sure, Van Buren received only about 145,000 less votes than his opponent out of the heavy popular total of almost 2,500,000. But Harrison had a majority of 174 in the electoral college, only 7 states out of 26 ranging themselves under the Democratic banner.[56]

There was an ominous note in the campaign. The Liberty Party, an organization of Abolitionists who believed in independent political action, had entered the fray, and its candidate, James G. Birney of New York, polled some seven thousand votes, principally in New York and Massachusetts. A portent of disaster for Henry Clay lay concealed in that movement, but for the present the Kentuckian was more interested in the question as to who should have the controlling influence in the new Administration.

[54] Clayton Papers, I, Clay to Clayton, May 29, 1841; Mallory, *op. cit.*, Vol. II, pp. 420–426; *Niles' Register*, Vol. LVIII, p. 228, July 4, 1840.
[55] Goebel, *op. cit.*, pp. 357–364.
[56] Stanwood, *op. cit.*, pp. 203–204.

CHAPTER XXI

THE CRISIS OF 1841

THE victory had been won, but it was pregnant with possibilities of disaster. Could the party hold together and pursue a constructive program or would its disparate elements, nationalists and states' rights men, Abolitionists and Southern planters, fall into confusion and discord? Whose influence, Clay's or Webster's, would predominate in the councils of a President whose health was none too good? Many of the Whigs were fearful, but the Democrats looked on in unholy glee. "Now our fun commences," wrote William Learned Marcy to an intimate friend.[1] Storm signals were flying everywhere, and, if he were to continue his leadership in the party councils, it behooved Clay to stride vigorously upon the field of action. An opportunity speedily presented itself, for, almost immediately after the election, the victorious candidate set out on a trip to Louisville and Frankfort, Kentucky.

Harrison's purpose was to confer with "the old Duke," Charles Wickliffe, a long-standing Whig enemy of Clay. The conference supposedly had to do with the affairs of a land company, but the Democratic press promptly heralded it as a sign of Clay's political impotence.[2] Furthermore, Harrison, who had at first courted a meeting with Clay, now wrote that, in the interests of party harmony, it might be better for them to communicate only through some mutual friend.[3]

On receipt of Harrison's first letter, Clay had determined

[1] W. L. Marcy Papers (Lib. of Cong.), VI, Marcy to Gen. P, M. Wetmore, Nov. 6, 1840; Kent Papers, Francis Lieber to James Kent, Dec. 1840. Cf. G. R. Poage, *Henry Clay and the Disruption of the Whig Party in 1841* (Doctoral Dissertation, Univ. of Chicago), pp. 1–2.

[2] G. R. Poage, *Henry Clay and the Whig Party* (Chapel Hill, N.C., 1936), pp. 16–17.

[3] Crittenden Papers (Duke Univ.), Clay to Letcher, Nov. 4, 1840; (Lib. of Cong.), Harrison to Clay, Nov. 15, 1840.

to meet the President-elect in Frankfort, and he did not allow "Old Tip's" perturbations to interfere with this plan. The Kentuckian went to the state capital, invited Harrison to Lexington, and during the following week that gentleman was in the company of Clay and his son Henry Junior, a goodly share of the time.

Harrison's demeanor during this experience was most affable. He made a speech at Versailles, praising Clay in the highest terms, and asserting that, if the Constitution allowed it, he would gladly invest the Kentuckian with the presidency and himself retire to his farm. Harrison intended to offer Clay the State Department, but Clay declined the offer before it was made and suggested Webster's name for the position. Old Tip did not open his heart on Cabinet appointments, but he made it clear that on questions of public policy his views coincided with those of Clay. In fact, the latter was so well satisfied that he left for the Senate while the President-elect was still in Lexington.[4] But there was no real prospect of permanence for these halcyon days.

The formation of the Cabinet, which was completed by the middle of February, gave a fair representation to Clay's friends. John J. Crittenden was chosen as Attorney-General, and Thomas Ewing of Ohio, dubbed "the Butcher" by his opponents because of the facility with which he swung the political axe, became the Secretary of the Treasury. They were stout Clay men both, and trusted advisers of the President. But the dark-browed Webster, Secretary of State, was also high in favor. He was not one to bow the knee to the imperious Kentuckian, and Clay strove desperately but unsuccessfully to broaden his own influence by securing a Cabinet position for another henchman, John M. Clayton of Delaware.[5]

The Kentucky leader was a prey to hope and fear. Well he knew that the road was slippery, that the Websterites were

---

[4] Henry Clay, Jr., Diary, entry of Nov. 29, 1840; Porter Collection, Clay to Porter, Dec. 8, 1840; Clayton Papers, I, Clay to Clayton, Dec. 17, 1840; Webster, *Correspondence*, Vol. II, pp. 90–91.

[5] Clayton Papers, I, Clay to Clayton, Dec. 29, 1840, Jan. 17, Feb. 12, 23, 1841.

hostile to Clayism, and that he must move with circumspection if he were to avoid arousing Harrison's touchiness on the subject of domination. "Mr. C. must look about him or the rogues will cheat him — " wrote Marcy, a shrewd observer of the Washington intrigues. "To safeguard against such a contingency he ought to take care of his *outposts*, and the collectorship of N.Y. is the most important among them." [6] There was in this observation a note of prophecy.

During the short session, Clay taunted the Democrats with their impending reduction to a minority. To the accompaniment of gibes and sneers at the fallen foe, he made clear his program for tariff reform, the distribution of public land sales, and the repeal of the Sub-Treasury, while states' rights Whigs, such as Henry A. Wise of Virginia, began to manifest open discontent on the floor of the House with the measures thus indicated. And in the midst of these alarums and excursions a struggle began which was destined to fill the first days of Harrison's short term with bitter frenzy.

Edward Curtis was a candidate for Collector of the Port of New York City, the most lucrative office, from the patronage point of view, at the disposal of the President. Curtis was something of a political free lance, having served on the staff of Democratic Governor Throop, solicited reappointment from Democratic Governor Marcy, then turned Antimason and finally Whig.[7] Hand-in-glove with the Weed faction, he had been a leader in the destruction of Clay's chances at Harrisburg. "A shrewd and managing man," he enjoyed a great reputation for political skill and was a close friend of Webster. That gentleman, Weed, and Governor Seward were ardent advocates of his appointment, and Weed even sought to persuade Clay that Curtis would work for Clay's election in 1844.[8]

But to Clay and his friends Curtis' appointment was anathema.

---

[6] Marcy Papers, VI, Marcy to Wetmore, Feb. 21, 1841.

[7] Marcy Papers, II, Curtis to Marcy, Dec. 21, 1832, VI, Marcy to Wetmore, Feb. 16, 1841; Porter Collection, Porter to Clay (copy), Jan. 4, 1841.

[8] Porter Collection, Porter to Clay (copy), Jan. 4, 1841. Clay threatened to show Weed's suggestion to Webster.

The Kentuckian saw in this move the destruction of his political influence in New York State, and his rage was violent in the extreme. "The winds blow *awful*," Curtis wrote to Weed,[9] and the character of the tornado may be judged by a conversation Marcy had with Clay. They were discussing the appointment, and Marcy concluded his remarks "by saying that I supposed in all these matters he would be *very much disposed* to take the *advice* and consult the *wishes* of his *true* and *faithful friends* at Albany, *Spencer Weed* and *Seward*. This strok took effect. As to them he spoke out & said what I am not at liberty to repeat. He has just views of their character, and motives of their conduct." [10] Three days after this outburst, Harrison arrived in Washington and promptly became the center of the storm.

The worn-out old General was conscientious and wanted to be fair to everyone, but he was also vain and exceedingly fearful of Clay's dominating ways. Harrison agreed, perhaps reluctantly, to a demand for an extra session of Congress which Clay had been urging impetuously and which the Whig Senators had approved,[11] but he was in no mood to receive dictation on appointments.

Clay sensed the delicacy of the situation. He made it a general rule to abstain from pressing the claims of candidates for office, but the Kentuckian could not afford to be quiescent in the face of appointments hostile to him. The Curtis affair was not the only one, but it was beyond question the most significant, and Clay carried the fight to the President in outspoken fashion. The Weed and Webster men rallied their forces, and the struggle continued through the month of February, and into the first two weeks of the new Administration. Leadership and party domination were involved, and nerves were frayed to the breaking point.

Never had the Kentuckian been more irascible, never had his sudden moods of violent bitterness and sunny amiability

[9] Weed Papers, Curtis to Weed, Jan. 27, 1841.

[10] Marcy Papers, VI, Marcy to Wetmore, Feb. 6, 1841.

[11] Benton, *op. cit.*, Vol. II, p. 229; W. H. Graham Papers (Raleigh, N.C.), Graham to Mrs. Graham, Jan. 25, 1841.

succeeded one another more swiftly. His nervous tension seemed to find outlet in attacks upon the opposition, and the sessions of the Senate, during the first two weeks of March, were marred again and again by his lashing diatribes against the Democrats. These insults were not tamely borne, and a duel with Senator William R. King of Alabama was averted only by the exertions of mutual friends and an apology from Clay, delivered in his happiest manner, on the floor of the Senate.[12] Harrison, too, was irritable. He complained of ungenerous treatment on Clay's part, and, on March 13, wrote to the Kentuckian that the latter was too impetuous, that there were others who had to be consulted, and that, in many cases, Clay's judgments could not be followed.[13] Clay replied, denying any suggestion of dictation in regard to patronage, asserting (in the face of his efforts for Clayton) that he had recommended no one for any office, and that he had not said that Curtis *should not* be appointed.[14]

A day or two later Nathan Sargent found the angry Senator pacing his room, a crumpled note from the President in his hand, exclaiming, "And it has come to this! I am civilly but virtually requested not to visit the White House — not to see the President personally, but hereafter only communicate with him in writing! The prediction I made to him at Ashland last fall has been verified. Here is my table loaded with letters from my friends in every part of the Union, applying to me to obtain offices for them, when I have not one to give, nor influence enough to procure the appointment of a friend to the most humble position!" [15]

The Senate ended its labors on March 14, but Clay remained in Washington two or three days longer, carrying on the struggle against his New York enemies with great vigor.

[12] *Cong. Globe*, 26th Cong., spec. sess., 231–257; Poore, *op. cit.*, Vol. I, p. 259; Marcy Papers, VI, Marcy to Wetmore, March 9, 10, 17, 1841; Hone, *Diary*, Vol. II, p. 532.

[13] J. W. Du Bose, *The Life and Times of William Lowndes Yancey* (Birmingham, 1892), p. 103; Clay Papers, XXII, Harrison to Clay, March 13, 1841.

[14] Clay Papers, XXII, Clay to Harrison, March 15, 1841.

[15] Sargent, *op. cit.*, Vol. II, pp. 115–116.

He visited our dinner table on tuesday [Curtis wrote to Weed], drunk, laughed, joked and was happy for hours, & at night bid me goodbye with a hearty shake of the hand & God *bless* you, Curtis — God bless you, and the next morning went to General Harrison to make his final *protest* in the most decisive terms against me — left town that day, & from Baltimore wrote to Gen. H. begging him not to appoint "that d—d fellow Curtis." [16]

Harrison turned the matter over to four Cabinet members.[17] They reported favorably to Curtis. He was then appointed, and Clay, after a brief but serious illness which had struck him down in Baltimore, made his way back to Kentucky, raging. Internecine war had broken out among the Whigs and the outlook for party harmony was dark. Clay's followers were infuriated, while the Websterians smiled in triumph as their henchmen proceeded to take possession of all the important appointments in New York City.[18]

What fate might have held in store for the Whigs under Harrison's leadership will always remain a mystery, for the burdens of office and the importunate hordes of officeseekers swiftly sapped the veteran's strength. On April 1, reports began to spread that the President was seriously ill, and at half-past twelve on the morning of April 4, he passed away. A courier was sent post haste to Williamsburg, where the Vice-President was staying; and on April 6, John Tyler, a friend and supporter of Clay, but a member of the states' rights Virginia school, became the Chief Executive of the United States.

Who would be leader now?

John Tyler was an outstanding figure in that states' rights group which the Whig leaders, pursuing bitter war against Jackson, had welcomed with open arms. His courteous and tactful manners, oratorical powers and courageous political beliefs had made him a great favorite in Virginia and the Old Dominion had gratified his ambition with a host of offices.

---

[16] Weed Papers, Curtis to Weed, March 28, 1841. Curtis "got the whole story" from Harrison after the appointment had been made.

[17] Ewing, Badger, Bell and Granger.

[18] Crittenden Papers, VII, Westervelt to Crittenden, March 26, 1841; Ogden Edwards to Clay, April 12, 1841.

He had a naturally friendly, rather simple nature, but his light blue eyes, which twinkled with pleasure over brilliant wit and facile conversation, could blaze upon occasion with the hard cold light of that jewel which he prized above all others — consistency. Tyler had a long record of opposition to the National Bank, the tariff, and internal improvements at national expense. This being the case, the admiration which he had cherished for Henry Clay could not have been based upon a love for the Kentuckian's principles. There is no question, however, that at this time the two men were on the best of terms.

The new President was troubled in spirit and somewhat doubtful of his ability to take the helm amid the dangers which his close associates were only too ready to point out to him.[19] It was his earnest wish to avoid friction, and his presidential address stressed the necessity of harmony. He retained Harrison's Cabinet, a significant gesture of good will, and did his best to place himself *au courant* with Clay. Tyler made clear his opposition to the policy that had been followed in New York, and used the appointing power in a manner designed to placate the Kentuckian. The new President even stated that he would not arbitrarily oppose a National Bank, if it were framed so as to meet Constitutional objections.[20]

There was little reason, however, for Tyler to feel that he had become the leader of his party. This man, whom the Whigs were soon to term "His Accidency," had become President only by the whim of fate. He had never been a national leader, and any desire to assume such a rôle now would be further handicapped by the Whig tradition of reverence for the prerogatives of the legislature and fear of "executive usurpation" which had arisen out of the struggle with Andrew Jackson.

[19] Tyler Papers, II, Tyler to Rives, April 9, 1841, Tyler to Tazewell, Oct. 11, Nov. 2, 1841. There was even some question as to his rightful powers, for he was the first Vice-President to be elevated by the death of his predecessor. But, with the advice of the Cabinet, he assumed all the robes of the Chief Executive.

[20] Clayton Papers, Ewing to Clayton, May 1, 1841; Ewing Papers, VI, Tyler to Ewing, May 14, 1841; Weed Papers, J. A. Hamilton to Weed, April 27, 1841; Bonney, *op. cit.*, Vol. II, pp. 173–174.

Such being the case, Tyler was condemned in advance to becoming either a tool or a destructive force.

Clay, on the other hand, was indubitably the outstanding leader of his party, now that Harrison was gone. The Whigs in Congress looked to him as their guide, and his confidence in his own position was in no wise diminished by Tyler's obvious desire to be friendly. The Kentuckian heard, through a variety of channels, that Tyler would accept all the Whig measures, tariff reform, land sales distribution and especially, a Bank. The future appeared to be singularly auspicious.

"I have a perfect Bank in my head," Clay had written to Clayton early in March, and this plan for an institution with branching power, limited dividends, full publicity for its proceedings, and Government ownership of twenty per cent. of the stock and appointment of one fifth of the directors, was being communicated to friends by the end of April.[21] Despite the lack of a Whig platform in 1840, and despite the pussyfooting on the Bank question in which Clay himself had indulged during the campaign, the Kentuckian chose to regard the result as a popular demand for a Bank — an attitude undoubtedly strengthened by the rampant pro-Bank sentiment which the Whig leaders found in the South, and especially in Kentucky during the spring of 1841.[22] Business had not yet recovered from the panic of 1837. Clay regarded his measures as essential to national prosperity. But by the end of the first week in May, he had heard directly from Tyler that that gentleman was absolutely opposed to "an old-fashioned United States Bank,"[23] and it was in a decidedly agitated frame of mind that the Kentuckian left for Washington and the extra session which had been called for May 31. It is very probable that he was beginning to foresee another attempt to wrest the leader-

[21] Clay Papers, XXIII, Ewing to Clay, May 8, 1841; Clayton Papers, I, Clay to Clayton, March 3, 1841; Miscellaneous Papers (N.Y. Pub. Lib.), Clay to B. O. Tayloe, May 1, 1841; Porter Collection, Clay to Porter, April 24, 1841.

[22] Ewing Papers, VI, Crittenden to Ewing, April 30, 1841; Cole, *op. cit.*, pp. 90–92.

[23] Tyler, *op. cit.*, Vol. III, pp. 92–94.

ship of the party from him, and was determined that this should not happen.

Clay reached Washington about a week before Congress convened. By the opening of the session, he had had a violent disagreement with Henry A. Wise, leader of states' rights Whigs in the House and a close friend of Tyler, over the tariff and the Bank. From this time on, Wise, Beverly Tucker and other Virginians worked unceasingly upon the President, urging him to stand out against Clay's "centralism."

The organization of Congress showed the Kentuckian's power. He headed the Committee on Finance in the Senate, and the Committee on Public Lands was put in charge of one of his henchmen. The most important committees in the House were in the hands of his friends, and the Speaker, White of Kentucky, was a Clay man with little else to recommend him.[24] Clay "has consummate nerve," wrote Wise, "and ability to stand alone; Webster has not, and flies before him. We humble the latter to us and must combat the former. Regard Clay as the opposition to Tyler's administration ultimately." [25]

Tyler's message, on June 1, 1841, acknowledged that Congress was best qualified to express the popular wish regarding a financial system, but reserved the right to reject any measure that, in his judgment, was unconstitutional. After it had been read, Clay moved that the part relating to currency and finance be referred to a select committee that should suggest a remedy for existing evils. On being asked what remedy he proposed, he replied "a National Bank." Two days later the committee was appointed and Clay was made its chairman. Immediately he began engineering the passage of a bill repealing the Sub-Treasury, and, on June 7, introduced a resolution directing the Secretary of the Treasury, Ewing, to submit a plan for a Bank or fiscal agent.[26] The states' rights men were exceedingly restive, and Clay was exceedingly autocratic. On June 12, Ewing's bill came down to the Senate, and it was then that

[24] *Cong. Globe*, 27th Cong., 1st sess., 11; Marcy Papers, Marcy to Wetmore, May 31, 1841.
[25] Tyler, *op. cit.*, Vol. II, p. 38.
[26] *Cong. Globe*, 27th Cong., 1st sess., 8f.

the breach between the President and the Senator became apparent to all.

Ewing had worked out a project for a Bank that met the approval of Tyler and the Cabinet. It called for the establishment of a Fiscal Bank of the United States, and its great variance from Clay's plan lay in a provision that the Bank should have the power to establish branches of discount and deposit only with the assent of the states. The plan was defective in many ways,[27] but two of its deficiencies were fatal, from Clay's point of view. It differed significantly from his own plan, thus making the Administration rather than himself the sponsor of the measure, and the limitation on the branching power might well destroy the effectiveness of the institution. "What a Bank would that be!" he wrote in disgust to Robert P. Letcher, and made up his mind that he would have none of it.[28]

Tyler informed Clay of his complete opposition to any "ultra-Federalist" bank, and urged the adoption of Ewing's plan,[29] but the Kentuckian remained adamant. He was "tired of experiments," and was convinced that his own proposal represented the wishes of the party. He assumed a confident air. "Tyler dares not resist. I will drive him before me," one report credits the Kentuckian with saying, but he saw clearly that a crisis was impending, and that there was reason to believe that the President might cast in his lot with the states' rights champions "and detach himself from the great body of the Whig party." [30] That, in the face of this threat, and in the face, too, of the support given by Webster and by the *National Intelligencer* to the Ewing measure, Clay continued to exhibit the most refractory temper and to demand his bill or none, is strong evidence of his determination to go to any lengths to preserve his leadership and reduce Tyler to subservience.

[27] See the comments by Kinley, *op. cit.*, pp. 44–45.

[28] Crittenden Papers (Duke Univ.), Clay to Letcher, June 11, 1841.

[29] Tyler Papers, II, Tyler to Tazewell, Oct. 11, 1841. Tyler, *op. cit.*, Vol. II, pp. 53–54.

[30] Autograph Letters, IV (Pa. Hist. Soc.), Clay to H. C. Carey, June 11, 1841; Crittenden Papers (Duke Univ.), Clay to Letcher, June 11, 1841; Tyler, *op. cit.*, Vol. II, p. 41.

The President was in a most difficult position. His ideas on finance were hazy,[31] and this hampered his movements. Clay's plan was abhorrent to him, and acceptance of it would mean political subjugation. Webster, jealous of Clay but anxious for some kind of Bank, was counseling support of the Ewing plan. The Virginia côterie of Tyler's friends, opposed to any National Bank whatever, was constantly hovering about the President. It was a situation full of danger. On every side, ambition was obscuring national welfare. "The question of successorship," wrote a New York Congressman to Weed, "is having a deep and baneful influence here now & the locos fan the flames." [32]

Every move on the part of Clay evinced a determination reckless of consequences. In the Senate, where the Whigs had a majority of seven at the most, he whipped his forces into line, controlling procedure with an iron hand, and browbeating the Democratic opposition with the greatest asperity. The portly Senator Woodbury of New Hampshire was advised to save "a little of his wind," which, Clay supposed, "was a commodity exceedingly useful to him." Arbitrary treatment of the proceedings of an anti-Bank meeting in Ohio brought on a quarrel with Senator Allen, and the Kentuckian indicated perfect readiness for a duel.

On one occasion, when rigorously controlling the proceedings of the day, Clay professed dislike for being "a dictator in any sense."

"You do it so well you ought to like it!" Buchanan shouted; and the exclamation "That's fair!" arose in various quarters of the chamber.[33]

On June 21, Clay brought in a majority report from the select committee on the currency, a report that recommended his own Bank proposal. He attacked the Ewing plan, asserting that it was ineffectual and dangerous; that a Bank whose operations were dependent upon the will of the states would be only

[31] Witness his groping after a plan, later in the year. — Tyler Papers, II, Tyler to Tazewell, Oct. 11, Nov. 2, 1841.

[32] Weed Papers, S. M. Gates to Weed, June 30, 1841.

[33] *Cong. Globe*, 27th Cong., 1st sess., 48, 51, 83–86.

another disastrous experiment; and that "a derivation of power to the General Government from the consent of particular States would be unsound in principle, and the committee apprehend dangerous in practice. Admit such consent to be a legitimate source of power, the Government would not operate equally in all the States, and the Constitution, losing its uniform character, would exhibit an irregular and incongruous action." He pleaded for his own plan, as Constitutional and necessary.[34] These were strong arguments and they were supported and expanded in the vehement debate that followed. The passage of Clay's bill seemed assured.

Then the states' rights Whigs played their trump card.

An amendment was offered by Rives of Virginia that required state assent for branching. It was very similar to the Ewing proposal, and was supported by Webster and Rufus Choate, who had succeeded Webster in the Senate. Choate intimated that the bill would not receive the President's signature without this amendment, and Clay, in a violent attack for which he apologized on the following day, tried vainly to force the Senator from Massachusetts to disclose the sources of his information.[35]

The situation was grave indeed, for Rives's action, coupled with Choate's support, had made clear the ominous threat to Clay's control over the Senate Whigs. Preston was wavering, Archer attacked the bill and the amendment as well. The Kentuckian, disturbed, then furious, saw yawning before his feet a pit which had been dug by Webster and the White House, leagued against him.[36] But the delighted Democrats came to his aid, and, on July 6, the amendment was defeated by a vote of ten to thirty-eight.

The situation remained dubious, however. Clay cracked the caucus whip, and a careful check, on the evening of July 9, showed that his bill could not pass the Senate at that time, even though his supporters, an overwhelming majority of the

---

[34] *Ibid.*, 27th Cong., 1st sess., 80–81.
[35] *Ibid.*, 27th Cong., 1st sess., 133, 351–355.
[36] Porter Collection, Clay to Porter, June 30, 1841; Marcy Papers, VI, Marcy to Wetmore, July 3, 1841; Adams, *Memoirs*, Vol. X, p. 498.

party, felt that his cause was the Whig cause, and were becoming more and more incensed against Tyler.[37] The President, meanwhile, had advanced to a position where even Ewing's original plan no longer pleased him.[38] He was rapidly drifting into delusions of grandeur about a triumph that would mean another term in the White House.

Peter B. Porter now arrived in Washington, and began supporting an amendment that, Porter felt, would ensure the passage of the bill and again make Clay the "Great Pacificator." This amendment gave each state an opportunity to prevent the establishment within its borders of a branch of the Bank, by having the state legislature pass an act to that effect at its first session after the passage of the Bank bill through Congress. Clay was obdurate, and for days Porter pleaded without success. Then Porter went to New York, rallied powerful Whig support there for the compromise, and at last Clay yielded.[39] This proposal was adopted, modified by the proviso that, if it were found necessary to the carrying out of powers granted in the Constitution, *Congress* should have the power to establish a branch in a state, regardless of the state's attitude. The bill, thus altered, passed the Senate on July 27 by a margin of three votes. It went to the House and there under a caucus decree admitting no amendments, it passed, one hundred and twenty-eight to ninety-eight, on August 6, 1841.

The most contradictory rumors were abroad as to what Tyler's action would be. "What he will do," Clay wrote to Porter, "is unknown to me or to his Cabinet. There is a most agonizing state of uncertainty in the public mind. It is impossible to foresee the tremendous consequences of a veto. If the bill should be approved, we shall probably carry all our great measures; if rejected, we may lose most of them." [40]

[37] Graham Papers, Mangum to Graham, July 10, 11, 1841, Graham to Mrs. Graham, July 19, 22, 24, 1841; Mangum Papers, X, Reverdy Johnson to Mangum, July 13, 1841.

[38] Ewing Papers, VI, Webster to Ewing, July 15, 1841; Tyler, *op. cit.*, Vol. II, p. 52.

[39] Porter Collection, Porter to Clay, *n.d.*, July 21, 23, 24, 1841, Clay to Porter, July 21, 1841.

[40] Porter Collection, Clay to Porter, Aug. 9, 1841.

Within less than a week, uncertainty began to disappear. Clay informed his son, Thomas, that Tyler would probably veto, and that this would mean his separation from the Whigs.[41] On August 16, against the advice of his Cabinet, Tyler sent the bill back to the Senate with his disapproval. The President had "fired upon the flag of truce sent from the Capitol," [42] and that night a crowd hissed its disapproval on the porch of the White House.

Tyler objected to the bill on three counts: the power of discount, the power of branching, and his consistently expressed personal belief that a National Bank, created "to operate *per se* over the Union," was unconstitutional.[43] He had a right, and was under provocation to act as he did. His duty is not so clear. The bill represented the opinion of the majority of Congressmen in regard to a Bank, and Tyler had admitted that Congress was better qualified than himself to express the wishes of the people in this matter.[44] He had run on the national ticket of a party that regarded the veto power with loathing and the wishes of the legislature with a tender regard. Such considerations might well have led him, if not to sign the bill, at least to let it become law without his signature. This he would not do, and the inference is inescapable that he turned against his party either for the sake of an idolatrous devotion to consistency, or because of an equally foolish belief that he could outgeneral Clay and replace him as a great national leader.

On August 19, Clay spoke to a crowded Senate on the veto. In temperate language, he pictured the necessity of the bill and his sorrow at its rejection. He understood that another measure, framed to meet the President's objections, was in process of formation, and announced that he would take no active part in this proceeding. If nothing could be accomplished at this ses-

---

[41] Clay Papers, XXIII, Clay to T. H. Clay, Aug. 15, 1841.

[42] Mallory, *op. cit.*, Vol. II, p. 586.

[43] Richardson, *op. cit.*, Vol. IV, pp. 63–68.

[44] *Ibid.*, Vol. IV, p. 46. As Clay pointed out, there was such strong sentiment for a powerful bank that the amendment to the bill had lost it several votes in the House.

sion, he hoped that, by limiting the executive power, or by increasing majorities in Congress, the way might be paved for future action.[45] Rives defended Tyler and Clay made a spirited reply, denying any intention of quarreling with the President or of breaking up the Whig Party, and accusing Tyler's friends of fostering enmity between him and Clay and trying to form a third party. The veto was sustained by a vote of twenty-five to twenty-four.

But the Whigs rallied to Clay. Adams was bitter against the veto. Seward wrote to Weed: "The veto has disgusted everybody with John Tyler but not with themselves and their party." Reverdy Johnson felt that the time had come to break with the President and unfurl Clay's flag. Mangum denounced Tyler's conduct. Even Edward Curtis was enthusiastic over Clay's "noble bearing" and his "services to his country."[46] There was no question as to where the great majority of the party leaders stood.

While another Bank bill was being drafted and started on its way, the Sub-Treasury was finally repealed, and a land bill, combining pre-emption with Clay's distribution plan, was passed by the House. This last measure was emasculated by an amendment suspending distribution if the tariff went above the twenty per cent. level, but the Kentuckian submitted, rather than see another veto and another failure chalked up against his legislative program. The Bank was his *sine qua non*.

The new Bank bill was framed as a result of numerous consultations between Tyler, his Cabinet and various members of the House, and there was a clear understanding that its main outlines had the President's approval.[47] This "Fiscal Corporation of the United States," so named in deference to Tyler's wish, was introduced in the House by John Sergeant of Pennsyl-

---

[45] Mallory, *op. cit.*, Vol. II, pp. 485–501.

[46] Adams, *Memoirs*, Vol. X, p. 533; Weed Papers, Seward to Weed, Aug. 22 [1841], Curtis to Weed, Aug. 21, 1841; Mangum Papers, X, Johnson to Mangum, Aug. 27, 1841, Mangum to Mrs. Mangum, Aug. 24, Sept. 5, 1841.

[47] Benton, *op. cit.*, Vol. II, pp. 344–345; T. Ewing, "Diary of Thomas Ewing," in *Amer. Hist. Rev.*, Vol. XVIII (Oct. 1912), pp. 99–103.

vania. The corporation was prohibited from making local discounts. But it was to have the right to establish "agencies" in the states to receive, disburse or transmit the public monies and to deal in foreign and interstate bills of exchange. For a few days fair weather signals flew, but suddenly another storm loomed in the offing. Congress and the President were not yet in accord.

Tyler had suggested a clause protecting the states against the establishing of agencies prohibited by their laws. This had not been included in the measure. He had understood that the bill would be submitted to him for final inspection, but this had not been done. Furthermore, the President was much aroused by the publication of a private letter, written by a Virginia member of the House, John M. Botts, a letter which described Tyler as false and treacherous to the Whigs and stated that he was to be "headed" by the new Bank bill. Whether by accident or by design, the Whig leaders in Congress had given deep offense to the President.

These grievances, important in themselves, were reinforced by another factor of considerable significance. The President was deeply committed to intrigues looking to a reorganization of the Cabinet and the formation of a new party.[48] Tyler certainly believed in the practicability of this scheme, and the delusion seems to have acted as a stimulant to his Constitutional scruples, and his offended pride. He began to back and fill, expressing doubts about the provision for exchange, which he had at first accepted, and urging the desirability of postponing the whole matter.[49]

On the night of August 28, a Whig gathering was held at the house of John J. Crittenden. The ladies were not invited,

[48] Marcy Papers, VII, Marcy to Wetmore, Aug. 22, 1841; McLean Papers, X, J. E. Miller to McLean, Aug. 25, 1841, Green to McLean, Aug. 26, 1841.

[49] Benton, op. cit., Vol. II, pp. 345–346; Ewing, op. et loc. cit., pp. 100–103; Richardson, op. cit., Vol. IV, p. 70. The provision for dealing in exchange, which would have given the Bank great power, had been thoroughly discussed in the Cabinet. To claim that Tyler had not then understood its significance is to convict him of incredible stupidity. To indict the Cabinet for hoodwinking him is equally far-fetched.

and liquor flowed freely. During the evening several of the guests went to the White House, which had been closed for the night, and prevailed upon Tyler to come over and join the frolic. Clay greeted him cordially with, "Well, Mr. President, what are you for?" and as Tyler paused, embarrassed, "Wine, whisky, brandy or champagne? Come, show your hand." The President, Senator Graham noted, chose whisky, and they drank together merrily, but that same day Mrs. Badger had told Graham that she and her husband expected to return to North Carolina soon, and that the dissolution of the Cabinet was likely to take place in the immediate future.[50]

The President's official household agreed to make an effort to postpone the bill, and Webster brought his influence to bear through the Massachusetts Senators to that effect, but Clay made clear his unalterable opposition to such a course. He was determined to force the President into action.[51] The Kentuckian was severely censured among the Whigs for his hot haste on the bill, and he must have felt this keenly, for he was convinced that his own conduct was not animated by any petty or selfish motive.

All here is uncertainty as to the course and designs of the President [he wrote to Henry Junior]. The general belief is that he will veto the new bank bill, if it be sent to him. We are to take it up tomorrow in the Senate. The present state of painful suspense is worse than any conceivable condition; and I sincerely hope that the President will soon define his actual position. I shall vote for the new bank bill upon the same grounds which all our friends will occupy — not because it is what we would have it, but because it has been framed to suit the President's views, as I understand they were communicated.[52]

Tyler welcomed the issue. He would not countenance an amendment, proposed by Rives, that would have vitiated the power to deal in exchange, for he wanted the bill to come be-

[50] Graham Papers, Graham to Mrs. Graham, Aug. 29, 1841; Adams, *Memoirs*, Vol. X, pp. 544–545. Adams heard that the President had chosen champagne, not whisky.
[51] Ewing, *op. et loc. cit.*, pp. 104–105; Benton, *op. cit.*, Vol. II, pp. 348–349; *Cong. Globe*, 27th Cong., 1st sess., 404, 417.
[52] McDowell Collection, Clay to Henry Clay, Jr., Aug. 31, 1841.

fore him without alteration. The measure passed the Senate by a strictly party vote.[53] On September 9, Tyler sent it back with a veto that concentrated its attack upon the provision for dealing in bills of exchange — a provision that he had been glad to accept three weeks before.[54]

The Cabinet felt itself placed in an untenable position. It had tried to frame a bill satisfactory to the President, and the attempt had ended in failure. It had not been consulted in the preparation of the veto message, and it was under pressure from the Whigs in Congress to resign. On September 11, 1841, all the members, save Webster, sent in their letters of resignation.[55]

The godlike Daniel was determined to stay in the Cabinet. It is true that he was anxious to see the Maine Boundary Question, then in the process of negotiation, brought to an amicable settlement. But even more than that, his long-felt jealousy of Clay now flamed up into open hatred. Webster was convinced that the Kentuckian, who "slept better of nights for being a candidate," had split the party deliberately in order to gratify his own ambition. Men would be no longer dictated to by Clay, Webster told Philip R. Fendall. The time had come to side with the President against a man who would take no advice or remonstrance from any save the subservient. It was war.[56]

When Ewing's resignation came in on September 11, Webster was in the President's office. He knew well the purport of the letter and asked, in his deep voice, "Where am I to go, Mr. President?"

"You must decide that for yourself, Mr. Webster."

"If you leave it to me, Mr. President, I will stay where I am."

Tyler rose, extended his hand and said warmly, "Give me

[53] Save for Rives, who voted against it.

[54] Richardson, op. cit., Vol. IV, pp. 1921–1925.

[55] There is no real proof that Clay directed this move, but he certainly did not oppose it.

[56] Fendall Papers (Duke Univ.), Diary, pp. 31f. Webster asserted that both Crittenden and Graves had told him that Clay would only listen to those who were subservient to him.

your hand on that, and now I will say to you that Henry Clay is a doomed man from this hour." [57]

The President was in error. It was he, himself, who was doomed to political oblivion.

Two days after this event, Congress adjourned, and Clay went home, breathing out his wrath upon Tyler's presumptuous use of the veto, which had prevented the establishment of a sound financial system and the separation of the purse from the sword. The Kentuckian honestly believed that Tyler was a traitor, who aimed at his own aggrandizement through the establishment of a new party.[58] Meanwhile, the President filled his Cabinet with men who, like himself, had been originally followers of Jackson, and prepared to ride out the storm.

The old Prince came back to Congress in December, 1841, weary and ill. It was generally understood that his resignation would not be long delayed, "getting off a while merely to get on better," as Letcher put it. Clay took little part in the debates during the following months, well content to be "a looker on at Verona" amid the general confusion, but resolutions that he introduced and the occasional speeches that he made indicated clearly the issues upon which he meant to wage the campaign of 1844. Restriction of the veto power, control of the Treasury by Congress, economy in Governmental expenses — these were double-edged weapons, fit to use against Jacksonism and Tylerism alike. In addition, the distribution of the public land sales was to be continued, and a tariff raised from the twenty per cent. level to thirty per cent. must be passed. This would defray the expenses of the Government and afford "incidental protection." Still "savage" for a National Bank in private conversations, he did not attempt to burden the party with an issue that would completely alienate the states' rights group.[59]

[57] Tyler, *op. cit.*, Vol. II, pp. 121–122.

[58] Clayton Papers, I, Clay to Clayton, Nov. 1, 1841; Porter Collection, Clay to Porter, Oct. 24, 1841; *Niles' Register*, Vol. LXII, pp. 87–88, 101, April 9, 16, 1842.

[59] *Cong. Globe*, 27th Cong., 2d sess., Vol. I, 164–167, 235, 268–270, 347–348, App., 322–329; Mallory, *op. cit.*, Vol. II, pp. 350–531; Porter

On the afternoon of March 31, 1842, before a crowded gallery and Senate chamber, Clay delivered his farewell. Old and careworn in appearance, his voice trembling at times with deep emotion, he pleaded the purity of his motives throughout his public life, and denied any wish to be a dictator. Perhaps the warmth and ardor of his nature had been mistaken, sometimes, for arrogance, but he hoped that he would be forgiven by his brother Senators, as he himself had forgiven, all wounds received in the heat and temper of debate. He must have stretched out his arms to them, as he said: —

May the most precious blessings of heaven rest upon the whole senate and each member of it, and may the labors of everyone redound to the benefit of the nation, and the advancement of his own fame and renown. And when you shall retire to the bosom of your constituents, may you receive that most cheering and gratifying of all human rewards — their cordial greeting of "Well done, good and faithful servant."

And now, Mr. President and senators, I bid you all a long, a lasting, and a friendly farewell.

Wright thought the speech egotistical and the audience unresponsive, but at its close Preston remarked that, judging by the deep and sympathetic sensation manifested, there was no desire to go into any business that afternoon. He moved adjournment, and the Senate rose for the day.[60]

The struggle with Tyler had shaken the Whig Party to its foundations, but Clay emerged from it, his leadership triumphant, the inevitable candidate for 1844. Tyler made desperate efforts to establish a following of states' rights Whigs and anti-tariff, anti-Bank men from both parties. This effort failing, he angled for the Democratic nomination, drew close to Calhoun, and began to curry favor in the South by championing the annexation of Texas — an issue full of dynamite

Collection, Clay to Porter, Jan. 16, 1842; Weed Papers, Greeley to Weed, Dec. 15 [1841].

[60] Mallory, *op. cit.*, Vol. II, pp. 562–568; *Cong. Globe*, 27th Cong., 2d sess., 376–378; *National Intelligencer*, April 2, 1842; Van Buren Papers, XLIV, Wright to Van Buren, April 2, 1842.

for Clay. Webster, his chances for the nomination hopelessly blasted, and suffering under a hail of abuse from the Whigs,[61] held grimly to his office until the Maine boundary had been settled. Then, differing with Tyler as to the expediency of annexing Texas, he resigned in the spring of 1843, and came back into the fold.

Once again, Clay had started on the path to the White House. But the path was perilous, and it behooved the old Prince to pick his way with care.

[61] Porter advised Clay to restrain the savage attacks that the Clay press made upon Webster. — Porter Collection, Porter to Clay, Feb. 17, 1842.

Chapter XXII

TEXAS

"THE old coon is really and substantially dead, skinned & buried — Clay's political career is closed forever. . . ."[1] This was Jackson's exulting cry from the Hermitage. But the fires of hatred had consumed the General's judgment, for never had the Kentuckian's political prospects looked brighter than after the great battle with Tyler. The demand for Clay steadily increased throughout the country. Everywhere Whig dinners, mass meetings, legislatures and state conventions vied in denouncing the President and demanding the leadership of the old Prince. The states' rights men in Georgia fell into line. Seward's coolness toward the Kentuckian as a candidate could not stem the tide in New York. The National Clay Club of Philadelphia epitomized the Whig spirit when it inscribed above its windows the motto "betrayed but not dismayed," and the budding candidacies of Scott, McLean and Webster were swept away like chaff before the wind.[2]

Clay really believed, at first, that he was indifferent to the nomination. "*He thinks honestly* he cares very little about the Presidency," wrote Letcher to Crittenden. "Well, that may be so, but about the *starting time*, I guess his feelings will undergo a slight change."[3]

There were, in truth, good reasons for Clay's retirement from the political scene. He was growing old, and was begin-

[1] Van Buren Papers, XLIV, Jackson to Van Buren, Nov. 22, 1842.

[2] Tyler Papers, V, G. R. Gilmer to T. W. Gilmer, June 29, 1842; Weed Papers, Seward to Weed, July 9, 22, 31, 1843, Jan. 22, Feb. 4, 1844; Journal of the National Clay Club (Lib. of Cong.), Nov. 14, 1842; Clayton Papers, I, Clay to Clayton, May 27, 1843. Seward's dissatisfaction was plain, but he assigned no specific reason, save Northern antislavery sentiment.

[3] Crittenden Papers, VIII, Letcher to Crittenden, May 19, 1842. *Cf.* the interesting, but unidentified newspaper clipping in T. H. Clay's Scrapbook, where an eye witness of a Whig meeting in Cincinnati recounts the story of an arduous attempt to push Clay into being a candidate.

ning to realize the necessity of conserving his energy. He found farming as attractive as ever, and was busily engaged at Ashland in the summer of 1842 with preparations for hemp production upon such a large scale that it might well have absorbed all of his attention.[4] In addition, 1842 found him confronted by serious financial difficulties. His son Thomas failed for thirty thousand dollars, a disaster in which Clay was heavily involved. The old statesman mortgaged his own property for twenty thousand dollars, made a trip to New Orleans to collect notes due, and to obtain contracts for rope and bagging, and upon his return to Lexington once again hung out his shingle as a lawyer.[5] But despite such efforts, his estate remained heavily encumbered with debt.

The political fever was in Clay's blood, however, and in the midst of his anxiety over financial matters, his interest in the next campaign remained keen. "The old Prince," wrote the irrepressible Letcher, "must hereafter remain a little quiet and *hold his jaw*. In fact he must be *caged* — that's the point — *cage him*. But he swears by all the Gods, he will keep cool and stay at home. I rather think he will be entirely prudent, tho' I have some occasional fears that he may write too many letters."[6] Letcher had evidently been giving some good advice, but Clay's temperament would not allow him to keep out of the political fight, and, despite his protestations to the contrary, his political activities steadily increased.

Van Buren, portlier than ever, stopped at Ashland for two days in the spring of 1842. He had been touring the South and came directly from the Hermitage. Clay liked the Little Magician, and on this occasion found him "interesting often and sometimes amusing." It seemed apparent that Jackson's

[4] Sweet Collection, Clay to Sargent, July 31, 1842; Clayton Papers, I, Clay to Clayton, Aug. 8, 1842.

[5] Clay Papers, XXIII, Clay to T. H. Clay, Dec. 12, 25, 1842, Jan. 22, 1843; Fayette County Court, Deed Book 21, p. 55, Nov. 15, 1842, H. Clay, mortgage to Madison C. Johnson; Van Buren Papers, XLV, McCalla to Van Buren, Jan. 11, 1843; Clayton Papers, Clay to Clayton, April 14, May 27, 1843. According to report, Clay was also badly involved in the failure of his son-in-law, James Erwin, in New Orleans.

[6] Crittenden Papers, VIII, Letcher to Crittenden, June 21, 1842.

mantle was to fall again upon the shoulders of the Red Fox, and it has always been suspected that, sitting in the library of Ashland over a bottle of port, or walking under the shade of the magnificent trees, the loose-jointed, impetuous Kentuckian and the smooth little New Yorker agreed to eliminate Texas from the approaching campaign. No better opportunity for such an agreement ever presented itself, but there is no proof that the deal was made.[7]

Shortly after Van Buren's departure, Clay made a political speech at a Lexington festival given in his honor. He defended his past record at all points and laid down a program of economy in government, sound currency, "reasonable" protection and distribution of land sales to the states. This obvious campaign argument was widely printed, and acted as a decided tonic to his supporters.[8]

The Kentuckian was determined that tariff and distribution should be tied together. The latter proposal was, of course, one of his pet measures, and its passage would make the tariff the great source of revenue, thus necessitating a considerable degree of protection. The Whigs in Congress tried to couple the two measures that summer, but Tyler, vigorously opposed to distribution, wielded the veto remorselessly. Clay exhorted the Whigs to stand firm, even if no revenue bill were passed, but this strange advice, based on the "principle" that the independence of the House in matters of taxation should be preserved at all costs, went down before the need for revenue and the threatened revolt of Whigs who held a tariff more vital than the continuity of party policy. The protective tariff of 1842 passed without the distribution feature, and Clay was forced to see a separate land bill go to oblivion by way of a pocket veto.[9]

---

[7] Clay wrote to Nathan Sargent that the visit had been made "without much conversation on party politics." Sweet Collection, Clay to Sargent, May 31, 1842.

[8] Mallory, *op. cit.*, Vol. II, pp. 569–594; McDowell Collection, Mangum to Clay, July 4, 1842.

[9] Crittenden Papers, VIII, Clay to Crittenden, July 16, 1842; Clayton Papers, I, Clay to Clayton, Aug. 8, 1842; Porter Collection, Clay to Porter, Aug. 29, 1842; Wellington, *op. cit.*, pp. 106–112; Coleman, *op. cit.*, Vol. I, p. 180. Clay had clung to his proposal, despite the fact that his hemp in-

The Kentuckian made a political tour through Ohio and Indiana that fall. He spoke at Dayton to an immense assemblage of Whigs, and a few days later addressed another great gathering at Indianapolis. While he was speaking to a large and sympathetic audience at Richmond, Indiana, an incident occurred that was ominous for the future.

One of the members of the crowd was a Quaker Abolitionist named Mendenhall. This gentleman came forward amid hoots and jeers, and presented a petition, signed by a considerable number of names, urging the Kentuckian to emancipate his slaves. Clay quieted the assemblage and then vigorously addressed himself to the petitioner and the question that he had raised.

Recognizing slavery as a great evil, the Kentuckian asserted, as he had so often done before, that colonization accompanied by very gradual emancipation was the only practical remedy. He respected the motives of the rational Abolitionists, but Abolitionism was only postponing the application of the remedy. Immediate emancipation would produce a dire struggle between blacks and whites for political supremacy, and an accompanying train of evils far worse than those of slavery. As to his own slaves, some would not accept freedom if it were given to them, others were his helpless charges, dependent upon him. All were well cared for. What would be their condition if he turned them loose upon the world? Clay waxed vigorous toward the close of his remarks, telling Mendenhall to "Go home and mind your own business, and leave other people to take care of theirs. Limit your benevolent exertions to your own neighborhood . . . and you will be a better and wiser man than you have this day shown yourself." [10]

terests were badly in need of protection. He finally admitted to Porter that it was wise to pass the separate tariff bill.

On Sept. 30, 1842, Webster made a speech in Faneuil Hall, defending Tyler, and attacking Clay's policies on the tariff and Bank and, by indirection, Clay himself. Clay thought of replying, but remained silent after Clayton sprang to his defense. — Clayton Papers, I, Clay to Clayton, Nov. 2, 1842; D. Webster, *The Works of Daniel Webster*, 6 vols. (Boston, 1851), Vol. II, pp. 117–140.

[10] Mallory, *op. cit.*, Vol. II, pp. 595–600; *Niles' Register*, Vol. LXIII, pp. 134–135, Oct. 29, 1842; *National Intelligencer*, Oct. 29, Nov. 12, 1842; L. S. Kenworthy, "Henry Clay at Richmond in 1842," in *Indiana Magazine*

This speech was a vigorous attack upon Abolitionism, and it could only inflame the feelings of the antislavery host. Already there was appearing in Congress a group of Whigs, — Giddings of Ohio, Slade of Vermont and others, — representatives of a moral crusade which put the extirpation of slavery above all else, and was reckless of consequences. Ben Wade of Ohio, shortly after the Richmond incident, was doing his best to prevent Clay's nomination, as one who could not be carried in that state, a man who had "committed the unpardonable sin against the North," and Seward was to comment sourly that "Mr. Mendenhall will reply audibly through the ballot boxes there [Indiana] to that most able and effective speech addressed to him last year by a certain candidate." [11]

The Slavery Question would not down, and it was soon to appear in a form that boded ill for Clay's ambition, and for the Union that he loved.

Shortly after his return from the Northwest, Clay went to New Orleans for the winter. His business affairs undoubtedly constituted the chief reason for this trip, but he was also concerned about his health (there was some talk of a trip to Cuba), and Southern politics were not entirely neglected. Enthusiastic admirers gathered about him everywhere he went, and the confident feeling which prevailed among the Whigs made his heart rejoice. [12]

The summer and fall of 1843 were spent at Ashland, a summer tour of the Atlantic Coast cities, urged by Clayton, being rejected as altogether too arduous. [13] But Clay found time to make a speech in Lexington designed to bolster Whig morale, and he kept up an ample correspondence. An invitation to visit North Carolina the following spring was accepted, and an itinerary was worked out that would take him to New

of History, Vol. XXX (Dec. 1934), pp. 353–358. According to one version of Clay's remarks, he told Mendenhall to "Go home and slop your hogs."

[11] Giddings Papers, Wade to Giddings, Jan. 2, 1843; Weed Papers, Seward to Weed, July 22, 1843. Cf. Clay Papers, XXIII, J. Davis to Clay, Oct. 14, 1843, and Ewing to Clay, Nov. 1, 1843.

[12] Crittenden Papers, VIII, Clay to Crittenden, Jan. 14, 1843; Clayton Papers, I, Clay to Clayton, April 14, 1843.

[13] Clayton Papers, I, Clay to Clayton, May 27, 1843.

Orleans, through the deep South to North Carolina, and then home by way of Washington.

The news of the invitation and its acceptance came out in the papers during the late summer of 1843. Seward commented sadly on the "strange infatuation" of the Whigs for Clay, in the face of lugubrious political news from Louisiana, North Carolina, Tennessee and Indiana, and a less restrained member of the party wrote to Mangum: —

Who the deuce among you is the author of asking old Harry to come to North Carolina? Sir, have you forgotten what these junketings of his cost us in Ohio & Louisiana? They only waken up popular animosity & prejudice. . . . If he would let himself alone, we should have less trouble in electing him. He & Scott are both too fond of their Epistolary style. Their letters will presently form a collection as vast as that of Horace Walpole. If St. Paul had been a candidate for the Presidency, I should have advised him to cut the Corinthians and not to let the Hebrews see even his autograph.[14]

But the die had been cast, and that spring Clay took the road to Raleigh.

Again and again, along the route through Alabama, Georgia and South Carolina, Clay was received with tumultuous enthusiasm; but the climax came when he arrived at Raleigh, on the evening of April 12, 1844. A blaring band, and thousands of cheering Whigs who had gathered in expectation of his arrival, escorted him through the illuminated city to the home of his host, Governor Morehead. It was an imposing welcome, and the hearts of his followers beat high with joy, but the perspective of history tinges the event with melancholy. The sacrificial victim was being crowned with flowers.

The following morning Clay was conducted to the Capitol, where he received an ovation and spoke to the great crowd. Then came a monster barbecue, where seven thousand pounds of meat were turning on the spits. When Clay appeared at the

[14] Weed Papers, Seward to Weed, July 31, 1843; Porter Collection, Clay to Porter, Sept. 17, 1843; Mangum Papers, XII, Edward M. Johnston to Mangum, Sept. 14, 1843. *Cf.* Granger Papers, Weed to Granger, April 8, 1844.

barbecue the crowd rushed toward him. The sixty-seven-year-old statesman was in danger of being overwhelmed, but he made for a tree and braced his back against it. Then, turning his eager smile upon the crowd, he called out "Ah! you have tree'd the old coon at last!" and an answering roar for Henry Clay rent the air.[15]

But the Raleigh visit had far greater significance than could be attributed to any display of Whig enthusiasm. For it was in that "City of Oaks" that Clay wrote the first of his letters on the annexation of Texas.

Texas was dynamite, but certain gentlemen were determined to meddle with it, and among them none had shown himself more eager than John Tyler. As obstinate an expansionist as he was a worshiper of consistency, Tyler had sought to pave the way to annexation before he had been a year in the White House. The move had been rebuffed by Senatorial and Websterian opposition. But, by 1843, the tales of growing British interest in the "Lone Star," the fears of the South that the constant admission of new Northern states would force the Southern scale to "kick the beam," and the ties of blood and friendship which made the Southwest palpitate at every rumor of a Mexican raid against the Texas pioneers had molded a popular sentiment that fitted Tyler's purpose. Abel P. Upshur, Secretary of State, had then made a formal offer of adoption. Texas had been coy, but had finally consented and in March of 1844 had sent a representative to Washington to draw up a treaty. Meanwhile, Upshur had lost his life in a gun explosion on board the battleship *Princeton;* but as avid an expansionist as ever drew the breath of life was ready and willing to carry on: John C. Calhoun took over the State Department, and, on April 12, the day that Clay came to Raleigh, the treaty of annexation was signed. Ten days later, it was sent to the Senate with a message urging ratification.

These proceedings had not taken place in a corner. Clay had known for months that the negotiation was on the cards,

---

[15] *Raleigh Register*, April 5, 16, 19, 1844; Mangum Papers, XIII, B. W. Leigh to Mangum, April 22, 1844.

and had deplored it.[16] As an individual, he would undoubtedly have been glad to see the Lone Star State annexed.[17] But as a national leader and a statesman, he saw the dangers involved in an acquisition that was bound to stir up the slavery controversy. We had enough territory, he felt, and it was much more important to harmonize and improve what we already had, than to attempt an acquisition that "would be inevitably attended with discord and dissatisfaction." His trip through the South had convinced him (he was always so easily convinced that his wishes and those of the people were identical!) that there was no burning anxiety there for annexation, and he had come to believe that he could treat the question in such a manner "as to reconcile all our friends, and many others, to the views which I entertain." [18]

According to tradition, he wrote the "Raleigh letter" of April 17 seated under a great white oak on East North Street. Annexation, he said, had not been called for by any general expression of public opinion; it was dangerous to the integrity of the Union; it was financially inexpedient because it would mean assumption of Texas' debt — at least thirteen million dollars; and it involved certain war with Mexico and possibly war with European powers. For these reasons he stood opposed "at the present time" to the acquisition of Texas.[19]

The letter was shown to Governor Morehead and other prominent Whig leaders at Raleigh. They agreed that it was Clay's duty to make it public and it was sent to Crittenden

---

[16] Crittenden Papers, IX, Clay to Crittenden, Dec. 5, 1843, Feb. 15, 1844.

[17] A. H. Stephens, *Recollections of Alexander H. Stephens*, Myrta L. Avary, ed. (N.Y., 1910), pp. 17–18; G. P. Garrison, ed., "Dipl. Corresp. of the Rep. of Texas," in *A. H. A. Ann. Report* (1907), Vol. II, p. 287, Hunt to Orion, Jan. 31, 1838; *Niles' Register*, Vol. LXVI, p. 439, Aug. 31, 1844. See also an interesting, although unidentified, newspaper clipping in the possession of Mrs. Annie V. Parker of Ghent, Kentucky, in which Clay is quoted as replying to a question on Texan annexation, addressed to him early in 1844 by a committee of the citizens of Ghent, that, "though *personally* inclined toward annexation, *politically* he opposed it."

[18] Crittenden Papers, IX, Clay to Crittenden, Dec. 5, 1843, March 24, 1844.

[19] *National Intelligencer*, April 27, 1844; *Niles' Register*, Vol. LXVI, pp. 152–153, May 4, 1844.

with instructions that it be published in the *National Intelligencer*.

Crittenden hesitated.[20] Clay insisted peremptorily, asserting as a fact that Van Buren stood on the same ground and that, even if Van Buren changed his position, the public mind was too fixed on the presidential question and the current was "running too strong and impetuous" to be affected by Texas.[21] There was nothing for Crittenden to do but yield, and on Saturday, April 27, the day after Clay arrived in Washington, the "Raleigh letter" appeared in the *National Intelligencer*. Van Buren's letter, also opposing annexation, came out in the *Globe* the same day. The prospective candidates for the Whig and Democratic nominations were evidently determined to avoid making an issue out of Texas.

On May 1, 1844, Clay was unanimously nominated at Baltimore by the Whig National Convention.[22] His running mate was Theodore Frelinghuysen of New Jersey, at this time Chancellor of New York University, a devout man, able in politics and law, and an ardent follower of the old Prince.[23] The Whigs at Baltimore were filled with confidence and joy, to mention only the milder stimulants. On the day following the nominations, a young men's national ratification convention marched through a city adorned with flags, banners, triumphal arches,

[20] Crittenden may have sensed the danger of such a stand in the South and Southwest. Less than a month before, a New York Whig had received a letter from him indicating his own opposition to the treaty of annexation. — Weed Papers, S. Blatchford to Weed, March 28, 1844.

[21] Crittenden Papers, IX, Clay to Crittenden, April 17, 19, 21, 1844. His certainty about Van Buren lends color to the idea of a secret agreement, for Van Buren had not yet come out.

[22] Clay had been distinctly cool to a national convention, fearing a repetition there of the intrigues of 1839. In his eyes, the Baltimore gathering should merely establish concert in measures for electing the candidate already chosen by the popular will, and see to the nomination of a vice-presidential candidate. — Clayton Papers, I, Clay to Clayton, Aug. 8, 1842, May 27, 1843.

[23] Clay had preferred Clayton. The Kentuckian had taken no part in the selection of the vice-presidential candidate. He had rebuffed an attempt to obtain his support for Webster's nomination to that office. — Clayton Papers, I, Clay to Clayton, Aug. 8, 1842, June 28, Oct. 10, 1843; Miscellaneous Papers (N.Y. Pub. Lib.), Clay to Frelinghuysen, May 22, 1844; Porter Collection, Clay to Porter, Oct. 3, 11, 13, 1843.

Clay hats and sticks and live coons. The action of the preceding day was endorsed with great enthusiasm, and tumultuous approval was given to a speech by Webster, pledging his support to the ticket. Similar meetings were held all over the country. Everything was going smoothly, and even Seward felt that the nomination was "as felicitous in manner as propitious in circumstance." [24]

Clay's letter on Texas, published on the eve of the convention, had produced no adverse effect upon his nomination, but the Democratic convention, also at Baltimore, was not held until May 27. By that time, Van Buren's stand had brought a fatal revolt against him in the South and Southwest. The opposition pushed through the two-thirds rule, first used in 1832 in connection with Van Buren's nomination for Vice-President, but now standing like a specter in his path. On successive ballots, the Red Fox slowly lost ground, and the convention finally stampeded for James K. Polk of Tennessee, a dark horse, but a fervent advocate of expansion.

Polk's unexpected nomination brought delight to many of the Whigs. Mangum wrote jubilantly that it was "a literal disbanding of the party for this campaign." Democrats who had gathered at the Capitol in Washington to hear the news transmitted over the new magnetic telegraph were dumb with amazement, and Benton groaned over the "d——d fools" at Baltimore who had betrayed the party. But Crittenden, who had a keener appreciation of popular sentiment in the South and Southwest than had Clay, felt certain that "we have a *great* battle to fight." [25]

As a matter of fact, Clay entered the campaign under a terrible misapprehension. His speeches and correspondence, from 1841 to 1844, show clearly his belief that the country could be wooed and won upon questions of internal policy alone. A

[24] Hone, *op. cit.*, Vol. II, pp. 695–699; *Niles' Register*, Vol. LXVI, pp. 181–203, May 18–25, 1844; *National Intelligencer*, May 2, 4, 1844; Weed Papers, Seward to Weed, May 7, 1844.

[25] Mangum Papers, XIII, W. P. Mangum to P. H. Mangum, May 29, 1844; *National Intelligencer*, May 30, 1844; Clayton Papers, Crittenden to Clayton, June 17, 1844.

tariff for revenue, with incidental but substantial protection (the tariff of 1842),[26] Governmental economy, a sound currency established and maintained by the creation of another National Bank, distribution of land sales to the states, a single term for the President and restrictions upon the veto power — these were the points which he emphasized repeatedly, and these were the points, with the exception of specific reference to a Bank, that were mentioned in the resolutions passed by the Whig convention.

The Democrats swore by the Sub-Treasury system and against a Bank, hedged on the tariff, upheld the veto power and denounced the distribution of land sales. But where the Whig resolutions avoided mention of expansion, the Democrats came out for the "re-annexation of Texas at the earliest practicable period." [27] And by that pronouncement, the fat was cast into the fire.

The Senate rejected the annexation treaty, June 8, by a vote of thirty-five to sixteen. All the Whigs save one voted against it, while fifteen of the twenty-two Democrats voted yea. Tyler appealed to the House for support, but no action was taken. Despite all of Clay's intentions and assurances, Texas had become a significant factor in the race for the presidency.

The campaign of 1844 opened with four candidates in the field. Clay and Polk headed the major parties. Tyler, nominated by a convention that consisted chiefly of officeholders, hung on doggedly until the middle of the summer, when he gave up hope and withdrew. But James G. Birney was running as the Liberty Party candidate, and he did not withdraw. Strong in New York and Massachusetts, numbering its devotees by the thousands in Pennsylvania and the Old Northwest, this antislavery group hurled its challenge to the hated institution from a thousand platforms. And as the fight grew

[26] *National Intelligencer*, July 18, 1842; *Niles' Register*, Vol. LXVII, p. 75, Oct. 5, 1844.

[27] Stanwood, *op. cit.*, Vol. I, pp. 199, 215–216, 220–221. "The reoccupation of Oregon" added emphasis to the expansionist note in the Democratic platform.

hotter, these "Mendenhalls" became an increasingly important factor in the contest.

Clay had returned to Lexington from his Eastern trip in good health and spirits. He felt that electioneering was beneath the dignity of a presidential candidate, and resisted all efforts to entice him into a speechmaking tour.[28] Nor did it appear that such efforts would be necessary. The Whig morale was good in all parts of the country. Seward had announced his full support of Clay before the nomination, and the venom of internecine strife among the New York Whigs, if it had not entirely disappeared, had at least suffered a dilution in the passage of the years.[29] Webster, though still bitter in spirit, was to take the stump in Pennsylvania.[30] A flood of Ashland hats and Ashland textbooks swept the country, and the Whig torchlight and transparency processions marched to the martial strains of the "Ashland Quick Step."

The whole party seemed to burst into songs celebrating the log cabin, the coon, and the virtues of their great leader.

> The moon was shining silver bright,
> The stars with glory crowned the night,
> High on a limb that "same old coon,"
> Was singing to himself this tune:—
>> Get out of the way, you're all unlucky;
>> Clear the track for old Kentucky!

And

Far from the west see the statesman advancing,
Whose voice in our cause has so often been heard;
Now his bright, beaming eye, towards the Whig standard glancing,
Is fixed on the gay-plumaged liberty bird.
Give him the helm of the fair ship Columbia,
And we'll laugh at the storm as we ride safely o'er

[28] *Niles' Register*, Vol. LXVI, pp. 161, 402, May 11, Aug. 17, 1844; *Lexington Observer & Reporter*, May 22, 1844.

[29] *Niles' Register*, Vol. LXVI, pp. 51–52, March 23, 1844; Weed Papers, Seward to Weed, July 27, 1844; Seward to Ruggles, 1844 (Lib. of Cong.); Graham Papers, Carroll to Graham, Aug. 27, 1844.

[30] Harvey, *Reminiscences*, pp. 215f.

All the high-swelling surges of life's troubled ocean,
Till *Protection* we find on our own native shore.
    Now to the lofty mast,
    Nail the Whig banner fast,
And let it fore'er on the wind's pinions play!
    None will the tempest fear,
    When with a hearty cheer,
We welcome on board, the brave mariner Clay.[31]

Ardent Clayites offered wagers of all descriptions, from money to farm produce and wearing apparel, and an enthusiastic merchant in Mississippi advertised as follows: —

To the world! — As far as my watches and jewelry goes, and any other articles I have for sale, can be had, payable for when Henry Clay is elected. If not elected, nothing. Clay I am, and unto Clay I will return, if defeated.

                                         EDWARD FRANCIS.[32]

But as the campaign got under way, the Clay forces found themselves confronting an extremely determined opposition that had no hesitation about the use of scurrilous attacks. The old charges of "bargain and sale" were spread before the public again, "blowing up the coals," as Adams put it, "to consume Clay's election hopes and my honest fame." Jackson published a letter renewing them, and Clay and his friends were again forced into the weary and unprofitable task of refuting the vicious allegations.[33] Nor was this the only attempt at defamation.

In 1838 a duel had taken place between two Congressmen, Cilley of Maine and Graves of Kentucky, in which the former had been killed. Graves had roomed in the same house with Clay and had sought and obtained the latter's advice, which appears to have been directed toward warding off the en-

    [31] *The National Clay Minstrel* (Phila., 1843).

    [32] *Lexington Observer & Reporter*, July 3, 1844.

    [33] *Niles' Register*, Vol. LXVI, p. 247, June 15, 1844; Adams, *Memoirs*, Vol. XII, p. 21; Mangum Papers, Vol. XIII, Willcox & Hardee to Clay, Aug. 27, 1844, Clay to Mangum, Sept. 11, 1844; *Lexington Observer & Reporter*, Oct. 12, 1844.

counter.[34] But Clay was now accused of having deliberately instigated the duel. His opponents made him out a murderer, and the charge certainly did him no good in New England.

A Democratic pamphlet, which had wide circulation, was headed in bold, black type: —

Christian Voters!
Read, Pause and Reflect!
Mr. Clay's
Moral Character.

Then followed a series of paragraphs expatiating upon "Mr. Clay's Gambling," "Mr. Clay's Profanity," "Mr. Clay — a Sabbath-Breaker," and "Henry Clay's Duels," with charges that his slaves were ill-treated thrown in for good measure.[35]

It was asserted that, when told of Polk's nomination, Clay had said, "beat again, by hell." The Kentuckian went to horse races and made bets on the Sabbath. He was immoral, a gambler and a proslavery man, cried the Abolitionists. Democratic processions carried banners inscribed "No Duellist," "No Gambler," and a Democratic member of the House of Representatives declared that Clay's standard should consist of his armorial bearings and that these ought to be "a pistol, a pack of cards and a brandy-bottle." [36]

Clay, said the Democrats of the South, was a friend of the Abolitionists, and was sacrificing Texas to them. Furthermore, all his measures, the Bank, the tariff and distribution, were in

[34] Sweet Collection, and Clay Papers, XXI, Clay to Sam'l Wood, Jr., March 22, 1838; *National Intelligencer*, March 8, 22, 1842; *The Campaign of 1844*, Sept. 14, 1844; Hone, *op. cit.*, Vol. I, p. 307; *Lexington Observer & Reporter*, Sept. 4, 1844. *Cf.* the account in B. H. Wise, *The Life of Henry A. Wise* (N.Y., 1899), pp. 80–86. The most that can be said fairly against Clay is that he might have interposed more vigorously and have been less sensitive about respecting Graves's sense of honor.

[35] This pamphlet was made accessible to me by the courtesy of its owner, William H. Townsend, Lexington, Ky. *Cf.* the North Carolina *Standard*, April 10, 1844.

[36] *National Intelligencer*, Aug. 1, 1844; Adams, *Memoirs*, Vol. XII, p. 45; J. P. Kennedy, Letters (Lib. of Cong.), Clay to Kennedy, Sept. 16, 1844; Hone, *op. cit.*, Vol. II, p. 712; *Niles' Register*, Vol. LXVII, p. 214, Dec. 7, 1844.

the Northern interest. The charge of being friendly to the Abolitionists had such effect in the South that Clay was forced to check the activities of his Abolitionist kinsman, Cassius M. Clay, who had gone into the North to campaign for him.[37]

The Whig press vigorously denied these allegations, and did its best to retort in kind. It denounced Polk. "Young Hickory" indeed! This was only the attempt of a very weak stick to trade on borrowed capital. Down with him! He stood for disunion, free trade and British influence. As to this last, what more could one expect, since "old Zeke" Polk, his father, had been a Tory in the Revolution.[38] By such charges the Whigs sought to counter the stream of abuse that was being poured out upon their candidate, but, though their intentions were good, they were handicapped by Polk's comparative obscurity and came out decidedly second best in blackguardism.

There were other factors as well that weakened Whig strength. The suspicions that the Clay men had entertained since 1839 toward the followers of Webster and Seward would not down entirely, and they were not conducive to the spirit of harmony within the Whig ranks.[39] The tendency of the Whigs in various quarters to ally with a growing Native American movement which was anti-Catholic and anti-immigration, coupled with the fact that Frelinghuysen was widely suspected of anti-Catholic leanings, hurt the Clay cause. This was especially true in New York City, where there was a strong Catholic element, and where Tammany Hall appears to have registered fraudulently thousands of alien voters.[40] Fi-

---

[37] Weed Papers, pamphlet, "The South in Danger," *Niles' Register*, Vol. LXVII, pp. 83–84, 140–142, Oct. 12, Nov. 3, 1844; C. M. Clay, *Memoirs*, pp. 80, 100–101; Greeley Papers (N.Y. Pub. Lib.), C. M. Clay to Greeley, Jan. 28, 1845.

[38] *The Campaign of 1844*, Nos. 13, 27, 28; *Lexington Observer & Reporter*, Oct. 19, 1844, et passim.

[39] Graham Papers, Carroll to Graham, Aug. 27, 1844; Bayard Papers, Clay to R. H. Bayard, Sept. 14, 1844; Weed Papers, Seward to Weed, Nov. 11, 1844.

[40] Clay Papers, XXIV, Ambrose Spencer to Clay, Nov. 21, 1844, Sargent to Clay, Nov. 26, 1844; Hone, *op. cit.*, Vol. II, p. 720; Weed Papers, J. T. H. to Weed, May 27, 1844; Mangum Papers, XIII, Carroll to Mangum, Sept. 8, 1844; Mueller, *op. cit.*, p. 113; McMaster, *op. cit.*, Vol. VII, pp. 374,

nally, the Democrats in the North, especially in Pennsylvania, brazenly declared that Polk was a better protectionist than Clay, and this had real effect, despite desperate Whig counter-attacks.[41]

But the fatal issue was Texas. The Democrats asserted that Clay opposed annexation, while Polk stood for it unequivocally, and a mounting tide of excitement in the South and in Clay's own state showed that this charge was having real effect.[42]

This attack was disingenuous, but it struck a vulnerable spot, for the Raleigh letter had been a straddle. It had stated at length the reasons for opposing annexation. It had thrown an additional sop to the foes of annexation by declaring that Texas should not be admitted against the wishes of any considerable portion of the Union. But it had not said that Texas should *never* be admitted. Clay had simply asserted that, for the reasons he outlined, he was against it "at the present time." The increasing antislavery sentiment in the North had received the utmost assurance as to the present. The Southern annexationists *could* easily interpret the letter as merely a plea for delay, and Clay had written confidently to Weed that "my opinion on the Texas question will do me no prejudice at the South." [43]

But in that belief, Clay had been terribly wrong. Vainly, his friends sought to defend him against the Democratic onslaught. They were howled down, and, in an attempt to keep

---

383, 385; Gustavus Myers, *The History of Tammany Hall* (N.Y., 1917), pp. 134–137. Louisiana was undoubtedly lost to Clay by election frauds. See "The Election Frauds in Plaquemine Parish in 1844," in *La. Hist. Quart.*, Vol. XX (July 1927), pp. 402–406.

[41] Mangum Papers, XIII, Sargent to Mangum, Aug. 21, 1844; Clayton Papers, I, Clay to Clayton, Aug. 22, 29, 1844; Mueller, *op. cit.*, pp. 103, 112–114; *Niles' Register*, Vol. LXVI, p. 192, Vol. LXVII, p. 30, May 28, Sept. 14, 1844; *National Intelligencer*, Oct. 8, 1844.

[42] Clayton Papers, I, Combs to Clayton, Nov. 30, 1844. For a discussion of annexationist sentiment in Kentucky, see Poage, *Henry Clay and the Whig Party*, pp. 123–125, 140–143.

[43] M. J. Lamb, "Unsuccessful American Presidents," in *Mag. of Amer. Hist.*, Vol. XII (Nov. 1884), pp. 385–413, Clay to Weed, May 6, 1844. *Cf.* Giddings Papers, III, Giddings to Maria Giddings, April 28, 1844.

his strength in the South from slipping away, Harry of the West began to explain and defend his position.

In a letter written to the editor of an Alabama paper, July 1, 1844, Clay asserted that, in objecting to annexation against the opposition of any "considerable portion of the Union," he had been thinking of states, not of the Abolitionists. He was not courting those people. He had no personal objection to annexation, but he would be unwilling to see the Union dissolved or seriously jeopardized for the sake of acquiring Texas. There was, said Clay, a party in South Carolina that was using the rejection of Tyler's "abominable treaty" as a pretext for dissolving the Union. If the nation were broken up, South Carolina, surrounded as she was by slave states, would suffer only "comparative evils." But what would be the condition of Kentucky, with her Ohio River boundary extending five hundred miles on three slave states, "in the event of the greatest calamity that could befall this nation?" The letter was an appeal to nationalist sentiment, and the old leader threw down the gage to the secessionists when he declared: "If anyone desire to know the leading and paramount object of my public life, the preservation of this Union will furnish him the key." [44]

The drift toward Polk in the South was not yet checked, more demands for explanation poured in, and, on July 27, Clay wrote a second "Alabama letter." Once again he pointed out the dangers involved in annexation "at this time," but he also took further steps toward the propitiation of the South. He would be glad to see Texas annexed, if it could be done without dishonor or war, with the common consent of the Union and upon just and fair terms. He did not think that slavery ought to affect the question, one way or the other. That institution was destined to become extinct at some distant day, "by the operation of the inevitable laws of population," and "it would be unwise to refuse a permanent acquisition which will exist as long as the globe remains, on account of a temporary institution." If elected, and the question of annexa-

[44] *Niles' Register*, Vol. LXVI, p. 372, Aug. 3, 1844; *National Intelligencer*, Aug. 8, 1844.

tion came up, he would be governed by the state of fact and public opinion and, above all, by the paramount duty of preserving the Union.[45]

A final letter, written to the *National Intelligencer* on September 23, defended his previous utterances against the charge of inconsistency, and repeated his opposition to immediate annexation.[46]

Clay's position was consistent throughout — a consistent straddle. No one could be sure from these letters what would be his future attitude toward annexation. He had made clear the fact that he considered the preservation of the Union the paramount issue, and that, at present, there were conclusive reasons why Texas should not be annexed. But as to the future, antislaveryites and rabid annexationists alike were given reason to hope and to fear. It was simply his old policy of patriotic compromise. "Truth and justice, sound policy and wisdom, always abide in the middle ground." So he had asserted at Raleigh [47] in speaking of the tariff, and it was middle ground in regard to Texas that he assumed during the campaign. But middle ground could not give him victory.

The Alabama letters, coupled with the fact that the Democratic platform stood for annexation only "at the earliest practicable period," enabled the Whigs to avert absolute disaster in the South and capture Kentucky and Tennessee. But in the pivotal state, New York, the letters produced a fatal drift of antislavery men out of the Whig ranks. "Things look blue!" Weed wrote to Francis Granger on September 3. "Ugly letter, that to Alabama. Can't stand many such." And Seward, campaigning in central New York, told Weed that "everybody droops, despairs. . . . I wish with you I was out of the Northern tour, but I am pledged." [48] The hopes of some of the New York Whigs were aroused by Clay's final letter to the *Intel-*

---

[45] *Niles' Register*, Vol. LXVI, p 439, Aug. 31, 1844.

[46] *Ibid.*, Vol. LXVII, p. 74, Oct. 5, 1844.

[47] *Ibid.*, Vol. LXVI, p. 298, July 6, 1844.

[48] Granger Papers, Weed to Granger, Sept. 3, 1844; Weed Papers, Seward to Weed, Sept. 2, 1844. Two weeks later, the New York Governor wrote that he was sorry to hear that Weed was really ill, and added "I thought you were only sick of an Ashland letter."

ligencer, but on October 22, after a trip through the state, Seward wrote to Weed that the Whigs were tacitly confessing "that New York is lost, and if you are right about Pennsylvania, then all is lost."[49]

The New York vote gave Birney 15,812, while Clay ran 5,106 votes behind Polk. So were the forebodings of the New York Whigs justified, and James K. Polk, with a plurality of 36,725 out of a total vote of 2,700,061, became a minority President of the United States.[50]

On the night that the news from New York reached them, the Clays were attending a wedding in Lexington. The New York mail came in at ten o'clock, and, as the hour approached, several of the gentlemen present went out to get the news. Upon their return they consulted together for a moment, and then one of them went up to Clay, who was standing in the center of a group, and handed him a paper.

He opened the paper [wrote Mrs. Robert S. Todd] and as he read the death knell of his political hopes and lifelong ambition, I saw a distinct blue shade begin at the roots of his hair, pass slowly over his face like a cloud and then disappear. He stood for a moment as if frozen. He laid down the paper, and, turning to a table, filled a glass with wine, and raising it to his lips with a pleasant smile, said: "I drink to the health and happiness of all assembled here." Setting down his glass, he resumed his conversation as if nothing had occurred and was, as usual, the life and light of the company. The contents of the paper were soon known to everyone in the room and a wet blanket fell over our gaiety. We left the wedding party with heavy hearts. Alas! our gallant "Harry of the West" has fought his last presidential battle.[51]

[49] Weed Papers, Seward to Weed, Oct. 22, 1844. *Cf.* the letters from various New York Whigs to Mangum in October. — Mangum Papers, XIII.

[50] A. C. McLaughlin and A. B. Hart, eds., *Cyclopedia of American Government,* 3 vols. (N.Y. 1914), Vol. III, p. 25. An analysis of the figures indicates that, had the Alabama letters not been written, Clay would probably have won New York and Michigan, but lost Tennessee and Kentucky. This would still have prevented his election. Either way, the Texas issue was fatal for him.

[51] Mrs. Robert S. Todd to Mary Todd Lincoln. A letter in possession of the Helm family, Lexington, Kentucky, and quoted by W. H Townsend, *op. cit.,* pp. 109–110.

The Democrats received the news with great rejoicing. Shouts of victory rang out from banquets and parades. Skinned coons hung from trees along main traveled ways, and the defeated candidate was deluged with letters of insult and of exultation over his downfall.

The gloom of Clay's staunchest supporters was as deep as the joy that filled his opponents. His friends had rallied around him, convinced that his turn had come, only to see him go down to defeat by the narrowest of margins. Many wept when they heard the news. Others used their fists upon the exultant supporters of Polk. One Kentucky bride and groom, on receiving the news of the election, changed their wedding trip from Washington to New Orleans. The groom became ill on the way, and the physician who was called in asked if the young man had suffered any great shock. He was told of Clay's defeat, whereupon he fell into the arms of his patient and they wept together.[52]

Clay preserved his outward composure. His Lexington friends were told that he was relieved from a load of anxiety and hoped to spend the remainder of his days in peace and quiet. Leading Whigs throughout the country were thanked scrupulously for their efforts in his behalf. But the iron of disappointment had entered his soul, and not infrequently his letters, filled with ominous forebodings for the country's welfare, were tinged with a more personal melancholy. Within the bosom of his family this grief found spontaneous expression. It is said that he and Mrs. Clay wept in one another's arms, and, in a letter to Henry Clay Junior, who thought of running for Congress in the Louisville district, Clay showed the depth of his hurt. "I hope," he wrote, "that your connection with me, if it do not benefit, may not injure you, should you determine to be a Candidate." [53]

For the time being, Clay saw no constructive means by which the victorious opposition might be unseated. He frowned upon an idea that was attractive to many of the Whigs, that

of amalgamation with the Native Americans. Recognizing the
logic of harmonious relations between the two groups, and privately admitting that he felt strong sympathies for the Natives,
he wisely regarded any attempt at fusion as bound to produce
discord and weakness, rather than strength. All that the Whigs
could do, Clay felt, was to fall back on the old ground of
criticizing Democratic measures. And repeatedly he asserted
his determination to retire from politics, once and for all.[54]
The White House was cloaked in shadow now, and he believed
that he had put away ambition. But his unconquerable spirit
only slumbered, and visions of national service and national
leadership were bound to haunt the dreams of the aging statesman.

[54] Crittenden Papers, IX, Clay to Crittenden, Nov. 28, 1844; Clayton
Papers, I, Clay to Clayton, Dec. 2, 1844.

CHAPTER XXIII

GATHERING SHADOWS

As the defeated "Sage of Ashland" surveyed the national scene during the winter months of 1844–1845, he found it gloomy indeed. The Democratic victory opened up prospects of lowered tariffs and lavish land policies that filled him with anxiety. Fearfully he watched the Methodist Church rend itself asunder over the Slavery Question. The stimulus that this division gave to sectional bitterness was plain to see, and Clay used his influence in a vain attempt to prevent the schism.[1] The annexation of Texas, and the war cloud gathering in the Southwest, produced at one time fears for the safety of the Union, at another gloomy forebodings as to military chieftains and an expansionist career that would absorb vast stretches of neighboring territory "until the identity of the Nation is lost in dilution." Passed and passing events, he wrote to Justice Story, filled him with "awful apprehensions. . . ."

If indeed this Nation be resolved to cast away the blessings which encompass it, and to add another sad example to those which History records, of the corruption and downfall of Republics, no organization of the Supreme Court, however enlightened, virtuous & patriotic its members might be, can avert the calamity.[2]

Nor were public affairs the only sources of Clay's despondency. His taxable property, listed in 1839 at close to one hundred and forty thousand dollars, was listed in 1844 at only fifty-one

[1] Alfred Brunson Papers (Wisconsin Hist. Soc.), Clay to Brunson, Dec. 5, 1844; Colton, *Correspondence*, p. 525.

[2] Crittenden Papers, IX, Clay to Crittenden, Jan. 9, 1845; Stoddard Collection (N. Y. Pub. Lib.), Clay to J. R. Thompson, April 23, 1845; Sweet Collection, Clay to Story, Feb. 5, 1845. The events of 1845 excited in William Henry Seward visions of the United States as an American colossus that, at some future time, would come to death grips with Great Britain *in Asia.* — Weed Papers, Seward to Weed, Dec. 20, 1845.

thousand dollars.[3] The business failure of his son, Thomas, and the necessity of finally settling the Morrison estate had forced Clay to dispose of thousands of acres of land holdings in Missouri and Kentucky, and to mortgage Ashland. A debt of fifteen thousand dollars to John Jacob Astor still hung over his head. Clay owed about forty thousand dollars and was on the verge of losing his home.[4]

Under these circumstances, his friends in the great cities of the East and in New Orleans came to his assistance. A stream of anonymous contributions poured in to the Northern Bank of Kentucky, where many of Clay's notes were held. The gifts amounted to at least twenty-six thousand dollars, perhaps considerably more, and the old leader was saved from falling into a financial slough of despond.[5] The matter was a delicate one, but the subscriptions had been delicately made. Clay accepted the money reluctantly, although with a pardonable feeling of pride in this concrete expression of the loyalty of his friends. He was deeply moved, and thereafter, according to his grandson, could never speak of this generous aid without having his eyes fill with tears.[6]

It was most unfortunate that the shadow of family tragedy should again appear, a kind of sinister accompaniment to the happiness engendered by these gifts. Clay's youngest son, John

[3] Fayette County tax lists. The lateness of the entry in 1844 appears to indicate difficulty in paying his assessment. The low point, 1843, was $48,400. In 1845, it was $64,305.

[4] Clay Papers, XXIV, D. M. Craig to J. Odenhamer, March 5, 1845; Col. Peyton, "Statement," in *Lexington Transcript*, June 27, 1889; Weed Papers, Jas. Bowen to Weed, Jan. 14, 1845.

[5] Clay wrote to Henry Clay, Jr., April 2, 1845, that the contributions amounted to $24,750. That same day John Tilford, of the Northern Bank, wrote to Clay that $5,000 had been received, but it is impossible to ascertain if Clay counted this amount in his reckoning to his son. Tilford wrote again, May 9, that $1,500 more had been received. — McDowell Collection; Clay Papers, XXIV. Not all the gifts were anonymous. — Clay Papers, XXIV, Abbott Lawrence to Clay, March 13, 1845. I have found no proof that Clay received as much as $50,000, an amount suggested in his grandson's biography. — T. H. Clay, *op. cit.*, p. 324.

[6] McDowell Collection, Clay to Henry Clay, Jr., March 17, 1845; T. H. Clay, *op. cit.*, p. 324.

Morrison Clay, twenty-four years of age, began to exhibit such wildness of conduct and signs of mental derangement that his heartbroken parents thought it best to put him in the Lexington asylum where Theodore was confined. The young man became rational again within a few weeks and returned to Ashland, but a dark and somber pall had been cast over Clay's happiness at relief from debt.

The next two years slipped away quickly and on the whole pleasantly. The old chieftain spent the winter seasons in New Orleans, and Ashland flourished under his care during the summer months. Improvements were made on the house and the ornamental trees and shrubs were carefully tended. The blooded stock, the rolling fields of wheat, hemp, rye and corn, bore witness to the fact that Clay was by no means a mere "gentleman farmer." Mrs. Clay busied herself in the garden and the dairy, the butter and cheese made under her supervision commanding a ready market and furnishing a considerable revenue. The Clays entertained in openhearted fashion, and on more than one occasion the big house was filled to capacity with visiting relatives and friends. Thomas and James lived at Ashland while their homes near by were being built. John was there. Henry Junior, melancholy and unsettled of purpose since his wife's death five years before, remained in Louisville but came frequently to visit his parents, and to see his two children who were staying with relatives in the home town.

During this period, the master of Ashland sat for two portraits by George Peter Alexander Healy. There is no way of knowing whether or not Clay was pleased by the results, but the chances are that he was not. His warm, impetuous spirit, quick to conceive, ready to execute, by turns arrogant and winning, was best revealed in the swift play of emotion across his mobile face, and Clay in repose was not Clay at all. He was wont to say that no likeness of him had ever been painted, and he was disgusted by tedious sittings that ended only in failure. "You can imagine," he wrote to Charles Edward Lester, "what repugnance one has to set [sic] to an artiste, who has submitted to that operation more than one hundred times." [7]

The Mexican War, which Clay had dreaded and which he did not cease to deplore, broke out in the spring of 1846. It brought heart-rending tragedy to the veteran statesman. Henry Junior promptly enlisted, was made a lieutenant-colonel in the Second Regiment of Kentucky Volunteer Infantry, and marched away to fight in a cause for which his father had no heart. Serving in Taylor's army, the young man was killed while gallantly leading his command at the battle of Buena Vista, and once again, as so often in the past, Henry Clay was forced to drink from one of the bitterest cups that can be held to the lips of man. It was, he wrote to Clayton,

one of the greatest afflictions which has ever befallen me, in a life which has been full of domestic afflictions. I have not had a heart to write to you; and now I can hardly trust myself in the performance of the task. If I could derive any consolation from the fall of my beloved son on the bloody field of Buena Vista, it would be from the fact that, if he were to die, I know he preferred to meet death on the field of battle, in the service of his Country. That consolation would be greater, if I did not believe that this Mexican War was unnecessary and of an aggressive character. My poor son did not however ever stop to enquire into the causes of the War. It was sufficient for him that it existed in fact, and that he thought the Nation was entitled to his services. [8]

And now Henry Clay turned at last to the spiritual comforts of the Episcopal Church. He had reached his seventieth year. The election of 1844 had been a source of bitter disappointment that had added to the sorrows engendered by domestic tragedy. He had never recovered wholly from Anne's death, and since then had come the death of her son, Henry Erwin, the sad spinal affliction of a favorite granddaughter,[9]

---

[7] McDowell Collection, Clay to Henry Clay, Jr., June 21, 1845; Crittenden Papers, IX, Clay to Crittenden, July 11, 1845; Washburn Papers, IV, fol. 68, Clay to Lester, Sept. 26, 1845; Mangum Papers, XVII, T. C. Johnston to Mangum, May 20, 1854.

[8] Clayton Papers, I, Clay to Clayton, April 16, 1847 (confidential).

[9] Lucy Clay, daughter of James B. and Susan J. Clay.

John Morrison Clay's trouble, and, above all, the loss of the son who had borne his father's name. It may well be that Clay had at last reasoned himself into accepting the Christian dogma, but it seems altogether probable that grief and trouble, of which he had seen so much, prepared the way. He was baptized in the parlor at Ashland, on June 22, 1847, by the Reverend Edward F. Berkley, rector of Christ Church, Lexington, and some two weeks later took his first Communion.[10]

Jackson had predicted that Clay would either join the Church or die drunk, a prophecy which Frank P. Blair now called to mind,[11] but the obvious inference as to Clay's political ambition which this remark contained was as vicious as it was unfounded.

Clay had not lost sight of politics while busied with his private affairs. Nor could he well forget the affectionate regard of his political admirers. Costly gifts poured into Ashland. Popularly subscribed silver vases, a casket of jewels for Mrs. Clay and other donations bore witness to his hold upon the affections of the people. His friends in New York were soon busy raising his standard. The letters he received from supporters who venerated him almost to the point of canonization, and the adulatory comments in the Whig press, soothed his wounded spirit and stimulated his ambition afresh. William Henry Seward, on a Western trip in the early spring of 1846, visited Lexington and called twice at the home of the old leader.

The Sage of Ashland [Seward wrote to Weed] is in vigorous health and joyous spirits. As confident of the nomination and of success next time as he was at the last. . . . You may depend upon it that the battle is all to be fought over again.[12]

There were other indications of the old leader's ambition. His private correspondence, while opposing any premature

[10] T. H. Clay, Scrapbook, unidentified newspaper reprints of letters from Berkley and T. H. Clay, Sr.; Historical Sketch of Christ Church (Lexington, Ky., 1898), p. 57. The sprinkling ordinance was used. Clay repeated the answers in the prayer book from memory.

[11] Van Buren Papers, LIV, Blair to Van Buren, Aug. 25, 1847.

[12] Weed Papers, Seward to Weed, April 24, 1846.

agitation of the presidential question, showed at least a receptive attitude. Published letters bemoaned the lowering of the tariff in 1846. A speech in Lexington that fall, lamenting the war and the "subversion" of the protective policy, betrayed "the smothered flame." Political expediency certainly approved the humanitarianism of an eloquent appeal, early in 1847, on behalf of the sufferers in the Irish famine. Whether or not with deliberate intention, Harry of the West had set his face again toward the White House.

But the great leaders of the Whig Party had other plans. There was grave doubt, even in Kentucky, as to the availability of a thrice-defeated candidate who would be almost seventy-two before he could possibly take office. His demonstrated vulnerability on the slavery issue was another serious drawback in both North and South. The natural course, inspired by the success of 1840, was to turn to the military, and as early as December, 1845, the leaders of the Congressional Whigs, Clayton, Crittenden and Mangum, had pronounced Clay *hors de combat* and were bent upon Scott and Corwin as the party ticket.[13]

The Scott boom faded, however, as another hero, crowned with the laurels of victory, appeared upon the scene. Before the Mexican war was two months old, Zachary Taylor had beaten the Mexicans at Palo Alto and Resaca de la Palma, and had crossed the Rio Grande. Popular enthusiasm for "Old Rough and Ready" at once began to manifest itself, and on July 5, 1846, John J. Crittenden wrote to Taylor, exulting in his victories and urging him on to still greater efforts: —

. . . Your highest ambition may be well satisfied if you can in the further prosecution of the War, sustain your present reputation. . . . Great expectations & great consequences rest upon you. And the people everywhere begin to talk of converting you into a political leader, when the War is done.

Taylor was urged not to give up his command.

[13] Weed Papers, Seward to Weed, Jan. 1, 1846. "How bitter will this desertion be felt by Mr. Clay," wrote Seward.

I know [said Crittenden] your devotion to your country, & should not presume to offer any useless exhortation as to that — But it is in respect to yourself & your own interest, that I would venture to express the hope, that you will retain the command, at whatever private sacrifice, till the close of the War. I wish to see you win & wear all its honors, from the beginning to the *end* — without a rival or competitor.[14]

John J. Crittenden, Clay's lifelong friend, was grooming Taylor as a candidate.

Buena Vista greatly accelerated the Taylor boom, but during the late summer of 1847 it began to waver. The old General, who could pen without a blush a page-long sentence which violated all the rules of syntax, betrayed a disconcerting tendency to write letters. Some of those spread dismay among the Whigs. If he were to run, he wished to be a national rather than a party candidate. He apparently preferred nonpartisan nominations, and showed an extreme coyness, which he frankly admitted arose from ignorance, about committing himself upon any political issue.

But powerful circumstances worked in Taylor's favor. He finally confessed that he was a Whig in principle and that, had he voted in 1844, it would have been for Clay. This dissipated the fears of the doubters. His popularity, privately fostered by Crittenden and other leaders, became tremendous in Clay's own state. Taylor was a Louisiana planter and a slaveholder, and the Southern Whigs, increasingly restive under Clay's leadership as they became more and more convinced of the necessity of resisting the antislavery movement in the North, rallied under the General's banner. The Northern Whigs, distrusting Clay's ability as a vote-getter and unable to unite upon any Northern candidate, began listening reluctantly to the siren song of Taylor's "availability."[15] The General's candidacy was making decided progress.

[14] Sweet Collection, Crittenden to Taylor, July 5, 1846.
[15] Hone, *op. cit.*, Vol. II, p. 795; Mangum Papers, XVI, Harvey to Mangum, June 3, Aug. 17, 1847; Clayton Papers, I, Clay to Clayton, April 16, 1847; Giddings Collection, Corwin to Giddings, Aug. 19, 1847; Clay Papers, XXV, Ullman to Clay, July 12, 1847; Weed Papers, Greeley to Weed,

Clay was disturbed and grieved by the Taylor movement, especially by its manifestations in Kentucky. The old leader was ready, as a last resort, to accept the General as the Whig candidate, but he coupled such private statements with scepticism as to the popular demand for Taylor, and grave doubts about the advisability of exalting a military chieftain.[16] An Eastern trip during the summer of 1847 elicited evidences of popular enthusiasm that could not but increase Clay's hopes. He still hesitated, however, to allow the use of his name as a candidate. He was waiting apparently for a great popular movement in his favor, a movement that had not yet appeared.

Up to this time, Clay had refused to credit the rumors as to the part Crittenden was playing. But, almost coincident with the return to Ashland, there came a direct warning. Joseph L. White, a New York politician who had been traveling in the West, wrote to Clay that Crittenden was lending himself to the Taylor movement in Kentucky, a movement which was doing more than anything else to keep Taylor's boom alive. Clay sent the letter to Crittenden, suggesting that he give it such consideration as he thought proper. Crittenden's answer, which was sent by Clay to White, has never been found, but it resolved all Clay's doubts. He wrote in reply: "I thought I understood you. I find I did; and to all such enquiries, I have made representations of your conduct substantially corresponding with your own account of it." White remarked, in a letter to Crittenden, that evidently he had been mistaken in believing that the latter had abandoned the support of Clay *"in any contingency."* Obviously, Crittenden's letter was so phrased as to give the distinct impression that Clay was Crittenden's own choice.[17] This was, of course, untrue. Crittenden had abandoned Clay as early as December, 1845. He had begun to groom Taylor in July,

Oct. 14, 1846, Seward to Weed, Aug. 27, 1847; Weed, *Autobiography*, pp. 571–582; Cole, *op. cit.*, pp. 126–129.

[16] Clayton Papers, I, Clay to Clayton, April 16, 1847; Mangum Papers, XVI, Harvey to Mangum, June 3, 1847; Colton, *Correspondence*, pp. 540–545.

[17] Crittenden Papers, X, White to Clay, Sept. 15, 1847 (copy), Clay to Crittenden, Sept. 21, 26, Nov. 18, 1847, White to Crittenden, Oct. 30, 1847, Crittenden to Clay, May 4, 1848.

1846. During the summer of 1847, Crittenden was counseling Taylor as to the proper course he should pursue to win the presidency, and Taylor acknowledged in reply, that, if he must be a candidate, it would be due to "the agency of some of the wisest heads & purest hearts in the whole land, yours among the most conspicuous," and added that, if elected, he would rely particularly upon Crittenden's advice and counsel.[18] The Senator from Kentucky was undoubtedly sincere in his belief that Clay was not the right candidate and that Taylor was; but, when the time arrived for him to make that avowal frankly, his courage had failed him.

Some two months after his correspondence with Crittenden, Clay made a speech at Lexington which was calculated to further his chances for the Whig nomination. The address dealt with the Mexican War and the additional territory which might be obtained as the result of that struggle. In order to understand the significance of his proposals, it is necessary to trace briefly the story of the Wilmot Proviso.

President Polk had requested Congress, in 1846, to appropriate two million dollars which could be used in paying Mexico for any territory ceded as a result of peace negotiations. The necessary appropriation bill had been promptly introduced in the House, but that body had tacked to it an amendment that became famous as the Wilmot Proviso. This stated that neither slavery nor involuntary servitude should ever exist in any territory acquired from Mexico, and with its introduction began the great battle over the extension of slavery. The Proviso failed to pass the Senate in 1846. It was defeated in that body in 1847. But the House had twice accepted it, and the passions of the North and South rose with the struggle in Congress. Already, before the war with Mexico had ended, the fatal effect which Clay had dreaded was beginning to appear. It was under these circumstances, together with the knowledge that the Congressional Whigs had attacked the war bitterly during the session of 1847, that Clay rose to speak.

Beginning with a reference to the gloomy day, so like the

[18] Taylor Papers, Col. J. P. Taylor to Zachary Taylor, Sept. 8, 1847; Crittenden Papers, X, Zachary Taylor to Crittenden, Nov. 1, 1847.

gloomy state of national affairs, and an allusion to the autumnal season of the year and of his life, Clay proceeded to denounce at length the war with Mexico as "unnatural," "lamentable," and brought on by deceit. He then developed the rôle which he believed Congress should play in the prosecution of the war, and ended with a summation in the form of eight resolutions. They declared that the annexation of Texas was the cause, Taylor's advance to the Rio Grande the immediate occasion of the war; that Congress was of right and duty bound to declare the purposes and objects of the war and to see to it that the President continued it for no other reasons; that under no circumstances should Mexico be annexed; that the United States should adopt a moderate and magnanimous policy toward her discomfited foe; that all that was wished was a just and proper fixation of the limits of Texas; and "that we do positively and emphatically disclaim and disavow any wish or desire on our part, to acquire any foreign territory whatever, for the purpose of propagating slavery, or of introducing slaves from the United States, into such foreign territory." [19]

This speech was really a bid for the nomination. Clay accepted the annexation of Texas, but he denounced the war as unjustifiable and manifested strong opposition to acquiring additional territory for the purpose of spreading slavery. Would not his speech and resolutions, Clay wrote in a confidential letter to Greeley, "represent me as a Western man (I protest being considered as a *Southern* man) with Northern principles?" He had not touched the Wilmot Proviso by name, he continued, because it was unnecessary, "and sufficient for the day is the evil thereof." His speech had been received with enthusiasm in Kentucky. Would it not be well, if the resolutions were approved in New York, to hold public meetings to sanction them? Taylorism, Clay felt, was on the decline. He expressed himself as "entirely friendly to Mr. Seward." That gentleman ought to hold high place in any Whig Administration, possibly receiving the nomination for Vice-President. Clay asked Greeley's advice as to whether or not he should try to get back

[19] *Niles' Register*, Vol. LXXIII, pp. 197–200, Nov. 27, 1847; McElroy, *op. cit.*, pp. 446–447.

some private letters favorable to Nativism that he had written in 1844. He had not decided about the use of his "poor name" as a candidate, but would decide "next Spring, or earlier if necessary. . . . I mean, if I should be a Candidate," the Kentuckian concluded, "to write no letters, make no speeches, and be mum. I expect, if that contingency should arise, to be as much abused for my *silence*, as I have been for my speaking or writing." [20] It was obvious that Clay hoped and believed that, as a result of his stand, popular preference would be fixed upon him. [21]

Clay's speech did produce a wave of enthusiasm. Whig mass meetings and newspapers throughout the country gave it warm commendation. They evidenced, as did an Eastern trip undertaken in the winter of 1847–1848, that Clay was still a popular idol. Weed, a shrewd observer, states that Clay's nomination was "generally expected." Toombs bore witness to Clay's popularity through the Union. [22] But the flood of popular nominations, so highly significant four years before, was not forthcoming.

Meanwhile, the Taylor leaders had been marshaling their forces. Alexander H. Stephens had secured the General's nomination in a Georgia Whig Convention. Other nominations had followed from the Whig legislators in Virginia and Tennessee, and from innumerable popular meetings throughout the country. Stephens and other Whig leaders in Congress set up in December a Taylor club known as the "Young Indians," and, fortified by Crittenden's hearty approval, opened an extensive correspondence. Old Rough and Ready's friends in Washington were full of confidence. Well they might be, for late in February, 1848, came the news that a meeting at Frankfort, Kentucky, had endorsed the General's candidacy while, at the same time, the Whig State Convention, assembled on the anniversary of Buena Vista, had refused to put any candidate in

[20] Porter Collection, Clay to Greeley, Nov. 22, 1847.
[21] This despite the fact that Clay wrote a letter, which was published, denying that the Lexington speech indicated presidential aspirations. — *Niles' Register*, Vol. LXXIII, p. 273, Jan. 1, 1848.
[22] Weed, *op. cit.*, p. 575; Phillips, *op. et loc. cit.*, pp. 103–105.

nomination.[23] The Taylor movement in Kentucky was bearing poisoned fruit for Henry Clay.

The old leader had not been able to make up his mind what course to pursue. When he had left Ashland for Washington in December, 1847, he had been ready to make a definite announcement that he was not a candidate. But at the Capital, the clamors of his devoted friends, and the guileful counsel of Horace Greeley, who came down from New York full of persuasive arguments, brought a change of heart.[24] From then on, despite the rebuff he received in Kentucky, despite Taylor's growing strength, despite a warning that he could not carry Ohio unless he came out more specifically against the extension of slavery, there was no more talk of withdrawal. The siren song of the presidency had again enthralled him, and, on April 10, 1848, he finally announced that he was a candidate for the Whig nomination.[25]

The Clay movement developed considerable strength, especially in the North, but the Taylor sentiment was too powerful and too well organized to be overcome. The General promptly announced that he would run, regardless of the result at either the Whig or the Democratic convention, and proceeded to publish a letter declaring that he was a Whig, even if he was not ultra, and that his Administration, uncontrolled by purely partisan considerations, would not attempt to dictate to

[23] Stephens, op. cit., pp. 21–22; "Letters of John Bell to Wm. B. Campbell," in Tenn. Hist. Mag., Vol. III (Sept. 1917), p. 209; Weed Papers, Seward to Weed, Dec. 14, 1847, Jan. 20, 1848; Crittenden Papers, XI, Letcher to Crittenden, Feb. 1848, Metcalfe to Crittenden, Feb. 8, 1848.

[24] Clay Papers, XXV, Clay to James B. Clay, Jan. 16, 1848, Clay to H. T. Duncan, Feb. 15, 1848, Clay to Lucretia Clay, Feb. 18, 1848, Stevenson to Clay, June 19, 1848; Lexington Observer & Reporter, April 12, 1848; Weed Papers, Seward to Weed, Jan. 20, 22, 1848. Greeley was playing a double game. He had raised Clay's standard in the Tribune, and was posing as an enthusiastic supporter, but Seward, who was in Washington at the time, wrote to Weed that "Greeley expects that all he can make out of this will be the exclusion of both Clay and Taylor, and he is beginning now to prepare for McLean. But this is a secret not to be whispered." Cf. Phillips, op. et loc. cit., pp. 103–104, Toombs to Thomas, April 16, 1848.

[25] Clay Papers, XXV, Stevenson to Clay, April 8, 1848, Clay to S. S. Prentiss, April 12, 1848, Clay to Brooks, April 13, 1848; Clay, Works (Fed. ed.), Vol. III, p. 462; Lexington Observer & Reporter, April 12, 1848.

Congress on questions of domestic policy. The movement for "Old Zack" continued to sweep the South. Crittenden, appealed to by Clay, replied gloomily that he judged Clay's candidacy unfortunate, and correspondence between the two men ceased.[26] Washington was a hotbed of anti-Clay sentiment. "Availability" was the slogan. Clay did not qualify, but Taylor did. As one erstwhile Clay supporter wrote: —

I have voted for Mr. Clay all the time, have *bet* on him, and lost, until I am *tired*, and have finally concluded that Mr. Clay is *too pure a patriot* to win in these *demagogueing* times — We must mix up a little "humbugging" with our glorious Whig creed, before we can expect a victory — and Gen. Taylor's *military fame* is about the best we can make use of at present . . .[27]

As Clay delegates came to Washington, en route to Philadelphia, they were met by Taylor men who talked in chorus about "availability," arguing that Clay lacked that necessary quality. Northern delegates favorable to Clay were told by Weed, Truman Smith of Connecticut and others at New York and Philadelphia, that, with the old Prince as a leader, the party must go down to inevitable defeat. The cry was raised that, if Clay were elected, the younger men would have no chance of preferment. Much was made of the fact that a majority (seven) of the Kentucky delegates were hostile to Clay. Delegates committed against Taylor were steered in the direction of Scott or Webster. There was no Clay leadership

[26] Crittenden Papers, XI, Clay to Crittenden, April 10, 1848, Crittenden to Clay, May 4, 1848. Crittenden later asserted that, from the time of Clay's pronouncement, he had pursued a course that was not in opposition to Clay, but it is distinctly probable that Crittenden had a hand in the formulation of the second Taylor letter mentioned above, the so-called "first Allison letter." — Crittenden Papers (Duke Univ.), Crittenden to Burnley, July 30, 1848; Coleman, *op. cit.*, Vol. I, p. 294. See the analysis in Poage, *Henry Clay and the Whig Party*, p. 177, note 20.

[27] J. R. Desha Papers, T. S. James to Desha, May 13, 1848. Toward the close of May, the proposal was made to put Scott on the Clay ticket as the vice-presidential candidate. Scott told a supposed Clay leader that he would be glad to accept, but, either because this information was deliberately withheld, or because of a report that Scott was dangerously ill, the movement produced no effect. Clay Papers, XXV, J. L. White to Clay, May 26, 1848, Scott to Clay, July 19, 1848.

capable of meeting this storm, and by June 7, when the convention assembled in the great hall of the Chinese Museum, the issue had been practically decided.[28]

When the voting began on the second day of the convention, the results of the politicians' intrigues quickly became manifest. New York, where the great majority of the Whig voters were undoubtedly for Clay, gave him 29 out of 36 votes, but New England gave him only 16, to 21 for Webster and 6 for Taylor. Pennsylvania divided more votes between Taylor and Scott than she gave to Clay. Ohio gave Clay 1 vote, while Scott received 20. As these results appeared, Clay men began to hiss and cries of "treachery" were heard in various parts of the hall.[29] The complete ballot gave Taylor 111, Clay 97, Scott 43 and Webster 22, with four-fifths of the Southern delegates for Taylor. A second ballot showed gains for Scott and Taylor and a loss of eleven votes for Clay. The Clay men then moved adjournment until the next day. The motion carried, but the delay was fruitless. On the third ballot, Truman Smith took Connecticut into the Taylor camp, and on the fourth Old Rough and Ready received the nomination. Then, as a sop to disgruntled Northern delegates who were raving against the nomination, Millard Fillmore of New York, a Clay man and an antislaveryite, was chosen as the General's running mate.[30] There was no platform.

Many of the Clay men were bitter and resentful. They asserted that they would not support a ticket that had been nominated by treachery and double-dealing.

A movement began for nominating their leader as an independent candidate — and Clay could have headed an insurrection that would have made Taylor's defeat certain.

Clay shared the resentment of his followers at the action of the convention. He felt that, principally due to the defection

[28] Clay Papers, XXV, Harlan to Clay, June 2, 1848; Lawrence to Clay, June 9, 1848; Weed, *Autobiography*, pp. 576–578; Oliver Dyer, *Great Senators of the United States* (N.Y., 1899), pp. 62–63, 69.

[29] Dyer, *op. cit.*, pp. 72–73.

[30] The Seward-Weed group in New York was displeased by the nomination of Fillmore. — Weed Papers, Seward to Weed, June 10, 1848.

of Kentucky, the party had nominated "the merest military man ever offered to the American people for that office." He was outraged and alarmed by the Whig tendency to regard the Bank and tariff questions as obsolete,[31] for he saw in the maintenance of those issues a safeguard against the sectional issue of slavery which was "ever ready to fill the vacuum." He refused to accept the seat in the Senate left vacant by the resignation of Crittenden,[32] and, nursing his wrath and disappointment with gloomy letters to his friends, he stayed in retirement at Ashland.

But, after all, the rejected leader was a Whig. Cass and Van Buren, the Democratic and Free Soil Party nominees, were out of the question for him. There was at least a chance, Clay felt, for a better Administration under Taylor than with either of them. And so, while he would take no steps to further Taylor's chances, Clay rejected running as an independent candidate. Stricken with a serious illness at the beginning of November, he was spared the ordeal of going to the polls. His sons voted for the Whig candidate, and, had Clay's health permitted, there is no question but that he, too, would have cast his ballot for Zachary Taylor.[33]

[31] The Democrats had restored the Sub-Treasury, and had lowered the tariff in 1846. Both the Sub-Treasury and the tariff were working well, and the Whigs made no great issue of either during the campaign.

[32] Crittenden ran as the Whig candidate for Governor of Kentucky in 1848, and was elected.

[33] Clay Papers, XXV, Clay to Louisville Committee, June 28, 1848, Clay to G. W. Curtiss, July 4, 1848, Clay to Meade and King, Sept. 11, 1848; Clayton Papers, II, Combs to Clayton, Nov. 12, 1848, W——— to Clayton [Dec. 1848]; Crittenden Papers, XI, Burnley to Crittenden, July 17, 1848; McClung to Crittenden [Jan. 6, 1849]; T. H. Clay, Scrapbook, Clay to Harvey, Aug. 18, 1848; Pa. Hist. Soc. Collection, Clay to White, Sept. 10, 1848.

CHAPTER XXIV

FOR THE UNION

CLAY's health was bad during the months following the election, and as had now become his wont, he spent the winter season in the more genial climate of New Orleans. While there, he received word that the Kentucky legislature had elected him to the United States Senate.

The possibility of his return to the Senate had been foreseen in Washington and more than one good Whig had written frantically to Kentucky in an attempt to prevent such action. They feared, as one of them expressed it, that Clay would "kick up a row" with Taylor, and the "Young Indians," particularly, were vociferous in their objections.[1] Their doubts and fears had found echo in Kentucky, but Clay's followers there had been determined. They had produced his assertion that, if elected, he would cordially support Taylor, and, calmed by this and by the belief that the veteran leader would either decline or serve only a short time, the Whigs had voted for him, practically with unanimity. After all, as Crittenden remarked, Kentucky could hardly refuse him.[2]

Clay was trying, apparently, to forget old scores. He was amicable toward Taylor, and cordial to Crittenden. Despite the dissatisfaction of some of his friends with Taylor's appointments, Clay was very cautious about attempting to use his influence in their behalf, although he solicited and obtained the mission to Lisbon for his son James. But the President and his

[1] Crittenden Papers, XII, Toombs to Crittenden, Dec. 3, 1848, Reverdy Johnson to Crittenden, Dec. 12, 1848, W. L. Dayton to Crittenden, Dec. 14, 1848; J. Pendleton to Crittenden, Dec. 22, 1848, XIII, Jefferson Davis to Crittenden, Jan. 30, 1849.

[2] Clayton Papers, II, III, IV, Crittenden to Clayton, Jan. 7, 30, 1849, Combs to Clayton, Jan. 22, Feb. 4, 1849, Letcher to Clayton, May 8, 1849.

Secretary of State, Clayton, crowed over this request, and Clay felt rightfully indignant.[3]

A cholera epidemic swept Lexington with deadly effect that summer, and at its height both Mr. and Mrs. Clay fell ill, although Clay believed that their sickness had no connection with the scourge. Late in the summer, the Kentuckian went to Saratoga Springs and Newport for rest and recuperation. He made a short stay with Van Buren at Lindenwald and then came back to Kentucky. The first of November found him traveling East again, for he hoped by this early start for the Capital to avoid bad weather. On the way, his carriage was overturned on the rough roads, but he escaped injury. He spent a few days in New York, living as quietly as possible, but dogged by admiring crowds wherever he went. By the first of December he was lodged in comfortable rooms at the National Hotel in Washington.

Age and ill health had taken their toll of Prince Hal. His cheeks were a bit hollow now, his nose had a pinched look, and his head was bald on the top. Absent-mindedness was growing upon him, and, when in repose, he looked quite old and shriveled. But his genial smile, his ready wit, his love of conversation and his great gift for drawing people to him still remained. "There is a peculiar power in his presence (I don't know how to describe it) which makes you admire and love him," wrote one who had long since rejected his leadership. Clay's power to command, with all its arrogance and all its charm, was with him still when, on December 3, 1849, he took his old seat in the Senate Chamber.[4]

The Kentuckian had come back to a session that will never be forgotten so long as Americans take an interest in their history. For, by December of 1849, the Union was facing

[3] *National Intelligencer*, Dec. 21, 1848; Clay to White, Feb. 8, 1849, Clay to Lewis, Feb. 9, 1849 (Pa. Hist. Soc. Collection); Clay Papers, XXVI, 1849, passim; Clayton Papers, V, Crittenden to Clayton, June 1, 8, 29, 1849; Crittenden Papers, XIII, Orlando Brown to Crittenden, June 23, 1849; Clay, *Works* (Fed. ed.), Vol. III, p. 496, Clay to Stevenson, July 21, 1849.

[4] Poore, *op. cit.*, Vol. I, p. 363; Salmon P. Chase Papers, XX, Chase to Mrs. Chase, Jan. 7, 1850; Giddings-Julian Collection, G. W. Julian to Isaac Julian, Jan. 25, 1850; Seward, *op. cit.*, Vol. II, p. 113.

a tremendous crisis. The South was moving toward secession, and the North, shouting for the Wilmot Proviso and inveighing against the evils of slavery, was fomenting the rising tide of Southern passion. Sectional rivalry had been violently accentuated by the outcome of the war with Mexico. The war had brought the fifteen-million-dollar purchase of California and New Mexico, and with that purchase had come the question foreseen and dreaded by Clay. Should slavery extend into the new territories? The South said Yes, the North said No. The peculiar institution, in all its manifold aspects, had taken the center of the stage, and the drums of hatred had begun to beat with redoubled fury.

Controversy over the rendition of fugitive slaves, over slavery in the District of Columbia, and over the Wilmot Proviso filled the land. Legislation upon any problem involving slavery had to be handled with the utmost care. Oregon Territory, where there was no question of servile labor, had been organized in 1848 only with the greatest difficulty, the South stubbornly opposing any territorial organization that expressly prohibited slavery. That same year, President Polk had urged the formation of territorial Governments for California and New Mexico with the extension of the Missouri Compromise line to the Pacific. But no agreement had been reached and the Thirtieth Congress had ended amid outbursts of torrid rhetoric, fist fights on the floors of both Houses, and the passage of a vital appropriation bill so late that Polk had signed it hours after his term of office expired.[5]

The first nine months of Taylor's Administration had brought only complications. California, her population swelled by the rush of the Argonauts to the newly discovered gold fields, had begun moving toward admission as a free state. A squabble between Texas and the people of New Mexico over their boundary line threatened an outbreak of violence. Sectional feeling was certain to produce havoc amidst the major parties in the Thirty-first Congress, and even if the Whig and Democratic lines could by some miracle hold together in the House,

[5] Von Holst, op. cit., Vol. III, pp. 454–455.

twelve Free Soilers held the balance of power between them.[6]

Meanwhile, President Taylor, honest and patriotic but utterly lacking in political experience and extremely jealous of the veteran statesmen of his party, had fallen under the influence of a Northern Whig leader whose antislavery views were pronounced. William Henry Seward was now United States Senator from New York. By clever management and the canny aid of Weed, Seward had succeeded in pushing the urbane Vice-President, Millard Fillmore, to one side, and, to the disgust and alarm of Southern Whigs and Democrats alike, had achieved a position of great power with the Administration.[7]

The South was in a ferment as 1849 drew to its close. Calhoun had fostered a project for a Southern convention, and out of Mississippi had come a call for a meeting of the Southern states at Nashville the following June. A formidable secessionist movement was developing throughout the slaveholding states, and the Union was on the high road to dissolution.[8]

Such was the situation when Clay came back to the Senate, where a galaxy of talent gathered for the fateful session. The semicircular chamber, with its red carpet and draperies, was crowded with the leaders of old days. Benton and Cass, Mangum and Berrien were there. Webster, his face stern and solemn above his resplendent dress, came to bear witness for the Union. Calhoun, wasting away in the last stages of consumption, harassed by the never-ending conflict of his love for the Union and his love for the South, answered to the first

[6] There were 112 Democrats, 105 Whigs and 13 Free Soilers in the House. The Senate had 34 Democrats, 24 Whigs and 2 Free Soilers. — *Cong. Globe*, 31st Cong., 1st sess., 1.

[7] Weed Papers, 1849, passim; F. W. Seward, *op. cit.*, Vol. II, pp. 100–108; Barnes, *op. cit.*, p. 175; F. W. Bancroft, *op. cit.*, Vol. I, pp. 215–216; Coleman, *op. cit.*, Vol. I, p. 365; Stephens, *Recollections*, pp. 25–26; Cole, *op. cit.*, p. 147.

[8] For a treatment of this movement see, among other authorities, H. D. Foster, "Webster's Seventh of March Speech and the Secession Movement," in *Amer. Hist. Rev.*, Vol. XXVII (Jan. 1922), pp. 245–270; A. C. Cole, "The South and the Right to Secession in the Early Fifties," in *Miss. Valley Hist. Rev.*, Vol. I (Dec. 1914), pp. 376–399. *Cf.* J. H. Hammond Papers, Nov. 1849–Jan. 1850.

roll call. Beside these veterans sat younger men: the keen-eyed Seward, the swart and energetic Douglas, Chase the opinionated, Davis the imperious, all alike in their eager ambition to share with the old warriors the heat and burden of the day.

Clay's fear for the safety of the Union had been accentuated by the march of events. In 1848 he had written to a friend predicting that Southern determination to introduce slavery into California and New Mexico would result in the formation of a sectional and Northern party with fatal results to the Union.[9] During 1849 he had striven to get a constitutional convention in Kentucky to agree on a plan for gradual emancipation in the state. The only result had been a torrent of abuse from Southern hotheads.[10] The situation in Washington was full of menace. Congress had no sooner met than a bitter contest over the election of officers filled the House with sound and fury. Sixty-three ballots were taken before Howell Cobb of Georgia was chosen Speaker. The election of a doorkeeper favorable or opposed to slavery threw the House into confusion for days. Taunts and insults flew between Northern and Southern men, and open threats of secession by Southerners filled Clay's heart with anguish. He sat beside Giddings to witness one of the debates in the House and, as the Southerners cheered Toombs for openly threatening a dissolution of the Union, Clay asked the Ohioan if the Free Soil and Northern members could not raise a hiss. "I told him we were too well bred to do that. He replied that perhaps ours was the better way. . . ."[11] It was under these circumstances that the old leader, secluding himself almost completely from the social life which was so attractive to him, began to work out a project for averting the menace of disunion.

Taylor stood for "non-action" by Congress, while, backed by Seward, the President urged California and New Mexico to apply as soon as possible for admission as states. But this proposal, which would have meant their coming in as free states,

[9] T. H. Clay, Scrapbook, Clay to Harvey, Aug. 18, 1848.

[10] *Ibid.*, Clay to Pindell, Feb. 17, 1849; Martin, *op. cit.*, pp. 126–130.

[11] Giddings Papers, IV, Giddings to G. N. Giddings, Dec. 14, 1849, Giddings to Maria Giddings, Dec. 16, 1849.

excited the bitterest opposition among the Southern leaders. Such a project was merely adding fuel to the flame that had already flared up over the Slavery Question.

By January 21, bills, resolutions and recommendations had been presented in Congress to reduce the boundary of Texas with compensation to her; to organize New Mexico as free territory; to skip territorial organization of California and New Mexico and admit them to statehood as soon as possible; to pass a more effective fugitive slave law; to resist the extension of slavery and exclude slavery from the District of Columbia.[12] If order were to be brought out of this chaos, it would have to be by way of compromise, and Clay determined to make the effort.[13]

Confident in the patriotism of Kentucky, hopeful that the Union men in Congress, regardless of party lines, would rally to his side, Clay slowly evolved his plan. On the evening of January 21, the Kentuckian, his lungs wracked by a cruel cough, braved the stormy weather and called, without appointment, at Webster's home. There, in an hour's interview, he outlined his ideas, and Webster, deeply moved, promised support in principle.[14] Eight days later, Clay, weak in body but strong in spirit, rose in the Senate chamber and began his last great struggle to save the Union that he loved.

Clay's plan, "founded upon mutual forebearance, originating in a spirit of conciliation and concession; not of principles, but of matters of feeling," was summed up in a series of resolutions that covered all the great controversial questions. Cali-

[12] *Cong. Globe*, 31st Cong., 1st sess., 91, 119, 165–171, 195.

[13] It is certain that Clay felt keenly the Administration's coolness toward him, and that he was privately critical of Taylor, but there is no evidence that such considerations prevented his support of the President's plan. *Cf.* Weed Papers, Seward to Weed, Dec. 7, 1849; Giddings-Julian Collection, G. W. Julian to Isaac Julian, Jan. 25, 1850; Van Buren Papers, LVII, H. D. Gilpin to Van Buren, Jan. 27, 1850; Crittenden Papers, XIV, Orlando Brown to Crittenden, April 19, 1850.

[14] Curtis, *op. cit.*, Vol. II, pp. 397–398; Colton, *Correspondence*, p. 593, Clay to Combs, Dec. 22, 1849; "Letters of John Bell," in *Tenn. Hist. Mag.*, Vol. III (Sept. 1917), p. 216, [Bell] to [J. H. McMahon], [1851]. Clay later asserted that he had consulted with Southern leaders, but with only one Northern man. — *Cong. Globe*, 31st Cong., 1st sess., p. 400.

fornia should be admitted as a state without any Congressional action as to the existence or nonexistence of slavery there. Since slavery did not exist by law and was not likely to be introduced into the territories acquired from Mexico, they should be organized without restriction or condition as to slavery. As to the boundary between Texas and New Mexico, Clay suggested a line that meant relinquishment by Texas of a goodly part of her claim, but coupled this with the proposal that the United States assume the public debt owed by Texas at the time of annexation. It was not expedient to abolish slavery in the District of Columbia while slavery continued in Maryland, without the consent of Maryland and the people of the District and without compensation, but it was expedient to abolish the traffic in slaves brought into the District for sale or transportation. The Federal Government should seek by law to render more effective the rendition of fugitive slaves. Finally, Congress had no power to meddle with the trade in slaves that went on between the slaveholding states.[15]

On February 5, his physical vigor fallen so low that he had to be assisted up the steps of the Capitol, Clay began his great speech in support of these resolutions. The Senate chamber was jammed to the point of suffocation, and, when the Kentuckian began to speak, was terribly overheated, the thermometer standing at one hundred degrees.[16] Clay spoke for nearly three hours and then, exhausted, gave way to an adjournment which enabled him to finish on the following day.

It was a speech replete with love for the Union, a challenge, then and now, to all doubters of the grandeur of patriotism. The great orator was pleading for his country. One by one, he took up his resolutions, defending them with consummate skill. Had not California the right to declare herself a free state? What surrender of principle did that represent, either to the North or to the South? As to the territories — "for the sake of peace," let the Northern states cease to demand the Wilmot Proviso. For in those territories slavery did not exist and nature forbade its introduction there. "What more do you want?"

[15] *Cong. Globe*, 31st Cong., 1st sess., 244–247.
[16] Harvey, *op. cit.*, p. 218.

he asked the free state men. "You have got what is worth more than a thousand Wilmot Provisos. You have nature on your side. . . ." The boundary line between New Mexico and Texas represented a compromise between those wishing to see slaveholding Texas constricted to its narrowest possible limits, and those who wished to see slavery extended to the source of the Rio Grande. It would give Texas a vast territory and, in addition, her public debt to the amount of about three million dollars would be assumed by the United States. The resolution as to slavery in the District conceded, practically speaking, all for which the South contended there. Prohibition of the slave trade in the District would meet a Northern demand, but it would be by action similar to that which had already been taken in most of the slaveholding states. The rendition of fugitive slaves was a duty enjoined by the Constitution upon the Federal and state governments and even upon the citizens of the country. The effective discharge of this duty would remove one of the most just grievances that the South had against the North. Finally, the acknowledgment that Congress had no right to interfere in the slave trade between the slaveholding states would be a distinct concession to the South on the part of Northern public opinion.

Compromise your demand for the sake of the Union. That was Clay's theme. In closing, he declared his solemn belief that no state or states had the right to secede. Secession, said the veteran patriot, would mean the establishment of rival and multiplying confederacies, a series of bloody and exterminating wars, and eventually the rise of a despot who would "crush the liberties of both the dissevered portions of this Union." Solemnly, he conjured his countrymen to pause "at the edge of the precipice, before the fearful and disastrous leap is taken in the yawning abyss below, which will inevitably lead to certain and irretrievable destruction. . . . And finally, Mr. President, I implore, as the best blessing which Heaven can bestow upon me upon earth, that if the direful and sad event of the dissolution of the Union shall happen, I may not survive to behold the sad and heart-rending spectacle." [17]

[17] *Cong. Globe*, 31st Cong., 1st sess., App., 115–127.

Tributes to Clay's oratorical powers rose from every side and considerable support at once developed for his plan. No aid was more welcome than that of his friend of early days, Tom Ritchie, now editor of a Washington newspaper. On Clay's initiative, a meeting between the two men took place and Ritchie agreed to stand shoulder to shoulder with his old friend, helping to save the Union.[18]

But the ultras, North and South, found little to commend in Clay's proposal. Davis, Mason and other Southern Senators attacked it promptly. Beverly Tucker, a Virginia hothead, denounced Clay, with his "sneaking compromises," as the "prince of humbugs, charlatans and traitors." In the North, Chase regarded "the Compromise" as "sentiment for the North substance for the South"; Giddings was certain it would "fall stillborn"; and Seward called it a "magnificent humbug."[19] Such attacks were the best possible proof of the essential fairness and justice of the plan.

The Senate began to discuss Clay's resolutions on February 11 and no formal disposition was made of them until April 18. Meanwhile, the giants of debate paraded all the weapons in their arsenals.

On March 4, the Senate listened to Calhoun's speech. Two weeks before, the South Carolinian, with that optimism peculiar to consumptives, had been confident that his health was entirely restored, but on the day assigned to him, he could barely struggle to the Senate, where he sat wrapped in flannels, his eyes half-closed, while his defense of the extreme Southern position was read by Mason of Virginia.[20] Three days later, Webster's seventh-of-March speech came to Clay's support

[18] Crittenden Papers, XIV, Morehead to Crittenden, March 30, 1850; Ritchie, *op. cit.*, pp. 7–10; Ambler, *op. cit.*, pp. 279–283.

[19] *Cong. Globe*, 31st Cong., 1st sess., 247–252; Hammond Papers, XVII, Tucker to Hammond, Feb. 2, 1850; Giddings Papers, V, Giddings to J. A. Giddings, Feb. 3, 1850; Chase Papers, XXI, Chase to E. S. Hamlin, Feb. 2, 1850; Weed Papers, Seward to Weed, Feb. 14 [1850]; *Cong. Globe*, 31st Cong., 1st sess., 405. Preston King wrote Gideon Welles that in Washington Clay's proposal was not regarded as any settlement of the question. — Gideon Welles Papers (Lib. of Cong.), King to Welles, Feb. 8, 1850.

[20] Hammond Papers, XVII, Calhoun to Hammond, Feb. 16, 1850; *Cong. Globe*, 31st Cong., 1st sess., 451. The Hammond Papers show clearly Calhoun's belief that disunion was almost inevitable.

with powerful arguments that, while they stung the Abolitionists to fury, found a responsive note among the commercial classes of the North. Seward and Chase followed, as ardent in their attack upon slavery as Calhoun was in its defense, but at one with him in opposition to the Compromise. But Douglas, powerful among the Democrats and chairman of the Committee on Territories in the Senate, took the same ground as did the Compromise proposals toward California, the territories and the fugitive slave law.[21]

Calhoun passed away "a little after sunrise" on March 31, and with the South's great champion stilled in death, the Compromise seemed to be gaining ground.[22] Day after day the Union men, Northern and Southern, Whigs and Democrats, assembled in caucus, with Clay in the chair, Cass seated on his right hand and Webster on his left.[23] Their efforts were aided by Douglas, who had taken action to end a raging filibuster inaugurated by Southern leaders in the House against an attempt there to push through a bill for the admission of California. The strife in the House was ominous when the "Little Giant" reached an agreement with Toombs, Stephens and others upon the basis of which he introduced, March 25, a bill for the admission of California as a free state, and another which provided for the establishment of territorial governments in Utah and New Mexico without reference to slavery but with a settlement of the Texas boundary question.[24] This was a distinct step toward putting Compromise principles into law.

[21] *Cong. Globe*, 31st Cong., 1st sess., App., 364–375.

[22] Chase Papers, XXI, Chase to Mrs. Chase, March 31, 1850; Hammond Papers, XVII, Tucker to Hammond, March 13, 26, April 18, 1850, Hammond to W. G. Simms, March 26, 1850; Marcy Papers, Marcy to Wetmore, March 17, 1850; Chase Papers, XXI, Chase to E. S. Hamlin, April 16, 1850; H. D. Foster, *op. et loc. cit.*, pp. 255–256, 265.

[23] Douglas, speech of Sept. 9, 1859, quoted in J F. Rhodes, *History of the United States since the Compromise of 1850*, 7 vols. (N.Y., 1899–1906), Vol. I, p. 173, note 2.

[24] *Cong. Globe*, 31st Cong., 1st sess., 592; George D. Harmon, "Douglas and the Compromise of 1850," in *Journal of the Ill. State Hist. Soc.*, Vol. XXI (1928–1929), pp. 472–474; F. H. Hodder, "The Authorship of the Compromise of 1850," in the *Miss Valley Hist. Rev.*, Vol. XXII (1935–1936), pp. 527–528.

But progress was still slow. Hatred between the sections continued to flame. The President, too, was hostile to compromise, in part because of an almost childish jealousy of Clay, and in part because of a conviction that Southern leaders, particularly his own son-in-law, Jefferson Davis, were hatching treasonable projects that must be sternly repressed.[25]

Meanwhile, a second plan of conciliation had been introduced by Bell of Tennessee. Another Southern Senator, Foote of Mississippi, proposed a select committee of thirteen, which should discuss the two proposals and attempt to establish a plan for the definitive settlement of the whole controversy,[26] and this proposition steadily gained in favor.

Clay gave his assent to this committee only with reluctance. He had believed at first that the Senate should accept his resolutions and that then they should be referred to appropriate committees where some of them might be combined in one bill. California, he felt, should be considered by itself, and as soon as possible. It seemed improbable to him, as late as March 13, that a committee could arrange a general scheme of adjustment that would command a majority.[27] But by the beginning of April, Clay became convinced that the speediest method of establishing a settlement of the questions at issue would be through the action of such a committee. He clashed with Benton (who was urging feverishly the admission of California) and led the way in championing Foote's proposal. In doing so, Clay made it clear that he would support a plan to combine California's admission with the establishment of a government for the territories, and perhaps with the adjustment of the Texas boundary. The tenor of his remarks in regard to this shows that one of the principal reasons for his taking this stand was the intense opposition of Southern members to the admission of California by itself.[28]

---

[25] Crittenden Papers, XIV, Brown to Crittenden, April 19, 1850; Barnes, *op. cit.*, pp. 177–181; Rhodes, *op. cit.*, Vol. I, p. 134.

[26] *Cong. Globe*, 31st Cong., 1st sess., 418, 509.

[27] Foote, *Casket of Reminiscences*, pp. 25–26; *Cong. Globe*, 31st Cong., 1st sess., 365–367, 510.

[28] *Ibid.*, 31st Cong., 1st sess., 652, 660, 722, 758. *Cf.* App., 614–615, 865.

The Senate agreed to the appointment of the committee of thirteen on April 18. The following day, its members were elected. Clay was chairman, and the body of the committee was made up of three Whigs and three Democrats from each section. All the bills on controversial subjects were referred to this group.[29]

Little that is authentic is known about the deliberations of the committee, but the report, which was read to the Senate by Clay on May 8, was in substantial harmony with the Kentuckian's Compromise resolutions. Three bills were presented. The first provided for the admission of California as a free state, for the organization of the territories of Utah and New Mexico without reference to slavery, and for adjustment of the Texas boundary, with compensation to Texas for relinquishing claim to an area of about one hundred and twenty-five thousand square miles. This was the true "Omnibus" bill. The second measure established provisions for the more effective rendition of fugitive slaves. The third prohibited importation of slaves into the District of Columbia for subsequent transportation or sale.

In framing these bills, the committee had relied almost wholly upon the work of others. The first tied together the bills introduced by Douglas on March 25, although, against Clay's wish, the Southerners in the committee had insisted upon adding a clause which forbade the territorial legislatures to take any action in regard to slavery. The second consisted of a measure already before the Senate, with some amendments. The third had not appeared before in Congress, but was framed on the model of a Maryland law.[30]

And now the question was, could the Omnibus be passed?

---

[29] Hodder, *op. et loc. cit.*, p. 529. Douglas opposed the appointment of this committee, believing a comprehensive plan of adjustment was impractical. Webster voted against it, preferring to see the Compromise adopted by means of amendments in the Senate.

[30] *Ibid.*, 31st Cong., 1st sess., 944–948, App., 571, 1410; Hodder, *op. et loc. cit.*, p. 529; Harmon, *op. et loc. cit.*, pp. 477–481. Hodder asserts that, even in the committee, "Clay had joined the two bills [the "Omnibus"] reluctantly, but the Southern members insisted upon doing so for fear that if the California bill passed first, Taylor would veto the territorial bill."

Douglas did not believe it, and the outburst of criticism from the ultras, as well as from some moderates, showed that his judgment was good.[31] But during the weary months that followed, Clay strove desperately to marshal his forces and put his measures through.

On May 13, Clay spoke for over two hours, defending the proposals of the committee, and arguing for the Omnibus especially, as a decidedly more practical solution than the Administration's policy of "non-action" in regard to the territories.[32] The debate, which began two days later, continued through a summer of blazing heat until the end of July. Almost every Senator took lengthy part in the struggle, but Clay was in the van of the battle for his measures. Faced by the opposition of extremists on both sides, and by the hostility of the Administration, the Kentuckian spent his failing energies without stint.

On May 21, stung by the attacks of newspapers favorable to the President, Clay made a vigorous assault upon Taylor's plan. There were five wounds, said the Kentuckian, "bleeding and threatening the well being, if not the existence of the body politic." The President proposed to heal one of them with the admission of California. The committee proposed to heal them all. Forcefully, Clay pointed out the inadequacies of the White House program and the dangers which it involved. The language of this speech, as printed in the *Globe*, was not intemperate, but it signalized his breach with the Administration. Seward found it "so insolent and so offensive" as to call for a vindication of "the Administration and the noble old chief." The breach between Clay and Taylor had opened wide, and gossip commented upon the similarity between 1850 and 1841.[33]

The chances of the Omnibus were by no means bright as June came on. Douglas, an astute judge of circumstances and

[31] *Cong. Globe*, 31st Cong., 1st sess., 948–956.

[32] *Ibid.*, 31st Cong., 1st sess., App., 567–573. *Cf.* the speech of Jefferson Davis, *ibid.*, 31st Cong., 1st sess., 1005.

[33] *Cong. Globe*, 31st Cong., 1st sess., App., 612–616, 1091; Weed Papers, Seward to Weed, May 22 [1850]; Crittenden Papers, XIV, Brown to Crittenden, May 23, 1850; Chase Papers, XXII, Chase to Hamlin, May 27, 1850.

a proponent of its individual measures, was certain that it would fail the Senate by a majority of ten. Chase noted that this "patchwork hardly seems to please anybody." Seward's judgment was that the North and South were falling back upon their original positions. "If Mr. Clay knew how to yield," the New Yorker wrote to Weed, "he would separate his bills now." The Kentuckian himself scarcely dared to hope, but he had never been one to give up a plan of action, once adopted, and he refused to do so now.[34]

The weary Senators leaned toward a week's adjournment that would afford a breathing space and give an opportunity to remove the heavy carpets and draperies of the chamber. Clay was stubbornly opposed. "He said," wrote Chase, "that he did not care about having the matting put down — he preferred the carpet — he would be content with the carpet all summer — it was of the utmost importance to push the Compromise bill through — he wanted to know its fate & the country would justly reproach us if we adjourned without coming to a decision." The Senate continued its daily meetings, and even acceded to Clay's wishes by convening at eleven o'clock each day instead of twelve.[35]

All through June the debate went on. Clay's health began to break, but he continued his attempts to push the Omnibus forward, while Benton, the ultras and the Administration men offered a flock of amendments that consumed the Senate's time and energy.[36] No one could be sure that the bill would pass or fail. Popular sentiment for the Compromise was growing, but its pressure had not as yet exerted any decisive influence upon the Senate.

Meanwhile, there were grave developments in other parts of the Union. Relations between Texas and New Mexico were

---

[34] F. W. Seward, *Seward at Washington*, Vol. II, pp. 132–137; Chase Papers, XXII, Chase to Hamlin, May 27, 1850; Clay Papers, XXVI, Clay to T. H. Clay, May 31, 1850.

[35] Chase Papers, XXII, Chase to Mrs. Chase, May 29, 1850; F. W. Seward, *Seward at Washington*, Vol. II, pp. 137, 141. The carpet and draperies were not removed until the end of June.

[36] See Clay's almost despairing comment, *Cong. Globe*, 31st Cong., 1st sess., App., 929. Also *Cong. Globe*, 31st. Cong., 1st sess., 1210–1211.

becoming more strained. There was increasing danger of open warfare over the boundary, with Southern aid for the Lone Star state bringing the North to the support of the territory. The much-heralded Nashville Convention met, June 3 to June 12. That gathering, it is true, gave evidences of the force of moderate sentiment in the South. Hampered by the condemnation received from many Southern Whigs, by the absence of six slave states and perhaps because, as Beverly Tucker sourly suggested, Old Hickory's ghost walked at Nashville, the Southern ultras were unable to take decisive steps toward secession. Nevertheless, the convention denounced the Compromise, called for the extension of 36° 30′ to the Pacific, and made arrangements to meet again. This was by no means, as Webster might have put it, "all lullaby and requiem." [37]

It is obvious that the true course of statesmanship was to unite moderate sentiment behind a conciliatory policy. Even passivity on Taylor's part would have been of inestimable value. But the President continued to stand doggedly by his own plan, a plan which was utterly unacceptable to the South. On July 3, Clay denounced Taylor for having prevented the passage of the Omnibus by "war, open war, undisguised war . . . against the plan of the committee." Three days later the Kentuckian ruefully confessed that a vote might be taken any time between then and Christmas. [38]

Then fate dealt a blow for the compromisers.

July 4 had been a day of blistering heat. President Taylor, participating in the patriotic exercises at the Washington Monument, had drunk ice water in large quantities, and on his return to the White House, had indulged himself with cherries

<hr>

[37] Hammond Papers, XVII, XVIII, June–Sept., 1850, passim; Mangum Papers, XVI, Atchison to Mangum, June 28, 1850; Giddings Papers, V, Giddings to his son, July 1, 1850; R. R. Russell, *Economic Aspects of Sectionalism*, pp. 73f; Cole, *The Whig Party*, pp. 158–164, 168–172, and "The South and the Rights of Secession in the Early Fifties," in *Miss. Valley Hist. Rev.*, Vol. I (1914–1915), pp. 376–399, 376–378; St. George L. Sioussat, "Tennessee, the Compromise of 1850, and the Nashville Convention," in *Miss. Valley Hist. Rev.*, Vol. II (1915–1916), pp. 313–347.

[38] *Cong. Globe*, 31st Cong., 1st sess., 1346, App., 1091–1093.

and iced milk.[39] An illness which began that evening, increased in violence, typhoid set in, and on July 9, the President breathed his last.

Millard Fillmore, the new President, was a kindly, cautious man, anxious to avert strife and convinced that compromise was the best policy.[40] His relations with Clay were friendly and confidential, and the Kentuckian was consulted as to the new President's Cabinet. Seward's power over the Administration was gone, and Webster was slated for the State Department. Clay's spirits bounded upward, and, summoning his failing energies to the task, he pushed hard for the passage of the Omnibus.

On Monday, July 22, the Kentuckian made his last great argument for the Compromise. For three hours he went over the whole ground of controversy, answering objections to his proposal and exposing the weakness of the ultras' demands. He urged the dangers involved in failure. War between Texas and New Mexico, developing into a war between North and South, was more than a probability. Even if this did not happen, the admission of California, without accompanying legislation to propitiate the South, would be certain to drive that section into a state of frenzy against Northern aggression. On the other hand, the Compromise would end agitation that played into the hands of the Abolitionists. It would bring peace after storm. Clay entreated his hearers to lay aside all jealousy and personal ambition.

The crowded Senate listened in breathless silence as the great orator brought into play all the magic of his eloquence.

Let us go to the limpid fountain of unadulterated patriotism, and, performing a solemn lustration, return divested of all selfish, sinister, and sordid impurities, and think alone of our God, our country, our consciences, and our glorious Union; that Union without which we shall be torn into hostile fragments, and sooner or later become the victims of military despotism, or foreign domination.

[39] Rhodes, *op. cit.*, Vol. I, p. 176.
[40] Marcy Papers, XVIII, Marcy to A. C. Campbell, July 18, 1850; Giddings Papers, V, Giddings to G. A. Giddings, July 22, 1850; F. H. Severance, ed., *Millard Fillmore Papers*, 2 vols. (Buffalo, 1907), Vol. II, pp. 321-324.

Mr. President, what is an individual man? An atom, almost invisible without a magnifying glass — a mere speck upon the surface of the immense universe — not a second in time, compared to immeasurable, never-beginning, and never-ending eternity; a drop of water in the great deep, which evaporates and is borne off by the winds; a grain of sand, which is soon gathered to the dust from which it sprung. Shall a being so small, so petty, so fleeting, so evanescent, oppose itself to the onward march of a great nation, to subsist for ages and ages to come — oppose itself to that long line of posterity which, issuing from our loins, will endure during the existence of the world? Forbid it, God! Let us look at our country and our cause; elevate ourselves to the dignity of pure and disinterested patriots, wise and enlightened statesmen, and save our country from all impending dangers. What if, in the march of this nation to greatness and power, we should be buried beneath the wheels that propel it onward? What are we — what is any man worth who is not ready and willing to sacrifice himself for the benefit of his country when it is necessary?

Clay made patriotism the dominant note, bringing it into the speech and the debate that followed with dramatic effect.

If there be any . . . before whose imagination is flitting the idea of a great Southern Confederacy to take possession of the Balize and the mouth of the Mississippi, I say in my place, never! *Never!* NEVER will we who occupy the broad waters of the Mississippi and its upper tributaries consent that any foreign flag shall float at the Balize or upon the turrets of the Crescent City — never — never!

And the gallery thundered applause when Clay, naming Robert Barnwell Rhett of South Carolina, exclaimed: —

I know him personally, and have some respect for him. But, if he pronounced the sentiment attributed to him of raising the standard of disunion and of resistance to the common Government, whatever he has been, if he follows up that declaration by corresponding overt acts, he will be a traitor, and I hope he will meet the fate of a traitor.[41]

The struggle continued until the end of July. Then came a strange climax. In order to gain three or four vital Southern votes, the friends of the Omnibus had agreed to eliminate the

[41] *Cong. Globe*, 31st Cong., 1st sess., App., 1405–1414.

provisions in regard to the Texas boundary. These were to be replaced by an amendment establishing a joint boundary commission representing Texas and the United States. Senator Bradbury of Maine offered this amendment. Then Dawson of Georgia tacked on a proviso stating that, until the boundary had been agreed upon, the Territorial Government of New Mexico established by the act should not go into effect east of the Rio Grande. This, too, was supposed to strengthen the bill. The Texas Senators were satisfied, the Bradbury Amendment with the Dawson Proviso was accepted, thirty to twenty-eight, and passage seemed certain.[42] Clay felt triumphant when the Senate adjourned on the evening of July 30, but the next day brought disaster.

Overnight, Northern moderates began to draw back, apparently afraid that too much had been conceded to Texas. Objection centered on the Dawson Proviso. In the session of July 31, James A. Pearce of Maryland, close friend and confidant of President Fillmore, offered a motion to strike out the whole section of the Omnibus that related to New Mexico, at the same time restoring all save the Proviso. It was obvious that such action might alienate hardly won Southern support, but, despite vehement protests from Clay and a warning that the Omnibus would go down in ruin, Pearce insisted upon his motion. The path to destruction was greased when Pearce, at the suggestion of an ultra, Yulee of Florida, agreed to divide his proposal into two parts. The first, to strike out, was then passed, thirty-three to twenty-two. Then Pearce moved to reinsert all that had been struck out, save the Dawson Proviso. Yulee offered an amendment striking out of the reinsertion the part which related to the appointment of a commission for the settlement of the Texas boundary. Here was the crucial test. Yulee's motion was agreed to by a margin of one vote — twenty-nine to twenty-eight. Then the motion to reinsert simply the part relating to New Mexico failed by a vote of twenty-eight to twenty-five. The Omnibus had been broken up, and Clay saw section after section stripped away,

[42] Van Buren Papers, LVII, F. P. Blair to Van Buren, Aug. 1, 1850; *Cong. Globe*, 31st Cong., 1st sess., 1481–1482.

until only the provision for establishing a territorial government in Utah remained to be voted on the following day.[43]

Utterly worn-out by his exertions, Clay now left for Newport, where he recruited his strength by rest and sea bathing.[44]
He did not return until the latter part of August, and during
his absence all the Compromise measures, save the District of
Columbia bill, were taken up and passed singly. This was done
under the leadership of Douglas and the Administration, with
a block of Northern and Southern moderates voting steadily
for all the measures.[45]

Clay took charge of the District of Columbia bill on
August 28. It passed the Senate eighteen days later. The other
measures had passed the House by that time, and on September 17 the District bill also passed the lower chamber. The
Spirit of Compromise had triumphed.

Douglas had believed from the first that the measures had
a better chance of passing singly than in combination.[46] He had
taken the lead in pushing them through after the Omnibus
failed, and full credit should go to him for that achievement.

Clay had stated repeatedly during the debate that his idea
and that of the committee was to achieve the passage of the
measures, whether separately or jointly. He had accepted the
Omnibus proposal reluctantly, as presenting the most feasible
means of passage, and, once accepted, had championed it ardently, bearing the brunt of the great battle through the torrid
summer of 1850. In doing so, he had rendered a national
service of the first magnitude.

---

[43] Van Buren Papers, LVII, Blair to Van Buren, Aug. 1, 1850; *Cong.
Globe*, 31st Cong., 1st sess., 1479–1482, 1489–1491, App., 1447–1491.
Pearce also seems to have been angered because he had not been consulted by
Clay or any other proponent of the Omnibus as to the advisability of the
Dawson Proviso. See Pearce's remarks in his quarrel with Clay over responsi-
bility for the failure of the Omnibus. — *Cong. Globe*, 31st Cong., 1st sess.,
App., 1488.

[44] Fillmore Papers, VII, Clay to Fillmore, Aug. 10, 1850.

[45] The Texas boundary bill, as finally passed, increased Texas some 30,000
square miles over the Omnibus bill provision. The state received, directly
and indirectly, $10,000,000.

[46] Save, perhaps, in regard to the territorial organization and the Texas
boundary, which he had incorporated in one bill.

It was impossible to tell at the beginning of the fight which method of procedure would be more effectual, and the use of the Omnibus plan had the merit of giving the bills two chances. They could be, as they were, taken up individually if unitary passage failed. More important than this, the combination emphasized the compromise aspect. At a time when passions were running high, and Taylor's policy was exciting rather than allaying Southern feeling, the measures were brought together for a discussion and interchange of opinion that tended to diminish rather than to increase sectional animosity. The long debate in Congress and in the newspapers gave an opportunity for popular opinion to form, and, as Foote and Dickinson bore witness, it was public opinion that was the real factor in pushing the Compromise through.[47]

In the formation of that public opinion, no man was more important than Clay. Wracked by ill health and the weight of advancing years, he had rallied his failing energies to plead for compromise in words that had echoed throughout the country. Harry of the West, still loved and revered by multitudes of followers, had stood foremost among the champions of that spirit of moderation which finally prevailed. Therein lay his great service to the Compromise, and to the Union.

[47] *Cong. Globe,* 31st Cong., 1st sess., 1829.

Chapter XXV

THE SHADOWS FALL

CLAY's vigor had been recruited only temporarily by his stay at Newport. The resumption of his duties in the Senate exhausted the strength that he had gained by his brief rest, and he left Washington shortly before the close of the session. He reached Lexington on the evening of October 2, 1850, to be met on the outskirts by a great crowd. The horses were unhitched from his coach and, amidst the ringing of bells and the firing of cannon, men with bared heads drew the vehicle down what is now Limestone Street and finally to the Phoenix Hotel. A speech was demanded, and Clay expressed his appreciation and affection.

"And now," he said, in closing, "I must ask you to excuse me, for, strange as it may seem, there is an old lady at Ashland whom I would rather see than all of you." [1] So he came at last to the home where he had longed to be. [2]

Kentucky delighted to honor him. About the middle of October, a barbecue was given to him at Lexington, men of all parties joining in the celebration; and a month later, while visiting at Frankfort, he was invited to address the houses of the Kentucky legislature. In his speech there, Clay defended the Compromise and declared that if it were necessary to form a new party in order to prevent a dissolution of the Union, he could be counted upon as one of its members. The moment Abolition became a part of the Whig creed, that moment he would "cease to be a Whig." [3] The preservation of the Union was now his dominant thought, although it may well be that

[1] J. O. Harrison Papers, Family Letters, Mary Harrison to George Harrison, Oct. 3, 1850; Madeleine McDowell, *op. et loc. cit.*, pp. 765–770.

[2] Clay Papers, XXVI, Clay to T. H. Clay, Sept. 6, 1850.

[3] J. O. Harrison Papers, Scrapbook, pp. 44–45, Clay to Harrison, Gratz, etc., Oct. 10, 1850; Clayton Papers, IX, Whittlesey to Clayton, Nov. 23, 1850; *National Intelligencer* (daily), Nov. 21, 27, 1850; Van Buren Papers, Blair

his hint at a new party and the stand that he took that fall in opposing life tenure for judges and defending their election by the people showed a desire to build up his forces in Kentucky against the strength of Crittenden.[4]

Clay went back to Washington in December. That winter his health was so poor that at times he was almost hopeless of recovery. A severe cold settled upon him shortly after reaching the Capital, and during the ensuing weeks he was tormented by a cough and by sleeplessness that would not yield to nightly doses of an opiate.[5] His social activities were reduced to a minimum, but he did attend a Jenny Lind concert in December, marching in after the overture ended, while the house rose and a thunder of applause dimmed the receptions that had just been accorded to Webster, Crittenden and Fillmore. It was a triumph that pleased the Kentuckian immensely.[6]

Considering the state of his health, Clay was surprisingly active in the second session of the Thirty-first Congress. There his attitude on public policies was characterized by a spirit of moderation. This was evidenced in connection with the strained relations that existed at the time between the United States and Austria.

The open expression in the United States of popular sympathy with the Hungarian struggle for independence, the sending of a special agent to Hungary in 1849 with discretionary powers of recognition, and the communication to the Senate in March of 1850 of the instructions and correspondence of this agent, had produced a vigorous protest from the Austrian Government. This had been presented by the Chevalier Hülsemann, Austrian chargé d'affaires in Washington, and the reply was Webster's famous "Hülsemann letter" of December

to Van Buren, Dec. 30, 1850. Considerable sentiment for a National Union Party was developing at this time among the Southern Whigs. See Cole, *op. cit.,* pp. 182–183.

[4] So thought Frank P. Blair, who talked with Clay after the latter's return to Washington. — Van Buren Papers, LVII, Blair to Van Buren, Dec. 26, 1850.

[5] Clay Papers, XXVI, Clay to Mrs. Clay, Dec. 26, 1850, Jan. 12, 1851.

[6] Buffalo Hist. Soc. Mss., Clay to Mrs. Hall, Jan. 23, 1851; Van Buren Papers, LVII, Blair to Van Buren, Dec. 26, 1850.

21, 1850. Couched in boastful and truculent language that was designed to inform the Europeans as to "who and what we are," and also to stimulate national pride among our own citizens, the letter defended our action, glorified American institutions, and took occasion to inform Austria that the United States held sway over a region "in comparison with which the possessions of the house of Hapsburg are but as a patch on the earth's surface." [7] This bombast aroused a chorus of praise in America, and a motion to print ten thousand extra copies was made in the Senate. Clay protested against this motion in a brief but trenchant speech. He pointed out that any interference in the affairs of a foreign state was a very delicate matter, that Hungary was doomed and that no useful purpose could be served by irritating further the Austrian Government. Such arguments had weight, and the motion to print the extra copies was defeated by a vote of twenty-one to eighteen.[8]

The Kentuckian's attitude toward domestic affairs was equally marked by a pacificatory tone. He was determined to preserve the Compromise of 1850, and to prevent the outbreak of more slavery agitation. His name headed a list of over forty members of Congress who signed a resolution pledging adherence to the Compromise and declaring that they would not support candidates for office who opposed that agreement.[9] Again and again, Clay moved to lay on the table petitions presented by Free Soil Senators praying for repeal or modification of the Fugitive Slave Law. He pulverized the argument that the Federal Government had no authority to enforce that law by expounding the necessity and validity of national powers logically derived from the powers specifically granted by the Constitution.[10] It was obvious that these poli-

[7] G. W. Curtis, op. cit., Vol. II, p. 537; Daniel Webster, The Writings and Speeches of Daniel Webster, 18 vols. (Boston, 1903), Vol. XII, pp. 165–178.

[8] Cong. Globe, 31st Cong., 2d sess., 136; Clayton Papers, VIII, John W. Houston to Clayton, Jan. 8 [1851].

[9] National Intelligencer (daily, Jan. 22, 1851; tri-weekly, Jan. 30, 1851); Cong. Globe, 31st Cong., 2d sess., 304.

[10] Cong. Globe, 31st Cong., 2d sess., 425, 436, App., 293, 294, 320–323. As the result of a slave rescue in Boston, Clay took an active part in moving

cies were adopted with a view to safeguarding the Union.

But though Clay's views on public matters bore the stamp of moderation, his conduct during the session was not always marked by philosophic calm. Aged and frail though he was, his love of leadership and his impatience of opposition had not forsaken him. The tone of his remarks in regard to the Hülsemann letter prompts a suspicion that he was not unmindful of the favorable effect produced by that missive upon Webster's popularity. The Kentuckian's tongue was still sharp when he could say of the New Hampshire antislavery Senator, John P. Hale: "I hope he will receive this surrender on my part of any ambition between him and me to contend for the palm of oratory, with the complacency with which he usually rises in this body and presents himself before us." [11] Clay appeared to take delight in compassing the defeat of Benton's attempt to obtain for Missouri two per cent. of the proceeds from the sale of public lands within that state. A vigorous, though unsuccessful, effort to obtain the passage of a rivers and harbors bill which was of interest to the Mississippi Valley brought out the Kentuckian's "zeal and hot temper" in a debate with Jefferson Davis wherein each man accused the other of "lecturing" to the Senate.[12] And Clay still kept an eye on the patronage, suggesting to the President its more equable distribution in courteous but decided terms.[13] The old leader of the Whigs was still true to character.

Clay intended to go straight back to Ashland at the close of the session. But his poor health and persistent cough, the report of bad roads, and the hope that he might find relief in a softer climate, finally prompted him to return home by way of Cuba and New Orleans.[14] He went from Washington to New York and, after a grand ball and supper at Niblo's, re-

---

an investigation by the Judiciary Committee of the need for further fugitive slave legislation. — *Cong. Globe*, 31st Cong., 2d sess., 580, 600, 660, 676.

[11] *Cong. Globe*, 31st Cong., 2d sess., App., 294.

[12] *Ibid.*, 31st Cong., 2d sess., 813, App., 329, 353f, 368, 381.

[13] Buffalo Hist. Soc., Letters to Millard Fillmore, XVIII, 128, Clay to Fillmore, March 10 [1851].

[14] Anderson Collection, Clay to John Morrison Clay, Feb. 27, 1851; Colton, *Correspondence*, p. 615.

plete with "the greetings and kisses of eight hundred ladies and gentlemen" who had been touchingly entreated to respect the state of his health,[15] the old leader sailed for Havana on the steamer *Georgia*. This trip, of about a month's duration, marked the third and last time that he was to journey into foreign parts.

Clay's health was somewhat benefited by the fortnight that he spent in Cuba, and during the summer and fall of 1851 he continued to take an active interest in the state of the country. Threats of secession were still emanating from various parts of the South, particularly South Carolina, and Clay did not hesitate in asserting his opinion that secession was treason and that such action should be met by force.[16] In October he wrote a letter to New York that was published widely. Only the Fugitive Slave Law was being seriously assailed in the North, he declared, but that law was an essential one and he believed that Northern opinion would see to its enforcement. The only basis for real uneasiness in regard to the South lay in the "general desire" in South Carolina to withdraw from the Union. He then examined the claim that the individual states possessed powers of Nullification and Secession. Clay asserted that Nullification derived only "an ambiguous and contested support" from the Virginia and Kentucky resolutions, and that those resolutions gave no countenance whatever to Secession. That doctrine, if applied, was a violation of the Constitution and utterly destructive of the Union. Open resistance to the Union, the Constitution and the laws could be answered only in one way. "The power, the authority, and dignity of the Government ought to be maintained, and resistance put down at every hazard." The Union was essential to the peace and prosperity of the country. "United we stand — divided we fall."[17] The letter was a powerful arraignment of the right of any state to secede from the Union.

[15] Hone, *op. cit.*, Vol. II, p. 915.

[16] Clay, *Works*, Vol. III, pp. 499–500, Clay to Stevenson, May 17, 1851

[17] *National Intelligencer* (tri-weekly), Oct. 21, 1851. Clay was decidedly cool toward the Southern desire for immediate annexation of Cuba. He wrote to a Southern lady: "With you I deprecate the cold-blooded massacre of ou

But anxiety over national affairs could not prevent Clay's thoughts from turning more and more toward the approaching end of life. Shortly after his return to Ashland, in the spring of 1851, he began to contemplate purchasing a final resting place in the Lexington cemetery. When the news of this got about, Mr. John Lutz, one of the founders of the cemetery corporation, presented Clay with four lots, a gift that was gratefully received.[18] Some six weeks later, July 10, 1851, Clay made his last will and testament. This left to his wife the use and occupation of Ashland, save for two hundred acres that were devised to his son John. Should Lucretia so desire and should the executors consent, Ashland might be sold during her lifetime, the proceeds to be invested, with the income from the investment accruing to her. Upon her death, the pecuniary legacies provided for in the will were to be paid out of this principal, the remainder passing into the residuary estate. The Mansfield estate went to Thomas, together with five thousand dollars and the canceling of any debts owed to his father. John received, in addition to the land mentioned, four slaves and a considerable amount of stock. Provision was made for Theodore, and liberal bequests were made to various grandchildren. The residuary estate, including the amount realized by the sale of Ashland, was to be handled by the executors as a trust fund. Out of the proceeds of this fund, Theodore was to be supported. The remaining income from it was to be paid in equal portions to Thomas and James, and the fund was to pass, in equal portions, to such persons as these two sons might direct in their wills. Mrs. Clay was made executrix, and Thomas A. Marshall and James O. Harrison executors of Clay's will. Perhaps the most interesting provision related to Clay's slaves. All the children born after January 1, 1850, were to become free, the males at twenty-eight, the fe-

countrymen at Cuba, although their engagement in the Lopez expedition was highly culpable. It is not yet time for us to get Cuba. It will come to us in due season, if we are wise, prudent and united." — Buffalo Hist. Soc. Mss., Clay to Mrs. Octavia Walton Le Vert, Nov. 14, 1851. This was essentially the same position that he had taken in regard to Texas in 1844.

[18] Filson Club Historical Quarterly, Jan. 1935, pp. 52–53. Lutz to Clay, May 23, 1851, Clay to Lutz, May 26, 1851. The originals of these letters are in the Filson Club archives.

males at twenty-five. For the three years before arrival at the age of freedom, they were to receive wages "at the fair value of their services, to defray the expence of transporting them to one of the African Colonies, and of furnishing them with an outfit on their arrival there. And I further direct that they be taught to read, to write and to cipher, and that they be sent to Africa." The issue of such females, if there were issue while the mothers were yet slaves, were to be deemed free from birth, apprenticed to learn farming or a trade, and at the age of twenty-one were to be sent to Africa. Thus Clay demonstrated his abiding faith in colonization as a remedy for slavery.[19]

The hot summer months at Lexington exhausted Clay's strength, and autumn weather brought no material relief. But his spirit was still strong, and he finally decided to go to Washington "for the last time."

The day before his departure, James O. Harrison, General John C. Breckenridge, and Major M. C. Johnson, President of the Northern Bank of Kentucky, called to pay their respects. They found Clay very feeble. When the gentlemen rose to go, their host accompanied them to the door. He touched Harrison on the shoulder, and, stepping back a few paces, said in a quiet voice: "Remember that my will is in the custody of my wife." Clay's voice broke as he said good-by and they all felt that it was their last farewell.[20]

The old leader answered to the roll call on the first day of the session, but the arduous trip across the mountains had weakened him still further. It was his last appearance on the

[19] The will was drawn up in Clay's handwriting, July 10, 1851. A codicil was added, November 14, 1851. It was admitted to probate, July 12, 1852. The original is in Will Book T, p. 474, July 12, 1852, Fayette County Court House, Lexington, Kentucky. There is a copy in the J. O. Harrison Papers, Scrapbook. Mrs. Clay wrote later to the executors that her husband took the advice of his son James in making this will. — J. O. Harrison Papers, Scrapbook, pp. 44–45, Lucretia Clay to Judge Thomas A. Marshall, and J. O. Harrison, Sept. 18, 1856.

[20] Fendall Papers, Clay to Fendall, August 1, 1851; Buffalo Hist. Soc. Mss., Clay to Mrs. Le Vert, Nov. 14, 1851; Van Buren Papers, LVIII, Jabez D. Hammond to Van Buren, March 29, 1852; J. O. Harrison Papers, Scrapbook, p. 28.

floor.[21] Thereafter, he remained closely confined to his room in the National Hotel, his superb constitution struggling against the cough and the loss of weight and strength so characteristic of the final stages of consumption. On December 17, he resigned his seat in the Senate, the resignation to take effect on September 1, 1852. This gave the Whig majority in the Kentucky legislature an opportunity to choose his successor, and forestalled the possibility of an appointment by the Democratic Governor in the event of Clay's sudden death. There was another reason as well. The old statesman knew that his political existence was almost at its close, but he told Frank P. Blair that he wanted to reserve the opportunity "to exert any possible usefulness that might remain to him." [22]

There were times during that tedious winter when Clay's health rallied. Occasionally he went out riding, and there were always visitors who talked politics, and, on occasion, heard him express his preference for Fillmore as the logical Whig candidate in 1852.[23] The Kentuckian was able to receive and address briefly a deputation from New York which presented him with a gold medal, and one day in January, he received a dramatic visit from Louis Kossuth.

The Hungarian patriot and exile had been hailed with great enthusiasm in the United States. He called upon Clay at the National Hotel, January 9, 1852; and, after describing the condition of Hungary and the situation in France, expressed the hope that the United States would intervene in the affairs of Europe. Clay made a brief reply, indicating the sympathy that he felt in any struggle for liberty, but protesting against American intervention in European affairs. Such action, said Clay, could do no good, and might bring irreparable harm to the United States through attacks by the conservative powers.

[21] *Cong. Globe*, 32d Cong., 1st sess., 1–4. Clay took part in seating Stephen R. Mallory of Florida, despite the claim of David L. Yulee. There was good reason for this action, but it is easy to surmise that Clay derived pain neither from this nor from the subsequent final rejection of Yulee's claim.

[22] Van Buren Papers, LVIII, Blair to Van Buren, Dec. 21, 1851; E. M. Coulter, "The Downfall of the Whig Party in Kentucky," in *Kentucky State Historical Society Register*, Vol. XXIII (May 1925), pp. 162–164.

[23] Colton, *Correspondence*, p. 628, Clay to Ullmann, March 6, 1852.

The greatest service we could render would be by continuing to set an example of the results of liberty. One version states that, at the close of his remarks, he said: "A dying man, I oppose your doctrine of intervention" — adding, as he grasped Kossuth's hand in farewell: "God bless you and your family! God bless your country! May she yet be free!"

An "official" version of this reply went into the newspapers, and thus Clay's last published utterance was a plea for American isolation from a Europe that was binding democracy in chains.[24]

Clay bore his tormenting cough, and the sleeplessness that harassed him, with admirable fortitude. Blair had urged him not to despond, and the Kentuckian's reply [25] — "Sir, there is no such word in my vocabulary" — was not belied by his conduct during the last months of suffering. For a long time he hoped that he could return to Kentucky to die, but by the close of April it was apparent that he would not be able to leave Washington. Thomas, summoned by telegraph on April 27, found his father unable to walk across the room and exhausted by five minutes of conversation. Thereafter the old statesman's health improved slightly at times, but the fatal course of his disease was apparent to all.[26]

---

[24] The "official" report of Clay's speech to Kossuth may be found in the *New York Daily Tribune*, Feb. 4, 1852. See also Clay, *Works*, Vol. III, pp. 221–224; *National Intelligencer* (tri-weekly), Jan. 10, 15, 1852; *New York Daily Tribune*, Jan. 13, 1852; Van Buren Papers, LVIII, Blair to Van Buren, Jan. 11, 1852; Sargent, *op. cit.*, Vol. II, p. 383; Collins, *History of Kentucky*, Vol. I, pp. 63–64. Kossuth later criticized Clay in a speech at Louisville, for allowing the publication of what Kossuth termed a confidential conversation. Clay replied, March 30, 1852, in a letter to a gentleman in New Orleans which asserted that the interview granted to Kossuth had been neither private nor confidential, and that the "official" publication had been given out because of the varying and sometimes contradictory reports that had appeared in the newspapers. — *National Intelligencer* (tri-weekly), March 20, April 17, 1852, reprints from the *New Orleans Picayune* and the *New Orleans Bee*.

[25] Van Buren Papers, LVIII, Blair to Van Buren, Dec. 21, 1851.

[26] Clay felt that the published accounts of his condition were thoroughly unreliable. He wrote in February to Mrs. James B. Clay that the family must not believe all that they saw in the newspapers, favorable or unfavorable. — Clay Papers, XXVI, Clay to Mrs. James B. Clay, Feb. 12, 1852, and Colton, *Correspondence*, p. 630, Clay to James B. Clay, March 22, 1852.

Dr. Samuel Jackson, summoned from Philadelphia during the first part of May, pronounced the case hopeless, but Clay was assured that his passing would be easy. He showed no fear of death, but occasionally spoke with regret of his inability either to rise up or to die. He was thin and weak, prostrated by coughing fits, his appetite almost gone and natural sleep only an occasional boon, but still life clung tenaciously to his wasted frame. Throngs of people, Democrats as well as Whigs, called to inquire after his health, and Clay was anxious that grateful messages be sent to them, repeating over and over "Be very kind, very kind." [27]

The passions of old days were spent at last. Blair was once more Clay's friend. Benton, writing his *Thirty Years' View*, was refuting the old slander about "bargain and corruption," and the Kentuckian, deeply touched, had told Blair that there was no bitterness in his heart. The old leader had taken pains to assure Van Buren of his friendship, and of his regret that, at the time of the West Indian treaty, he had allowed partisan excitement to provoke him into bitter speech.[28] Crittenden's desertion in 1848 no longer rankled. The shadow of death was stealing into the National Hotel, and even the nomination of General Scott, attended by ominous signs of the Whig Party's dissolution, could not matter too much when life was slipping away.

On the evening of June 28, Clay was heard to murmur, "My mother, mother, mother!" and then, as though Lucretia stood by his side, "My dear wife!" [29] The next morning, at his own expressed desire, he was cleanly shaven. Shortly thereafter, his servant James summoned Thomas to the bedside. "Sit near me, my dear son," said the dying man. "I do not wish you to leave me for any time to-day."

[27] George Bancroft, "A Few Words about Henry Clay," in the *Century Magazine*, new series, Vol. VIII (July 1885), pp. 479–481; Colton, *Correspondence*, pp. 633–636; J. O. Harrison Papers, Scrapbook, an unidentified newspaper clipping signed "E. R."

[28] Van Buren Papers, LVIII, Blair to Van Buren, Dec. 11, 21, 1851, Jan. 11, 1852, Benton to Van Buren, Jan. 11, 1852, Van Buren to Blair, Jan. 16, 1852.

[29] Henry Clay, "Personal Anecdotes, Incidents, etc.," in *Harper's Magazine*, Vol. V (Aug. 1852), pp. 392–399.

An hour passed, broken only by a request for a drink of water. Then he said, "I believe, my son, I am going." Five minutes later he asked to have his shirt collar buttoned. Thomas did so, and Clay caught his son's hand in his own. He held it for some minutes, then his grasp relaxed and gradually, peacefully, he ceased to breathe. It was seventeen minutes after eleven o'clock on the morning of June 29, 1852.[30]

Funeral services were held in the Senate chamber on July 1, and Whigs and Democrats united in their grief and praise. Every face was sad, and no one appeared to be more deeply affected than Webster. He was "the Saddest I saw at the ceremonies of the Senate," wrote Blair to Van Buren, "& not withstanding all his wishes towards Clay while he lived, I cannot but believe his sorrow was unfeigned." [31]

A committee of Senators attended the remains to Lexington. There, on July 10, in the midst of a city swathed in crape and a crowd of thirty thousand people whose mournfulness symbolized a nation's lamentation, the "Mill Boy of the Slashes" was laid to rest in the Lexington cemetery.

The character and principles of Henry Clay illustrate two great forces in American life. His freehearted, openhanded ways, his dash and daring, whether at the card table or on the battleground of politics, his belief in a predominantly agricultural nation, and his keen interest in the public lands and internal improvements, were characteristic of the West as it was in his day. But there is another side to the picture. Champion of financial interests at the very beginning of his career, conservative in his economic views, recognizing the value of political support from men of business, Clay rapidly developed a keen appreciation of industrial progress as an essential factor in national prosperity. Sympathetic in spirit with the agrarian West, he was also a protagonist of the rising industrialism of the East, that industrialism which was to fructify after the Civil War in the barbaric splendor of the Gilded Age. These two forces, the agricultural and the industrial, Clay sought to

[30] Colton, *Correspondence*, p. 636, Thomas Clay to his wife, June 29, 1852; Ranck, *op. cit.*, p. 206; J. O. Harrison Papers, Account Book.
[31] Van Buren Papers, LVIII, Blair to Van Buren, July 4, 1852.

unite under his leadership, and his ambition stimulated his belief that the democracy of the West and the conservatism of the East could be drawn together under the banner of the American System.

The concept of such a union was reasonable enough. The Republican Party was to embrace it with marked success in later years, and at a time when the divergence of interest between East and West was decidedly more obvious than it was in the Middle Period. But, logical though his position was, Clay's political rôle was confined chiefly to leadership of an opposition which caustically attacked the policies enacted by others. He never became the triumphant leader of the nation.

The reasons for this are not far to seek. Mistakes in judgment at crucial times had serious effects. Such a mistake was the acceptance of the State Department, the attempt to force recharter of the Bank, the belief that the annexation of Texas was not a vital issue. The difficulty of uniting the heterogeneous Whig Party under a leadership based upon political principles was a factor. Clay's party functioned best while in opposition, finding it well-nigh impossible to agree upon a constructive program under a forceful leader. Practical politicians of the Weed stripe sought to avoid this handicap by raising the standards of military heroes. In 1840 and 1848, when chances of success were brightest, the Whigs turned to "available" candidates and the old leader was denied the nomination that he craved. The Slavery Question also, a problem for which Clay could find no effective answer, vitiated his strength and helped to compass his defeat in 1844.

Deeper than these reasons lay the fact that he was the conservative leader of forces that were fundamentally conservative, whether they styled themselves National Republican or Whig. The Democratic tide of the Middle Period found Clay in sympathy with the well-to-do, defending the National Bank, sponsoring the maintenance of high prices for public lands, linking himself with the industrial interests of the East. Democracy turned to Jacksonism, and the Kentuckian was left behind.

Frequently rash in attacking his opponents, too often arrogant and dictatorial, brilliant rather than profound in his analysis of public questions, ambitious for preferment, Henry Clay was far from perfect, either as a party leader or as a statesman. But, despite his faults, the Kentuckian remains a shining figure in American history. Bowed down again and again by family tragedy and by anxiety over financial matters, he never lost his ardor for public service. Magnetic and eloquent, quick in perception, daring in execution, he commanded an affection that was almost idolatry from tens of thousands of devoted followers. His services as Speaker, his long career as leader and watchful critic in the House and Senate, the part played at Ghent, the pacificatory influence exercised over the Senate's attitude toward foreign policy in the later phases of his career, were valuable contributions to the development of our national life. His ready sympathy was ever extended to peoples seeking freedom from political oppression, and Latin America remembers gratefully to-day the support he gave in her great struggle against the yoke of Spain. Above and beyond these attributes lay his devotion to his country, a devotion that was an integral part of his emotional and intellectual life. The day may come when patriotism will cease to be a virtue, but until that time Clay will be honored as a man who gave himself earnestly to the task of making the United States a prosperous and an enduring nation. Often stubborn and intractable in questions of private or party policy, he was always among the first to urge the need of compromise when the rise of passion threatened his country's welfare, and always foremost in using his great influence to guide the nation safely through stress and storm.

One hundred years ago, the clouds of sectional strife darkened the American horizon, harbingers of civil war which Henry Clay strove stanchly to prevent from bursting upon the land. To-day we hear the mutterings of a class struggle, ominous in the potentialities that lead to conflict. The present never exactly reproduces the past; but now, as then, men may gain inspiration from the career of one who stood valiantly in defense of human freedom and of the Union that he loved.

BIBLIOGRAPHY

(Necessarily an abbreviated list)

MANUSCRIPT MATERIAL.

1. Archives: —

> Department of State. Instructions, Vols. X–XII; Domestic Papers, Vols. XXI–XXII; Panama Congress, 1826–1827; Miscellaneous Letters, 1825–1829; Despatches to Consuls, Vols. II, III; Notes to Foreign Legations, Vols. III, IV; Ghent, *etc.* American Commissioners, 1813–1816; Archives of the Embassy at Ghent, 1814, Negotiations.
>
> Fayette County Court House, Circuit Court Records, Will Books, Order Books, *etc.*
>
> Great Britain. Public Record Office. F.O. 5, Vols. 199–248. Despatches. (Photostats in the Library of Congress.)
>
> Virginia State Library. Court Records, Hanover Co., 1783–1792; Land Tax Book, Hanover Co., 1782–1802; Hanover Property Book, 1782–1791.

2. Library and Private Collections used in whole or in part: —

> M. William Anderson Collection. Lexington, Kentucky.
>
> James A. and Richard H. Bayard Papers. Library of Congress.
>
> Nicholas Biddle Papers. Library of Congress.
>
> Breckinridge Papers. Library of Congress.
>
> Mrs. Jouett Taylor Cannon Collection. Frankfort, Kentucky.
>
> Salmon P. Chase Papers. Library of Congress.
>
> Henry Clay Papers. Library of Congress.
>
> John M. Clayton Papers. Library of Congress.
>
> John J. Crittenden Papers. Partly at the Library of Congress, partly at Duke University.
>
> Lyman C. Draper Collection. Wisconsin Historical Library.

Ferdinand J. Dreer Collection. Pennsylvania Historical Society.

Robert T. Durrett Collection. University of Chicago.

Etting Papers. Pennsylvania Historical Society.

Joshua R. Giddings Papers. Ohio State Historical and Archæological Society.

William A. Graham Papers. North Carolina State Historical Commission.

Simon Gratz Collection. Pennsylvania Historical Society.

James H. Hammond Papers. Library of Congress.

James O. Harrison Papers. Library of Congress.

Andrew Jackson Papers. Library of Congress.

Joseph S. Johnston Collection. Pennsylvania Historical Society.

James Kent Papers. Library of Congress.

Samuel Larned Papers. American Antiquarian Society.

Anne Clay McDowell Collection. In possession of Mrs. Thomas S. Bullock. Lexington, Kentucky. Includes among other items about one hundred and twenty-five letters from Henry Clay to Henry Clay, Junior. Also the latter's diary.

John McLean Papers. Library of Congress.

Willie P. Mangum Papers. Library of Congress.

William L. Marcy Papers. Library of Congress.

Peters Manuscripts. Pennsylvania Historical Society.

Timothy Pickering Papers. Massachusetts Historical Society.

Peter B. Porter Collection. Buffalo Historical Society.

F. G. and F. H. Sweet Collection. Battle Creek, Michigan.

Zachary Taylor Papers. Library of Congress.

Transylvania University Collection.

John Tyler Manuscripts. Library of Congress.

Martin Van Buren Papers. Library of Congress.

Noah Webster Papers. New York Public Library.

Thurlow Weed Papers. University of Rochester Library.

Gideon Welles Papers. Library of Congress.

Robert C. Winthrop Papers. Massachusetts Historical Society.

PRINTED MATERIAL.

1. Newspapers, Periodicals and Pamphlets: —

African Repository. 68 vols. Washington. 1826–1892.

Anderson, D. R. "The Insurgents of 1811," in *American*

Historical Association Annual Report, 1911, Vol. I, pp. 165–176.

Argus of Western America. Frankfort, Kentucky.

Clay, Thomas H. "Two Years with Old Hickory," in *Atlantic Monthly,* Vol. LX (Aug. 1887), pp. 187–199.

Coleman, C. B. "The Ohio Valley in the Preliminaries of the War of 1812," in *Mississippi Valley Historical Review,* Vol. VII (June 1920), pp. 39–50.

Coleman, R. T. "Jo Daveiss, of Kentucky," in *Harper's Magazine,* Vol. XXI (1860), pp. 341–356.

Coulter, E. M.
"The Downfall of the Whig Party in Kentucky," in *Kentucky Historical Society Register,* Vol. XXIII (May 1925), pp. 162–174.

"The Genesis of Henry Clay's American System," in *South Atlantic Quarterly,* Vol. XXV (Jan. 1926), pp. 45–54.

Durrett, R. T. "Early Banking in Kentucky," in *Kentucky Bankers Association Proceedings, 1892,* pp. 35–45.

Ewing, Thomas. "Diary of Thomas Ewing," in *American Historical Review,* Vol. XVIII (Oct. 1912), pp. 97–112.

Frankfort [Kentucky] *Commonwealth.*

Harmon, George D. "Douglas and the Compromise of 1850," in *Journal of the Illinois State Historical Society,* Vol. XXI (1929), pp. 453–499.

Harrison, J. O. "Henry Clay, Reminiscences by His Executor," in *Century Magazine,* Vol. XI (Dec. 1886), pp. 170–182.

Hockett, Homer C. "Western Influences on Political Parties to 1825," in *Ohio State University Bulletin,* Vol. XXII (Aug. 1917), pp. 1–157.

Hodder, Frank H. "The Authorship of the Compromise of 1850," in the *Mississippi Valley Historical Review,* Vol. XXII (1935–1936), pp. 525–536.

Hopkins, Halford L. "The Hispanic-American Policy of Henry Clay, 1816–1828," in *Hispanic American Historical Review,* Vol. VII (Nov. 1927), pp. 460–478.

Hunt, Gaillard. "Joseph Gales on the War Manifesto of 1812," in *American Historical Review,* Vol. XIII (Jan. 1908), pp. 303–312.

Lexington [Kentucky] *Intelligencer.*

Lexington [Kentucky] *Observer & Reporter.*

National Intelligencer.

Niles' Weekly Register.

Parmelee, Theodore N. "Recollections of an Old Stager," in *Harper's Magazine*, Vols. XLV–XLVII, Aug. 1872–July 1873.

"Philo-Jackson." *The Presidential Election.* Frankfort, Kentucky. 1823–1826.

Rammelkamp, C. H. "The Campaign of 1824 in New York," in *American Historical Association Annual Report, 1904*, pp. 177–201.

Ritchie, Thomas. *Reminiscences of Henry Clay and the Compromise.* Richmond, Va., 1852.

Roseboom, E. H. "Ohio in the Presidential Election of 1824," in *Ohio Archæological and Historical Quarterly*, Vol. XXVI (April 1917), pp. 157–223.

Smith, Justin H. "Poinsett's Career in Mexico," in *Proceedings of the American Antiquarian Society*, Vol. XXIV (1914), pp. 77–92.

Taul, Micah. "Memoirs of Micah Taul," in *Kentucky State Historical Society Register*, Vol. XXVII (Jan., May, Sept. 1929), pp. 343–380, 494–517, 601–627.

Truth's Advocate and Monthly Anti-Jackson Expositor. Cincinnati. 1828.

Webster, C. K. "Castlereagh and the Spanish Colonies," in *English Historical Review*, Vol. XXVII (Jan. 1912), pp. 79–99.

Weed, Thurlow. "Recollections of Horace Greeley," in the *Galaxy*, Vol. XV (March 1873), pp. 372–382.

Western Monitor (Lexington, Kentucky).

Whiteley, Emily Stone. "Between the Acts at Ghent," in the *Virginia Quarterly Review*, Vol. V (Jan. 1929), pp. 18–30.

2. Books: —

Abdy, E. S. *Journal of a Residence and Tour in the United States.* London, 1835.

Abernethy, Thomas P. *From Frontier to Plantation in Tennessee; a Study in Frontier Democracy.* Chapel Hill, 1932.

Adams, Henry. *Life of Albert Gallatin*. Philadelphia, 1879.

Adams, John Q.

    Memoirs; Chas. Francis Adams, Ed. 12 vols. Philadelphia, 1874–1877.

    Writings; W. C. Ford, Ed. 7 vols. N.Y., 1913–1917.

Ambler, Charles H. *Thomas Ritchie, A Study in Virginia Politics*. Richmond, 1913.

Barnes, Gilbert H. *The Antislavery Impulse, 1830–1844*. N.Y., 1933.

Barnes, Thurlow W. *Memoir of Thurlow Weed*. Boston, 1884.

Beatty, Adam. *Essays on Practical Agriculture*. Maysville, Ky., 1844.

Benns, F. L. *The American Struggle for the British West India Carrying-Trade, 1815–1830*. Bloomington, Ind., 1923.

Benton, Thomas H. *Thirty Years' View*. 2 vols. N.Y., 1863.

Binney, Charles C. *The Life of Horace Binney*. Philadelphia, 1903.

Bradford, Gamaliel. *As God Made Them*. Boston, 1929.

Brown, Everett S.

    The Missouri Compromises and Presidential Politics. St. Louis, 1926.

    William Plumer's Memorandum of Proceedings in the the United States' Senate, 1803–1807. New York, 1923.

Brownlow, W. G. *Sketches of the Rise, Progress and Decline of Secession* (Parson Brownlow's Book). Philadelphia, 1862.

Bruce, William C. *John Randolph of Roanoke, 1773–1833*. 2 vols. New York, 1922.

Bungay, George W. *Crayon Sketches and Off-Hand Takings*. Boston, 1852.

Butler, Mann. *A History of the Commonwealth of Kentucky*. Louisville, 1834.

Calhoun, John C. *Correspondence of John C. Calhoun;* J. F. Jameson, Ed. *American Historical Association Annual Report, 1899*. Vol. II. Washington, 1900.

Catterall, Ralph C. H. *The Second Bank of the United States*. Chicago, 1903.

Clark, Allen C. *Life and Letters of Dolly Madison*. Washington, 1914.

Clay, Cassius M. *The Life of Cassius Marcellus Clay* — Memoirs, Writings and Speeches. Cincinnati, 1886.

Clay, Henry.
  Private Correspondence; Calvin Colton, Ed. Cincinnati, 1856.
  The Works of Henry Clay; Calvin Colton, Ed. 6 vols. N.Y., 1855. 7 vols. N.Y., 1897. 10 vols. (Fed. ed.) N.Y., 1904.
  An Address of Henry Clay to the Public, Concerning Certain Testimony in Refutation of the Charges Against Him Made by General Andrew Jackson Touching the Last Presidential Election. Washington, 1827.

Clay, Thomas H. *Henry Clay.* Philadelphia, 1910.

Cole, Arthur C. *The Whig Party in the South.* American Historical Association, 1914.

Coleman, Mrs. Chapman. *The Life of John J. Crittenden.* 2 vols. Philadelphia, 1871.

Coleman, J. Winston, Jr.
  Masonry in the Bluegrass. Lexington, Ky., 1933.
  Stage-Coach Days in the Bluegrass. Louisville, Ky., 1935.

Congdon, Charles T. *Reminiscences of a Journalist.* Boston, 1880.

Cox, I. J. *The West Florida Controversy* (1798–1813). Baltimore, 1918.

Darby, William. *The Emigrants' Guide to the Western and Southwestern States & Territories.* N.Y., 1812.

Dixon, Mrs. Archibald. *The Missouri Compromise and Its Repeal.* Cincinnati, 1903.

Du Bose, John W. *The Life and Times of William Lowndes Yancey.* Birmingham, 1892.

Dyer, Oliver. *Great Senators of the United States Forty Years Ago.* N.Y., 1889.

Edwards, Ninian. *The Edwards Papers;* E. B. Washburne, Ed. Chicago, 1884.

Eiselen, M. R. *The Rise of Pennsylvania Protectionism.* Univ. of Pennsylvania, 1932.

Fish, Carl R. *The Civil Service and the Patronage.* N.Y., 1905.

Flint, Timothy. *Recollections of the Last Ten Years.* Boston, 1826.

Follett, M. P. *The Speaker of the House of Representatives.* N.Y., 1909.

Fuller, H. B. *The Purchase of Florida: Its History and Diplomacy.* Cleveland, 1906.

Gammon, Samuel Rhea, Jr. *The Presidential Campaign of 1832.* Baltimore, 1922.

Goebel, D. B. *William Henry Harrison.* Indianapolis, 1926.

Greeley, Horace. *Recollections of a Busy Life.* N.Y., 1868.

Grigsby, Hugh B. *Discourse on the Life and Character of the Hon. Littleton Waller Tazewell.* Norfolk, Va., 1860.

Hamilton, Thomas. *Men and Manners in America.* 2 vols. Edinburgh and London, 1834.

Hammond, Jabez D. *Life and Times of Silas Wright.* Syracuse, N.Y., 1848.

Harvey, Peter. *Reminiscences and Anecdotes of Daniel Webster.* Boston, 1877.

Hilliard, Henry W. *Politics and Pen Pictures at Home and Abroad.* N.Y., 1892.

Hone, Philip. *Diary;* Allan Nevins, Ed. N.Y., 1927.

Hunt, Gaillard. *Life in America One Hundred Years Ago.* N.Y., 1914.

Inman, Samuel G. *Problems in Pan-Americanism.* N.Y., 1921.

Jervey, Theodore D. *Robert Y. Hayne and His Times.* N.Y., 1909.

Johnson, L. F. *History of Franklin County, Kentucky.* Frankfort, Ky., 1912.

Kendall, Amos. *Autobiography of Amos Kendall;* William Stickney, Ed. Boston, 1872.

Kentucky State Archives. *Journal of the House of Representatives, 1801–1810.*

Kinley, David. "The Independent Treasury of the United States," in *National Monetary Commission Reports,* 1910, Vol. VII, No. 2. Sen. Doc. 587, 61st Cong., 2d sess.

Lanman, Charles. *Haphazard Personalities.* Boston, 1886.

Littell, John S. *The Clay Minstrel; or, National Songster.* N.Y. and Philadelphia, 1842.

Littell, William, comp. *The Statute Law of Kentucky.* 5 vols. Frankfort, Ky., 1807–1811.

Little, Lucius P. *Ben Hardin: His Times and Contemporaries*. Louisville, Ky., 1887.

Lockey, J. B. *Pan-Americanism: Its Beginnings*. N.Y., 1920.

Lynn, Harry Richmond. *Henry Clay and Transylvania University*. Master's thesis, Univ. of Ky., 1930 (unpublished).

McCaleb, F. *The Aaron Burr Conspiracy and New Orleans*. N.Y., 1903.

Mallory, Daniel. *The Life and Speeches of Henry Clay*. 2 vols. N.Y., 1844.

Manning, William R.
The Early Diplomatic Relations between the United States and Mexico. Baltimore, 1916.
Diplomatic Correspondence of the United States Concerning the Independence of the Latin-American Nations. 3 vols. N.Y., 1925.

Marshall, Humphrey. *History of Kentucky*. 2 vols. Frankfort, Ky., 1824.

Martin, Asa E. *The Anti-Slavery Movement in Kentucky Prior to 1850*. Louisville, Ky., 1918.

Martineau, Harriet.
Retrospect of Western Travel. 2 vols. London and N.Y., 1838.
Society in America. 3 vols. London, 1837.

Maury, Sarah Mytton. *The Statesmen of America in 1846*. London, 1847.

Meyer, Leland Winfield. *The Life and Times of Colonel Richard M. Johnson of Kentucky*. N.Y., 1932.

Michaux, François A. *Travels to the West of the Alleghany Mountains*. London, 1805, reprint Cleveland, 1904.

Moore, Brent. *The Hemp Industry in Kentucky*. Lexington, Ky., 1905.

Page, Roswell. *Hanover County; Its History and Legends*. Richmond, 1926.

Paxson, F. L. *The Independence of the South American Republics*. Philadelphia, 1903.

Peck, Charles H. *The Jacksonian Epoch*. New York, 1899.

Peter, Robert. *History of Fayette County, Kentucky*. Chicago, 1882.

Poore, Ben: Perley. *Perley's Reminiscences of Sixty Years in the National Metropolis*. 2 vols. Philadelphia, 1886.

Power, Tyrone. *Impressions of America; during the years 1833, 1834 and 1835.* 2 vols. Philadelphia, 1836.

Pratt, Julius W. *Expansionists of 1812.* New York, 1925.

Plumer, William, Jr. *Life of William Plumer.* Boston, 1857.

Poage, George Rawlings.
"Henry Clay and the Disruption of the Whig Party in 1841." Ph. D. dissertation at the University of Chicago, 1923. (Unpublished.)
Henry Clay and the Whig Party. Chapel Hill, 1936.

Prentice, George D. *Biography of Henry Clay.* New York, 1831.

Quisenberry, Anderson Chenault. *The Life and Times of Hon. Humphrey Marshall.* Winchester, Ky., 1892.

Ranck, George Washington. *History of Lexington, Kentucky.* Cincinnati, 1872.

Richardson, James D. *Messages and Papers of the Presidents.* 20 vols. New York, 1897–1927.

Rippy, J. F. *Latin America in World Politics.* New York, 1928.

Rogers, Joseph M. *The True Henry Clay.* Philadelphia, 1904.

Sargent, Nathan. *Public Men and Events.* 2 vols. Philadelphia, 1875.

Schmucker, Samuel M. *The Life and Times of Henry Clay.* Philadelphia, 1860.

Schurz, Carl. *Life of Henry Clay.* 2 vols. Boston and New York, 1887.

Seward, Frederick W. *Seward at Washington, as Senator and Secretary of State.* 3 vols. New York, 1891.

Simms, Henry H. *The Rise of the Whigs in Virginia.* Richmond, 1929.

Smith, Margaret Bayard. *The First Forty Years of Washington Society;* Gaillard Hunt, Ed. New York, 1906.

Smith, William H. *Charles Hammond.* Chicago Historical Society, 1885.

Smith, W. T. *A Complete Index to the Names of Persons, Places and Subjects Mentioned in Littell's Laws of Kentucky.* Lexington, Ky., 1931.

Smith, Zachary F. and Clay, Mary Rodgers (Mrs.). *The Clay Family.* Louisville, Ky., 1899.

Stanwood, Edward. *American Tariff Controversies in the Nineteenth Century.* 2 vols. Boston, 1903.

Stephens, A. H. *A Constitutional View of the Late War between the States.* 2 vols. Philadelphia, 1870.

Stickles, Arndt M. *The Critical Court Struggle in Kentucky, 1819–1829.* Auspices of Graduate Council, Indiana University, 1929.

Story, William W. *Life and Letters of Joseph Story.* 2 vols. Boston, 1851.

Temperley, Harold W. V. *The Foreign Policy of Canning, 1822–1827.* London, 1925.

Townsend, William H. *Lincoln and His Wife's Home Town.* Indianapolis, 1929.

Turner, F. J. *The Significance of Sections in American History,* N.Y., 1933.

Tyler, Lyon Gardiner.
  "George Wythe, 1726–1806," in *Great American Lawyers;* Wm. D. Lewis, Ed. 4 vols. Philadelphia, 1907.
  The Letters and Times of the Tylers. 3 vols. Richmond, 1884–1896.

Updyke, F. A. *The Diplomacy of the War of 1812.* Baltimore, 1915.

Van Deusen, John G. *Economic Bases of Disunion in South Carolina.* N.Y., 1928.

Vigne, Godfrey T. *Six Months in America.* Philadelphia, 1833.

Warfield, Ethelbert Dudley. *The Kentucky Resolutions of 1798.* N.Y. and London, 1887.

Webster, Daniel. *Writings and Speeches;* national edition. 18 vols. Boston, 1903.

Weed, Thurlow. *Autobiography of Thurlow Weed;* Harriet A. Weed, Ed. Boston, 1884.

Weld, Isaac Jr. *Travels Through the States of North America, and the Provinces of Upper and Lower Canada, during the Years 1795, 1796, and 1797.* 3d ed. 2 vols. London, 1800.

Wellington, Raynor Greenleaf. *The Political and Sectional Influence of the Public Lands, 1828–1842.* Cambridge, 1914.

Winthrop, Robert C. *Memoir of Henry Clay.* Cambridge, 1880.

Wise, Barton H. *The Life of Henry A. Wise.* N.Y., 1899.

Wise, Henry A. *Seven Decades of the Union.* Philadelphia, 1872.

Young, Sarah S. (Mrs.). *Genealogical Narrative of the Hart Family.* Memphis, Tenn., 1882.

Zimmerman, J. F. *Impressment of American Seamen.* N.Y., 1925.

INDEX